EUROPEAN STUDIES SERIES

General Editors   Colin Jones
                     Richard Overy

Series Advisers   Joe Bergin
                     John Bruilly
                     Ruth Harris

This series marks a major initiative in European history publishing aimed primarily, though not exclusively, at an undergraduate audience. It will encompass a wide variety of books on aspects of European history since 1500, with particular emphasis on France and Germany, although no country will be excluded and a special effort will be made to cover previously neglected areas, such as Scandinavia, Eastern Europe and Southern Europe.

The series will include political accounts and broad thematic treatments, both of a comparative kind and studies of a single country, and will lay particular emphasis on social and cultural history where this opens up fruitful new ways of examining the past. The aim of the series is to make available a wide range of titles in areas where there is now an obvious gap or where the existing historical literature is out of date or narrowly focused. The series will also include translations of important books published elsewhere in Europe.

Interest in European affairs and history has never been greater, *European Studies* will help make that European heritage closer, richer and more comprehensible.

EUROPEAN STUDIES SERIES

Published

Robert Aldrich — Greater France: A History of French Overseas Expansion

Yves-Marie Bercé — The Birth of Absolutism: A History of France, 1598–1661

Janine Garrisson — A History of Sixteenth-Century France, 1438–1589

Michael Hughes — Early Modern Germany, 1477–1806

Martyn Lyons — Napoleon Bonaparte and the Legacy of the French Revolution

Pamela M. Pilbeam — Republicanism in Nineteenth-Century France, 1814–1871

Richard Vinen — France, 1934–1970

Greater France

A History of French Overseas Expansion

ROBERT ALDRICH

St. Martin's Press
New York

GREATER FRANCE
Copyright © 1996 by Robert Aldrich
All rights reserved. No part of this book may be used or reproduced
in any manner whatsoever without written permission except in the
case of brief quotations embodied in critical articles or reviews.
For information, address:

St. Martin's Press, Scholarly and Reference Division,
175 Fifth Avenue, New York, N.Y. 10010

First published in the United States of America in 1996

Printed in Malaysia

ISBN 0–312–15999–4 (cloth)
ISBN 0–312–16000–3 (paperback)

Library of Congress Cataloging-in-Publication Data applied for à tous mes amis français

Contents

List of Maps   viii
Preface   ix
Maps   xi

Introduction   Reading and Writing about the Colonies   1
Prologue   The First Overseas Empire   10
1 The Conquest of Empire: Africa and the Indian Ocean   24
2 The Conquest of Empire: Asia, the Pacific and
   the Austral Regions   68
3 Ideas of Empire   89
4 The French Overseas   122
5 The Uses of Empire   163
6 The French and the 'Natives'   199
7 Colonial Culture in France   234
8 Colonial Nationalism and Decolonisation   266
Epilogue   After the Empire   307

Notes   326
Bibliographical Essay   343
Index   352

List of Maps

The French Empire in 1930   xi
North Africa   xii
French West Africa (AOF) and Togo   xiii
French Equatorial Africa (AEF) and Cameroon   xiv
French Indian Ocean Colonies   xv
Indochina   xvi

Preface

This book is an introduction to French colonial history with an emphasis on the 'new' empire created in the nineteenth century. It does not presuppose knowledge of the colonies which France acquired and administered, but the reader may find that some background on the history of modern France and on the history of European overseas expansion will be useful.

Because of the vast size of the empire and the complexity of examining different aspects of French involvement with overseas countries, this book does not pretend to be either exhaustive or authoritative. I have often opted to examine particular cases or examples rather than trying to be encyclopaedic. I have tried to take account, so far as possible, of recent research on the history of French expansion, a field which has attracted renewed interest from researchers and writers. However, notes have been kept to a strict minimum; they do not give a complete account of works consulted or sources available, but alert readers to major studies in English and French. The bibliographical essay provides a list of only a few of quite literally thousands of books on the colonies.

Rendering non-European names is difficult, as spellings change over time and from French to English. I have generally used French names for smaller African locales (and some other places) since independent Francophone countries have usually preserved such spellings: thus 'Tombouctou' rather than 'Timbuktu'. I use 'Guyane' for French Guiana to avoid confusion with British and Dutch Guyana. The government of the Côte-d'Ivoire prefers its French name even in other languages. When a country has changed names (Dahomey to Benin, Upper Volta to Burkina Faso), I use the name current in the colonial era. Soudan here refers to the old French colony, largely part of contemporary Mali, not to the north African country of the Sudan. I use 'native' for the indigenous inhabitants of the colonies because that is how Europeans thought of them in an ethnocentric way; I intend no disparagement to Africans, Asians or inhabitants of other colonised regions by using the word.

Some readers may find this text asymmetrical, and I have indeed devoted more attention to the French experience of expansion than to the way colonialism was experienced by indigenous populations. Space and coherence, I believe, justify doing so. But the interested reader will find that fascinating and valuable accounts – ranging from fictional literature to ethnohistory – provide perspectives from the 'other side'.

I would like to thank my publishers for their patience in awaiting this book, Julie Manley for her fine work in preparing the manuscript, John Connell for a careful reading of it, John Roberts for preparing the maps, Iain Walker for doing the index, and friends who came to my rescue when, in my reading and writing, I was struggling through tropical jungles, lost in Saharan sands or stranded on remote islands.

ROBERT ALDRICH

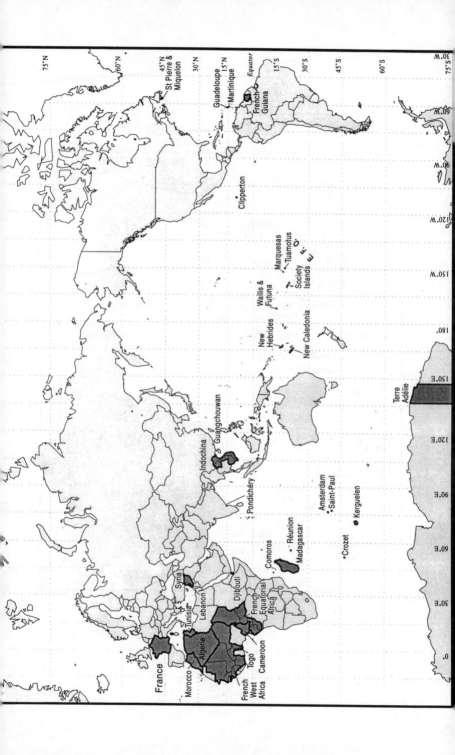

NORTH AFRICA

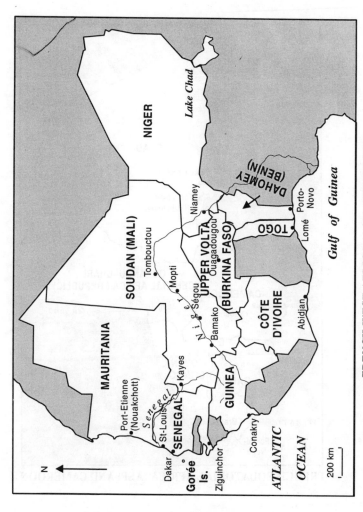

FRENCH WEST AFRICA (AOF) AND TOGO

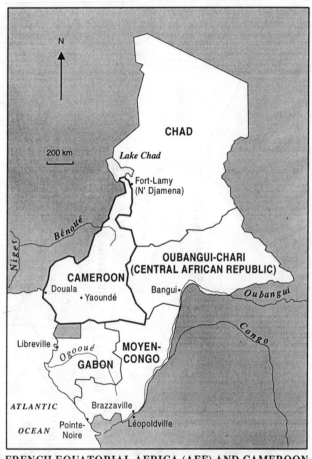

FRENCH EQUATORIAL AFRICA (AEF) AND CAMEROON

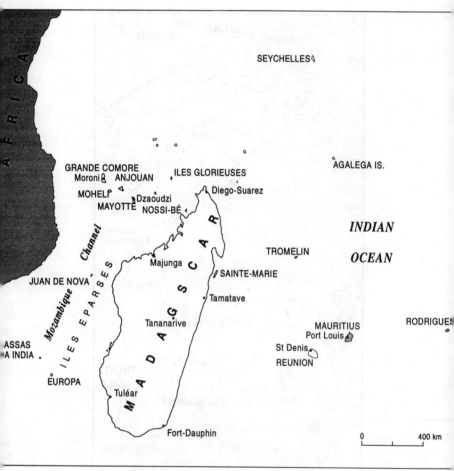

FRENCH INDIAN OCEAN COLONIES

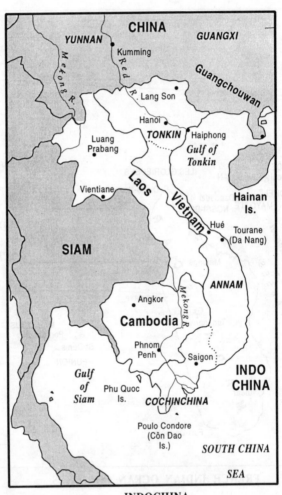

INDOCHINA

Introduction: Reading and Writing About the Colonies

At its apogee in the 1920s and 1930s, France and its overseas domains – what some called 'greater France' (*la plus grande France*)[1] – encompassed 11 million square kilometres of land and over 100 million inhabitants; Paris controlled the second largest empire in the world, second only to that of Britain. France's possessions included African and South American jungles, islands in the Caribbean, the Indian Ocean and the Pacific, vast expanses of Saharan desert and Antarctic ice, enormous colonies such as Indochina and Madagascar, remote little-known outposts such as Wallis and Kerguelen, and toeholds in India and on the Red Sea. The French tricolour flag flew over the fabled city of Tombouctou and the legendary island of Tahiti. Colonial promoters lauded the benefits of an empire they said provided international prestige, a secure place for investments, a market for France's products, a source for raw materials and a reserve army of soldiers. Popular literature recounted the exploits of hardy explorers, courageous soldiers, kindly doctors and missionaries, pioneering farmers and miners, loyal natives. They promised an eternal marriage between France and its outposts over the seas. Anti-colonialists dissented, speaking about invasion of foreign countries, brutal conquest and exploitation, mistreatment of indigenous populations, appropriation of labour and natural resources, spoliation of land, and concerted attempts to destroy non-Western cultures, largely for the benefit of a few rapacious settlers and profiteering capitalists.

By the early 1960s, most countries in the French empire had gained independence, though some had been forced to fight for their sovereignty. Except for a handful of generally small territories

1

scattered around the globe, France had withdrawn from its empire. The age of colonialism seemed to have come to an end, even if ties between France and its former colonies were not always severed. Nevertheless, only 130 years after France took over Algiers, less than a century after it annexed Cochinchina and the Congo, less than 50 years after it proclaimed a protectorate over Morocco, 'greater France' was no more.

Writing or reading the history of colonialism is a formidable task. Such study covers several centuries of history in each of the world's continental land masses and in dozens of islands. Colonial history must look at societies conquered by France as different as North Africa and Southeast Asia, and it must reflect on the political, economic and cultural imperatives in Europe which motivated the powers to scramble for colonies and carve out empires. It must try, as well, to see the history of colonialism from the vantage point of those who were conquered, whose countries and cultures were so profoundly and permanently affected by foreign overlordship.

Writing about the Colonies

The amount of material on areas colonised by France is truly massive – one scholar has counted over 3000 volumes published just on the Algerian war of independence (fought between 1954 and 1962). Hundreds of men and women associated with the colonies have written memoirs. Generations of scholars have examined the French overseas possessions, which provided a laboratory for anthropologists, geographers, ethnologists, economists and other social scientists, as well as historians. The committees and institutes which promoted the colonies, and the anti-colonial organisations, published journals, newspapers and books. Since the end of empire, colonised people have examined their own past, often pioneering new methods and theories and providing different perspectives than those of European writers.

The French empire produced reams of documents. The French overseas archives contain thousands of hefty cartons filled with government reports, statistical compilations, newspaper clippings, personal letters and other primary material. The French National Archives, the archives of the army and navy, Catholic and Protestant missionary archives and other collections contain countless documents. The independent former colonies all conserve archives and library materials. Historians have also increasingly used non-traditional sources such as interviews and oral history, art, cinema and music to examine the colonial past.

The extent of the published sources can be seen in the library catalogue of the Académie des Sciences d'Outre-Mer, the former Colonial Academy, in Paris. Among works published during the colonial era are the erudite tomes of the Association for the Development of Cotton in the French Colonies, the National Committee for Colonial Timber, and the Research Institute for Palm Oil. There are books on colonial telegraphy, refrigeration in the colonies, the mineral resources of the empire, currency in the empire, the first veterinarians in the colonies, the postal history of the French possessions. There are the publications of the Society of Friends of French Explorers and the Society of French Colonial Artists. There is a pamphlet entitled 'Advice to Europeans and Natives to Warn Them about the Dangers of Alcohol in the Tropics', a handbook on colonial artistic and architectural styles, magazines on colonial clothing and fashion. Not the least interesting artefact is a colonial cookbook with descriptions of tropical fruits and vegetables, and recipes for Vietnamese rice dishes, West Indian curries, North African couscous – and, no doubt to create a shiver in European chefs and gourmets – monkey meat roasted with groundnuts.[2]

Most such works were far from devoid of ideological intent: they aimed to inspire interest in France's far-flung domains and alert the public to the economic and political potential of the colonies. They formed a body of writing about the empire that included works of pure propaganda, technical monographs and fiction.

Colonial Historiography

The first professional colonial history was written during the age of expansion.[3] Often the authors were administrators, settlers or academics who had lived in the colonies. Their writings generally celebrated French achievements and exalted expansion. Such works usually betrayed the Eurocentric (or outright racist) attitude of colonialists convinced of their mission to develop newly found resources and to bring civilisation to the savages and Christianity to the heathen. Views which now seem objectionable do not necessarily detract from the seriousness of such authors' research and the usefulness of their books; as with any history-writing, the writers' ideology and the context in which the works were published must be taken into account.

The tone of such books is clear in an authoritative history of the colonies edited by two highly respected academics in the 1930s. Gabriel Hanotaux announced his sentiments in the introduction, 'The Civilising Expansion of France in the World':

> The history of France is not truly complete if it does not include the history of French colonisation and French expansion in the world. France has always tried to extend itself outwards. In doing so from age immemorial, it has not responded to an egotistic instinct, not even to an appetite for conquest, but a singular need to know men and the world, to propagate, to found, to create.[4]

After six lengthy volumes, Hanotaux concluded that French expansion was a case of 'true colonisation, which is the mother-country offering itself to these young peoples, these children' in an act of 'association, mutual comprehension, mutual respect, common labour among children of the same family'. France was the country known universally as liberator; wherever France had passed, 'the indigene found himself at peace, fed, reared, healed and multiplied by French presence'.

Africa provided an example. After the glorious period of Roman penetration, Hanotaux wrote, Africa had sunk into barbarity: 'All manner of evils, piracy, raids, slavery, the slave-trade, cannibalism had brought an unhappy destiny, and the night of darkness had struck people with a new curse.' There remained only 'dark feasts by the light of fires, erotic dances performed to the tom-tom of drums, monstrous apparitions of nudity magnified by masks shining in the firelight, infinite lamentations carrying across the oceans and trailing after ships like the unending cry of hopeless unhappiness.' Then came the Europeans – missionaries, administrators, soldiers – and Africa was rescued: 'France conquered ignorance. . . . She saved the black, educated him, hovered over him and presented this child with civilisation.' France had undertaken programmes of development with extraordinary 'progress', an 'admirable achievement' which the French ought to acknowledge with pride.[5]

Parallel to the stream of pro-colonial writing ran a current of anti-colonial literature. French public opinion was never unanimously in favour of the colonial enterprise. Some scholars kept their distance from colonial policy or were frankly opposed to imperialism. Until the 1950s, however, anti-colonial historians formed a tiny band in opposition to colonialists aided by the government, given university positions and publishing contracts, and feted by colonial promoters. The work of Charles-André Julien, a specialist on North Africa and professor at the Sorbonne, stands out among the relatively few professional histories critical of the colonial adventure.

Most anti-colonial writing came from outside the ivory towers. Journalists such as Albert Londres revealed abuses of native labour in equatorial Africa and inhumane conditions in the penal colony of Guyane. Novelists portrayed colonial exploitation, and some, like André Gide, wrote scathing non-fiction reports based on travels overseas. Political activists, many on the left of the ideological spectrum, published pamphlets and articles damning colonialism. Intellectuals among colonised populations authored manifestos; one published by Nguyên Ai Quôc, who later took the name Ho Chi Minh and led the Indochinese nationalist movement, denounced French business profiteering, physical violence against Indochinese, the brutal inefficiency of administrators, and the pernicious government promotion of opium-smoking (since the government collected precious tax revenue from its opium monopoly).[6]

Anti-colonialists gained greater voice, in both scholarship and politics, after the Second World War. Scholars took part in the heated debate on colonialism and decolonisation in the 1950s, and a few earned notoriety for opposition to French control in Algeria and elsewhere. Jean-Paul Sartre, the existentialist philosopher, stood in the forefront of the anti-colonialist campaign, and the journal he established, *Les Temps modernes*, provided a major forum for serious critical articles on colonial issues. Respected social scientists, such as the ethnographer Michel Leiris, wrote widely and articulately in opposition to colonialism; the black West Indian psychiatrist Franz Fanon and the Jewish Tunisian intellectual Albert Memmi analysed the nefarious psychological effects of colonialism on Europeans and non-Western peoples alike.

Whether pro- or anti-colonial, colonial history was never either the *avant-garde* or the centre of attention in French historical research – but the colonies themselves were seldom the centre of French public life. After the decolonisation of France's major overseas territories, colonial history faced renewed problems. Historians from colonial universities joined others who returned to France from the former possessions, yet their background placed them in an ambiguous academic position. Conservative political and university leaders continued to deny senior posts to those who had criticised the empire too severely. Some episodes of decolonisation had been so painful that the French were hardly eager to reopen old wounds by investigating a colonial past that was not always praiseworthy; a virtual embargo existed on certain studies of Algeria. Colonial archives were not always easily accessible, either left behind in fragile conditions in overseas countries or left uncatalogued and disregarded in France. Moreover, the new social history popular in the 1960s and 1970s concentrated on the metropole – quantitative history, family history, regional history, labour history, the history of collective attitudes. Colonial history withdrew to the periphery of the historical profession.

Yet traditional colonial history attracted a small band of devoted researchers, while others flocked to the burgeoning field of non-European history. New centres of African, Asian and Magrebin studies, as well as journals and conferences, focused on the former colonial world, generally attracting scholars more sympathetic to anti-colonial than pro-colonial points of view. These scholars sought to advance understanding of non-European countries and redefine the history of contact between European conquerors and colonised peoples. Their colleagues in European history re-examined the motives and ideologies of imperialism and the impact of colonial expansion on France itself.

Several historians pioneered new theoretical perspectives. Henri Brunschwig, dean of French colonial historians, in a seminal book in 1960 questioned the accepted idea that economic imperatives lay behind the French imperial venture. Brunschwig broke ground in studying the individuals and groups who had promoted colonialism in France. He examined the history of both Europeans and indigenous people in the empire, looking at local resistance to and collaboration with French rule. He also wrote histories of modern Africa and of German expansion.[7]

Among other historians in the 1970s, Raoul Girardet systematically traced the history of the colonial idea in France. Girardet was also one of the first to discuss the history of colonial imagery, such as photographs. Charles-Robert Ageron examined support for colonialism in France to determine whether France was a profoundly colonialist country or whether a small group of adamant promoters had succeeded in convincing leaders to adopt pro-colonial policies. Ageron pioneered the history of anti-colonialism. As well, he wrote numerous works on Algeria. Others returned to the economic history of colonialism. Jacques Thobie and René Girault looked at French commercial activity outside the empire and, with Jean Bouvier, developed theories about the economic complementarity of formal colonial possessions and other areas of French business. Jacques Marseille undertook the most detailed investigation of French economics and empire; one of his most striking new arguments was that the smaller, more fragile French companies, rather than the industrial giants, gained the most from overseas colonies in the age of monopoly capitalism. Other historians focused on particular areas of French expansion, producing in-depth studies of many areas of the empire, especially black Africa; Catherine Coquery-Vidrovitch's and Marc Michel's works stand as fine examples.

By the mid-1980s colonial history had made a definite comeback. The work of lonely scholars in the 1960s and 1970s had stimulated interest among a new generation of students. The 'Third World' continued to attract attention. As the 'new social history' and 'new cultural history' no longer seemed so new, historians moved into alternate areas; older specialities, such as political history, returned to favour. By the 1990s the 30 years which had passed since the independence of Algeria, and almost 40 since the independence of Indochina, created a certain historical distance from pro- and anti-colonial positions. More archival material became accessible as time passed: classified sources from recent periods could be consulted, new materials were located, and the French colonial archives were consolidated at the Archives d'Outre-Mer in Aix-en-Provence.

Revived interest in the history of French expansion inspired stacks of monographs on particular colonies and themes. Areas previously bypassed by historians, such as the French territories in the West Indies and the South Pacific, became subjects of theses and books. Historians explored new domains. The history of women in the colonies attracted long overdue attention, and the study of images of colonialism in literature and the visual arts achieved prominence. Studies of exoticism and French concepts of 'the other' proliferated in historical and literary disciplines. Books treated issues as diverse as colonial medicine and sport. Decolonisation emerged as a growth area in colonial studies.[8]

The French were not the only ones to study French colonial history. Increasing numbers of Africans, Asians and islanders made contributions, as did writers in the English-speaking world. William Cohen wrote an impressive study of the French encounter with Africans, as well as a volume on French administrators and their training. Raymond Betts, whose study of the policies of assimilation and association, published in the early 1960s, had become a classic, pioneered work on colonial cities. C.M. Andrew and A.S. Kanya-Forstner produced works on the colonial lobby. Others published monographs on particular areas of French overlordship.[9]

There were, as well, general histories of French colonies,[10] and overviews of France's whole colonial history,[11] albeit they were rarer in English than in French. By the 1990s, shelves started to become laden with works which summarised previous research, presented new approaches and provided briefer or lengthier surveys. One publishing house issued a five-volume history of expansion under the general title 'The Colonial Adventure of France', as well as a companion series on the 'crossed destinies' of colonisers and colonised.[12] Another synthesis came in a two-volume, 1500-page study.[13] Yet another two-volume study weighed in at 1721 pages.[14] Several more succinct studies appeared,[15] supplemented by such useful works as an encyclopaedic dictionary of expansion.[16]

Writers on expansion, traditional or innovative, have faced a number of problems – the availability of sources, relative proximity to hotly debated and sensitive issues, the very extent of the domain conquered by Europeans. The most persistent issue has been the deceptively straightforward question of what precisely is colonial history, the history of imperialism, or the history of overseas expansion. (Even the nomenclature is troublesome.) Is it primarily a history of the colonising power, its ideology and its efforts? If so, pride of place may go to debates in domestic policy, the formulation of political doctrines and decisions taken on strategies of conquest and rule, biographies of Europeans overseas, business histories of colonial companies. By contrast, if history concentrates on regions brought under European control, it may emphasise domestic developments in those countries: power struggles among local elites, receptivity or opposition to contact and cooperation with foreigners, the structures and evolution of non-European societies, biographies of African, Asian or islander leaders. Should the focus be on Europeans or indigenous peoples, on the 'centre' or the 'periphery'? Recent histories of European expansion try, to different degrees, to combine these approaches and search for the link between the national history of the colonising power and the societies which it colonised.[17] It seeks to understand the interaction of the two, even if due stress must be placed on the basic fact that the expanding power always exercised domination over the countries which it conquered. The 'new colonial history' is thus a history of the colonisers and the colonised, of images and realities of conquest and control, of ideologies and imperial actions, of individuals who played a primary role in the acquisition and administration of empire and of underlying political, economic, social and cultural forces which led Europeans to take over distant domains.

Prologue: The First Overseas Empire

Finding the first episode of French international expansion is a matter of choice. Charlemagne, crowned Holy Roman Emperor in the year 800, created a multinational European empire. In the eleventh century, the French expanded overseas when William the Conqueror defeated the British and occupied England in 1066; 26 years later, Normans established a kingdom in Sicily which lasted for 200 years. The French ventured even further afield during the Crusades, the campaign to liberate the Christian holy land from infidel Arabs and, not coincidentally, to win glory, booty and political influence for the crusaders; from 1099 to 1187, Frenchmen ruled the kingdom of Jerusalem. From 1192 to 1372, another French dynasty reigned over Cyprus, and for a brief period at the beginning of the fourteenth century, a French adventurer lorded over the Canary Islands.[1]

These early episodes of expansion contained, in embryo, aspects of later incursions into foreign lands – the search for power and prestige, often overlaid by religious or cultural justification, conquest of territories by force of arms, the installation of new governments (and, sometimes, settlers), and in many cases rebellion and eventual loss of French control. Yet several of these prototypical outposts remained under French domination for longer periods than did later conquests.

From the end of the fifteenth century, European attention turned to the New World of the Americas and the islands of the West Indies. First contact with local residents confirmed European belief in their cultural, political and technological superiority to 'savage' civilisations – a constant in future expansion – and sparked hopes of finding hordes of precious metals and other riches. The

10

Spanish led the way in exploration of the New World, and conquistadors claimed large territories for God and the Spanish monarch. In the 1490s, the pope, as arbiter of disputes among Christians, divided the recently discovered and still unknown world between Spain to the west and Portugal to the east of a meridian passing through South America. The angry French king, François I, remarked that he was unaware that the last will of Adam had so cleaved the world, and that the sun shone on the French just as it did on the Iberians.

During François' reign in the early 1500s, the French made their first forays into the Americas. Most notable was the 1534 voyage of Jacques Cartier, who explored Hudson Bay and the area that became New France, although attempts to stake claims or found colonies along the Atlantic coast of the Americas came to naught. At the end of the sixteenth century, King Henri IV renewed interest in the overseas world by chartering a company for exploration, colonisation, trade and the administration of territories brought into the king's realm. Such domains should be developed, primarily through agriculture, to provide gain for France. Henri demanded that the French should respect and befriend indigenous peoples. On these bases – though the principle of friendship between Europeans and 'natives' was often honoured in the breach – the seventeenth century witnessed substantial French expansion in Canada and the Antilles.

Colonial Conquest

New France: the French in Canada

In 1603, the French monarch gave the Huguenots, French Protestants, a monopoly on fur trade in Acadia, a region which included a portion of the present-day American state of Maine and the Canadian province of Nova Scotia. Six years later Samuel de Champlain founded the city of Québec, and in 1642 a French outpost was established on the site of the future city of Montréal. French presence in North America nevertheless remained small scale. In 1626, New France, as the territory was called, counted only 100 French settlers, and their number had, at most, tripled by mid-century. Most numerous were traders in furs and skins, who obtained their wares from Indians for shipment to France.

Important as well were Catholic priests; the first Jesuits arrived in
Québec in 1625. The colonists lived precariously, faced with extreme cold, isolation and threats from Indian raids. From the
mid-1600s onwards, however, the colony began to flourish. Paris
turned New France into a royal province, promoted settlement,
and tried to develop farming and forestry. Some 10 000 French
men and women, including soldiers, female orphans, illegitimate
children and prostitutes sent to America, prisoners and free settlers, migrated to Canada from 1608 to 1760. The French gradually pushed back the frontier of exploration and foreign control
and established trading outposts and forts in the Great Lakes area
and south to the Gulf of Mexico and New Orleans.

France's perennial rival, Britain, firmly established on the eastern seaboard of North America, had designs on French possessions. Skirmishes in America and dynastic wars in Europe pitted
the powers against each other on two continents. Wars at the
end of the seventeenth century ended to French advantage, but
Paris did less well in the new century. France's colonial efforts
suffered a dire blow when it lost the War of the Spanish Succession, and the Treaty of Utrecht, in 1713, forced France to abandon Acadia. Many French settlers subsequently emigrated, mostly
to Louisiana, where local pronunciation of 'Acadians' turned the
refugees into 'Cajuns'.

Another war proved even more disastrous for the French. In
Europe the 'Seven Years War' from 1754 to 1763 again set the
French against the British, each side marshalling its North American colonists and Indian allies. The British gained the upper hand
at the end of the 1750s. By the Treaty of Paris, signed in 1763,
France renounced all claims to Canada. Even before the treaty
was signed, in 1762, France had ceded its enormous, if precariously held, territories west of the Mississippi River, including
Louisiana, to the Spanish.[2]

The 1763 treaty left France with a small (242 km^2) consolation
prize, the islands of Saint-Pierre and Miquelon off the coast of
Newfoundland. In 1604 the first French fishermen had established
on the islands a seasonal camp for fishermen coming from France
to catch cod for export to the Caribbean colonies. The loss of
the islands in 1713 hardly troubled Paris, but the restitution of
Saint-Pierre and Miquelon 50 years afterwards allowed France to
maintain a sovereign toehold in North America. Treaties also gave
Frenchmen the right to catch fish and process their haul on land

facilities on the so-called 'French Shore' of Newfoundland. Colonists on Saint-Pierre and Miquelon, who braved isolation, cold climate and the fragility of an economy based on a single resource, numbered at most several thousand and formed one of the least regarded of France's outposts. The islands nevertheless remain a French overseas territory.[3]

The Antilles and Guyane

The islands of the Caribbean (also called the West Indies or Antilles) sparkled as the real colonial treasures in the seventeenth century.[4] Many had fine harbours for trade and defence. The local Carib and Arawak Indian population had been largely killed by the Spanish through war and disease, and little effort was needed to secure foreign control. Fertile soil and warm climate provided perfect locations for cultivation of such tropical crops as indigo, tobacco, rice, cotton and, above all, sugar, a highly prized commodity.

The French government chartered companies in the 1620s to prospect for sugar islands and in the 1630s occupied Saint-Christophe (St Kitts), Martinique, Guadeloupe and its smaller neighbours (Les Saintes, Désirade and Marie-Galante), Dominique (Dominica), Sainte-Lucie (St Lucia), Tobago and, the largest possession of all, Saint-Domingue (Haiti), the western part of the island of Hispaniola. The companies recruited 8500 colonists for the West Indies by the mid-1600s, but settlers did not provide sufficient workers for the labour-intensive and back-breaking job of producing sugar. Europeans found a labour force in Africa, and thus began the long and horrific history of slave-trading. The need for slaves provided an incentive for the establishment of outposts in western Africa, especially on the Gulf of Guinea. The island of Gorée, off the coast of Senegal, became the most infamous of the ports from which kidnapped or purchased slaves were loaded onto ships for transport to the New World; as many as a third perished on the voyage. Survivors were sold on the auction block, legally the property of their new owners in much the same way as household belongings or livestock. The harsh conditions on plantations are now well known but worried few Europeans at the time. Slaves worked long days under a punishing sun and generally received no wages. Housing and nutrition were inadequate. Africans, torn from their own cultures and traditions and separated from kith and kin, were forced to live together with no concern for their family or ethnic origins. Slave-owners encouraged women to have as many children as possible, for each child was a new source of wealth for the owner. Plantation owners enjoyed rights to discipline and punish slaves, including corporal punishment, branding, mutilation and imprisonment. Police forces captured runaway slaves and returned them to owners for suitable chastisement.[5]

Some, if not all, French planters grew rich from their estates and became an entrenched white aristocracy (the *Békés*) in the Antilles. Shippers made a profit from the slaves they transported to the New World, the tropical goods they transported from the Caribbean to France, and the sale of European manufactured goods (textiles, metal wares and baubles) to Africans: a great triangular trade. Businessmen in French Atlantic ports, such as Nantes, La Rochelle and Bordeaux, were enriched by such commerce.

The West Indian colonies prospered, as France's outposts in North America stagnated. In Martinique, for instance, the number of white residents grew from 4770 in 1683 to 14 000 in 1756, while the number of slaves soared from 14 500 to 65 000. In Saint-Domingue, the number of slaves was even larger: 24 100 in 1717 and 172 000 in 1752. Half a million slaves, in total, toiled in the French Antilles in the mid-1700s; 600 French ships ploughed the seas between Europe and the West Indies. The Antilles produced 40 per cent of the world's sugar and half its coffee. The French possessions in the West Indies were the richest colonies in the world.

France had one other colony in the New World, Guyane, a large continental possession on the northeastern shore of South America. Europeans had first visited the area in the mid-1500s, but not until 1637 did the French take possession. Thereafter, the history of Guyane was a series of efforts at colonisation, each defeated by the insalubrious site, torrid weather, impenetrable Amazonian forest, tropical diseases and lack of resources. A few hardy individuals did manage to survive, though by the early 1700s settlers numbered only 600. Guyane also counted 3000 slaves, most of whom worked on sugar plantations which never knew the success of those in the islands; an indeterminate number of indigenous Indians lived in the tropical jungle. Another effort to colonise Guyane occurred in 1763–65, when Paris sent 12 000 settlers to the colony; within several years, 8000 had died from typhoid or yellow fever.

Africa and the Indian Ocean

The French presence in Africa was closely tied to the operation of West Indian plantations. The first attempts to set up trading posts – in the Gambia River region in 1612, further south at Ouidah on the Gulf of Guinea in 1623, at the future Senegalese city of Rufisque in 1635 – came to naught. The first successful French settlement occurred in 1638, when a Norman company set up an outpost on Gorée. Two decades later, in 1659, the French established the city of Saint-Louis, a port in what is now northern Senegal. By 1780, it boasted a population of 6000. Saint-Louis remained the centre of French activities in Africa for the next two centuries, a base for purchases of slaves, arabic gum and other products, and the spearhead for penetration of sub-Saharan Africa.[6]

The islands of the Indian Ocean also attracted French interest as ports for trade in spices and pepper, coffee, resins, cowrie-shells, natural dyestuffs, textiles and saltpetre as well as produce from eastern Asia, such as Chinese silks and teas and Japanese copper, and sites for sugar plantations.[7] Louis XIV established the East India Company (*Compagnie des Indes Orientales*) in 1664, granting it a monopoly on trade in India and the Indian Ocean for 50 years, as well as control over territories it occupied in India or Madagascar. The company did not thrive, and a second East India Company, organised in 1719 by a Scottish expatriate in France, John Law, was soon compromised by Law's bankruptcy, although it was reorganised and continued activities until 1769.

The French established three colonies in the Indian Ocean. In 1642, the French took possession of an uninhabited island which they named the Ile Bourbon after the ruling French dynasty. (After the Revolution, the name was changed to La Réunion.) It took 12 years for the first French colonists to arrive, and by 1700 the island still counted only 1500 inhabitants. Most were African slaves, imported to work on sugar-cane plantations and in the production of tropical spices for the French market; by the 1770s the island's population had risen to 8800 whites and 37 000 slaves. France also took over neighbouring Mauritius, another island without a native population which had first been occupied by the Dutch in 1598. After the Dutch withdrew at the beginning of the 1700s, France took possession in 1715 and renamed Mauritius the Ile de France. Although development was slow, the Ile de France, with much arable land and one of the best harbours in the Indian Ocean, was a promising site. Governor Mahé de la Bourdonnais, in the 1730s, created port facilities and built the city of Port-Louis, which served as capital for both the Ile de France and the Ile Bourbon. The Ile de France became a major trading entrepôt and, like its sister island, a prosperous plantation island; on the eve of the Revolution, the population included 4690 whites and 36 000 slaves. In 1756, France annexed the Seychelles archipelago, north of the Ile Bourbon and the Ile de France. Settlement was slow; in 1789 the total population was 600, five-sixths of them slaves. Trade, sugar and cotton provided a livelihood to the inhabitants.

French adventurers also attempted to establish settlements on a far larger island, Madagascar. An official of the East India Company set up a colony at Fort-Dauphin, in southern Madagascar, in 1643. Several dozen colonists followed, but possibilities for development were limited and relations with Malagasy chieftains tense. The settlement did not prosper, and the arrival of 2000 colonists in 1667 failed to revive the fledging outpost. Disputes among the French and violent confrontations with Malagasy caused the deaths of a number of Europeans. Many others fled the settlement, and the last detachment of colonists abandoned Fort-Dauphin in 1674. A century later, another aspiring colonial promoter, an officer in the Ile de France garrison, persuaded the government to provide funds and soldiers for another settlement at Fort-Dauphin; this colony lasted only from 1768 to 1770. The *ancien régime* saw one final try at colonisation. In 1774, the French minister of the navy invited a Hungarian adventurer called Beniowski to set up an outpost. Two years later, he sailed back to France, where he claimed to have established a city and won recognition for his claim on Madagascar from local chiefs; an enquiry proved his claims false. Not until 100 years later did the French make a successful attempt to take over Madagascar.[8]

India

India had excited European interest from time immemorial. In the 1600s, the British, French and Portuguese established toeholds in India, and a long struggle between the British and the French ensued for domination of the Indian subcontinent, a contest eventually won by the British. The dreams of some French colonialists of carving out a new empire in India were doomed to failure.

France nevertheless kept hold of five Indian *comptoirs*, small trading posts over which the French held sovereign rights. Acquisition of the *comptoirs* dated back to the age of Louis XIV, when the East India Company hatched a plan for a colony in India. In 1673, a French naval captain persuaded an Indian ruler to grant France rights to establish a *comptoir* at Pondichéry. Under Governor Joseph-François Dupleix the post prospered in the mid-1700s. The French extended their holdings through occupation of other *comptoirs*, including Chandernagor in 1674, Mahé in 1721, Yanaon in 1723 and Karikal in 1739. By 1742, France counted 12 outposts in India, though some were only tiny trading stations over which the French flag flew. Over the next 50 years, the vagaries of imperial rivalry in India saw France lose, win and exchange various outposts.[9]

The Revolution of 1789 and the Colonies

On the eve of the Revolution of 1789, France was left with its trading outposts in India and Senegal, Saint-Pierre and Miquelon, and the plantation colonies of the West Indies and the Indian Ocean. Recent years had seen unparalleled prosperity in the plantation colonies, and the status quo, including slavery, benefited the overseas possessions.

The storming of the Bastille on 14 July 1789, traditionally taken as the start of the French Revolution, brought little immediate change to the colonies. The Declaration of the Rights of Man and Citizen proclaimed equality for all, but law-makers did not imagine such principles to extend to colonial domains or slaves. The institution of a constitutional monarchy did not diminish the powers held by the metropolitan government; it gave the elected assembly the right to legislate on colonial issues, but legislators considered colonial issues a low priority. Nevertheless, the very existence of colonies posed serious questions about the governance of France and the particular problem of what role settlers would play in their own government. Were French settlers overseas, once subjects of the king now citizens of France, eligible to elect members to the national assembly? Must they follow France in the path of Revolution, even though a majority were hostile to the events which had taken place in Paris? Should colonies enjoy autonomy or self-administration? The major issue was the future of slavery. Before the Revolution, liberals in France had called for termination of the slave-trade; a few went further and called for emancipation of slaves. Such demands faced strident opposition from planters and slave-traders, who expressed concern about the local economic effects (and repercussions on the French mainland economy) of precipitate ending of slaving or freeing of slaves.

News of the taking of the Bastille reached the colonies only three months after 14 July, but settlers in Saint-Domingue soon formed provisional local councils. Violent incidents occurred, and insurrections threatened by slaves or mixed-blood (*mulâtre*) residents demanding rights. By 1791 Saint-Domingue was in a state of virtual war between slaves, *mulâtres* and whites.

Meanwhile, the issue of slavery divided legislators in Paris. The Society of the Friends of Blacks (*Société des Amis des Noirs*), founded just before the Revolution, gathered together opponents of the slave-trade and emancipationists. Planters and their supporters formed the Club Massiac. In 1792, with the arrival in power of the radical Jacobins, Paris stepped up efforts to restore authority in the Antilles, while legislative opinion veered towards emancipation. The Jacobin-dominated Convention, in September 1793, timidly decided to remove government subsidies to the slave-trade. Then, after much debate, the Convention unanimously voted for the abolition of slavery on 4 February 1794. Hope that freed slaves would volunteer to join the war against the British, and that conditions in the West Indies would calm down was more of a motivation for the action than desire to free slaves.

The British soon captured Martinique and Guadeloupe and attacked Saint-Domingue. Toussaint Louverture, a former slave who had led a black rebellion on Saint-Domingue, rallied to the French, and British conquest of France's largest West Indian possession was averted. The French went on the offensive and retook Guadeloupe and Martinique. For the remainder of the 1790s, the Caribbean islands continued to suffer civil unrest, British attacks and periodic occupation, and economic reversals caused by disruption to Atlantic trade.[10]

France's colonies in the Indian Ocean had been spared some of the troubles of the West Indies. *Mulâtres* and slaves had not mounted insurrections, and government officials purely and simply did not apply the emancipation decrees. The British Navy threatened the islands, and the economy took a downturn, but the islands struggled through the first years of the Revolution without undue disruption. In Africa, the residents of Saint-Louis, Gorée and Rufisque, like other French citizens, welcomed the decision by the revolutionary legislature to enact free trade in 1791; not surprisingly, they were less pleased with the abolition of slavery. In any case, the abolition decrees were never fully applied.

Despite the relative stability of the French government under the Directory (1795 to 1799), Paris had little time to devote to colonies. The government was busy fighting a war and restoring order to a country which, in a brief time, had seen multiple changes in government, the overthrow and execution of the king, and major economic and social upheaval.

Napoleon's Empire

The period of Napoleon's rule, as First Consul from 1799 to 1804 then as emperor until 1814 (and during the 'Hundred Days' of 1815), saw the shrinking and temporary disappearance of France's overseas empire through British conquest, colonial rebellion and the inaction of Paris. Napoleon lacked a real colonial policy, but he saw overseas possessions as complementary to the continental empire he sought to create in Europe. He maintained a sentimental attachment to the West Indies, partly under the influence of his first wife, Joséphine de Beauharnais, who was from Martinique. Yet Napoleon's re-establishment of slavery in the Antilles and in Guyane in 1802 and 1803 had more to do with desire to ensure the fortunes of planters and reap as much profit as possible from the West Indies than with any emotional consideration. Napoleon proved unable to restore French control and slavery in Saint-Domingue. In 1799, Toussaint Louverture began a campaign for independence; after four years of fighting, the defeated French withdrew in 1803, and Saint-Domingue gained independence under the name of Haiti.

Elsewhere, Napoleon was not an ardent colonialist. He showed indifference to France's huge claim in the Mississippi valley of North America. In 1803, the territory was restored to France after 40 years of Spanish rule, but the French flag flew for only a few months before Napoleon sold the colony to the United States. Napoleon displayed only casual interest in other overseas colonies, although considering possible expansion in Egypt or Algeria to compensate the nation for the loss of Saint-Domingue. He expressed general commitment to reconquering a French empire in India, but the plan came to naught. Vague projects to establish a French presence in lands as far apart as Muscat, Sind and Mozambique were all abandoned.[11]

The most ambitious of Napoleon's overseas ventures was an expedition to Egypt in 1798. Strategists saw French action there as a way to curb the efforts of Russia and Britain to gain influence in the Ottoman Empire, which held nominal sovereignty over the country. A French base could also provide a transit point for voyages to India and would endow France with a replacement for the West Indian colonies occupied by Britain. Since plans for a canal through the Suez isthmus had already been mooted, Egypt looked to hold great potential as a trading entrepôt. Finally, French takeover would safeguard the interests of the small French community in Egypt.

Commanding 13 ships and 36 000 soldiers and sailors, Napoleon set sail from Toulon in June 1798, conquered Malta *en route*, then landed in Alexandria; his troops fanned out to secure posts along the Nile delta before penetrating Cairo. Napoleon remained in Egypt for 14 months, but French rule lasted until 1801, when disease, demoralisation and the ever-increasing primacy of Britain forced them to evacuate the erstwhile colony.[12] For the remainder of his rule, Napoleon's attentions turned away from overseas empire – except to recover and defend the West Indian possessions – to favour expansion in continental Europe.

At the end of the disastrous Napoleonic Wars, France was left with not a single overseas colony. The victors deprived France permanently of several possessions, notably the Ile de France (Mauritius), the Seychelles, and various smaller Caribbean islands. Restored to France were Martinique and Guadeloupe in the West Indies, Guyane in South America, Saint-Pierre and Miquelon in the Atlantic, the Ile Bourbon, the five *comptoirs* in India, and the island of Gorée and city of Saint-Louis in Senegal. Compared with Britain's empire – Canada, British Honduras in central America, British Guyana in South America, India, Australia, a host of islands in the Caribbean, Atlantic and Indian Ocean, and various outposts in Africa – France was a much reduced imperial power.

The Vieilles Colonies *in the Nineteenth Century*

In the wake of Napoleon's defeat and the Congress of Vienna in 1814–15, the French government needed to devise plans for its recovered possessions. Paris sent a convoy of settlers to Senegal, but the shipwreck of one of the vessels, the *Méduse*, in 1816, compromised the project. A survivor, Julien Schmaltz, appointed governor of Senegal, tried to stimulate agriculture and transform Saint-Louis's hinterland into a plantation colony to replace Haiti as a source of tropical products. The initiative did not succeed, and Saint-Louis resumed its life as an entrepôt. New traders gradually arrived from France; most were merchants from Bordeaux, led by the Maurel and Prom company. Despite restrictions on slave-trading and a fall in the export of arabic gum, business boomed. With sales of European goods, and purchases of an assortment of African products, the private import-export business grew sevenfold from 1818 to 1844; the number of merchants grew from 4 to 30, and the number of middlemen working in trading climbed from 30 to more than 200. By the 1840s, Saint-Louis had a population of 12 000.

The plantation colonies of the West Indies and Réunion saw declining prosperity in the early 1800s. The impossibility of shipping sugar to Europe during the Napoleonic wars, when naval battles and blockades disrupted sea routes, had prompted the development of beet sugar in France as a substitute for the cane sugar of the colonies. The 'war of the two sugars' pitted metropolitan and colonial interests against each other, reducing colonial sales and the influence of the colonial lobby. Criticism of slavery foreshadowed threats to labour supply in the islands. New French settlers remained few.

One of the major achievements of the French Revolution of 1848 was the abolition of slavery. Abolitionists, led by Victor Schoelcher, won a battle against colonial interests in the heady days of revolution and republicanism. Slaves themselves were restive and, before the emancipation decrees reached the West Indies, a slave revolt erupted in Martinique. Whether abolition of slavery was thus a noble humanitarian gesture by a nation convinced of the evils of enslavement, an inevitable development because of declining profits, or freedom which might have been won by the slaves themselves, it led to the liberation of a quarter of a million slaves. Slaves were also given the vote – henceforth all French men in Martinique, Guadeloupe, Guyane and Réunion, whether white, mixed-blood or black enjoyed the suffrage – but they did not get land, training or capital. Many blacks continued to work in conditions which differed little from slavery, although some acquired small plots of land and became farmers. The *mulâtres*, generally already free and benefiting from access to education, emerged as the new professional elite. Nevertheless, Europeans in the islands retained their land, capital, rum distilleries and trading contracts, even if they never received full compensation for the emancipation of their slaves.

Labour was the great problem in the post-abolition plantation economy since the former slaves, other than in dire circumstances, avoided plantation work. Planters located a new source of labour in India, both the French *comptoirs* and British India. Recruiters took 25 000 Indians to Martinique from 1850 to 1914, 37 000 to Guadeloupe and 8000 to Guyane; 68 000 labourers arrived in Réunion from India (including some from China, Madagascar and Africa). They added to the demographic complexity of the old colonies, sometimes intermarrying with blacks or Europeans. Their labour helped assure the primacy of sugar production in the islands for a century after emancipation.[13]

Guyane experienced a different development. In 1851, the French government created a penitentiary in Guyane and continued to send prisoners there until 1932; the penal establishment did not officially close until 1945. As many as 70 000 prisoners were transported to South America, both common criminals and political prisoners, such as Captain Alfred Dreyfus, the Jewish officer whose conviction for treason – although he was later proved innocent of the crime – at the end of the nineteenth century became a *cause célèbre* in France. The inhospitable natural conditions of Guyane made the penitentiary a 'green hell' for both prisoners and warders, and Devil's Island attained notoriety. The only other resource of Guyane to be exploited, apart from its use as a prison camp, was gold, discovered in 1855. By the end of the nineteenth century, gold accounted for nine-tenths of Guyane's exports (though it represented less than half a percent of the world's total gold production) and occupied most of the free labour force in the colony. Yet as deposits reached exhaustion, after 1916, the gold rush came to an end.[14]

The Revolution of 1848 also brought about the end of slavery in Senegal. Fortunately, from the point of view of Saint-Louis's businessmen, the same year saw the first successful pressing in industrial quantities of oil made from groundnuts. Production of groundnuts, which developed substantially from the mid-1860s onwards, provided a new lifeline for the economy. What was required for successful production and export of groundnuts was French control over a larger region of Senegal. In 1854, the businessmen of Saint-Louis persuaded Paris to appoint as governor a young army officer, Louis Faidherbe, who had recently established control over Podor, a strategic post on the Senegal river east of Saint-Louis. Faidherbe's military skill, interest in Africa and enthusiasm for expansion promised to push the French African frontier further into the interior and to transform France's Senegalese outposts from coastal trading stations into the bases of a continental empire in black Africa.[15]

The Treaty of Paris of 1815 left France with five *comptoirs* in India – Pondichéry, Mahé, Yanaon, Karikal and Chandernagor – where it could transact business, maintain local military forces (with a handful of European officers) and exercise sovereignty. The *comptoirs* were geographically separate; indeed each consisted of several non-contiguous concessions of land – a difficult and awkward challenge to administration and economic development. The population of the *comptoirs* was large and growing, and Indians greatly outnumbered Europeans; in 1857, of 215 887 residents, French India counted only 707 Europeans. The economies of the *comptoirs* were based on production of goods for this large population and on exports of groundnuts, copra, pepper, onions, tobacco, cotton and indigo; contraband played a large role in local commerce. Labour became a prime export of the French outposts after 1848, but the *comptoirs* themselves remained somnolent and generally forgotten French possessions. The *comptoirs*, like most of the older outposts, diminished in importance after France, beginning in 1830, began the conquest of a new overseas empire.

1 The Conquest of Empire: Africa and the Indian Ocean

Only 15 years after the defeat of Napoleon, France again became involved in an overseas adventure of conquest and colonisation. The invasion of Algiers marked a new step in the creation of an empire in Africa, although it took over 80 years for France to gain control over Algeria, the protectorates of Tunisia and Morocco, and the large expanses of sub-Saharan Africa administered as French West Africa (*Afrique Occidentale Française*, AOF) and French Equatorial Africa (*Afrique Equatoriale Française*, AEF). In addition, France established an outpost on the horn of Africa, in the east, and took over the enormous island of Madagascar and the small archipelago of the Comoros in the Indian Ocean. France thereby claimed its share – a generous portion – of the 'Dark Continent'.

The Maghreb

Algeria

Algeria, directly across the Mediterranean from France's southern coast, had been a sphere of French commercial activity since the early 1500s, when its ruler had granted merchants the right to establish a trading post, the *Bastion de France*, near the present-day city of Annaba. From this entrepôt, goods from Africa and the Middle East, including gold, spices, ostrich plumes and other exotic commodities, found a transit-point to Europe. The fortunes of the *Bastion de France* varied over the next centuries and the *ancien régime* made no effort to expand French dominions from this base.

The situation changed in the early nineteenth century. The conquest of Algiers in 1830 represented a response to a domestic political situation more than a direct start to commercial expansion or colonisation, although merchants in Marseille enthusiastically supported intervention. In the early 1800s, the Ottoman emperor ruled the Regency of Algiers through a local dey, but Constantinople's authority was more nominal than real. Political quarrels and financial problems beset the Regency, which depended for its income primarily on the activities of slave-traders and corsairs, pirates who raided international shipping and provoked British attacks on the 'Barbary coast'. France kept its distance from British bombardments, but a financial matter festered between Paris and Algiers. During the wars of the 1790s, Jewish financiers in Algiers had arranged for grain to be shipped to southern France and to Napoleon's troops in Italy and Egypt; a French debt of 7 to 8 million francs to the merchants remained outstanding. One of them, who himself owed money to the Regency government, convinced the dey that he was unable to pay his own debt until the French settled their long-standing account. Paris, angry at the amount of interest levied on the loan and unwilling to accept full responsibility for the debts of the revolutionary regime, postponed payment even after the dey made an official request that the question be settled.

On 29 April 1827, the French consul in Algiers visited the dey to pay his respects during a festival marking the end of the Muslim month of fasting. When the dey asked about French repayment of the loan, the consul allegedly answered in a high-handed way that the august French king could not condescend to enter into correspondence with a North African potentate on a question such as debt. The dey took offence, lost his temper, swatted the consul six times on the arm with his ceremonial fly-whisk and ordered him out of the reception hall. Soon French ships arrived in Algiers to demand an apology; the dey then destroyed the trading posts at the *Bastion de France*. This constituted a serious blow to French Mediterranean commerce, the cost to be borne by Marseille traders. The diplomatic conflict remained a stand-off.

Meanwhile, in France, opposition mounted to the increasingly reactionary government of the unpopular Restoration monarch. The king tried to appease his opponents by appointing a moderate government, which in 1829 sent an emissary to Algiers to suggest an armistice. Algerian ships, however, fired on the ambassador's ship as it left the Regency after inconclusive talks. This provided an excuse for King Charles X to dismiss his moderate government and adopt an ultraconservative line, with the effect of fuelling opposition still further. The new prime minister, Jules de Polignac, tried to pressure the Ottoman sultan to bend the will of the Algerian dey, then he attempted to provoke the ruler of Egypt – technically also a vassal of the sultan but harbouring expansionist urges in North Africa – to act against Algiers. Neither proposal stimulated a response.

Coercion had failed, revolt threatened the French monarchy, the distressed merchants of Marseille pleaded for French action against the dey, and political analysts warned of the rising menace of British seapower in the Mediterranean. In March 1830, King Charles X announced he was ready to redress the insult to France which the fly-whisk incident of 1827 symbolised. A fleet of 635 French ships loaded with 34 184 soldiers and 3389 noncombatants, in addition to sailors, left Toulon on 25 May and, after a delay caused by bad weather, began landing in Algiers on 14 June. Some 43 000 North African forces fought valiantly against the French, but on 4 July the defenders evacuated the fortress of Algiers. The following day the French raised their flag over the kasbah. Five days later the dey went into exile. French soldiers, despite official policy to the contrary, pillaged Algiers, committed violence on men and women, desecrated mosques and cemeteries, and confiscated land and houses.

The conquest of Algiers proved popular at home, but the victory was not enough to save the French king. An election held just as the French troops occupied Algiers returned an opposition majority. The government's decision to invalidate the results of the voting set off a three-day revolution in Paris which toppled the Restoration monarchy and led to the establishment of the July Monarchy under King Louis-Philippe, who ruled until another revolution in 1848. Charles X's last-minute effort to save the Restoration by overseas expansion had failed, but it gave France its first new foreign possession since Bonaparte's ill-fated conquests.

French rule of Algeria in 1830 was limited to the coastal cities of Algiers, Oran (to the west) and Bône (Annaba) (to the east). The next 40 years saw the extension of French control along the Mediterranean littoral from the Moroccan to the Tunisian border, inland towards the Atlas Mountains and eventually into the Saharan interior. Conquest was costly and gradual; it took 40 years for the French to secure their hold throughout Algeria and 'pacify' remaining pockets of resistance. In doing so, Paris had to wage war against numerous chiefs, notably Abd el-Khader.

Emir Abd el-Khader was the 23-year-old son of the head of an Islamic confraternity in Mascara. He had made a pilgrimage to Mecca, studied in Muslim institutes in Cairo, Baghdad and Damascus, and taken part in an anti-Ottoman movement under the aegis of the Moroccan sultan. El-Khader was in the process of extending his area of political influence when France invaded Algeria. In 1834, after a number of skirmishes, the French commander in Oran signed a treaty with el-Khader. The Algerian agreed to free French prisoners, recognise French sovereignty over Algiers, Oran and Bône, and grant foreigners trading privileges in his zones of domination; in return, the French recognised el-Khader's sovereignty over a region extending from the Moroccan border to central Algeria. Despite several subsequent battles between French and Algerian forces, another agreement in 1837 extended the area over which France recognised the emir's control to roughly two-thirds of Algeria.

The 1840s saw major French campaigns to push back the frontiers of empire in North Africa. Led by General Bugeaud, an army which occasionally comprised a third of all French troops eliminated resistance, extended French control and consolidated authority in areas already conquered. El-Khader commanded resistance but suffered great losses; the French also put pressure on the sultan of Morocco, the emir's mentor, to declare him an outlaw. In December 1847, el-Khader surrendered. He was exiled to France and held prisoner until 1852, when Emperor Napoleon III released him and accorded him an annuity. El-Khader moved to Syria, where he helped defend Christians from Muslim attack in 1860. France's former enemy won recognition as an ally; his pension was increased, he made a triumphal visit to Paris and was awarded the Legion of Honour before his death in 1883.[1]

Meanwhile, the French continued military subjugation of Algeria, attacking nationalist commanders, millenarian religious movements and chieftains in remote mountain regions and desert oases who refused to accept French authority. Bugeaud and his successors burned countless villages, slaughtered livestock and destroyed the olive groves, fig orchards and wheatfields which provided peasants' livelihood. Algerians were thus starved and terrorised into submission in a manner which provoked criticism even by some colonial promoters. Simultaneously, the expropriation of much Algerian land and the installation of numerous colonists – the European population of Algeria soared from 37 000 in 1841 to 279 700 only 30 years later – turned Algeria into a colony of settlement and further sapped the strength of the resistance. In 1871, France repressed the last major nationalist movement, led by el-Mokhrani, and extended control over the hold-out Kabyle region east of Algiers.[2]

Conquest of Algeria gave France an immense domain in North Africa, a territory of 2.4 million square kilometres – although seven-eighths of the country was desert. The coastal bands provided fertile agricultural land, and Algiers, Oran and Bône became centres of trade and administration. Algeria formed the most important site of French colonial activity. Promoters saw Algeria as the extension of metropolitan France to the other shore of the Mediterranean. So important was Algeria to France, at least in colonialists' eyes, that it became constitutionally and legally an integral part of France. By the late nineteenth century, with farms and vineyards, French-style cities and European settlers, Algeria was well on the way to becoming *Algérie française*. The indigenous Berbers and Arabs had been relegated to the background, a picturesque population living on the fringes of their own country.

Tunisia

France did not enlarge its Maghreb domain beyond Algeria for half a century. The next area for expansion, at the beginning of the 1880s, was Tunisia. With an area of 155 000 square kilometres, Tunisia was a small prize. But it occupied strategic importance, across the Algerian frontier and only 150 kilometres from Sicily; Tunisia offered good port facilities, especially at Bizerte. France and Italy, as well as Britain, counted significant expatriate communities in Tunisia and maintained consulates there. Ties were also commercial; France had advanced a major loan to Tunisia in the mid-1800s and had trading interests.

Tunisia formed a province of the decaying Ottoman Empire but enjoyed a large measure of autonomy under a bey. Central administration, however, was weak. Tax collection was devolved onto tax-farmers, and only one-fifth of the revenues ever reached the national treasury. Many hill tribes and desert nomads lived in quasi-independence. Economic conditions deteriorated through the 1800s, as foreign fleets curbed corsairs, and droughts perennially wreaked ill effects on production of cereals and olives. Because of accords with foreign traders dating back to the sixteenth century, customs duties were limited to 3 per cent of the value of imported goods; yet manufactured products from overseas, primarily textiles, flooded Tunisia and gradually destroyed local artisan industries.

In 1861, the Tunisian prime minister made an effort to modernise administration and tried to increase revenues by doubling taxes. The major effect, only fully felt by 1864, was widespread rural insurrection, coupled with great misery. The government had to negotiate a new loan from foreign bankers. In 1867, an attempt to secure money failed; government revenues were insufficient to meet annual interest payments on the national debt. Tunisia plunged towards bankruptcy. Two years later, France, Italy and Britain set up an international finance commission to sort out Tunisia's economic problems and safeguard Western stakes. Their actions enjoyed only partial success, largely because of opposition from foreign traders to increases in the sacrosanct customs levy. In 1873 the Tunisian prime minister again undertook reforms and attacked the widespread financial abuses within the bureaucracy. The results were initially promising, but bad harvests and palace intrigues led to his downfall. Tunisia seemed more unstable than ever.

In 1877, Russia declared war on the Ottomans. Russian victory foreshadowed the dismemberment of the empire, including independence for several Balkan possessions and international discussions about the future of the North African provinces. At the Berlin Conference of 1878, convened to resolve the Ottoman question, Britain opposed total dismantling of the Ottoman empire but acceded to French requests for control of Tunisia. Germany, seeing the French claim as a way to divert French attention from revengeful action in Europe (where France had suffered defeat at Prussian hands in 1870–1) and little concerned about the southern Mediterranean, agreed to allow France overlordship in Tunisia. Italy strongly opposed the plan, but its ambassadors proved unable to impose their will, much to the discontent of the Italian public.

Paris did not act immediately; parliament remained in an anti-colonial mood and no groundswell of popular opinion mandated

a takeover of Tunisia. Several developments spurred France to
action. In 1880, the British owners of the railway linking Tunis
with the coast put their company up for sale. An Italian concern
successfully bid for the enterprise, leaving France worried about
possible Italian intervention. Another incident, also in 1880, concerned the sale of a 100 000-hectare property by a former Tunisian
prime minister. Negotiations involved complicated arrangements to forestall pre-emption of the sale by the bey's government or by proprietors of adjacent tracts of land. A French
consortium buying the property believed the deal had been completed, but a British citizen, ostensibly representing neighbouring landholders, pre-empted the sale and occupied the land (though
without paying for it). A judge sent by London to investigate discovered that the British purchaser was acting on behalf of the
bey's government and Italian businessmen; moreover, he discovered
that the Briton had used fraud to stake his claims. The sale was
cancelled, and French buyers got the property. Paris moved to
protect French claims, as London and Berlin gently warned that
if France did not act, they might reconsider their go-ahead for
French occupation.

French diplomats scrambled to convince unenthusiastic parliamentarians and bureaucrats, all the while looking for a new
incident to precipitate intervention. In March 1881, a foray by
Tunisian Khroumir tribesmen across the border into Algeria caused
the deaths of several Algerians. Here was the incident for which
the French had hoped. By mid-April, French troops had landed
in Tunisia and, on 12 May 1881, forced the bey to sign the Bardo
Treaty granting France a protectorate over Tunisia. Although
soldiers took until May 1882 to occupy the whole country and
stamp out resistance, France's empire counted a new domain.
Germany and Britain remained silent; Italy was outraged but
powerless.

The protectorate was different, at least on paper, from French
annexation of Algeria. The bey remained in office, and Tunisia
retained its legal status as an independent country; existing treaties with other states continued in force. Yet the powers of the
French Resident were great: he was prime minister, comptroller
of the country's finances and commander of its armed forces.
The energetic Resident appointed in 1882, Paul Cambon, soon
curbed the considerable prerogatives of foreign consuls, reduced
the bey's government to a rubber stamp for French decisions,

and brought in enough French administrators to reorganise the justice and finance systems. France for all practical purposes ruled the country as another colony.[3]

Morocco

Of all the North African countries, Morocco had the most ambiguous relationship with Europe. Morocco's Islamic dynasty had for more than seven centuries ruled much of southern Spain; not until 1492 did Catholic Spaniards complete the 'reconquest' and end Muslim rule in southwestern Europe. The sultan, who possessed a large realm in North Africa, then conquered the Songhay kingdom in the western Soudan. Morocco remained an international power. The Spanish and Portuguese continued the campaign against the Moroccans, however, with incursions into North Africa and the takeover of several enclaves on the seacoast.

Europeans looked to Morocco for wool and other local products as well as goods from black Africa, all the while greatly resenting the activity of corsairs off the Moroccan coast. Morocco favoured trade links with Europe which provided government revenue. As an independent country, Morocco treated on equal terms with its commercial and diplomatic partners. European leaders showed respect for the sultan, whose prestige was enhanced by direct descent from the prophet Muhammed. Despite occasional financial difficulties by the late 1700s, trade between Europe and Morocco boomed.

Morocco did not fare so well in the early nineteenth century, victim to droughts and plague, revolts by Islamic confraternities and trading difficulties. French conquest of Algiers sent shock waves through Morocco. The sultan's support for Abd el-Khader provoked French ships to bombard Tangiers and Essaouira; Bugeaud's soldiers crossed the border from Algeria and vanquished Moroccan troops at the battle of Isly in 1844. Chastened, the sultan withdrew backing from el-Khader and formalised borders between Morocco and French Algeria.

Europeans demanded increasingly better terms of trade from Morocco. In 1856, London signed a treaty which assured British merchants preferential rights in the sultanate. Spain tried more militant tactics: an army of 50 000 men occupied Tetuan. Morocco managed to keep losses to a minimum in the resulting negotiations, but the sultan agreed to pay an indemnity to Madrid.

Without sufficient revenues to do so, the Moroccan government
was forced to contract a loan with the British. In the wake of the
Spanish war, the French also secured preferential trading arrangements in 1863.

Defeated on the battlefield and economically weakened, Morocco struggled to maintain its political independence while the
situation worsened. Merchants, led by French traders from Marseille, supported by Paris, pressed for further concessions. In
particular, they demanded that foreign consuls be allowed to
exercise extra-territorial authority not only over their own nationals
but also over employees of consulates and foreign business-houses
in Morocco, and even over trading intermediaries and some producers of export goods in the countryside. Such protection generally exempted Moroccans from payment of various taxes to the
sultan and military service in the Moroccan forces. Confirmed by
international conferences in 1877–8 and 1880, these arrangements
led to widespread abuses, as numerous Moroccans gained foreign
protection (and foreign earnings); the sultan's treasury stood
deprived of needed income. The Europeans seemed temporarily
satisfied with their gains. The British prime minister in 1895,
however, commented that the European powers might eventually
carve up Morocco. At the very end of the century, the French
army in Algeria made incursions and captured several Moroccan
oases with impunity. The young sultan who ruled from 1894 to
1908, Abdelaziz, proved unpopular because of inability to stand
up to the Europeans, his imposition of new taxes, a hedonistic
private life, and criticisms of slack religious practice. Rebels, pos-
ing as restorers of Islam and warriors against Europeans, became
virtual warlords in certain areas by the early years of the twentieth century.

French commanders in Algeria undertook expansion on their
own initiative, despite the reluctance of authorities in Paris to
sanction their moves. Early in 1903, using the pretext of a border incident, troops moving from Algeria occupied a further Moroccan post. Later in the year, an intrepid French officer, Hubert
Lyautey, who had previously served in Madagascar and Indochina
and had just won promotion to the rank of general, marched
westwards and occupied Béchar. The action specifically violated
boundaries recognised in Franco-Moroccan treaties of the 1840s.
The following year, Lyautey's troops moved further onto Moroccan soil, this time in direct disobedience to orders from the Min-

ister of War, Lyautey's superior. The general threatened to resign if Paris did not condone his action.

The Minister of Foreign Affairs, whose portfolio included relations with Morocco, issued only a vague disavowal of Lyautey's move, because he was concerned about the prominence of Britons among Abdelaziz' advisers and he had been attempting through international negotiation to reinforce France's position in Morocco. In 1904, the British foreign minister assured France of London's acquiescence to Paris's Moroccan manoeuvres in return for French willingness to give Britain free rein in Egypt. The French minister had already signed a secret accord with Italy giving Rome *carte blanche* in Tripolitania (part of Libya) in return for the Italians leaving the French alone in Morocco. France acceded to Spanish plans to extend their foothold in northern Morocco, albeit much to the outrage of the French colonial lobby, which organised a Moroccan Committee in 1904 to promote French influence in the sultanate. Germany watched the goings-on with vigilance which, French colonialists feared, foreshadowed action.

The Moroccans became more thoroughly indebted to French financial interests because of renewed need for loans. In 1904, the sultan signed an agreement with a French bank for a large advance, much of which was used simply to pay off existing loans; the bank took over 60 per cent of Morocco's customs revevues for 35 years to assure repayment. The next year, the French ambassador presented a list of financial demands to the sultan which included a French monopoly on various public works projects, supervision of exports and imports, and the creation of a national bank.

The sultan found an unexpected ally in the German kaiser, Wilhelm II, who visited Tangiers in 1905. The German emperor was said to favour the maintenance of Morocco's territorial integrity and independence, and the visit produced a confrontation with the French. The upshot of the so-called First Moroccan Crisis was the resignation of the French foreign minister and the convening of an international conference on Morocco. At Algeciras in 1906, thirteen powers, including Morocco, recognised the country's sovereignty and unity, although they dictated stringent political and financial terms to the sultan. France won a preponderant position in managing Moroccan ports and customs, and in constituting the new national bank. Takeover of Morocco and a European war were narrowly averted.

The Algeciras Treaty calmed the great powers, but dissidents in Morocco accused the sultan of capitulation to the Europeans. Some called for a holy war, and parts of the country rose in open rebellion. Early in 1907, a prominent French doctor in Marrakesh was killed, having been suspected, probably rightly, of conspiring to lay the groundwork for French takeover of Morocco. In response, Lyautey sent soldiers across the border to occupy the important town of Oujda. Meanwhile, another incident occurred on the Atlantic coast of Morocco. As part of the Algeciras Treaty, the French obtained the right to enlarge port facilities at Casablanca and build a railway line from the central city to the port. Local residents suspected, possibly correctly, that the tracks would cut through and desecrate a Muslim cemetery. Moroccans attacked the worksite and killed seven labourers. French ships thereupon bombarded Casablanca, destroying much of the city and killing between 600 and 1500 people. The ships then landed soldiers, whom Moroccans accused of pillage, rape and brutal reprisals for attacks on Europeans in Casablanca.

Moroccan outrage targeted the French and the sultan, Abdelaziz, impotent in the face of European gunpower. A month after the Casablanca massacre, government and religious leaders deposed Abdelaziz in favour of his brother Moulay Hafid. Although buoyed by popular support and riding on a surge of anti-European sentiment, he proved as powerless as his predecessor. At the beginning of 1909, he formally accepted the Algeciras Treaty. The French moreover forced the sultan to accept continued occupation of Oujda and Casablanca, finance the costs of the occupation and pay an indemnity to the victims of the bombardment of Casablanca. Trying to profit from Moroccan submission, Spanish troops mounted an expedition to enlarge Spain's territory in North Africa, but gains were few.

Part of the settlement was another major loan, largely by French banks, to the Moroccan goverment in 1910. As surety, creditors pocketed 95 per cent of Moroccan customs receipts and held a monopoly over profitable sales of tobacco, hashish and opium. French, German and Spanish mining companies gained rights to prospect and exploit Morocco's considerable mineral resources. Faced with political and financial domination, and military occupation of several cities, Moroccan dissidents hatched a plot to attack the capital, Fès, take Moulay Hafid into custody and mount a war on both foreigners and sultan. The rebels managed only to besiege Fès in March 1911. Using the pretext of danger to French residents and inventing an appeal from the sultan to justify their action, French troops occupied Fès.

This action provoked Germany, which had until then acquiesced to French moves. In the Second Moroccan Crisis of July 1911, Berlin sent a ship, the *Panther*, to Agadir, ostensibly to protect German nationals and businesses, but in reality to confront the French. France and Germany again averted war with a last-minute gentlemanly exchange: in return for allowing France a free hand in Morocco, Germany was ceded a portion of the French Congo. With France's imperial rivals bought off and the sultan supine, nothing stood in the way of France's assuming political control over Morocco.

The treaty inaugurating a protectorate came into force in 1912. A band of soldiers revolted, accusing Moulay Hafid of having sold Morocco to foreigners, and as many as 20 000 lay siege to Fès. Paris called in Lyautey to break the siege, then appointed him French Resident-General in Morocco. Moulay Hafid abdicated at the end of 1912, replaced by a docile brother; although receiving a handsome pension from the French, he symbolically destroyed symbols of royal authority before joining another brother, the former sultan Abdelaziz, in internal exile in the international zone of Tangiers. Resistance to French conquest persisted in remote districts; not until 1934 was the country entirely pacified.[4]

French West Africa (AOF)

The acquisition of Algeria, Tunisia and Morocco gave France a large empire in North Africa, and France also accumulated colonies in black Africa. Unlike the Maghreb, sub-Saharan Africa – except for a few coastal outposts – was still largely virgin territory for Europeans in the early 1800s. Much of the interior remained unmapped, European commercial interests were limited to the slave trade and the barter of manufactured goods for tropical commodities, the possibilities for colonial settlement were few, and Christian evangelisation was uncertain. Yet, the conquest of Africa south of the Sahara, the 'scramble for Africa' which reached an apogee in the last decades of the nineteenth century, became synonymous with the 'new imperialism'. European invasion and occupation left all of the African continent (other than Liberia and Ethiopia) under foreign control. Conquest, however, was a long process of creeping expansion from already established bases, military expeditions across desert and jungle, and agreements signed in European capitals to draw lines across maps of distant countries.

The major bases for French expansion were Senegal (Gorée and Saint-Louis, which the French had held since the 1600s), the old slave-trading entrepôts on the Gulf of Guinea where France established a new toehold, and the cities of the North African coast. French expansion in sub-Saharan Africa, like that of its colonial rivals, did not begin in earnest until the 1880s; it then took a good 20 years for Africa to be divided. France's aim was to gain control of western Africa moving inwards from the coast of Senegal, the Gulf of Guinea and Algeria. Further south, France took over a portion of equatorial Africa, Gabon and the French Congo.

However logical the territorial consolidation of the AOF and AEF might seem, there existed no grand plan for achieving it, and most land was acquired at the expense of armed forays, negotiations with African chieftains and great efforts to secure posts over which the French flag had tentatively been raised. Such endeavours took place in the face of persistent African resistance, hardships imposed by difficult terrain, tropical disease and inadequate supplies, and divided opinion at home about the value of expansion. Colonialism in sub-Saharan Africa was an incremental achievement made possible only by the determination of colonial promoters, explorers and military officers, the force of arms, an ideology of racial domination, and the fear that if France did not take over new territories, its rivals would step into the brink.

Senegal and the Casamance

One of the most illustrative episodes of French penetration was the move into the Casamance, 28 000 square kilometres of territory in present-day Senegal wedged between the British colony of the Gambia (itself a thread-like possession on either side of the Gambia River) and the Portuguese colony of Guinea. Portuguese traders had done business in the Casamance since the sixteenth century and founded its main city, Ziguinchor. Portuguese control nevertheless remained nominal, and from the 1820s onwards, French officials and traders in Senegal expressed interest in moving into the Casamance.

French authorities persuaded African chiefs to permit them to establish outposts, but a fort built upriver from Ziguinchor in 1842 attracted only five European settlers and exhausted no fewer than 22 commanders in fifteen years. Several French companies purchased rice for Gorée and Saint-Louis and bought cotton, wax and palm-nuts for export from the region. Their success inspired other initiatives, and gradually French influence, thanks to various individuals, extended eastwards along the Casamance River. One Emmanuel Bertrand-Bocandé pioneered French expansion from Karabane, a post established in 1836. Bertrand-Bocandé meddled in local African affairs and got himself accepted as mediator in a tribal conflict which had produced armed raids and pillage of Karabane. He persuaded the governor of Senegal to dispatch a warship after a particularly bad bout of livestock-raiding in 1850. The combatants were not impressed with the single French gunboat, so Bertrand-Bocandé convinced the governor to send extra vessels and a detachment of soldiers. The show of force worked, and the chiefs accepted a treaty recognising French sovereignty over Karabane. Bertrand-Boucandé emerged as the hero of the moment, rewarded with a concession of land and the Legion of Honour.

Such stories were repeated as private traders or military officers secured treaties from local rulers, sometimes after giving them money, dabbling in local disputes or using sheer force. Incidents could usually be found to justify intervention: the pillaging of a French ship which had run aground in Djembering in 1864 provided an excuse to send in soldiers, occupy a village, levy a fine on its inhabitants, institute a head-tax, then sign a peace treaty. Similar documents ceded further land and trading rights, and promised the submission of local chiefs to France. The colonial government in Saint-Louis warned against undue haste in expansion, but French control pushed steadily onwards. By the 1880s France controlled much of the Casamance; in 1886, Portugal renounced sovereignty over Ziguinchor in return for French cession of a tract further south. The following year, the British and French signed a convention defining the boundaries of their respective colonies of Senegal and Gambia.

Unlike some other areas conquered in western Africa, the Casamance presented distinct commercial potential. French firms in the early 1800s bought agricultural products and sold sugar, flour, beer, wine, textiles and – not without grave effects on local warfare – armaments. After the middle of the century, the cultivation of groundnuts became the primary export activity. Rubber took over in the 1880s, production soaring from 59 tonnes in 1883 to 252 tonnes sixteen years later. Firms such as the Casamance Commercial and Agricultural Company, established in 1880, paid the government an annual rent in return for the right to gather rubber, build roads and develop the territory for profit. The harsh working conditions to which the company subjected African labourers provoked criticism from the colonial officials – and a counter-charge by the company's director that the government always took the side of the native against the European. But as business prospered, the Casamance proved one of the more valuable French possessions in western Africa.[5]

Guinea

The Southern Rivers Region (*Rivières du Sud*), which became French Guinea, had attracted Europeans for several centuries before the French established a permanent colony there. Europeans obtained slaves, elephant skin and ivory, arabic gum, hardwoods, rice, palm oil, coffee, kola nuts and groundnuts in exchange for textiles, alcohol, armaments, iron, tobacco, glass and other manufactured goods. The Guinea coast provided a market for trade between Europeans and coastal peoples, and the terminus for supplies arriving by caravan from the African interior.

In the mid-nineteenth century, French authorities in Senegal decided that trading treaties had not sufficiently 'pacified' the Southern Rivers and in the 1860s began a war of conquest against Lat Dior, ruler of the Cayor region. The pillaging of French vessels and attacks on merchants were trumped up to justify the imposition of protectorates, which facilitated exports of groundnuts and rubber. Military action, persuasion or monetary rewards secured the submission of local chiefs – one chief was taken to Paris, fêted and given the Legion of Honour (then subsequently arrested and exiled to Senegal). French control moved steadily inland with the expansion of trade, claims on territory and efforts to prevent German and British expansion. By the 1880s, France had successfully curbed German influence in Guinea and signed a treaty with London delimiting the border between Guinea and British Sierra Leone.

One of the more challenging areas for conquest in the Guinea hinterland was Fouta-Djalon, a theocratic Muslim state with rich supplies of groundnuts, sesame, lemons and livestock. French troops advanced from both Senegal and the south, encircling Fouta-Djalon in order to link Senegal and Guinea. The army pressured the ruler to accept a French protectorate in 1881. The language of the treaty was suitably high-minded but almost laughably hypo-critical:

> Fouta-Djalon, which a long and ancient friendship has united to France, and knowing that the French people do not intend to extend their possessions in Africa but only maintain friendly relations designed to favour commercial exchanges, and hav-ing long known that the French never meddle in the internal affairs of their allies and that they absolutely respect the laws, traditions, customs and religion of others,

welcomed the proclamation of French overlordship. The French promised salaries to various chiefs of the region – salaries which were never paid.

In the years following, French troops made further incursions on Fouta-Djalon; in 1888 a new treaty replaced the salaries the French were supposed to pay with gifts to the chiefs. The great powers of Europe did not delay in recognising the treaty. French authorities, however, made no effort to complete military occu-pation. Ironically, British trading expanded significantly under the noses of the French. The French finally became annoyed that trade in Fouta-Djalon was being directed towards Sierra Leone, and they exacted yet another treaty, in 1891, in which chiefs 'for-mally agree to make all their purchases from the French'. France promised security and more money. Three years later, after re-ports of pillaging, officials resolved to establish effective control over Fouta-Djalon, though straining financial and military resources to do so. The way for development of rubber exports was now open.[6] Such a lengthy period of conquest and the signing of treaties, often negotiated and frequently violated, was typical of European expansion in Africa.

Dahomey

In the 1600s, French, Portuguese, British and Dutch captains es-tablished fortified trading posts along the coast of what became Dahomey (present-day Benin), especially at Ouidah. Profitable slave-trading from these outposts continued through the early nine-teenth century. French interest in Dahomey renewed in the 1840s with the explorations of Commander Bouët-Willaumez and the activities of the Régis firm of Marseille, which collected palm oil from Dahomey (and other regions).

Through treaties in the 1860s with the major chief of Daho-mey, Gléglé, France obtained coastal concessions around Grand Popo in the west and Porto-Novo in the east. Cotonou and the central coast remained under African control. In 1890 the French mounted a military campaign, which failed to wrest the central coast from Béhanzin, Gléglé's son and successor. Two years later, under the command of General Dodds, the French tried again. Béhanzin, whom even opponents recognised as a proud and brave warrior, wrote defiantly to the French about their intentions to take several villages in his realm:

> I have just been informed that the French government has declared war on Dahomey.... The first time [I fought two years earlier] I did not know how to make war, but now I do know. I have so many men that you would say that they were worms coming out of their holes. I am the king of the blacks, and the whites have nothing to say about what I do. The vil-lages of which you speak are indeed mine, they belong to me and they want to be independent.... I would like to know how many independent French villages have been attacked by me, King of Dahomey. Please remain calm, carry out your trade in Porto-Novo, and we will thus always remain at peace, just as before. [But] if you want war, I am ready.

French firepower bested Dahomey's armies, and Béhanzin fled northwards to his inland capital at Abomey. A third French cam-paign, in 1893—4, resulted in the capture of Béhanzin, who was exiled to Martinique with five of his wives and his favourite son and daughter. (After his death in 1906, Béhanzin's remains were returned to Dahomey to be interred with full honours in the presence of the French governor.)

The French placed a tame successor on Béhanzin's throne, and set up a colonial administration. It proclaimed freedom of com-merce, abolished slavery and human sacrifice (a feature of some traditional ceremonies), established a head-tax, and promoted missionary activities. French businesses, led by Régis, exploited oil-producing resources, which accounted for over 90 per cent of Dahomey's exports.[7]

The Côte-d'Ivoire

The central region of the Gulf of Guinea was called the Ivory Coast, the Côte-d'Ivoire. In 1637, a small band of French Capuchin priests settled at Assinie, although they enjoyed little success in converting Africans. Fifty years later, a French firm opened a trading post, and two Dominican priests landed. Neither businessmen nor missionaries prospered, and in 1705 the French abandoned Assinie. Other Europeans continued to trade in the area, primarily in slaves, and the British became well established in the area which became Ghana.

Commander Bouët-Willaumez, who had raised the French flag in other locations along the Gulf of Guinea, took possession of Grand Bassam in 1842; the following year he claimed Assinie. The conquest, accomplished by agreements with local chiefs, was straightforward, although Africans besieged Grand Bassam in 1852; the governor of Senegal sent in troops under an energetic young commander, Faidherbe, later responsible for much French expansion in west Africa. The new possessions did not prove profitable. After the Franco-Prussian War of 1870–1, the debilitated French evacuated the Côte-d'Ivoire for the second time. Paris did not relinquish sovereignty, but consigned Assinie to a British company and delegated control of Grand Bassam to Arthur Verdier, a shipper from La Rochelle. Over the next few years, Verdier alone represented French commercial and administrative concerns in the area. Trade in palm oil from Grand Bassam, and in gold dust from Assinie, provided profits to French and British traders.

The French return to the Côte-d'Ivoire, and enlargement of territorial claims in the 1880s, was due to two individuals: Marcel Treich-Laplène, an employee of Verdier's company, and Louis-Gustave Binger, an officer in the colonial army. In 1887, the two set off on exploratory missions, Treich-Laplène heading north from Grand Bassam, Binger going southeast from Bamako (Mali). The two met at Kong, in northeastern Côte-d'Ivoire, in 1889, having advanced French claims along their 4000-kilometre journey. Effective French control remained limited to coastal settlements.

In the 1890s French forces moved steadily northwards, where they encountered opposition from one of the great defenders of

Africa against foreign invasion, Samory Touré. Born in Guinea in 1830, Samory converted from animism to Islam and recruited an army to conquer a realm for himself. For three decades after 1860, he carved out an empire in the countries bordering the bend in the Niger river. Samory's initial skirmishes with the French took place in the early 1880s, just as French forces returned to the Gulf of Guinea and made their first forays inland. The long contest between Samory and Binger, appointed the first governor of the Côte-d'Ivoire when it became a separate colony in 1893, turned into fierce rivalry for mastery over the large northern region of the Côte-d'Ivoire and adjacent areas. Samory, after his earlier victories, was now handicapped by over-extension, revolt by vassals, lack of funds and superior French firepower. He suffered final defeat in 1898, was interned in Gabon, and died two years later.

Senegal, Guinea, Dahomey and the Côte-d'Ivoire provided coastal colonies for the French, but explorers and colonialists wanted to move further inland to discover the legendary cities of the African interior, explore the Sahel and Sahara, prospect for new resources and raise the French flag over ever widening areas. The conquest of the enormous band of land-locked territory lying between the Maghreb in the north and the Gulf of Guinea in the south – Upper Volta, Sudan (Mali), and Niger – was the most dramatic bout of French expansion.[8]

Upper Volta (Burkina Faso)

To the north of Côte-d'Ivoire, Ghana, Togo and Benin lies Upper Volta. In the late nineteenth century, this was unclaimed territory on which imperialists looked with interest. The British in Ghana, the Germans in Togo and the French in the Côte-d'Ivoire and Dahomey all hoped to explore and conquer the area beyond their coastal outposts.

European adventurers and officers made incursions into Upper Volta from the late 1880s onwards; Binger, who visited Ouagadougou, Upper Volta's main city, in 1887, was among them. Europeans paid court to African chiefs through whose domains they passed, sometimes signing commercial treaties or extracting grants of protectorates. The region remained officially undivided by the foreigners, although the French held an increasingly dominant position thanks to persuasion, military campaigns and lucky advances over rival explorers and troops from 1895 to 1897. French soldiers advanced in the path pioneered by explorers, coming to the eastern part of Upper Volta from Dahomey; to the west, from the Soudan. Britain and Germany recognised French overlordship by the late 1890s. The country, at the intersection of French routes of conquest, remained an odd administrative unit. The newly claimed regions were first governed as military territory, then in 1904 incorporated into the Soudan colony. In 1919, Upper Volta became a separate colony, then one region was transferred to Niger in 1927; five years later, Upper Volta disappeared, its remaining territory divided among the Côte-d'Ivoire, Soudan and Niger. Not until 1947 was Upper Volta put back together again.

Soudan (Mali)

No single place so excited explorers and would-be conquerors as the mythical African city of Tombouctou (Timbuktu). Founded on the Niger river in the twelfth century, Tombouctou dominated the caravan routes which carried salt and gold to the coast, served as a meeting point of Arabic and black African civilisations, and was a major Islamic cultural centre. In the late fifteenth and sixteenth centuries, Tombouctou was also the centre of the Songhay empire before it fell under the control of Moroccans, supplanted in turn by nomadic Tuaregs. Reports reaching Europe described the supposed wealth and magnificence of Tombouctou, embroidered by legends about rivers of gold, and snakes which slaked their thirst on gold dust. Yet the course of the Niger river remained uncertain, and no Europeans had visited Tombouctou. Every adventurer to the mystical city seemed doomed; one English explorer died on the very outskirts of Tombouctou in 1805, and another succumbed on reaching the city 20 years later. A Frenchman, René Caillié, in 1828, was the first European to return alive, only to pronounce himself disappointed with the city. The report did not staunch fantasies, and other expeditions followed. Many explorers fell victim to nomad warriors or illness, and French efforts to reach Tombouctou again in the 1850s and 1870s failed miserably.

As French troops dug further into Africa, new hopes of gaining Tombouctou surfaced – perhaps the city could be reached from the west via Bamako or the north. Potential explorers debated whether a land route or a river route would be more successful. In 1884 a specially constructed ship set sail up the Niger river, making frequent stops to negotiate safe passage with local chieftains. In 1885 the French reached Djenné, 500 kilometres south of Tombouctou, but their boat sank; although the explorers survived and salvaged the vessel, the expedition came to a halt. The next year colonial officials ordered a new boat; since the steam engine did not arrive from Paris in time the explorers set off again with their old ship. Resistance from Tuaregs forced the ship to make an about-turn to Bamako. The delay provided time for the new boat to be completed, but illness intervened: ten of the eighteen explorers succumbed to disease.

Ship and crew were ready in 1888, but the French regional commander, less keen on exploration than his predecessor, ordered the project abandoned. His successor proved willing to support the voyage, and an expedition departed in 1889. Two gunboats and two rafts with six months of supplies and 10 tonnes of coal left Saint-Louis and sailed up the Senegal river to Kayes, where explorers and their *matériel*, along with 300 porters, were loaded aboard rail carriages for transport to a navigable stretch of the Niger. One gunboat had to be left behind at Mopti, and further along, the expedition bogged down because seasonal rains had not yet inundated channels deeply enough for the boats and rafts to pass. Expedition leaders considered trying to reach Tombouctou on foot. With only ten men and twelve weapons, they reconsidered and returned to Mopti, only to discover that the vessel they had left behind had already departed for the coast. More voyages from 1889 to 1892 met with similar lack of success.

Governor Archinard, enthusiastic for expeditions, was nevertheless preoccupied with military pacification in Djenné and Mopti; authorities in Paris, who had specifically instructed him to use diplomacy rather than military means, recalled the governor. Archinard remained set on being the conqueror of Tombouctou, and he left behind orders which were vague about whether or not to pursue the campaign to reach the city. The interim governor, a 37-year-old officer named Eugène Bonnier, nourished hopes of reaching Tombouctou himself and saw Archinard's absence as a chance to make his mark on history. Bonnier planned to march on Tomboutou by a land route rather than sail there by river, but his departure was postponed by African insurrection. This delay gave yet another hopeful conqueror of Tombouctou, the military commander of the region, Boiteux, an unexpected stroke of good fortune; he saw an opportunity to outrun Bonnier. Boiteux got a head start, and in 1893, with the tacit approval of the colonial secretary in Paris, left Mopti with two well-equipped gunboats, thirty native soldiers and nine French soldiers. Upriver the convoy braved a Tuareg attack; only 7 kilometres from Tombouctou, Boiteux received an envoy from Tombouctou saying the city's black residents had called on their enemies, the Tuaregs, to defend the city against the French, and had also sent a message soliciting Moroccan aid. Eight days of negotiation followed, then Boiteux decided to attack. With cannon fixed on the city, French officers entered Tombouctou on 16 December 1893, leaving behind other sailors in the ships. They took Tombouctou without gunfire and raised the French flag. Bonnier, at the head of a company of 600 men, had meanwhile pursued his plan to arrive at Tombouctou by foot. The soldiers had marched from Bamako to Ségou and headed furiously towards Tombouctou, when they learned they had been beaten to the post by Boiteux. Bonnier also found out, to add insult to injury, that he had been dismissed as interim governor.

The conquerors' troubles were not over. Bonnier, gaining second place in the run to Tombouctou, paraded through the city gates. Outside the city, Bonnier's deputy, who remained behind with some of his men, ordered a salvo of gunfire against Tuaregs; the Tuaregs attacked and the 19 Frenchmen fled, only to be captured in marshes several hundred metres away and massacred. Boiteux, aboard a gunboat with a detachment of troops, heard his compatriots' gunfire and hurried to their rescue, but arrived too late. They nevertheless killed 15 Tuaregs and sent word to Ségou to plead for reinforcements before being surrounded. Bonnier came to their help from Tombouctou, reinforced by extra soldiers from Mopti. Boiteux and Bonnier argued bitterly, as Bonnier claimed credit for conquering Tombouctou. Bonnier, Boiteaux's superior, ordered him arrested for insubordination. Word of the unseemly rivalry grew into a scandal back in Paris as the press indicted adventurous expansion. Meanwhile, Bonnier led another expedition against the Tuaregs; he figured among 84 soldiers killed. In response, a column of soldiers, led by a future marshal, Joffre, left Ségou to secure the Tombouctou area, but lack of water and food retarded arrival – and cost the death of eight African porters. Joffre collected the remains of Bonnier and his comrades, fortified Tombouctou and gave chase to the

Tuaregs, killing over a hundred and capturing 1500 cattle. For his actions, Joffre won promotion; Bonnier's remains were interred in France; Boiteux committed suicide in 1897. Various commentators wondered whether Tombouctou, which was an arid, poor and desolate town, not the gold-filled capital of legend, was worth the deaths of so many men. The conquest had endowed France with a colony largely devoid of use except prestige.[9]

Niger

The French actually acquired the area which now forms Niger on paper before they conquered it. Covering 1.2 million square kilometres, the landlocked country was one of the larger African territories. The sparse population – when first counted in 1960, it numbered just under 3 million – was composed of sedentary black Africans in the south and nomadic Tuaregs in the desert which covers the northern third of the country. The most important state in Niger in the 1800s was the Sokoto caliphate. Warfare constantly punctuated tribal conflicts, and raids on the trans-Saharan slave trade which dominated the economy were frequent. Ethnic groups engaged in a never-ending process of territorial aggrandisement, and in areas under their control, Tuaregs dominated black Africans with colonial severity.

Niger presented little commercial interest for Europeans; searing desert sands, lack of water and temperatures that reached 50°C, combined with apparent lack of agricultural or mineral resources, hardly made Niger promising. As a link between northern and central Africa and between the western and eastern Sudan, however, it held strategic importance. French explorers yearned to reach Lake Chad, at the extreme eastern extent of present-day Niger on the Chad frontier, and colonialists dreamed of stretching French control all the way to the Red Sea. Control of Niger would also connect Algeria with Dahomey.

The British flag flew over Nigeria, south of Niger. In 1890, during a moment of Franco-British détente, Paris and London worked out a gentleman's agreement to divide Niger and Nigeria and drew lines on the map to demarcate their territories. Britain came out ahead, acquiring the coastal area and the lion's share of land on the basis of a fake treaty with the Sokoto caliphate which, London convinced Paris, implied African recognition of British sovereignty.

The French soon realised that they had been duped and sent an expedition from Dahomey to investigate the boundaries and reconnoitre the interior. Throughout the 1890s, other expeditions followed; all failed to budge boundaries but did secure French occupation of Niger. Considered among the most heroic of the exploratory campaigns in Africa, the Niger missions were accomplished at great expense and provoked heated controversy. The French movement eastwards also worried the British, concerned more than ever about French ambitions to link western Africa with the east coast and prevent the British from gaining control of the eastern Sudan (the route from Egypt to British eastern Africa). The head-on march of a French expedition, led by Marchand, and British forces under the command of Kitchener, culminated in a famous stand-off at Fashoda in 1898. France, eager to preserve peace with Britain, backed down, bringing to an end hopes of conquering a corridor to the coast but averting war between the two powers.[10]

The Fashoda incident did not stop exploration of the Sudan, including one of the most infamous of all expeditions. The Voulet–Chanoine campaign, which left western Niger in 1899, immediately encountered drought, severe shortages of supplies and strong African resistance. Reacting with brutality, Voulet and Chanoine led their troops steadily eastwards, occasionally trespassing on British claims. One disgruntled member of the expedition posted a letter to France telling of atrocities committed by its leaders. The Ministry of Colonies decided to arrest and court-martial Voulet and Chanoine even though the allegations remained unproven; authorities wanted to forestall further violations of British territory and avoid discrediting colonial expansion. A lieutenant-colonel named Klobb, already appointed to replace Voulet, was ordered to join the expedition near Lake Chad. When he arrived, Voulet ordered his soldiers to fire on Klobb's party. Klobb was killed, then Voulet and Chanoine's soldiers revolted and killed Voulet and Chanoine themselves. Greater scandal was avoided by evidence that Voulet and Chanoine were deranged.

Although France established Niger as a military territory in 1900, in the next few years, the French had to quell Tuareg revolts; not until 1908 was Niger pacified. The usefulness of the territory, except to secure France's control of west Africa, was not evident. In 1922, the colony counted only 220 resident non-Africans and remained one of France's poorest and least productive overseas domains.[11]

Mauritania

One of the last countries conquered by France was Mauritania, an area twice the size of metropolitan France. Nine-tenths of Mauritania is Saharan desert. Mauritania offered little economic potential to the French, although Europeans had traded with coastal merchants for arabic gum, slaves and a few other products since the 1500s. Only at the very end of the nineteenth century did France decide to take control of Mauritania in order to link together French possessions and to forestall any other power from occupying the sandy expanses. France convinced its rivals to give Paris a free hand in Mauritania in return for recognition of Italian rights in Libya, British sway in Egypt and Spanish control of the western Saharan littoral (Rio de Oro). In the early 1900s, French authorities used shows of strength and financial incentives to make peace with nomadic chieftains and black African leaders. The French later took recourse to military action to consolidate control, although pacification was not completed until 1934.

Conquest, in Mauritania as elsewhere, meant the establishment of colonial administration, although governance of nomads was necessarily less interventionist than authority exercised over sedentary peoples. The French declared some changes, notably the abolition of slavery, a prohibition nevertheless honoured in the breach; household servitude persisted until Mauritania's independence in 1960. The French instituted arbitrary justice, allowing administrators to detain wrong-doers and assess fines without judicial consideration. They made Mauritanians pay taxes, a head-tax for sedentary inhabitants, a tax on livestock for nomads. The need to pay imposts forced many Mauritanians to search for ways to earn money, usually by sales of livestock or agricultural products, or salaried employment, but the revenues did little to enrich French coffers. Tax-earnings covered a quarter of the colony's budget in the mid-1920s, but right to the end of the colonial period, the budget registered a deficit. Indeed, there was little money to be made in Mauritania. The major colonial economic activity, fish-drying and exporting in Port-Etienne, gave employment to fewer than fifty Mauritanians. Of so little interest did Mauritania seem that the French continued to administer it from Saint-Louis until the final years of the colonial era.[12]

Mandated Territories: Cameroon and Togo

The last African acquisitions of France were former German colonies consigned to Paris after the First World War under mandates from the League of Nations. France thereby gained control over part of the the former German colony of Togo and a German protectorate, Cameroon. Britain also won control of part of the countries.

French Cameroon was a relatively large territory; after several boundary changes between British and French Cameroon and between French Cameroon and the AEF, the land area totalled 429 000 square kilometres. No fewer than 173 ethnic groups lived in the French zone. Cameroon's economy was typically tropical, with exports of palm oil (the major commercial product), rubber, coffee, cocoa, bananas, tobacco, cola nuts and manioc. France easily established authority over Cameroon without need for conquest or warfare, although recalcitrant chiefs were replaced by ones more amenable to the French. Several pockets of resistance to French rule were pacified in the early 1920s, and a campaign was undertaken to wipe out residual pro-German sentiment. Tight political control, including restrictions on foreigners in the territory and press censorship, was particularly important since certain political groups in Germany wanted Cameroon to be returned to its old colonial master. Some in Cameroon who had converted to Lutheran Christianity and received German education felt sympathy for such goals. With the victory of Hitler in 1933, German policy avowedly promoted the restitution (and even enlargement) of Germany's overseas domains. France, not surprisingly, refused to consider such demands not only because of general opposition to relinquishing colonies and eagerness to reap economic benefits from them, but also because of the strategic dangers cession would create by allowing a German military presence in west Africa. France continued to rule Cameroon essentially as another of its colonies.[13]

The French had established a nominal protectorate over Togo, a small country sandwiched between British Ghana and French Dahomey, several years before German colonialists arrived in west Africa, but Paris had never implemented the takeover and willingly ceded Togo to Berlin in 1884. German, British and French missionaries had been active in Togo since the mid-1800s, and the colony counted a substantial Christian population. Foreign slavers had worked in Togo since the 1700s, but with the end of the slave-trade few other products presented great interest. Togo held no deposits of minerals (except small quantities of iron); the country was too densely populated for foreign settlement and extensive plantations. By 1900, nevertheless, the indigenous populations had been subdued and Togo soon became a model colony. Exports of palm oil were sufficient for the colonial government to balance its budget.

At the outset of the First World War, Britain and France conquered Togo and divided the spoils. Although officially administrated under mandates from the League of Nations, the British incorporated their portion into Ghana, while the French ruled their share of Togo as a separate colony. The French inherited the infrastructure left by the Germans. French missionaries and teachers replaced Germans, and the new rulers used both the indigeneous elite and African officials from Dahomey to run the colony. Production of cotton and groundnuts expanded during the interwar years, and the French undertook various public works projects. The French had to counter German demands for return of Togo, but the country remained a quiet and rather peaceful backwater of the French empire.[14]

French Equatorial Africa (AEF)

Smaller, poorer, less well known, and generally less well regarded than French West Africa was French Equatorial Africa (the AEF), the name given in 1910 to the Government-General which covered four colonies in central Africa: Gabon, Moyen-Congo (the present day Congo), Oubangui-Chari (now the Central African Republic) and Chad. The first two border the Atlantic coast of Africa. The French Congo lies north and west of the river from which it takes its name; south and east is the former Belgian Congo, a much larger country now known as Zaïre. The capitals of the French and Belgian colonies, and the independent countries, Brazzaville and Kinshasa (ex-Léopoldville), face each other directly across the Congo river. Oubangui-Chari is a landlocked country further north, and Chad, also landlocked, stretches north from the border with Oubangui-Chari and Cameroon across the Sahara to the Libyan frontier.

Gabon and the Congo

French occupation of equatorial Africa began in Gabon, where in 1839 Captain Bouët-Willaumez signed a treaty with a local chief, whom the French called King Denis. He ceded land along one bank of the Gabon estuary for French port facilities and a trading station; another treaty in 1841 gave France an outpost on the opposite bank. In 1849, France founded Libreville as a settlement for freed slaves, and thereafter enlarged its holdings along the coast. As explorers moved inland from the 1850s onwards, France gained further territory.

Lambaréné, on the Ogooué river, occupied in 1872, became the launching-pad for expeditions into the interior. These treks, which laid French claims to much of what became the AEF, were largely the work of Pierre Savorgnan de Brazza, most famous of French explorers. Brazza was born in Rome in 1852, the son of a count who worked as a museum curator. A childhood meeting with the Marquis de Montaignac, a French admiral, whetted Brazza's appetite for both France and exploration. In 1868, he enrolled at the French Naval Academy and six years later was naturalised as a French citizen. By that time, Brazza had completed his first voyages to the South Atlantic, Algeria (where he witnessed the 1871 Kabyle uprising) and West Africa.

In 1875, Brazza undertook his first expedition up the Ogooué river, a two-year journey commissioned by Montaignac, now Minister for the Navy. The major discovery was that the Ogooué was not, as had been believed, a branch of the Congo. On his second expedition, from 1879 to 1882, Brazza obtained a treaty from the chief of the Batéké peoples, Iléo (also known by the title of Makoko), which granted France the territory which formed the bulk of the Moyen-Congo colony. Brazza founded Franceville and the city that came to bear his name, Brazzaville. A third expedition followed from 1883 to 1885.

Brazza's expeditions were models of European exploration. His reports, published in instalments in the French illustrated newspaper *Le Tour du monde*, provided accounts of the dangers and adventures faced by explorers, tempered by Brazza's reflections on African culture and European enterprise. Brazza called his first trip up the Ogooué a 'veritable odyssey'. Plagued by mosquitos, serious illness, accidental sinking of canoes, utter lack of familiarity with the country through which they travelled, needing to bargain at each stop along the way for directions and help, Brazza, his European colleagues (a doctor, sailor, naturalist and geologist) and 160 African porters packed into nine canoes, faced a forbidding journey through dense jungle.

Brazza held many racialist attitudes about Africans, their unpleasant physical appearance ('a face recalling that of a monkey ... hands with a white palm which is repulsive to see'), lack of morality and capacity for deceit. Yet he admired their physiques and strength, as well as their prowess at navigation, bridge-building and carving. He observed that rumours of cannibalism, which excited and nauseated those who devoured literature on Africa, were grossly exaggerated. (Europeans might think Africans cannibals, but Brazza found that some Africans believed Europeans bought slaves to eat and that European wine was made from slaves' blood.) Brazza was keenly aware of the mutual incomprehension which existed between Europeans and Africans. If Europeans found Africans exotic, so Africans thought Europeans weird. Brazza recalled how some tribesmen, as yet unacquainted with Europeans, waited around at night until he had removed his heavy leather boots to ascertain that he had five toes on each foot, and he recounted how a woman brought her infant for him to touch, seeming to feel that he was endowed with magical powers.

Brazza had insight into the ironies of contact between different peoples. Wherever he travelled, Brazza handed out cheap blue beads which a French geographical society had provided as presents to Africans:

I admit that I myself ended up finding these modest blue beads splendid. They were coveted by all the women in regions where a bead belt played the same role as our diamond jewellery. I began to see that there was not a lot of difference between a bead and a sparkling piece of pure carbon. And indeed was there? Our European precious stones had value only because they were rare, and blue beads were very rare in the Ondoumbo country! And were not diamonds and blue beads both often traded for human flesh anyway?

Brazza also found it 'difficult to make [Africans] understand that the goods we had were the products of our industry. When I told them that we whites came from a country where we lacked nothing, they could not understand why we had left it.'

His conclusion about Africans was that 'in declaring them defiant, lying and incorrigibly disloyal, have we grasped the primitive aspect of their character? Would not any people placed in the same environmental conditions and [position of] weakness not also see in the initiatives of the whites just as serious a danger for the preservation of its privileges and would it not as well try to acquire arms?' Uncontrolled European trading activities troubled Brazza. Slavery, still widespread among African populations, horrified him; he purchased and freed as many slaves as his means allowed, giving them refuge in outposts he founded along the way.

Brazza made clear to Africans that he offered friendship but was capable of force as well. Renowned for completing his expeditions without killing any Africans, Brazza explained that he preferred 'prestidigitation and pyrotechnics' to terror, a show of force rather than the use of it. His comments on convincing Africans to serve as guides summarise European power and amibition:

> If it is dangerous to show force, it would be worse still to appear to be afraid. I convoked several chiefs for one last discussion, and I arrived holding in one hand several articles of merchandise in token of a gift, in the other a bullet. I briefly stated my requests. Naaman [a chief] responded, protesting that despite his personal friendship for me, he could not take responsibility for guiding me to the interior. So, very calmly, I enumerated the riches that we wanted to carry on our boats and the superior forces which we had at our disposal in case of war: 'The white', I said, 'has two hands: one full of presents for his friends, the other that death itself arms against his enemies – there is no alternative'.

The explorer wrote enthusiastically about the wealth of the Congo. The 'great fertility' of the land 'only demands a little effort' to develop it; Africans, he thought, were the only labour force which could do so in harsh tropical conditions. It would be possible to grow coffee, cocoa and sugar cane, produce palm oil and dyestuffs, collect rubber, fell sandalwood and ebony trees and buy ivory. A network of trading posts stretching from the coast inland could provide a conduit for such commodites to be exported from the African interior to Europe.[15]

Brazza's expeditions coincided with intense imperial rivalry over central Africa, marked by the entry of an aspiring colonial power into the 'scramble'. King Léopold II of Belgium cherished hopes of increasing the power and prestige of his small country through imperial aggrandisement. Efforts to expand in various parts of the world met with little initial success; the British opposed a Belgian settlement in the Transvaal, in southern Africa, and the Spanish declined Léopold's offer to buy the Philippines. The Belgian monarch saw greater prospects in central Africa, and in 1876 formed an organisation ostensibly to promote exploration and the eradication of slavery, the International African Association. Although grouping together national committees with similar objectives – Ferdinand de Lesseps, builder of the Suez Canal, presided over the French committee – the association was, in reality, a cover for Léopold's ambitions. The king also recruited Henry Morton Stanley, an English-born American journalist famous for his search for another explorer, David Livingstone. Soon Léopold's association had achieved quasi-official international status as a colonising power in its own right.

Brazza, on behalf of the French government, and Stanley, in the employ of the Belgians, were thus engaged in more than just exploration in the Congo. The situation was even more complicated, however, because the British were not content to be left out of the division of central Africa, the Portuguese claimed rights to the Atlantic coast north of Angola, and the Germans soon became involved in African colonial politics. Brazza's second expedition, and the treaty with the Makoko, was thus particularly important in staking French claims. Two years after the French parliament, in 1882, had tardily ratified the treaty, the German government called a conference, attended by 13 European powers and the United States, to discuss European intervention in Africa.

The Berlin Conference adopted provisions guaranteeing free trade on the Niger and Congo rivers, suppressing slavery and setting out appropriate procedures for making colonial claims. Subsequent agreements gave final and formal recognition to the division of most of black Africa. On the western coast between the British colonies in Nigeria and South Africa, Germany got Cameroon and Namibia; Portugal received Angola (including the small but strategically significant Cabinda territory north of the Congo river); Spain kept the tiny enclave of Rio Muni; France's claim to most of the right bank of the Congo, Gabon and the northern hinterlands was confirmed; and an enormous territory on the left bank of the Congo became the Congo Free (or Independent) State with Léopold as king. (The 'Belgian' Congo remained the personal colony of the monarch until, after revelations of scandals concerning treatment of Africans, Belgium annexed it in 1906.)

With the various claims sorted out, the French government in 1886 appointed Brazza Commissioner-General in Equatorial Africa with authority over the Congo and Gabon, a position he held until 1898. Conflict with French businessmen led to Brazza's recall,[16] but he returned to the Congo in 1905 as head of an official investigation into abuses committed by the companies which had obtained government monopolies on economic activity in the AEF. Having completed the enquiry, Brazza set out for Paris, only to die – in suspicious circumstances – in Dakar. All ten copies of his report, probably highly critical of the concession companies, were 'lost'.[17]

Oubangui-Chari

North of the French and Belgian Congo was Oubangui-Chari. Various explorers, including Brazza, trekked across the region in the decade after 1889, when the French founded an outpost at Bangui. A treaty between the Congo Free State and France recognised French sovereignty over the territory north of the Oubangui River in 1894, although the delimitation of the frontier between Oubangui-Chari, Chad and German Cameroon altered on several occasions. Acquired with relatively little effort as an annex to the Congo, Oubangui-Chari remained one of France's poorest and least-known colonies except for scandals surrounding the imposition of a head-tax, the murderous use of Africans as porters for caravans between navigable rivers, and the activities of concessionary companies. The Oubangui-Chari had almost no economic or strategic significance, and no other colonial powers challenged France's claims.

Chad

The push towards Lake Chad was a pet project of several French bodies, including the Paris Geographical Society, the Marseille Chamber of Commerce and the Committee for French Africa, which outfitted expeditions to do the deed. Their brief, in addition, was to conquer new territory, secure an opening into central Africa, open trade links and – perhaps most importantly – forestall expansion by Britain, represented on the fringes of the region by missionaries. Expedition succeeded expedition, hobbled by harsh terrain, African hostility, the occasional murder of leaders and lack of porters. The French finally reached Lake Chad in 1897; they raised the flag but did little else. Two years later, another expedition arrived; this time, according to the Committee for French Africa, 'the goal was to initiate serious commercial transactions, to establish permanent trading posts, to organise regular trading caravans, to extend our influence by essentially peaceful means through international treaties'. Indeed in 1899, after the Fashoda affair, Paris and London signed a convention delimiting the frontiers between their claims.

The Chad expeditions took on heroic colours. Both the French commander François Lamy and the African ruler Rabah were killed in action. An officer reported the deaths in prose guaranteed to inspire patriotism and a thrill of horror at home: 'In comparison with the loss of a great soldier and a great patriot such as Commander Lamy, what did the end of a negro as common as Rabah represent? His head had been brought [to us] during the day. . . . It showed the most ignoble bestiality.' Commander Gentil, leader of a later expedition, trumpeted his men's accomplishments – 'a glorious moment in colonial history occurred on 24 March 1900', he wrote, when three French expeditions, one coming from the Congo, one from Algeria and the third from the Soudan, met on an island at the confluence of the Chari and Logoné rivers: 'This manifestation of the vitality and energy of the ancient French race filled us with an immense joy.'

After the applause died, authorities had little idea of what to do with the newly conquered territories. Gentil admitted that Chad was so arid that finding drinking water was difficult. He confessed: 'I said to myself, when I was alone, that it truly was not worth having killed so many and having suffered so much to conquer such a forsaken country.' The military territory of Chad played home to only 20 Europeans at the turn of the twentieth century. Mostly non-commissioned officers, their responsibility was to administer a territory which measured almost 1000 km from north to south and 400 km from east to west. Forced labour and various taxes imposed on the population produced revenues equal to half the cost of administration. A single French businessman, who traded in ivory and rubber, represented French commerce. The capital, Fort-Lamy, was but a military outpost with a few artisans and a company of French African soldiers. Supplies ran short; hardship was evident. The Africans suffered the burden of French occupation. A French commander posted to Fort-Lamy complained: 'At the price of what hesitations, what sacrifices of money, and, alas, of what atrocious suffering, have we guaranteed supplies for this military territory? The population, decimated by work far beyond its strength, prefers death to porterage.... How many corpses line the route from the Possel fortress to Fort-Crampel, and yet projects for a roadway and a rail are under study and said to be indispensable for the future of the colony!' Promoters in Paris called for greater efforts, but in the early twentieth century, dissenting voices, not all anti-colonialist, called for outright abandonment of a colony which seemed to lack even potential.[18]

Djibouti

France boasted one outpost in eastern Africa. The 'conquest' of Djibouti – also known as the French Somali Coast and the Territory of the Afars and Issas – exemplifies the strategic imperatives of imperial expansion, the role a particular individual could exercise, the reaction of one power to the initiatives of another, and the often exaggerated claims of colonial propagandists.

For centuries the area around the Red Sea provided Europeans with such exotic products as myrrh, incense, khol, ivory, musk oil and ostrich plumes. With plans to cut a canal through the isthmus of Suez, the Red Sea littoral took on added importance. Toeholds on either side of the Bab el-Mandeb strait would allow Europeans stopping-off points on the route from Suez to the Indian Ocean and the Orient. The British led the way with the acquisition of Aden, in Yemen on the Arabian peninsula, in 1839.

A Frenchman named Henri Lambert, a trader from Nantes who had settled in Mauritius, pioneered French intervention on the horn of Africa. In 1855 Lambert moved to Aden and got himself appointed French consular agent. He then journeyed to the other shore of Bab el-Mandeb to visit Zeila, Tadjoura and Obock, coastal areas controlled by Muslim chieftains on the fringes of the largely Christian Abyssinian empire. Lambert persuaded one of two rival leaders to cede the port of Obock to him on behalf of France. The Minister for Algeria and the Colonies, Jérôme Bonaparte, took to the idea of a Red Sea colony:

> The horrible massacre [of Muslims in 1858] in Jedda, the serious events taking place in India and China, the grand project for building a canal in the Suez isthmus, and the position of France in the Mediterranean seem to me to impose on the Government... a duty not only to make an appearance but also to show our power in the Red Sea before it becomes the great route to the Far East.... The result would be to provide a regular and frequent link for steamships travelling between the metropole and our colonies in the Indian Ocean. If such a project is successful, thanks to our steamships and the cruisers of the imperial navy, our flag will float from the Nile delta to the coasts of Madagascar; under their surveillance and thanks to our prestige, our political and commercial influence will develop rapidly.... One or the other shore of the Red Sea could offer a precious source of free labour for our colonies.... The advantage for our country in occupying an area on the Red Sea is not, I would say, for a counterweight to British influence but as a rallying-point for our warships, a coaling station and water supply for our steamers, [a place to] look after our commercial affairs and an encouragement for our fellow Christians and supporters.

Naval officers remained dubious about Lambert; one commander cautioned that Lambert was more intent on advancing his own fortunes – he was shipping livestock from Ethiopia to Mauritius – than those of France. The Ministry of Foreign Affairs and the Navy pursuaded Napoleon III, despite Jérôme Bonaparte's arguments, to decline Lambert's offer of a colony.

Lambert soon met his fate: the rival of the chieftain who had ceded Obock had Lambert killed in 1859. Paris sent a delegation to investigate the murder, though without undue haste. In 1862, a treaty gave Obock to France in return for 5500 gold francs. The change of policy perhaps reflected reconsideration of Prince Jérôme's views and the progress of the Suez Canal project. Yet for the next two decades a lone agent represented France in the new possession; the opening of the Suez Canal in 1869 failed to spark development.

The situation changed in the 1880s. Britain declared a protectorate over Egypt in 1882, and established a colony in Somalia in 1884. The Abyssinian empire, or Ethiopia, seemed ripe for takeover, but the Abyssinian emperor was manoeuvring to extend his influence over coastal regions. The Egyptian khedive was meanwhile trying to push his sphere of influence further southwards. From 1883 to 1885 France was involved in military action in Indochina and needed a supply station for ships heading for Vietnam; the British refused to let the French use facilities in Aden. In 1885, the French convinced chiefs in Djibouti, across the Tadjoura bay from Obock, to cede Djibouti and thereby provide a finer port than Obock. Djibouti became the centre of French commercial and administrative activities transferred from Obock.

The colony soon contained modern port facilities, and a French shipping company regularly served Djibouti. A salt-mining company, two chalk quarries, a cigarette manufacturer and various shops did business. Two new activities developed. One was the construction of a rail line from Djibouti to the Ethiopian capital of Addis-Ababa. The project took 20 years and cost 155 million francs, and the coast was not connected to Addis-Ababa, 783 kilometres distant, until 1917. But already in the last decades of the nineteenth century, the rail, and the inland trade which followed it, stimulated Djibouti's economy; Djibouti became the link between Ethiopia and the outside world. The other new activity was arms-running, with the Ethiopian emperor as the major client. Some 17 000 weapons and several million shells were sold just in the first four years of the twentieth century, and arms merchants reaped good profits.

The small colony thrived at the turn of the century. The number of Europeans grew from only 51 in 1892 – 27 soldiers and officials, 4 nuns, 3 priests and 10 traders, as well as 7 non-Frenchmen – to 1000 at the end of the decade. The total population, mostly ethnic Afars, Issas, Somalis and some Yemenites, exceeded 10 000. A Djibouti newspaper championed the colony's merits:

Djibouti is the essential outlet for all of the products of a country as vast as France and populated by 8 to 10 million inhabitants eager for relations with the Christian world [Ethiopia]. Djibouti is the key to Ethiopia, now placed under the politically impartial safeguard of the French nation. Djibouti is ... the main artery for the scientific, industrial and commercial penetration [of eastern Africa], and the extension of [the rail line] will one day cross the Nile and join up with the railway in the Congo. Djibouti provides mooring for the French fleet and entry and exit to the Suez Canal. Djibouti is the coaling station for all French naval service to India, Cochinchina, Annam, Tonkin, China and Japan and onwards towards Australia and New Caledonia, to Madagascar and its dependencies. . . . Djibouti is an admirable front line of colonial expansion which – without recourse to foreign capital, without subsidy from the metropole, without government support – has earned the respect and welcome of all by the sole force of the irresistible impulse which it creates. Djibouti is the most remarkable example of the colonising virtue of France. . . . Djibouti is the east African Le Havre with a salubrious climate, where the port which can be used in all seasons, jetties thrust out to the wide ocean, an ice factory, comfortable hotels, immense docks, vast workshops, countless shops, a market overflowing with foodstuffs, a hospital and the multiple government services all already offer amenities which cannot be found anywhere else between Egypt and India. Soon there will be telegraphs, telephones, tramways, a new shipping terminal for larger vessels, more frequent postal services and a municipal water system which will multiply the number of fountains and decorate public squares with greenery, giving the illusion of the charms of Marseille to the shores of this torrid zone.

In describing a frontier outpost in an arid zone where summer temperatures climbed to 45°C, the word illusion is perhaps most relevant about the aspirations of colonial promoters.[19]

The Indian Ocean

Madagascar

The largest island in the Indian Ocean, Madagascar has a bigger land area than France. It counts some 18 peoples among its population, most of whom are historically of Malay rather than African origin. The dominant group, the Imerina, had gradually extended their control from the capital of Antananarivo (Tananarive) throughout much of the country by the nineteenth century, subjugating other ethnic groups but failing to form a unified state. A monarch, often a woman, ruled over Imerina in a feudal society capped by a class of nobles who descended from the sovereigns. At the bottom were slaves, both indigenes from Madagascar and African captives. The power of the monarch depended on a heavenly mandate. Religious observances, such as death ceremonies and the 'feast of the bath', held great significance, as did reverence paid to ritual talismans, the most important, the *Kelimalaza*, a wood carving festooned with scarlet cloth and silver chains.

King Andrianampoimerina, whose reign inaugurated the nineteenth century, represented the zenith of Malagasy autonomy and Imerina power. His successors reinforced royal control through campaigns of terror; during the 30-odd years that Queen Ranavalona I ruled, as many as 400 000 people died from poison administered by judges to prove loyalty to the monarch and detect witchcraft. While tightening control at home, the Malagasy sovereigns opened the country to the outside world. A treaty with Britain in 1817 paved the way for cordial relations between London and Antananarivo. Frenchmen from nearby Réunion traded with Malagasy for rice, cattle and (until the ending of the slave-trade) slaves; French shippers operated from Malagasy ports, and one French businessman, Joseph Lambert, maintained close ties to the Malagasy dynasty. By the 1860s, Christian missionaries – Anglicans, Methodists and Quakers from Britain, Catholics from France and Lutherans from Norway – had won a substantial number of disciples. In 1869, they converted Queen Ranavalona II and her prime minister, Rainilaiarivony, the island strongman and later the queen's husband. The *Kelimalaza* and other talismans were burned and missionaries became palace advisers.

The French had been attracted to Madagascar since the *ancien régime*, although attempts to found settlements in the 1600s and 1700s came to naught. France maintained a nominal claim on Sainte-Marie, a tiny island off the east coast of Madagascar ceded to France in 1750, then abandoned shortly afterwards. Reoccupied in 1818, Sainte-Marie provided a post for French reconnaissance of the Indian Ocean, although without significant trade and no settlement. In 1840 a French naval commander persuaded a chief to cede the island of Nossy-Bé to the French. Lying off the northwest coast of Madagascar, the 290-square-kilometre island attracted a few Réunionnais sugar-planters and served as a base for later

French attacks on the Malagasy mainland. French control of the two outposts on either side of the *Grande Ile*, as Madagascar was known, gave Paris a launching-pad for further activities.

In the early 1880s, a businessman and *député* from Réunion, then serving briefly as French Navy Minister, convinced the government to extend its influence in Madagascar. A slight to a French colonist, and the breakdown in subsequent negotiations for compensation, provided an excuse for bombardment of Tamatave and Majunga in 1883. An ultimatum demanded acceptance of a French protectorate over northern Madagascar, the end of prohibitions on sales of land to foreigners and a sizeable indemnity. The newly-crowned queen, Ranavalona III (who wed her step-father Rainilaiarivony) rallied troops. Hostilities between French forces and Malagasy troops (led by a British mercenary) continued until 1885, when the French succeeded in forcing the queen to accept a partial protectorate, allow the appointment of a French Resident, pay a huge indemnity and cede the coveted northern port of Diego Suarez. A large Paris bank lent money to the Malagasy government to pay the indemnity to France.

The queen begrudgingly collaborated with the French, as did Catholic Malagasy nobles, while Protestants remained in opposition. Domestic problems wracked the government in Antananarivo, partly because of the despotic rule of Rainilaiarivony and rivalry among his potential successors. The French practised a 'hands-off' policy, though increasingly worried about growing friendliness between some Malagasy authorities and the British. British recognition of the French partial protectorate in 1890 (in return for France's acquiescence to British dominance in Zanzibar) defused the issue, but over the next several years, Madagascar drifted into anarchy.

In 1894, the French National Assembly authorised a military expedition to subdue the island. General Duchesne, with 15 000 soldiers and 7000 porters, landed in the western port of Majunga in December, while a fleet of gunboats bombarded Tamatave in the east. Not until the end of September 1895 did French forces take Antananarivo, after battles with the Malagasy army as the invaders crossed the island. Only 20 French soldiers died in the fighting, but 6000 perished from disease – the conquest of Madagascar stood as France's most costly colonial venture in lost lives.

Duchesne coerced Ranavalona into signing a treaty granting France a full protectorate, and he exiled Rainilaiarivony to Algiers. Within weeks of the French victory, rebels attacked a provincial city and killed the family of a Quaker missionary. This touched off a broadly-based uprising by the *menalamba*, or red shawls (so called because insurgents smeared their garments with red earth to symbolise attachment to the motherland). The rebels were anti-colonial, xenophobic and generally anti-Christian, although proclaiming loyalty to Ranavalona. They burned churches and brought out for worship talismans hidden since the royal conversion of 1869. The French, in reprisal, burned rebel villages and rice-paddies. Through early 1896, the rebellion flourished with support from provincial governors and much of the populace. Higher officials nevertheless collaborated with the French, who kept the queen silent. In August 1896, General Gallieni reorganised French forces, captured and executed several rebel leaders, encouraged nascent rivalries among others, freed slaves and, in early 1897, abolished the Malagasy monarchy and exiled Ranavalona to Réunion. The departure of the queen removed the major rallying-point for nationalist insurgents, and the French quickly established control of Imerina strongholds. Gallieni, assisted by an able young deputy, Hubert Lyautey, extended French control to areas which had traditionally resisted Imerina administration. Complete pacification by 1899 led to the replacement of the protectorate by annexation.[20]

Comoros Islands

The Comoros are a chain of four main islands – Grande Comore, Anjouan, Moheli and Mayotte – located in the Mozambique Channel between Madagascar and the African mainland, inhabited by a Muslim population. European traders and pirates visited the islands in the 1600s and 1700s, but Malagasy raids wreaked greater devastation, as slavers bought or captured labourers for plantations. Poverty and civil wars among supporters of rival sultans created additional hardship. By the beginning of the nineteenth century, the islands lay devastated.

In the mid-1800s European powers searched for ports and refuelling stations for their mercantile and military fleets. With the accord of the local sultan, who feared the designs of rivals, the French governor of Réunion annexed Mayotte in 1841 and soldiers occupied it two years later. Mayotte had only 3000 inhabitants, relatively poor soil, inadequate harbour facilities and no infrastructure; it seemed to hold little promise, despite talk about the island becoming a French Hong Kong or Malta. A French company nevertheless acquired several thousand hectares of land, planted sugar cane, hired a hundred workers and made large investments. Returns were small. Only 200 Frenchmen, mostly officials and soldiers, lived on the island. Authorities largely ignored the local population, although in 1857 the government abolished slavery. Emancipation, ironically, led to greater impoverishment of the masses and the emigration of some nobles. The former slaves considered the contract labour which they were offered as little better than servitude and rose in rebellion against colonial administrators and planters; represssion was severe. The plantations gradually failed – only two were left in 1903 – and ships rarely called at Mayotte. One official wrote after 40 years of French occupation: 'One is led to draw the conclusion that Mayotte is one of the last spots on earth which one should try to colonise.'

The histories of the other islands, especially the smallest, Moheli, contain themes of adventure, speculation and avarice. Rumours circulated in the 1840s that Britain might occupy Moheli to counter the French presence on Mayotte. The Moheli regent, who held power during the minority of the young queen, Djoumbé, was well disposed to the French. He hoped to marry the queen to her cousin, the future king of Madagascar. The island's chief minister, however, was anti-French and wanted the queen to wed a nobleman from Zanzibar (where British influence was strong). The commander of the French Indian Ocean fleet promised to protect Moheli's independence. Meanwhile, the administrator of Mayotte appointed one Madame Droit, the *mulâtre* widow of a French planter, as French agent charged with winning favour with the queen; Madame Droit intended the queen to marry a government employee from Mayotte to cement ties between the monarch and France. But Madame Droit was expelled in the midst of a riot in 1851 and died soon afterwards, perhaps poisoned. The chief minister then married the 15-year-old queen to his Zanzibar ally, and France's star fell. Soon the minister fell out with the prince consort, and expelled him from Moheli; he later returned, only to be expelled again. Djoumbé took a Malagasy lover.

In 1860, a Frenchman tried to colonise Moheli. Joseph Lambert, a moneyed trader in Mauritius and kinsman of the French entrepreneur in Djibouti, was also the adopted brother of Djoumbé's princely cousin in Madagascar. Lambert, with French government approval, sent his confidence man to Moheli to investigate business possibilities. Djoumbé smuggled out a letter saying she was held prisoner by her chief minister and asking for French protection. France, still worried that Moheli might fall under British influence (especially after a British ship visited the island in 1861), first offered her refuge in Mayotte, then sailed a warship into Moheli to spirit away the chief minister. Lambert went to interview Djoumbé, who said she was in love with her Malagasy cousin and did not want her husband to return from Zanzibar. The cousin, however, was assassinated in 1863. The French then proposed Djoumbé's marriage to a pro-French prince from Anjouan. She and Lambert, however, became lovers. In 1865, Djoumbé signed a convention giving Lambert a 60-year concession on most arable land in Moheli in return for an indemnity and 5 per cent of total production. She adopted a new flag featuring the French Tricolour in the canton.

In opposition to Lambert and the queen, Djoumbé's sons undertook a pro-Zanzibar campaign. The queen began to live – perhaps in an intimate relationship – with her step-son, although she still sent letters to Lambert, who was frequently absent in Réunion. When Djoumbé decided to withdraw Lambert's concession and abdicate in favour of one of her sons, the French sent a gunboat to fire on Moheli. Zanzibar also sent ships, which observers thought foreshadowed takeover of the island, especially since Zanzibar's ambassador invested Djoumbé's son with the kingly symbols of sword, flag and horse. Nevertheless, Lambert returned, rallied local chiefs and ruled Moheli from 1868 to 1871 as regent for Djoumbé's son, now the official sultan. Djoumbé went overseas, first to Zanzibar, then to France, where she spent eight weeks as an exotic celebrity (and, to French alarm, met with the British ambassador). French authorities fell out with Lambert and bribed him to resign his position as regent. In 1871 Djoumbé returned, as the French fleet fired salutes to caution good behaviour. Djoumbé moved into a cottage on the property of her son, still nominally sultan. She married a Malagasy, who soon returned to Madagascar; Djoumbé perhaps resumed her affair with Lambert, who died in 1873. The following year the sultan died and Djoumbé again assumed power. Lambert's affairs were now in the hands of the 30-year-old son of a French admiral, Emile Fleuriot de Langle. In 1875 he and Djoumbé married; she bore two sons before her death at the age of 42, in 1878, bringing to an end a saga of love, intrigue and imperial designs.

While the French had gained control over Mayotte and jostled for position on Moheli, a British consul gained influence on Anjouan. Grande Comore was rife with civil strife, and the French sent gunboats to the island in 1864 and 1871. By the 1870s the situation remained confused. In Anjouan, the British consul lost his position, an American captain paid court to local rulers, and a rumour spread that a sultan would cede the island to Egypt. In the early 1880s, the island dissolved into civil war. Yet another French adventurer, Léon Humblot, made several scientific voyages to Grande Comore on behalf of a Paris museum. He also began producing perfume essences, thanks to a concession of land from a sultan and subsidies from the French government. Humblot convinced the sultan to ask France for a protectorate, but the response from Paris was vague.

The chaos which reigned in the islands, combined with British and now German and Italian interest in eastern Africa, stirred the French into action. In 1886 France proclaimed protectorates over Grande Comore, Anjouan and Moheli. This consolidation forestalled other foreign intervention and shored up Humblot on Grande Comore. Humblot, injured in a revolt by workers in 1893, took the incident as an excuse to get rid of the sultan and establish an autocracy. Humblot used his political position as the sultan's regent to lend the sultan's slaves to the plantation company owned by Humblot the businessman, a deal authorised by Humblot the French Resident; the contract was duly recorded by the island's official secretary, Humblot's brother-in-law, who was also treasurer of Humblot's company. The company's security guards were the only law force on the islands, and Humblot presided over the local court, assisted by Comoran syndics in his employ. Islanders hated the French for corruption, disciplinary brutality, the practice of paying salaries only every six months and levying fines. Finally, in 1895, the French government carried out an enquiry into Humblot's conduct and replaced him as Resident the following year. The new administrator tried to clean up the island, oversaw the reorganisation of Humblot's Grande Comore Company and despatched the chief sultan to Paris on a goodwill visit. In 1912, Humblot's unsavoury activities were tardily disclosed in Paris and the affair erupted in Parliament. The scandal contributed to the decision to turn the protectorates over the Comoros

Islands into annexation.[21] In a fitting coincidence, in the same year, France secured control over the Comoros and Morocco, dissimilar poles of France's conquests in Africa and the Indian Ocean.

2 The Conquest of Empire: Asia, the Pacific and the Austral Regions

European colonialism moved into the Asia–Pacific region as well as into Africa and the Indian Ocean. The vast markets of China beckoned to European producers, intrigued since the time of Marco Polo by the size, wealth, exotic products and culture of the Middle Kingdom. Neighbouring areas appeared promising stepping-stones to China which could be developed in their own right. The western expansion of the United States, striving to meet its self-appointed 'manifest destiny' to spread from the Atlantic to the Pacific, and the British occupation and settlement of Australia in 1788, pulled world attention towards the Pacific basin. The forced opening of Japan and China to western trade focused interest on Asia. The building of a canal through the isthmus of Panama – discussed from the 1830s onwards though not actually completed until 1914 – promised to shorten travel distances and costs across the Pacific.

By the 1880s, promoters proclaimed that the centre of gravity in the world's economy was shifting from the Atlantic to the Pacific, just as it had moved from the Mediterranean to the Atlantic in an earlier period of exploration and conquest. Writers such as Paul Deschanel, promoter of French expansion in the Pacific, argued that the economic, political and strategic rivalries of the future would be contested in an Asia–Pacific arena. The coming century, in short, was proclaimed to be the century of the Pacific, and it behoved European (and other) powers to secure a presence in this theatre.

The Pacific Islands

The Pacific had fascinated Europe ever since traders had begun making the long sea voyage from Europe to the East Indies, and Spanish conquistadors had discovered the eastern coast of the Pacific and then run galleons from Mexico to Manila. The islands lying between the Americas and Asia remained unexplored until the great voyages of the late eighteenth and early nineteenth centuries. If Captain Cook was the most famous of the Pacific seafarers, numerous Frenchmen – Bougainville, La Pérouse, d'Entrecasteaux, Baudin and others – played a major role in the European charting of the South Seas. French rulers sponsored explorations to conduct scientific research, investigate trading possibilities, keep an eye on Britain's activities and possibly reconnoitre locations for future French bases. They brought back tales of both the supposedly idyllic societies that inspired Rousseau's writings on the 'good savage' and, in marked contrast, reports of fierce cannibals and less noble primitives.

France, embroiled in revolution and war in the 1790s and early 1800s, was hardly in a position to seize the opportunity of establishing a colony to rival Britain's Australian settlements, and most policy-makers saw little reason to do so. In 1840, a private French company underwrote and organised an expedition to found a French settlement in still unclaimed New Zealand. The British, who had wind of the French initiative, were *en route* to take possession of the country and pipped French ships to the post by only a week; a small French group nevertheless settled, under the British flag, on the Akaroa peninsula of New Zealand.

British acquisition of the Australian continent and New Zealand left France in a decidedly inferior position, despite some successful evangelisation of Polynesians by French Catholic missionaries from the 1820s onwards. The smaller Pacific islands did not seem to offer vast resources to colonisers, although promoters imagined that successful plantation economies could be established and argued that products such as copra could create prosperous trade. They claimed, furthermore, that French outposts in Oceania were necessary for commercial and strategic purposes, as refuelling and provisioning stations for the French navy and merchant marine.

Tahiti, most fabled of Polynesian islands, well situated on trade routes and with a reasonably large land area, held particular lure.

Britain had won a privileged position in the realms of Queen
Pomaré (which included Tahiti and many of the Society Islands).
Protestant missionaries had successfully proselytised Tahitians since
the 1790s, and London's consul in Papeete, George Pritchard,
himself a missionary, exercised great influence over the local
monarch in the 1830s. In 1835, a French religious order tried to
set up a Catholic mission on Tahiti, but the government denied
the priests permission to land. The following year, two missionaries
managed to get ashore, but Pritchard convinced Pomaré to ex-
pel them. A French warship called at Papeete to demand an apology
for the affront; the apology was duly proffered, and the French
appointed a consul, but failed to win rights for Catholic evangelisation. French resentment of Pritchard, the British and the Tahitian government festered. Rumours circulated that Pritchard was
lobbying for London to declare a protectorate over the islands.

In early 1842, pursuing a new policy of acquiring strategic ports,
a French naval commander, Dupetit-Thouard, acting more on his
own initiative than on precise orders from Paris, annexed the
Marquesas Islands. The Marquesas, far to the north of Tahiti but
generally considered by Europeans as belonging to the same geographical ensemble, were small mountainous islands inhabited by
Polynesians. The action provoked little reaction or interest in either
the islands or France. Dupetit-Thouard then sailed to Tahiti, which
he reached in August 1842; Pritchard, propitiously, was absent in
London. The French consul summoned the Tahitian chiefs and
delivered an ultimatum demanding rights for French citizens and
Catholic missionaries to settle, trade and proselytise. Under dur-
ess, the chiefs acceded to establishment of a French protectorate.

Pomaré's realm thereby passed under French control, although
it took several years of warfare against rebellious chiefs (and a
generous payout to Pomaré) for the French to defeat resistance,
and even longer to reduce British influence in Tahiti. Britain
was outraged at the French protectorate, and Australian and New
Zealand colonists clamoured about the dangers of French presence
in the South Pacific. Sabres rattled in London and Paris, but war
between the two powers was averted. France gradually extended
its hold on eastern Polynesia; by the end of the century the
Tuamotu, Gambier and Austral Islands were securely in French
hands. In 1880, the protectorate over Tahiti and its neighbouring islands gave way to annexation, and the territory – compris-
ing the Society, Marquesas, Tuamotu, Gambier and Austral islands

– was organised as the French Oceanic Establishments (*Etablissements Français d'Océanie*, EFO).

Further west, in Melanesia, were New Caledonia and the Loyalty islands. Unlike Polynesia, Melanesia did not enjoy a high reputation in Europe; French missionaries had been rebuffed in the 1840s, and local populations were deemed inhospitable. Nevertheless, the New Caledonian mainland, one of the largest South Pacific islands, endowed with stretches of fine pasture land, a good harbour at Nouméa and a useful strategic position near Australia, looked a good site for a French outpost. In 1853, a navy commander took possession of the New Caledonian mainland, and French control was subsequently extended to the Loyalty islands. The French government justified the act: 'The takeover had as its goal to assure France the position in the Pacific that the interests of the military and commercial fleet require and the views of the government on the penal system.' New Caledonia, like Guyane, became infamous as a penal colony. Indeed, because Guyane's climate proved murderous to convicts, soldiers and administrators, Paris was looking for a new location for a penitentiary distant from France. Since the model of Britain's settlement of Australia with transported convicts lay before the French, penal settlement of New Caledonia seemed an opportunity to create a French colony and, at the same time, deal with criminals and political prisoners in France. From the 1860s to the 1890s, France shipped thousands of convicts to New Caledonia; the government also encouraged free settlement. Colonialists hailed New Caledonia as the only true French society of settlement other than Algeria.

France's third possession in Oceania consisted of the tiny Polynesian islands of Wallis and Futuna, located in the central Pacific between Tahiti and New Caledonia. Although devoid of good harbours and marketable natural resources beyond copra, the islands had attracted French Catholic missionaries in the 1830s. Priests soon converted the entire population and established a virtual theocracy in Wallis and Futuna, though leaving local chieftains in office. Paris turned a deaf ear to persistent requests from missionaries for a protectorate until the late 1880s. By that decade, Britain, Germany and the United States had taken possession of a number of Oceanic islands. Paris instituted a protectorate to forestall takeover by another power, leaving missionaries in control of the islands.

Another French outpost – though only partly French – was the

New Hebrides. A Melanesian archipelago north of New Caledonia, the New Hebrides attracted Protestant missionaries from Britain and Australia and Catholic priests from France, as well as traders from Australia and planters from New Caledonia. John Higginson, an Irishman who became a French citizen, spearheaded French claims. His company bought nominal title to a third of all land in the New Hebrides, and he tirelessly campaigned for French takeover. Australian and British colonialists stood guard against any French move while trying to persuade Britain to annex the archipelago. London and Paris, well aware of the conflicting interests present on the island, hesitated to provoke each other by a *prise de possession.*

The New Hebrides remained in legal limbo until the establishment of a Franco-British Condominium in 1907. In a unique imperial arrangement, France and Britain both renounced sovereignty over the New Hebrides. Their Residents in the islands' main centre, Port-Vila, exercised jurisdiction over their respective nationals; 'optants', citizens of other nations, chose to be governed by either British or French regulations. Two flags flew over the condominium, two currencies circulated, the few schools which existed taught in English or French. Native Melanesians remained ineligible for either British or French citizenship and, in international law, were stateless. Legal affairs concerning Melanesians were judged by a joint court with a French and a British magistrate and a Spanish president – for the simple reason that the Spanish had been the first Europeans to discover the islands. The awkward and sometimes comic-opera Condominium, renamed 'pandemonium' by a later nationalist, endured until the New Hebrides gained independence in 1980.

The other Oceanic possessions taken over in the 1800s, French Polynesia (as the EFO were renamed), New Caledonia, and Wallis and Futuna to this day remain overseas territories of France. So does Clipperton island. France claimed Clipperton, a desolate rock island far off the western coast of Mexico, in 1858. Plans were mooted to exploit guano for phosphate, but nothing eventuated. Mexico contested French sovereignty, and in the early years of the twentieth century sent a handful of settlers to Clipperton. They were soon forgotten, and the half-starved and deranged survivors were rescued by a passing American ship during the First World War. In 1931, France and Mexico submitted the question of ownership of Clipperton to the arbitration of the King of Italy, who found in France's favour.[1]

Indochina

Compared to the small islands of Oceania, Asia loomed as a inexhaustible treasure trove for Europeans. Traders dreamed of tapping the extraordinary wealth of the Orient, securing the much desired products of the East and carving out markets in this most populous area of the globe. Missionaries had visions of converting millions of Asians to Christianity. Politicians hoped to gain sway for their countries in China and its vassal states in southeastern Asia. The Portuguese, who acquired Macao in 1557, established the first permanent foreign presence on Chinese soil. The Spanish, although by the 1800s a much reduced colonial power, remained entrenched in the Philippines. The Dutch monopolised trade in the Spice Islands, maintained a major port at Batavia (Jakarta) and claimed sovereignty over the whole East Indies (Indonesia). The British had in India an ideal base for expansion further eastwards and had, since 1819, controlled Singapore, the crossroads of many trading routes. British acquisition of Hong Kong in 1842, which gave France's greatest rival a signal advantage in the Orient, made it more apparent than ever that the French lacked a foothold in the Far East.

Indochina looked the best remaining prize in Southeast Asia. Vietnam, composed of the three regions of Tonkin, Annam and Cochinchina under the loose control of the Annamese emperor, promised much bounty. Haiphong and Saigon afforded fine harbours, and the Mekong and Red Rivers provided a conduit to the interior of Vietnam and, it was hoped, to China beyond. Vietnam had arable land, a wealth of natural resources, a large population of potential labourers and consumers. West of Vietnam lay Cambodia and Laos, largely unknown but with many ties to Vietnam.

Missionaries led the way in French involvement in Asia. A priest, Alexandre de Rhodes, spent a quarter-century in Annam in the early 1600s, making a impressive number of converts and inventing a method of writing Vietnamese in Latin characters rather than in Chinese ideographs. His reports to Paris inspired hope for further evangelisation. In the 1660s, soon after de Rhodes' death, the Society for Foreign Missions (*Société des Missions Etrangères*) dispatched missionaries to Annam and Siam (Thailand). In the 1670s, despite opposition from Portuguese Jesuits who considered eastern Asia their preserve, the Vatican sanctioned the French priests' work.

Meanwhile, the French East India Company had undertaken trading expeditions to the Orient, though without brilliant success. Then in 1748 a former priest, Pierre Poivre, led a commercial delegation to Annam, where he negotiated a treaty with the Vietnamese emperor which granted France trading privileges. Few merchants took advantage of the opportunities, and French interests continued to be represented primarily by missionaries. Missionaries, however, did not hesitate to intervene in political affairs. In the 1780s, Bishop Pigneau de Béhaine, leader of the Vietnamese Catholics, allied with a fugitive pro-Catholic prince manoeuvring to gain the Vietnamese throne (as he eventually did under the name Gia Long). On a visit to Paris in 1787, the bishop, accompanied by the prince's son, convinced Louis XVI to sign an alliance with the Vietnamese.

When Pigneau returned to Annam, he found his protégé well on the way to winning his crown. This augured well for French influence and the missionaries' activities. Small-scale French trading indeed prospered in the early years of the nineteenth century. But Gia Long's successors were little interested in French business, and they turned hostile to Christianity. From the 1820s onwards, Vietnamese rulers persecuted Catholics, executing several priests. Subsequent rulers proved more or less tolerant of Catholics, although generally less so. The French, again embroiled in political upheaval at home, lacked the wherewithal to commit great resources to Asian expansion, despite a Catholic religious revival which quickened missionary fervour. Great success for the foreign mission society came in the 1830s and 1840s, when the pope granted the French control of half a dozen vicariates (proto-dioceses) in China and Indochina, as well as missions in Korea and Manchuria. French Catholics became the leading missionary group in eastern Asia. Obstacles still lay in their path, particularly the sometimes unfriendly attitude of the Chinese government and authorities elsewhere.

The 1840s saw renewed French political interest in Asia, partly inspired by the same effort to secure naval supply stations and trading posts around the globe which motivated the takeover of Tahiti, partly precipitated by British occupation of Hong Kong. French consuls in Macao and Manila urged the government to secure a foothold. In 1844, a French delegation arrived in China to investigate persecutions of Christians – clerics had importuned the French navy to protect their rights, by gunboat diplomacy if necessary – and to try to obtain a base comparable to Hong Kong. After lengthy negotiation, some coercion and possibly bribery, it persuaded the Chinese emperor to legalise Christianity, thus safe-guarding the missionaries.

Finding a French base was less easy. The French first considered the island of Basilan in the Sulu archipelago between the Philippines and Borneo. The capture of five French sailors who landed there in late 1844 (two of whom were killed) provided an excuse for sending in warships and forcing the ruling sultan to cede the island. But the substantial bill for remuneration to the sultan caused concern in Paris, as did the reaction of Spain, which claimed sovereignty over Basilan. The French found it prudent to retract the takeover. An alternative, Chusan Island, which the British occupied but planned to quit, was also abandoned because of strong British and Chinese opposition.

French activities over the next few years remained in a holding pattern. In the early 1850s, interest in China resurfaced. Paris appointed diplomatic representatives to China, and a consul convinced authorities to grant the French a 'concession' in Shanghai. Such a 'concession', accorded to several countries during the nineteenth century, provided an almost inviolate enclave for foreign activities. The immediate advantages were more symbolic than real, since the French community in Shanghai in 1850 consisted of ten people, half of whom belonged to the consul's family. Three years later, in the midst of the Taiping rebellion against the Chinese government and attacks on missionaries, French and British ships bombarded Shanghai. Other incidents – some revolving around minor, but incipient, conflicts such as whether the French had the right to fly their flag in Shanghai or why a French envoy was not seated in exactly the same sort of chair as a Chinese minister who received him – seemed episodes from an operetta but showed the determination of foreigners to win favour in China, by peaceful or belligerent means.

In Vietnam, the tide once more turned against Catholics in the 1840s, as a group of priests were implicated in a plot to overthrow the emperor. Several priests were arrested, sentenced to death, then exiled; they returned, were again arrested and again deported. French gunboats sailed to Vietnam but departed when the situation calmed. The next emperor, Tu Duc, was ardently anti-Catholic, and in 1848 banned further missionary activity. Three years later, he decreed that priests should be executed and that

Catholic Vietnamese should have their property confiscated and the word 'infidel' branded on their cheek; two French priests were put to death in 1851 and 1852.

French diplomats in China, who kept watch on Indochinese developments, entreated Paris to act, and Napoleon III, influenced by his pious wife Eugénie, agreed in 1856 to protect the missionaries. The French consul in Shanghai, Montigny, after consultations in Paris, hurried back to Asia to negotiate with the emperor of Annam. On the way, Montigny stopped in Bangkok and won trading privileges for the French in Siam; various blunders by the French led to almost immediate Siamese recension of the treaty. Montigny, however, had moved on to Cambodia, where he hoped to win from the Cambodian king tolerance for Catholics and the cession of Koh Doat (Phu Quoc), an island off the Cambodian coast which might provide a French outpost. The Siamese angrily learned of the French overtures; the Vietnamese also expressed opposition, so the project was dropped.

The French gunboat *Catinat*, which had preceded Montigny to Vietnam, had by now arrived in Annam. An officer attempted to deliver a message to the emperor asking for revival of good relations and closer ties; the letter implied that if the Vietnamese did not accept the French terms, they would suffer the consequences. The Vietnamese emperor returned the message from the French emperor without having opened it. The French then occupied a small island in Tourane (Da Nang) harbour and gunned Vietnamese forts. After several weeks of occupation, French forces departed for Macao. Montigny, who arrived from Cambodia two months later, lacked the firepower to take further action. France suffered humiliation.

Missionaries tried to persuade Paris to mount a full-scale incursion into Indochina to reverse the failure of the Montigny embassy. Bishop Pellerin, primate among Catholic bishops in Indochina, journeyed to Paris to put the missionaries' case to the emperor, and at the end of 1857, he decided to move. French forces, in collaboration with British troops, were diverted to China, where the allies used the execution of a French priest and capture of a British gunboat as justification for temporary occupation of Guangzhou (Canton). They forced the Chinese to give additional latitude to foreign missionaries and traders.

In August 1858, a force of 14 ships and 2500 men (mostly black African recruits), under the command of Admiral Rigault de

Genouilly, arrived in Indochina. They took Tourane with little effort and few casualties. The plan had been to move on to the Vietnamese capital at Hué, but the French lacked the flat-bottomed boats necessary to sail upriver. Furthermore, fever, dysentery and typhus savaged the French troops – for each man killed in battle, 20 succumbed to disease. The French had established a base in Indochina but seemed hardly able to maintain it, much less expand further.

Genouilly decided to transfer most of his men and firepower south to Saigon, an excellent port where missionaries were firmly installed. Over two weeks in February 1859, Genouilly occupied Saigon. The intentions behind the takeover – both the issue that served as justification and France's long-term interests – are evident from the admiral's statement on the *prise de possession*:

> The Annamese government has put itself outside the pale of civilised nations. War is again beginning; as the first act of war, I am placing the city of Saigon and its territory under French authority.... The laws and customs of the country will be respected, but the courts and the police will act under French authority. The measures which I will take will bring great commerce to the city. The justice of our administration, which will equatably protect the interests and the rights of all, will attract numerous residents.

French expansion in Vietnam came to a halt as other affairs beckoned. Napoleon III in 1859 declared war on Austria and invaded Italy, which netted French territorial expansion in Europe – in 1860 France annexed Nice and Savoy. The French emperor fomented a plot to place his puppet on the throne of Mexico.[2] French troops went to the Middle East in 1860 to protect Christians against Muslims. In the same year, the French joined with the British in military action in China. In 1861, a new French navy commander arrived in Saigon to relieve the troops holding the city and negotiate a treaty. Signed in 1862, the treaty ceded Saigon and the three eastern provinces of Cochinchina, as well as the island of Poulo Condore (Côn Dao), to the French; it granted freedom of action to Catholic missionaries and opened three ports (including Tourane) to French trade. The emperor renounced Vietnamese territorial claims to Cambodia. After formally agreeing to the treaty, Tu Duc immediately tried to get the French to reconsider their position by offering a protectorate over all six provinces of Cochinchina in return for French repudiation of the annexation of Saigon and the three ceded provinces. Paris refused.

France was now in possession of a major port, which promoters hoped would become the French Hong Kong; considering its strategic value, some observers labelled Saigon a French Gibraltar. Authorities in Paris were less than enthusiastic about devoting men and money to the new colony, and there was talk of abandoning the possession. The opposite course eventuated, as the French consolidated their hold on Cochinchina over the next several years. In 1867, the French commander in Saigon, though without direct orders from Paris, annexed the three western provinces of Cochinchina, bringing the whole southern region of Vietnam under the French flag.

The French were also intent on expanding beyond Cochinchina, still looking for a path to the markets of China. In 1866, the French commissioned a young lieutenant, Doudart de Lagrée, to lead an expedition up the Mekong River in the hope of finding a route to Yunnan. The journey, a heroic mission lasting two years and garnering much attention in France, took the explorers from Saigon to Angkor – where they visited the famous Khmer temples – and on to Laos, where they discovered that the Mekong was not navigable as far as China. Disappointed, the mission returned; Doudart de Lagrée died from illness during the journey.

The Mekong expedition did establish a French claim on Cambodia. Cambodia, a large country with imprecise borders and a relatively small population of 1 million, lay between Siam and Vietnam. Buddhism and the heritage of Indian influence fused the country together. Angkor Wat stood as a reminder of a period when Cambodia had been a powerful state, but the jungle had overrun the ruins, a commentary on the country's fate. The geographical position of Cambodia had sealed its destiny, because both the Vietnamese emperor and the Siamese king considered it a vassal state and obliged the Cambodian king to pay regular tributes. The Cambodian monarch tried to preserve a modicum of independence, but the complicated division of authority in the royal family, by which various members held control over different provinces but succession to the throne remained largely a matter of the king's personal choice of heir, made for administration beset with inefficiency and rivalry. Much of Cambodia's population lived in a condition of servitude, a modernised economic infrastructure was notable by its absence, and international trade was limited.

In 1860, the Cambodian king who had ruled for much of the early nineteenth century died, leaving his son Norodom, a 20-year-old reared in Siam, as successor. The new king's step-brothers, Sisowath and Si Votha, contested Norodom's authority, and Sisowath led open rebellion. Chaos threatened. The French viewed the situation with alarm because of danger that Siam, where France's great rival Britain exercised strong influence, might take over the country. The governor of Cochinchina, Admiral Bonard, announced French determination 'to ensure that the archaic governments which have for so long succeeded each other in Cambodia make no incursions into the territory of Cochinchina and that this state of affairs does not become for our provinces a source of ruin rather than prosperity'.

In 1863, the French persuaded Norodom to sign a treaty according France a protectorate over his country. France took control of foreign affairs and the accreditation of consuls, and promised to defend Cambodia against outside intervention. Norodom extended freedom of action to Christian missionaries and foreign traders. Behind the back of the French, the king signed a treaty with Siam with significant concessions to Bangkok and tacit acknowledgement of Siamese suzerainty over Cambodia. France was nonetheless able to establish control, but conflict loomed as the date for Norodom's coronation approached. The king wanted the ceremony held in Bangkok, where the Cambodian crown and royal sword were stored, a plan to which the French objected; ultimately, the ceremony took place in Cambodia – the Siamese king gave the Cambodian king his official reign title, while the French representative presented his crown.

Over the next few years, the French worked assiduously to secure their rule. They convinced Norodom to name his still estranged but openly pro-French step-brother Sisowath as heir, and they sent forces to rout Si Votha, who was attempting to raise a peasant army. The French provided various emoluments to Norodom, including the villa Empress Eugénie had used in Egypt for the opening of the Suez Canal; disassembled and shipped to Cambodia, the house became one of the king's favourite palaces. To make certain the Siamese accepted French overlordship of Cambodia, the French signed a treaty with the King of Siam in

1867 ceding the western Cambodian provinces of Battambang and Siem Reap to Thailand. (They were returned in 1907.) The Siamese conveniently forgot the treaty they had signed with Norodom. Despite a rebellion against the French in Cambodia in the mid-1880s, which was easily subdued, few henceforth contested France's domination.[3]

The next push in Indochina came in 1873, this time commanded by another of the explorers who so marked the history of French expansion. Francis Garnier had been a member of Doudart de Lagrée's mission, where he had met Jean Dupuis, a French trader, who convinced him that the Red River, which ran through Tonkin, would be the avenue to China. In 1872, Dupuis travelled to Hanoi to try to pry open the doors to trade in Tonkin. Refusal by local officials to allow him to leave the city with a cargo of salt served as pretext for French intervention. Garnier, with authorisation from the governor in Saigon, hurried to Hanoi, where he bullied Vietnamese officials, secured the release of Dupuis and officially declared the Red River open to foreign commerce. Garnier then occupied Hanoi's main fortress, but within weeks he was killed in fighting. Tu Duc's forces attacked Christian Vietnamese villages, massacring as many as 20 000 Catholics. The French evacuated Hanoi in return for confirmation of their sovereignty over Cochinchina and a vaguely worded unofficial protectorate over Annam.

France slowly but surely reinforced control of Cochinchina and Cambodia but, suffering from defeat in Europe in 1870–1 and rebuff in Tonkin, was incapable of advancing further in southeast Asia. Colonial promoters bemoaned the failure of the Garnier invasion and over the next decade pressed for renewed action to secure northern Vietnam.[4]

In 1883, under the prime ministership of Jules Ferry, an enthusiastic expansionist, the government decided to try again to take control of Tonkin. Authorities aimed to establish a formal protectorate over Annam and Tonkin and gain better access to China. Tonkin bordered the Chinese provinces of Yunnan, Guangxi and Guangdong, thought to hold great mineral wealth and commercial potential. Colonialists hoped to obtain raw materials and, if successful in procuring a railway concession from Haiphong and Hanoi to Yunnan, to take the lion's share of trade in southern China. Occupation of Tonkin would provide added glory for France in eastern Asia in these heady days of imperial conquest.[5]

On a pretext of attacking pirates – action permitted according to a Franco-Vietnamese treaty – the governor of Cochinchina sent Henri de Rivière and two companies of soldiers to Tonkin. They easily captured Hanoi's citadel and occupied part of the city. The pirates, however, counter-attacked, capturing and beheading Rivière. The French were stunned that ten years after the murder of Garnier, France had again suffered humiliation. Ferry ordered an all-out assault to take Tonkin. The fragile dynastic situation following the death of Tu Duc aided the French, who dictated terms to the Vietnamese. By the treaty of Hué, the new emperor recognised a French protectorate over Annam and Tonkin; the nominal power of the local government was maintained, but France gained control of foreign relations and enjoyed the right to station troops in the protectorate.

Frightened at the prospect of a strong European imperial power on its doorstep, China moved troops towards Tonkin. Various border incidents followed, the most serious at Langson, where on 28 March 1885, Chinese troops wounded the French commander. Panic spread, and a subordinate French officer ordered troops to evacuate the town. The incident was reported in Paris as a signal defeat for the French army. Parliament revolted and overthrew the government of Prime Minister Ferry, thereafter saddled with the nickname 'Ferry-the-Tonkinese'. Despite Ferry's fall and critical debate on the policy of imperial expansion, France held on to its new protectorate.

In the 1880s France was faced with the task of wiping out resistance and organising administration in Vietnam. French forces combated a rebellion of Vietnamese nationalists led by mandarins. Colonial authorities engineered the replacement of several Vietnamese emperors until a suitably pro-French child was placed on the throne. The setting-up of the Government-General of Indochina in 1887 brought together administration of the colony of Cochinchina and the protectorates of Tonkin, Annam and Cambodia. Royal power checked, rebellions under control and administration regrouped, France could claim, after almost 30 years, to have established a secure, promising and extensive empire in southeastern Asia.

France's last, and least controversial, acquisition in the region was Laos. Lying land-locked along the Mekong River west of Vietnam, in the nineteenth century Laos was a collection of principalities loosely organised as a kingdom. Isolation and poverty were the lot of most Laotians. Burma, Siam, Vietnam and China wielded political influence in Laos, and all but Burma collected tribute from the king; the Siamese maintained a garrison in the royal capital, Luang Prabang. In the 1890s, the future of the country remained undecided despite the presence of the French in eastern Indochina and the British in Burma; there was talk of retaining Laos as a buffer zone between the two imperial powers.

French takeover of Laos was largely the work of Auguste Pavie. A former military officer, Pavie by 1879 was working as a French postal official in Cambodia, when authorities commissioned him with several exploratory missions. Success inspired him to set up a training school for Cambodians, forerunner of the Ecole Coloniale, during a trip to France in 1885. In the same year, the government appointed Pavie vice-consul in Luang Prabang, although he did not take up the position until two years later. Pavie used deft diplomacy to win favour for the French with Laotian authorities, suppress Chinese banditry and reconnoitre the country. He devised a treaty, signed in 1889, by which Siam agreed to respect the status quo in Laos. For the next two years, Pavie triumphantly toured Laos – 'I have known the joy of being loved by the people among whom I passed', he remarked. Named French consul in Bangkok in 1892, Pavie continued to defend Laotian autonomy, despite continued Siamese designs on the country.

The movement of French troops into an area of the Mekong delta which Siam claimed, after the death of a French official there in 1893, provided the opportunity for French action. French gunboats needed only a short blockade of Bangkok to convince Siam's leaders to renounce claims on Laos. In 1895, China similarly relinquished its claims, and in 1896 the British recognised French control over Laos. Largely through Pavie's personal popularity, buttressed by gunboat diplomacy and a gentleman's agreement between imperial rivals, Laos became a French protectorate. In 1897 it was incorporated into the Government-General of Indochina.[6]

Other French Domains in Asia

France acquired two other domains in Asia. One was a small parcel of land in China. Given the impossibility of dividing China in the same way as they had carved up southeast Asia, the great powers put pressure on Beijing at the end of the nineteenth century to grant them long-term leases on small portions of territory. Russia, Britain (which already held Hong Kong), Germany and France thereby got rights to Chinese land. France signed a 99-year lease in 1898 for Guangzhouwan (Kwangchowan), an 840-square-kilometre peninsula and two islands in the bay opposite the larger Hainan island and Tonkin. Guangzhouwan, administered by French authorities in Indochina, counted a population of 210 000, almost all Chinese, by the early 1930s. Two main centres, the most important called Fort-Bayard, contained French-built roadways, a French school and hospital. The manufacture of fireworks and sales of exports from Hong Kong formed the main economic activities, but the small territory never proved of great commercial or military worth to France. More important were the French 'concessions' in Shanghai, Guangzhou and Hangzhou (Hanchow). France did not enjoy sovereignty over these enclaves, but a few French residents engaged in commercial and cultural activities. The great claim to fame of the French reserve in Shanghai – 1000 hectares with 460 000 inhabitants in 1930 – was the founding of the Chinese Communist Party there in 1921.

The other territory France added to its empire, located at the other extremity of the Asian landmass, was Syria and Lebanon.[7] At the end of the First World War, the victors divided the Middle Eastern territories of the dissolved Ottoman Empire. The League of Nations gave Britain a mandate over Iraq, Palestine and Transjordan, while France was assigned Syria and Lebanon. The mandates did not extend sovereignty over the countries to the administering powers, which were charged with proclaiming constitutions, developing representative institutions and promoting economic development; France, like Britain, was obliged to present regular reports to the League on its conduct. The mandated powers nonetheless treated territories much as other colonies.

The Ottoman Empire had traditionally been an area of French interest. French creditors held almost two-thirds of the Ottoman public debt in 1914; merchants associated with the Lyon Chamber of Commerce bought 90 per cent of Syria's large silk production, and entrepreneurs placed great hopes in the development of cotton plantations. France also maintained cultural and military links with the region. Since the eighteenth century, France had posed as protector of the Christian minority in Syria and Lebanon, where Islam dominated. The large Catholic community in Lebanon, the Maronites, kept especially strong ties with French religious orders, and French Jesuits operated a university in Beirut. In 1860, the Druze, a break-away sect of Muslims, attacked the Maronites, and the clash led to the deaths of as many as 10 000 Christians. France sent an expeditionary force to Lebanon to defend the Christians, and Paris pressured Ottoman rulers to grant autonomy to a Christian-dominated province created in Lebanon. Such connections paved the way for the French mandate over Syria and Lebanon, which lasted until the mid-1940s.

Uninhabited Islands

In addition to France's inhabited continental and island colonies, its empire included a number of small, remote and unpopulated islands, as well as a portion of Antarctica, Adélie Land (Terre Adélie), to which a French captain laid claim in 1840. In the Mozambique Channel between Madagascar and the African coast, France claimed a number of tiny and uninhabited islands, the Iles Eparses (Les Glorieuses, Juan de Nova, Bassas da India and Europa), as well as the Tromelin reef north of Réunion. Among other island outposts were the sub-Antarctic archipelagos lying between Australia and Africa, the main islands of which are Kerguelen, Saint-Paul, Crozet and Amsterdam.

The most important is Kerguelen, a mountainous and windswept island – gusts climb to almost 300 kilometres an hour – 4800 kilometres west of Australia. The navigator Yves-Joseph de Kerguelen discovered and took possession of the islands in the name of King Louis XV in 1772. Kerguelen mistakenly thought he had discovered the great southern continent of which explorers dreamed and, on his return to Paris, lauded its potential. He suggested that Acadians who had been exiled from former French possessions in North America could be resettled on the island that came to bear his name. Kerguelen received a warm reception, promotion in the Navy and a royal decoration. His star soon fell when he was accused of excesses of military discipline and other misdeeds (including stowing away a woman on his ship).

The French paid little attention to their southernmost possession; only one French ship visited the island between Kerguelen's second voyage in 1773 and a new French *prise de possession* in 1893. Vessels of other nations did call at Kerguelen, including a small flotilla which arrived to witness the transit of Venus in 1874. Whaling ships sometimes used the island's port for repairs and refuge, and one English whaler, lost in a shipwreck in 1825, survived there for two years. The island seemed unpromising, but various promoters or entrepreneurs formulated plans for development. A British company floated the idea of creating a coaling station; a Frenchman suggested establishing a penal colony there.

Two brothers, Henri and René Boissière, who acquired concessional rights from the French government to develop the islands, ventured the most ambitious plans. In 1908, the Boissières leased their rights to a Norwegian company, headquartered in Cape Town, which planned to hunt and process whales. For a brief period, the company maintained 140 employees on Kerguelen, but the project ended when the company decided it was easier to process whales on board ship than on land; the workers were repatriated. The Boissières then proposed to raise sheep on Kerguelen. The brothers had lived in Argentina, where their father ran a seal oil factory, and had studied sheep-raising in the Falkland Islands. In 1913, they brought a thousand sheep from the Falklands to Kerguelen; the herds did not thrive and were abandoned the following year. After the First World War, the Boissières signed a contract with an English company for whaling, but it never produced results. Undaunted, they turned their attention away from Kerguelen to Saint-Paul island, 2000 kilometres distant from Kerguelen, where they intended to fish for crustaceans. In 1929, seven Bretons were sent to the island, but after the fishing season were forgotten. The Boissières went bankrupt and when a ship was finally sent to rescue the fishermen, in 1931, only three were still alive.

Plans for Kerguelen continued to be mooted. A proposal to make part of the island a national park was put forward in 1924. Three policemen and their families, who lived on Kerguelen from 1927 to 1931, upheld French occupation. In 1932, an economics journal suggested that Kerguelen could support a settlement of 400–500 persons, but calls for migrants went unheeded. Kerguelen and other islands in the Southern Ocean remained uninhabited until the installation of temporary scientific missions after the Second World War. The landscape, nevertheless, was littered with the ruins of various earlier initiatives and the graves of several explorers, Chinese coolies and Comoran labourers who died on the island, testimony to the grand plans which could be affixed even to the most desolate imperial outposts.[8]

Lines of Conquest

France acquired possessions around the world through various ways. In some cases, the declaration of a protectorate or annexation simply confirmed a predominant position already established by private interests. Catholic missionaries had a strong hold on Wallis and Futuna when Paris established a protectorate in the 1880s, French traders held the reins of local economies in several of the Comoros Islands before they were taken over in the late 1800s, and French military forces buttressed the presence of commercial interests before the declaration of the Moroccan protectorate in 1912. In Syria and Lebanon, France posed as the guardian of Christians and dominated trade long before it received the League of Nations mandate. In other cases few French residents or commercial or cultural interests were present in colonies over which France raised the flag; this was true in much of the French Soudan. In yet other regions, the French had to compete, even after the *prise de possession*, with representatives of other powers: in Tahiti British influence persisted after 1842, while in Tunisia Italian influence did not disappear with the protectorate of 1881; the French *comptoirs* in India remained isolated enclaves in the British Raj. In short, trade – and the activities of missionaries or other Frenchmen – as often preceded the flag as followed it, and in some cases was not apparent either before or after takeover.

Paris had no master plan for colonial acquisition. Although the great powers drew lines on maps to divide desert sands or wild jungles, as happened at the Berlin conference of 1884–5, for example, European chancelleries seldom had precise schemes for colonial expansion. Private interests, or an organised colonial lobby, argued for expansion in particular zones, but the government sometimes turned a deaf ear to their requests or heeded them only tardily. Acquisition of colonies was often a matter of fortuitous circumstances, mutually agreeable arrangements among the great powers, or individual actions by hardy commanders in the field. France gained Niger through the map-making of European diplomats, and added Togo and Cameroon to its colonial portfolio as victor's booty after the First World War. Yet French control of Morocco, Tahiti and Tonkin owed much to army and navy officers who occasionally exceeded their briefs to acquire colonies for the motherland.[9]

Specific incidents provoked invasions or takeovers. Officials found it almost ridiculously easy to manufacture such incidents or to find some past episode to justify intervention. The swatting of a French consul by the dey of Algiers in 1827 justified the beginnings of French takeover of Algeria three years later; the expulsion of Catholic priests from Tahiti in 1836 became a reason for French takeover of the Society Islands in 1842. Officials trumped up border confrontations to act in Algeria, Morocco and many parts of sub-Saharan Africa. Seldom were such incidents the real reasons for takeover, as many similar clashes were routinely ignored. They simply provided the appropriate occasion for action, especially in cases where naked French expansion might not win approbation from other powers.

Expansion usually proceeded from an already established base. The French outposts in Senegal, established in the 1600s, provided the point of departure for conquest of much of western Africa, as explorers, soldiers and traders moved eastwards. The French moved southwards from Algeria; moreover, Algeria offered a base (and a reason) for French expansion to Morocco in the west and Tunisia in the east. Outposts on the Gulf of Guinea, in Dahomey, provided similar staging-posts for expansion northwards. Takeover of coastal areas in Gabon and the Congo allowed moves into the interior of equatorial Africa. Réunion served as a base for conquerors and entrepreneurs who moved from the island to Djibouti, Madagascar and the Comoros. The annexation of Cochinchina led to expansion into Annam, Tonkin, Cambodia and Laos. By the 1890s, a prime motive for continued conquest was to consolidate already established colonies and link together France's overseas possessions. Exploration and establishment of control over the hinterlands of the AOF and AEF aimed at joining these possessions with each other and with French North Africa, and the march towards the eastern Soudan unsuccessfully pursued linkage of France's western domains with the outpost on the Red Sea.

If expansion reached a fevered pitch in the 1890s, extension of French control had been continuous during the nineteenth century: Algiers in 1830, Nossy-Bé in 1840, Tahiti in 1842, Mayotte in 1843, New Caledonia in 1852, Cochinchina in 1859, and so on. The avidity for expansion increased in the 'new imperialism' of the last decades of the 1800s, but precedents had been set well before them. By the end of the century, foreign flags waved over almost all areas which could be taken over, even uninhabited islands such as Kerguelen and Clipperton. Only particularly thorny imperial conflicts, such as Morocco and the New Hebrides, awaited resolution.

In few cases did the raising of the Tricolour assure effective French control, and years or even decades were often required for France to quell resistance, establish control over interior regions or explore the new possessions fully. Resistance to French invasion occurred almost everywhere and 'pacification' was a lengthy and costly process. Force, actually used or simply brandished, represented the only assurance of French conquest and continued control. Gunboats poised to bombard coastal cities, military garrisons installed in major settlements and mobile columns of troops ready to punish rebels, inflict damage on recalcitrant populations and fight imperial rivals were the necessary agents and guarantors of French takeover. Colonial expansion, in short, relied on arms and soldiers to secure areas reconnoitred by explorers, missionaries or traders.

But the period of French rule was often surprisingly short. Chad gained independence barely 60 years after the first European explorers traversed that large country, and Mauritania became independent less than 40 years after it became a separate French colony. Less than a quarter-century passed between the last French efforts at pacification of Morocco and its independence. France ruled Indochina for less than a century. Conquering an empire was, in the case of some colonies at least, the major part of the imperial adventure.

3 Ideas of Empire

The French acquired some of their overseas possessions in seemingly piecemeal fashion, others after years of preparation and reflection. Not surprisingly, one single theory, ideology, or practice did not guide French expansion from the beginning to the end of empire. Policies and the ideas which underlay them metamorphosed considerably even over a few decades. Colonialists, in fact, chastised the government for failing to articulate a more coherent policy of expansion and colonial development.

The great disparities present in an empire which included holdings in Africa, Asia and the Antarctic, as well as islands in the North Atlantic, Pacific and Indian Oceans, the Caribbean, and the sub-Antarctic zone made a simple and inclusive policy difficult to devise. France's empire comprised colonies of settlement and uninhabited islands; tropical jungles, burning deserts and desolate icefields; areas securely held and those where French presence was more tenuously maintained; regions with Christian, Muslim, Buddhist, Confucianist and animistic populations; subsistence economies and bustling commercial centres.

Moreover, French expansion occurred in connection with – and often in response to – actions by France's international rivals. Throughout the eighteenth and nineteenth centuries, France and Britain battled for colonial supremacy, a continuation in foreign lands of centuries-long competition in Europe. Britain surged ahead in the 1700s with acquisition of India and Australia, though it lost the colonies which became the United States. Napoleon's defeat at Waterloo reduced the French empire to ruins, though France recouped losses in Africa and the Pacific. By the late 1800s, new colonial contenders appeared, such as the United States and Italy.

Germany emerged as the strongest new political, economic and colonial power, defeating France at war in 1870–1, outpacing France in industrial development, surpassing France in population and birth rate, and threatening France in the wider world. Fear of Germany brought about a French *rapprochement* with Britain; defeat of Germany in the First World War gave France new colonies as booty. By the 1930s, Japan posed a colonial threat in Asia and the Pacific, Germany clamoured for restoration of its colonies and Italy yearned to enlarge its small domains. After the Second World War, calls for decolonisation besieged France from the United Nations, the United States and the Soviet Union. French colonial policy could never be separated from overall French foreign policy.

As global affairs changed dramatically, so did France's domestic situation. From the conquest of Algiers in 1830 to decolonisation of Algeria in 1962, France endured significant political turmoil, several revolutions and a bewildering number of regimes: Restoration, July Monarchy, Second Republic, Second Empire, Third Republic, Vichy collaboration and German occupation during the Second World War, the Fourth Republic, and the Fifth Republic. During this time, France also underwent profound social and economic changes, including the industrial revolution, the emergence of new elites and a new proletariat, substantial urbanisation, increasing secularisation and many other developments rather facilely subsumed under the heading of 'modernisation'.

A final bar to maintenance of a unified colonial policy was lack of unanimity inside France about the proper course of action to follow in expansion, or indeed whether it suited France to acquire and preserve far-flung imperial domains at all. Colonialism was always a subject for debate, even though the empire seldom held centre-stage in parliament or the public arena. Colonial promoters faced a long and uphill battle to convince a sceptical political class and wider electorate of the merits of spending money, risking lives and diverting resources to distant and sometimes unpromising colonies. Not until the second or third decade of the twentieth century did anything approaching consensus reign – notwithstanding piercing and sustained anti-colonialist critiques – that empire was basically a 'good thing'.

Colonial Assumptions

Certain assumptions underpinning expansion nevertheless remained constant.[1] The most straightforward and unquestioned was that colonies should serve France. They must return profits by providing useful raw materials, purchasing French goods and attracting French investments. They should cost as little as necessary to conquer and administer and, as far as possible, raise the revenues necessary to cover their own expenses. They must extend France's power and prestige against international rivals, securing benefits in the balance of power in Europe and other continents. If colonies were not useful, they must be made to be so, or otherwise they could be traded, sold or abandoned. French metropolitan interests, however, must take precedence over the concerns of indigenous peoples or overseas settlers.

Furthermore, colonies must contribute to the solution of national problems. Social reformers hoped that at least some colonies would provide homes for landless peasants, the urban unemployed, and even orphans. Those convicted of criminal offences or political crimes could be transported to the colonies to rid France of dangerous elements in the body politic, supply the empire with settlers and rehabilitate wrongdoers. Empire would revive and revitalise a France threatened by self-satisfaction, lethargy and loss of national will. Missionaries added that evangelisation of natives would counter growing anticlericalism and secularism. Overseas business would supplement domestic markets which were becoming saturated, allow France to make up for what was often perceived as economic retardation, and provide guaranteed trading advantages in times of heightened economic competition and protectionism.

A corollary was that the empire must provide fields of opportunity. Technologists and engineers saw the empire as a vast worksite for bridges and canals, ports and railways. Social engineers dreamed of creating model settlements, from refuges for monarchists to communities inspired by the doctrines of utopian socialists, from a 'new France' established on the southern shores of the Mediterranean or on a Pacific island to a multinational and multiethnic empire in which liberty, equality and fraternity would be extended to black, brown and yellow French men and women across the seas. Moralists said the empire would provide a terrain for the exercise of youthful energies, manly virtues and the pioneer spirit. The empire would be a training ground for the army and navy, a workshop for business, a laboratory for research, and an experiment in social reform.

Behind the search for new opportunities lay certainty about France's right to take over foreign countries and the superiority of French civilisation to non-European cultures. Colonial expansion, in whatever fashion it was practised and wherever it led, implied a notion of cultural inequality – no matter France's sacrosanct revolutionary slogan. Europeans, in brief, were superior to Indochinese, Maghrebins, black Africans, Malagasy, Oceanic peoples and any other populations not blessed with a Graeco-Roman heritage, Christian religion, the legacy of the Enlightenment and Revolution, modern science, a capitalist economy and white skin. Colonialists suggested cultural, moral and biological proofs for European superiority, though they debated the possibilities of raising inferior peoples to the level of Europeans. Nevertheless, Europeans bore a responsibility to bring civilisation to the uncivilised; this *mission civilisatrice* (civilising mission) provided a moral mandate for expansion.[2]

To bring civilisation to the 'savages', religion to the 'benighted heathen' and modernity to the 'primitive' – English expressions with equivalents in French – meant conquest. Another assumption was that conquest, usually by military means, though also by coercion, purchase, cession or other forms of takeover, was legitimate. Expansion occurred in a context where if might did not make right, it was at least permissible. Most Europeans did not question the use of the gun to take over and control foreign countries, defend the motherland and expand national territory. Despite the growth of pacifist movements in the late 1800s, and shock at the horrors of the First World War, Europeans still thought of military campaigns as heroic, military officers as noble, the use of arms as justified in international conflict, and correction of offenders by physical punishment and the death penalty as a valid form of justice. The increased technical sophistication of the European military – new types of tanks, cannon and rifles, iron-clad ships, motorised conveyances, aeroplanes, radar and other intelligence devices – provided improved tools to advance and speed up conquest. Few thought that such weapons should be used indiscriminately, and even the most ardent colonialists expressed concern about the unrestrained violence of many soldiers and settlers. Almost none, however, disagreed with the principle of using force to expand territory and subdue foreign populations.

Thus belief that colonies should be useful to the metropole, help solve national problems and provide opportunities for national energies coupled with assurance about the right of Europeans to take over the lands of inferior peoples. On many other issues, disagreement predominated. Writers and decision-makers differed on whether France should primarily set up trading posts or societies of settlement; whether the establishment of protectorates or outright annexation was the preferable method of taking possession; whether administration should be delegated to chartered companies, placed entirely in the hands of officials appointed by Paris or devolved to colonists (or, in a late debate on policy, to the colonised); whether France should pursue rigorous assimilation and *francisation* (Frenchification) of peoples whom it conquered or build on indigenous social structures and cultures to associate conquered countries with France; whether colonies must rely on their own capital resources or receive large injections of money to stimulate development. Many other areas remained the object of contention, and seldom did unanimity reign among the politicians, economists, military strategists, colonial promoters and academics who discussed colonial issues.

Nineteenth-Century Ideologies and Policies

Conquest of Algiers in 1830 was more a reflection on the desperate political straits of King Charles X and an attempt to preserve his regime through foreign glory than an embodiment of a new policy of colonialism. Marshal Bugeaud's slogan, *Ense et Arato* ('By the Sword and the Plough'), summed up his approach: to conquer Algeria by force of arms and introduce native populations to sedentary agriculture. Policy-makers in Paris decided that Algeria could also serve as a depot for rebels after the Revolution of 1848 and the *coup d'état* of 1851, and made various attempts to encourage free settlers to move there. Otherwise, governments in the first decades of French occupation enunciated few precise policies for Algeria except to stamp out resistance to continued French expansion and pursue European settlement on land taken from Algerians.

In 1863 Napoleon III announced plans for an Arab kingdom in Algeria, claiming, 'I am as much the emperor of the Arabs as emperor of the French'. Two years later the Senate proclaimed

Algeria an 'Arab kingdom, European colony and French camp'. Napoleon considered giving the title King of Algiers or viceroy to his kinsman Jérôme Bonaparte or even to Abd el-Khader, but settlers and government officials were opposed. Questions about whether military officers, colonists or indigenous representatives should rule Algeria set the pattern for later debates on colonialism. But Algeria, a large country close to France and rapidly attracting European settlement, remained something of an anomaly among French colonies. In fact, French officials did not consider Algeria strictly as a colony. The three Algerian *départements* were integrated into the French administrative system, and the ministries which handled colonial affairs generally did not include Algeria in their briefs. (The Saharan district, in Algeria's south, which remained under military control, more closely resembled 'colonies' proper.)

The 'Points d'appui'

In the 1840s, under the July Monarchy, politicians began to devise a more definite policy of expansion. One of the most important statements of colonial policy came in an 1842 speech to the National Assembly by King Louis-Philippe's chief minister, François Guizot:

> I am inclined to believe, in general, that it is little befitting the policy and genius of France to essay new and great colonial establishments at a great distance from our territory and, for their sake, to engage in long struggles either against natives of these countries or against other powers. What is appropriate for France, what is indispensable, is to possess at points on the globe which are destined to become great centres of commerce, sure and strong maritime stations to serve as a support for our commerce, where the fleet can obtain provisions and find a safe harbour.[3]

Guizot opposed French conquerors raising flags over large tracts of continental territory; he favoured takeovers of coastal enclaves or, better still, islands which could serve as supply depots, storehouses and sources of essentials for sailing ships. Colonies were primarily of use as accessories in international trade and military manoeuvres. The perfect support station (*point d'appui* or *point de relâche*) was situated on a busy sea lane, could be defended easily and provided food and water for sailors and traders. Guizot argued that France would benefit greatly from a chain of such ports around the globe.

Guizot's view paralleled the policies of other powers. Spain, Portugal, the Netherlands and Britain held on to considerable areas acquired in earlier bouts of expansion, but had not taken over additional large continental territories by 1840 – British occupation of Australia in 1788 represented a notable exception. Britain's navy ruled the waves, but France's navy wanted a larger share of the ocean. The British *prise de possession* of New Zealand in 1840 pointed to the difficulty France faced in challenging British mastery, but also the need to secure outposts if France were not simply to accede to British hegemony. France already possessed good ports in the Antilles, Réunion in the Indian Ocean, and Saint-Louis and Gorée in Senegal, and the government wanted to supplement them with other *points d'appui*. The possible building of canals through the isthmus of Suez and central America encouraged hopes for increased ocean commerce. Britain's rapid industrialisation made it vital for France to secure new sources of raw materials and markets for manufactured goods. The time was ripe, in short, to raise the flag over islands and coastal enclaves which could enhance trade and prestige.

Guizot's 1842 statement nicely justified, *a posteriori*, acquisition of port facilities in Gabon in 1839 and takeover of the Indian Ocean islands of Nossy-Bé in 1840 and Mayotte in 1841, as well as *prises de possession* of the Marquesas islands and Tahiti in 1842, and of Grand-Bassam and Assinie in the Côte-d'Ivoire the same year. It foreshadowed establishment of a French toehold on the Gulf of Guinea, at Ouidah in Dahomey, in 1851, and occupation of New Caledonia in 1853. Only attempts to gain a base in eastern Asia, such as the effort to procure Basilan island in 1853, failed; the French waited until the early 1860s to obtain Saigon. In 1862, the same year the French secured Cochinchina, they also claimed Obock on the horn of Africa.

In a quarter-century, France thus had founded a network of outposts dappled across the tropical latitudes. Few brought immediate rewards. Mayotte did not provide a good harbour, and Obock was a hot arid wasteland; the South Pacific and African possessions did not develop dramatically (and France later abandoned several of the African enclaves). Areas outside the expanded empire attracted more French attention than the new domains. For instance, French trade with Australia, a major supplier of wool, easily outweighed trade with the Oceanic islands in the mid-1800s. French commercial, political and cultural contacts with Central America surpassed in importance involvement in some of the small possessions over which the Tricolour flew.[4] France's key links remained ones with its European neighbours, growing ties with the Russian and Ottoman empires,[5] and connections with developing countries such as the United States and the South American republics. France's major military adventures in the middle of the century were campaigns in Italy and Crimea in the 1850s, and interventions in Mexico and Syria in the 1860s; only in Algeria (and, to a smaller extent, in Tahiti) did France wage war to subjugate local populations.

French control of islands and enclaves did not demand great expenditure of manpower or money. More or less willing cession of land by local chiefs and the proclamation of protectorates gave France territories which required few soldiers to capture and few administrators to govern. Trade fared more or less well, as did missionary work, and navy vessels called at French overseas ports as regularly as possible. If returns from the *points d'appui* were small, so were costs to keep them.

French colonialists nevertheless began to depart from Guizot's injunctions to establish *points d'appui* by the 1850s and 1860s. Bugeaud's successors in Algeria pushed the French colony deeper into the Atlas mountains and beyond to the Sahara. Early nineteenth-century efforts to promote plantations and settlement in Senegal had come to naught. But Governor Protet, who administered the colony from 1850 to 1854, and his successor Faidherbe, who held office from 1854 to 1865, advanced the frontiers of French control steadily eastwards and southwards from Saint-Louis, to bring the hinterland of Senegal under French rule and found Dakar in 1857. With the first convoys of prisoners in the mid-1860s, New Caledonia became more than just a South Sea island port. The conquest of Cochinchina and Cambodia gave France a continental base in southeast Asia and promised further movement into Indochina.

France's attention was drawn back to Europe with war in 1870–1. Prussian troops bested France on the battlefield and besieged Paris. Napoleon III abdicated, and the revolutionary Commune held Paris for several months before being savagely put down by conservative provincial troops. The victorious Prussians forced France to cede the rich provinces of Alsace and Lorraine and pay a heavy indemnity; to add insult to injury, the Prussians crowned their king Emperor of Germany in the palace of Versailles. French politics over the next decade were marked by recrimination over the debacle, debates about whether France should be a republic or a kingdom (and, if so, under which dynasty) and a pause for *recueillement* - literally 'recollection' but more a licking-of-wounds - in international affairs. The disastrous attempt by Francis Garnier to establish French control over Tonkin in 1873 reinforced French despair.

Failure in Tonkin did not put all the French off colonial expansion. Only a year after Garnier's defeat, Paul Leroy-Beaulieu, son of a Saint-Simonian thinker and an economist in his own right - he held a chair at the prestigious Collège de France - published *De la colonisation chez les peuples modernes*. Leroy-Beaulieu saw a difference between colonies of settlement, which he judged of limited use in the modern world, and trading establishments, which were vital to commercial success in the contemporary economy. France, he concluded in agreement with Guizot, must find new trading outposts. Although Leroy-Beaulieu enjoyed only limited political influence, his theories kept expansion on the agenda. A few other writers began to promote overseas expansion as a way to recoup losses in Europe and gain leverage against Germany.

Jules Ferry and the 'New Imperialism'

In this context - although eight years after Leroy-Beaulieu's book - came another effort to conquer Tonkin in 1882-3. France succeeded in establishing a protectorate, but controversy over expansion, and particularly the clashes along the border between China and Vietnam, brought down the government of Prime Minister Ferry in 1885. In justifying his expansion in Tonkin, Ferry defended colonialism and provided the single most cogent statement of the reasons for French overseas expansion yet made in the French parliament. Listing three motives for overseas expansion, Ferry's arguments encapsulate French colonial ideology in the late nineteenth century. First, he said:

Colonial policy is the daughter of industrial policy. In rich states,

where capital abounds and accumulates rapidly, where the manufacturing system is undergoing continual growth and is drawing in if not the majority of the population then the most dynamic
and active component, where agriculture is itself required to
industrialise in order to survive, export is an essential factor in
public prosperity. The field of action for capital, like the demand for labour, is measured by the size of the foreign market.

If nations could divide different industrial activities among themselves, frenetic international competition could be avoided. But
with fiercely competitive trade and increased need to produce
and sell both agricultural and industrial products, business had
to search widely for markets and raw materials. Economic growth
depended on successful production and export, especially since
industrialisation had so dramatically transformed European manufacturing capacities, and railways and steam-powered ships sped
commodities from one region and one continent to another, while
Germany, and even the United States and Russia, were fast becoming France's commercial rivals. Colonies provided a suitable
market: 'The establishment of a colony is the creation of a market', Ferry stated on another occasion.

The second aspect of Ferry's doctrine was 'the humanitarian
and civilising side of the question', the *mission civilisatrice*. 'Superior races have a right *vis-à-vis* inferior races', but they also
have a duty to bring civilisation – Western government, education, medicine, morals – to other peoples and, in so doing, to
control what might become the unbridled activities of traders and
other foreigners. Ferry asked his fellow legislators:

> Can you deny, can anyone deny that there is more justice, more
> material and moral order, more equity, more social virtue in
> North Africa since France carried out its conquest? When we
> went to Algiers to destroy piracy and assure freedom of com-
> merce in the Mediterranean, were we doing the work of cor-
> sairs, of conquistadors, of destroyers? Is it possible to deny that
> in India, despite the unfortunate episodes which have been
> encountered in the history of its conquest, there is today infi-
> nitely greater justice, enlightenment, order, public and private
> virtue since the English conquest? Is it possible to deny that it
> is the good fortune of the miserable population of equatorial
> Africa to come under the protection of the French nation or

the English nation? Is not our first duty, the first rule that France has imposed on itself, . . . to combat the horrible traffic of the slave trade and the infamy of slavery?

Ferry's justifications for European intervention – to combat piracy, the slave trade and other injustices – did not convince contemporary anti-colonialists, but in the late 1800s, they provided a charter for European takeovers. Since France had abolished slavery, although only in 1848, Paris took responsibility for wiping out slavery within Africa. If the French enjoyed egalitarian justice through law codes and impartial courts at home, could they stand by while Africans suffered arbitrary and inhumane punishments, Ferry's argument implied. Because France was a civilised nation (by its own definition), it had the duty to spread civilisation overseas.

The third imperative for expansion was political; rivalry between nations in Europe found another battlefield outside Europe. A nation which wished to survive must compete in both forums:

In today's Europe, in this competition of the many rivals whose power we see growing around us, sometimes because of military or naval improvement, sometimes by an unceasingly expanding population, in such a Europe, or rather in such a universe, a policy of recollection or of abstention is, very simply, the road to decadence! In the times in which we live, nations are only great in accordance with the activities which they develop. Exerting ourselves without action, without intervening in the affairs of the world, in trying to stay apart from European alliances, in regarding all expansion in Africa and the Orient as a trap or an adventure, to live in this way, believe me, is to abdicate [our position] and, in a shorter time than you think possible, to tumble from the first to the third or fourth rank [of nations].[6]

Ferry's speech was neither an authoritative nor an exhaustive list of the imperatives for colonial expansion, but it underlined the triple economic, cultural and political impetus repeated time and again by later colonial promoters. Although Ferry's arguments clearly related to precise developments in Europe – the downturn in the economy since the mid-1870s which led to calls for heightened tariff barriers, protected markets and neo-mercantilist trade wars, Prussian defeat of France, criticism of the Indochinese campaign – his speech, uttered as justification after his fall from power, sounded a clarion call to colonialists. It provided a mandate for acquiring large continental domains, not just small outposts.

Ferry's ideas remained more a profession of faith than a detailed programme. They summarised arguments advanced over the last decade rather than pioneering new ideological ground. A host of later theorists (such as Paul Louis, who invented the term 'colonialism' in 1905) refined the ideas, but the substance changed little. What remained was to convince the French to accept such views and throw their weight behind expansion.

The Colonial Lobby

It would be easy to imagine that the French enthusiastically and almost unanimously supported overseas expansion. This was far from true. A few specialists vaunted the merits of colonies, especially after the 1870s, but the books of Jean Duval, Lucien Prévost-Paradol, Paul Gaffarel and Leroy-Beaulieu were almost as obscure to contemporary readers as their names are to later ones. Many politicians scorned overseas expansion, often with bitter humour; to the argument that winning overseas territory would compensate France for losing Alsace and Lorraine in 1871, the conservative *député* Paul Déroulède snapped, 'I had two sisters and you are offering me two domestic servants'. (In a variation, he said: 'I had two daughters, and you are giving me twenty Negroes'.) Others argued that France was wasting its 'gold and blood' in distant countries, or that government should attend to pressing national and European problems rather than searching for foreign outposts of uncertain worth. The majority of the public probably remained indifferent to colonialism, more concerned with employment and wages, family and community, local politics and domestic questions than with goings-on in foreign countries.

That support for expansion gathered strength inside government circles and among the public can be credited largely to the so-called *parti colonial* (colonial party), or colonial lobby. Never unified into a single organisation, a large number of different groups and individuals composed a promotion team for colonialism. Through propaganda, lobbying and steady efforts to wield influence, they put forward the case for expansion. By the first decades of the twentieth century they enjoyed remarkable success in persuading French men and women to rally round the empire.

An informal group of explorers, colonialists and geographers met every week at the Petite Vache *brasserie* from 1873 to 1896 to talk about the need for conquest, but by the 1890s, the colonial lobby became more formally organised. (Colonialists retained a love of banquets, however; 'the colonial party', punned one wit, 'is the party where one dines'.) Practically every colony or group of colonies enjoyed the support of a Paris committee: the Committee for French Africa established in 1890, the Committee for Madagascar founded in 1895, the Committee for French Asia set up in 1901, the Committee for French Morocco organised in 1904, the Committee for French Oceania which followed in 1905. (There was, as well, a Committee for Egypt, set up in 1895.) They held lectures, undertook research, awarded prizes, sponsored exhibitions and hosted visitors. They called on ministers to press colonial concerns. They published thick journals highlighting the potential offered by the colonies, detailing the achievements of governors and settlers, business people and missionaries, doctors and engineers. They pleaded for increased funds to build up colonial infrastructure, more settlers to develop local resources, greater efforts to address problems besetting the possessions. They strenuously tried to avoid earlier explorers' and writers' romanticisation of foreign parts and endeavoured to present the colonies as a domain for 'real life' work and success.

Not all groups limited their work to particular colonies or regions. The French Colonial Union (*Union Coloniale Française*), founded in 1893, brought together representatives of more than 400 French companies active in the empire. The *groupe colonial* in the Chamber of Deputies, established in 1892, was a caucus of pro-colonial members of the lower house of parliament; a similar group formed in the Senate in 1898. Many other groups, such as the Colonial Youth League, founded in 1894 to promote colonial careers, focused on specific issues. Chambers of commerce, especially in Marseille and Lyon, acted as informal colonial pressure groups, as did religious congregations (such as the Marists, *Spiritains*, *Picpuciens*, Jesuits and 'White Fathers') engaging in missionary work.[7]

The undisputed leader of the colonial lobby in the last years of the 1800s and early 1900s was Eugène Etienne, born in the Algerian city of Oran in 1844, the son of a military officer. Etienne worked for the Messageries Maritimes, one of the largest French shipping companies. At the age of 37, he won election to the French parliament as *député* from Oran, a seat he kept from 1881 to 1919; he was then a French senator until his death in 1921. Etienne devoted most of his public life to the colonies. He served as Under-Secretary of State for the Colonies intermittently from 1887 to 1892, during which time he set up a training school for colonial administrators and organised the Government-General of Indochina. He founded the *groupe colonial* in the Chamber of Deputies and served on numerous parliamentary committees. He was variously Minister of the Interior, Minister of War, and vice-president of the Chamber of Deputies. Etienne lent support to the Committee for French Africa and set up the Committees for French Asia and Morocco. He became president of the Colonial League in 1907, presided over a group studying the feasibility of a Trans-Saharan railway, and headed committees on French overseas exhibitions, the military and sport. He wrote articles for many periodicals and founded a newspaper, *La Dépêche coloniale*. Etienne was also president of the Paris omnibus company and the Tréfileries et Laminoirs du Havre, a company which specialised in construction in the colonies.[8]

Etienne's career illustrates the overlap of government, business and journalism which characterised the colonial lobby. Prince d'Arenberg, president of the Committee for French Africa, for instance, was president of the Suez Canal Company and the Paris–Lyon–Mediterranean railway, and vice-president of a mining company. Charles Roux, head of the French Colonial Union, was president of the Compagnie Générale Transatlantique (a shipping line) and the Marseille Chamber of Commerce. André Lebon, a lawyer from Dieppe and professor of political science in Paris, was a *député*, Minister for Commerce and Industry, Minister for Colonies, member of the Committee for French Asia, vice-president of the Suez canal company, president of the Messageries Maritimes, and president of the Algerian, Malagasy and Syrian land banks.

The colonial lobby was not just a mouthpiece for colonists or colonial business interests. An analysis of members of the parliamentary *groupe colonial* from 1889 to 1914 shows that only 20 per cent represented colonial constituencies, and another 30 per cent represented French port cities. If just under 29 per cent had very strong business connections with the colonies, over 41 per cent had none. Professionally, the largest group of parliamentarians in the *groupe colonial* were lawyers (28 per cent), followed by businessmen (18 per cent), journalists (13 per cent) and public servants (10 per cent).[9] Analysing members' backgrounds has helped determine whether one particular interest group dominated the colonial lobby and, by extension, whether a single motive played an outsize role in French expansion – particularly whether economics was the primary incentive for conquest. Ultimately it is not possible to single out one particular reason as providing a sufficient explanation for expansion. Many of those in the colonial lobby had varied interests in the empire, although commercial links were undoubtedly strong. But different motivations, both individual and collective, were intimately interlocked in the *parti colonial* and the colonial adventure. The combination of interests and clienteles – academic, business, political, social – may partly account for the strength and success of the lobby.

One particular group which promoted overseas exploration and conquest was geographers. The Paris Geographical Society (*Société de Géographie de Paris*), founded in 1821, was the first of such organisations which half a century later counted tens of thousands of members worldwide. The 200 enthusiasts who set up the Paris society, generally privileged men who could afford the organisation's steep annual dues, shared a fascination with exotic places and heroic exploits. Their mission was to promote voyages of exploration and give financial assistance and moral support to those who undertook them, to publish a journal and hold meetings at which scholarly papers were presented, and to award prizes to accomplished explorers and geographers. Only three years after its establishment, the society offered a handsome prize, including a medal and 7000 francs, to the first person to reach Tombouctou and report back on its geography and trade; in 1828, René Caillié fulfilled the conditions.

The Paris Geographical Society was as yet not the ardent promoter of conquest it later became: in the early 1800s exploration provided its own justification. Once the first flush wore off, by mid-century, the Society stagnated, losing members and facing financial difficulty. Great expeditions, now that the Pacific had been charted and equatorial Africa seemed stubbornly impenetrable, no longer seduced a public whose attentions were drawn to other issues. Nevertheless, a few individuals kept the flame alive.

From the 1860s onwards, renewed interest in geography, aided

by increasing literacy and greater access to schooling, revived the
society's fortunes and transformed it into a pressure group with
close connections to the government. Prosper Chasseloup-Laubat,
former Navy Minister and briefly Minister for Algeria and the
Colonies, assumed the helm of the Society in the mid-1860s. In
the two decades after 1864, its membership grew tenfold to over
2000 members. Other Parisian and provincial geographical organisations multiplied, including a Society for Commercial Geography (founded in the 1870s), with primary interest in the economic
utility of overseas regions. A popular magazine, *Le Tour du monde*,
began publishing illustrated articles on expeditions. By the mid-
1880s, France boasted more geographical societies than any other
country.

The geographical movement attracted public servants, military
officers, clerics and (albeit tardily) businessmen – there were only
two women members in the late 1800s – who found the society a
vehicle for promoting their different causes. The Paris society remained apolitical in a strict sense; its membership rolls included
men affiliated with many mainstream political parties, including
occasional Socialists, and from a variety of middle and upper class
professions. (Aristocrats were especially numerous.) Yet it made
its pro-colonial views known to the government and public, and
the presence of such members as Brazza, de Lesseps and Ferry
himself left little doubt as to its stance. Speakers at the Society's
fortnightly gatherings reiterated the need to press on with explorations and the *mission civilisatrice*, even if most of their audience
were just armchair travellers.

The link between geography and colonial expansion became
clear in an 1884 article in the Society's journal, which expressed
the organisation's admiration for those 'brave men who ... are
consolidating our colonial empire'. The president argued power-
fully for colonialism during the inauguration of the Society's new
headquarters:

Sirs, Providence has dictated to us an obligation to know the
earth and to conquer it. This supreme order is one of the great
duties prescribed for our intelligence and our efforts. Geography, this science which inspires such fine devotion, and to which
so many victims have been sacrificed, has become the philosophy of the planet.... Abstract science does not suffice in
human activity. The great motive of civilised people in their

enterprises consists above all in the accumulation of wealth, wealth which can only be produced by an increase in transactions and exchange. It is to this end that commercial and economic geography have recently been created.

From the late 1880s geographers argued that the world overseas could be made profitable and that indigenous populations could be civilised. Expansion would increase the glory of France and the well-being of its citizens. The academic interests of geographical societies coincided neatly with the ambitions of traders, conquerors and powerbrokers; the Marseille Society for Geography added the words 'and Colonial Studies' to its name. Almost none baulked when geography placed itself in the service of politics.[10]

Explorers, geographers and a small group of theorists thus cleared a path for the colonial lobby to emerge in the 1890s. Promoters of expansion drew on the arguments and services of individuals and groups who found in the empire satisfaction for their ambitions – to proselytise natives, make money, increase French power, claim land, enrich knowledge or, for some of the stay-at-homes, indulge in a hobby. As France acquired an empire and invested human and financial resources into it, more sceptics converted to the colonial movement. Promoters put forward even stronger arguments for expansion: the resources that were discovered, the advances of France's rivals which must be countered, slights to French honour which must be challenged, the successes of France's settlers. A particularly persuasive argument was the fighting potential of colonial troops.

Suffering defeat by the Germans, France saw Berlin's military strength grow dramatically while France, because of falling birth rates, stood in danger of being unable to produce sufficient soldiers to match Germany's army should another war occur. In 1910 General Mangin, in *La Force noire*, argued for the creation of an army recruited in France's black African empire; military service might civilise Africans and could save France. Mangin's calls seemed prescient when the First World War erupted. France called for volunteers from the empire, then began conscripting soldiers. In four years of war, 555 091 colonial soldiers (not counting Europeans from Algeria) fought for France: 78 116 died. The Maghreb sent 256 778 soldiers to the battlefields; black Africa and Madagascar, 211 860; Indochina, 49 000; the *vieilles colonies* 37 423; and the tiny Pacific possessions a thousand men (a third of whom were killed). In addition, the empire dispatched 183 928 civilians for work in factories on the home front.[11] The valour of colonial soldiers finally convinced many doubters of the value of empire.

Colonial Policy, 1880s–1920

From Brazza's treaty with the Makoko in 1880, which gave France part of the Congo, the Treaty of Bardo which established a protectorate over Tunisia in 1881, and the takeover of Tonkin in 1883 through to the protectorate over Morocco in 1912 – barely a generation – France acquired the bulk of its new overseas empire. But raising flags did not suffice to extract the benefits colonial promoters promised from new conquests.

The first order of business after takeover was generally an extension of French influence and 'pacification'. Lightning raids to push back the frontiers of the empire as quickly as possible seldom provided long-lasting gains, and colonial officers, particularly Gallieni and Lyautey, devised a tactic which they termed the 'spot of oil' (*tâche d'huile*) method: claims should be based on effective rather than nominal occupation, which should ooze forward like an oil slick. Soldiers should set up forward posts as they advanced, giving indigenes a chance to accept their presence, opening markets, schools and medical stations in order better to consolidate their authority. Advance might be slowed but real control would be more assured.

Another tactic was the 'racial policy' (*politique des races*), also practised by Gallieni and Lyautey in Indochina and Madagascar and similar to British 'divide and rule'. Colonial officers and administrators tried to separate ethnic groups from each other, negotiating with different chieftains, reinforcing divisions among tribes, clans or other groups, and attempting to keep one from dominating the other. This allowed colonialists to play on traditional rivalries and court support from isolated groups even if entire populations were not amenable to conquest; it also diminished the chance for unified resistance. In some places, the *politique des races* meant creating or exaggerating ethnic and cultural differences between neighbouring populations, as between Berbers and Arabs in North Africa.

Yet another strategy for entrenching French positions was to use local institutions as foundations for colonial control, and local chiefs as intermediaries between the French and the masses. In protectorates such as Tunisia and Morocco, indigenous governments retained titular authority, though French Residents held the real power. Even in annexed colonies, the French devolved some responsibilities such as tax-collecting onto local chiefs; the compensation they received, it was hoped, would encourage support for the French. The French saved on manpower and administrative costs. The French also attempted to win the hearts and minds of colonised people, what one writer in 1892 termed the 'moral conquest' (*conquête morale*) of indigenous populations; education, health care, new sources of income, arbitration of disputes and abolition of slavery were intended to show the French as humane and kind rulers. When such tactics did not work, France resorted to violence to pacify resisters and rebels.[12]

Control of a region secured, the French had to face the task of governing conquered territories. The exact structure of administration varied widely according to time and place. Some acquisitions were colonies, others protectorates; in China, France had overlordship of small 'concessions' which formed neither colonies nor protectorates, and the French ruled the New Hebrides with Britain under a unique 'condominium'. After the First World War, France gained territories under mandate from the League of Nations. Algeria was divided into metropolitan-style *départements*. Some possessions (including the small and uninhabited islands) fell under the administrative control of officials in neighbouring outposts.

Navy and army officers usually took command of colonies from the initial *prise de possession* until pacification was complete. Admirals served as colonial governors until the 1880s in the Pacific. Many African territories – especially newly conquered regions, frontier territories (such as the Algerian Sahara) and areas with sparse populations and few European interests (such as Mauritania) – remained under military control long afterwards. From the late 1880s, however, France gradually set up civilian governments, drew more definite colonial boundaries (although they often subsequently changed) and established bureaucratic hierarchies. The largest colonial units were federations of colonies under a governor-general, the senior category of colonial administrator; France established a Government-General in Indochina in 1887, the AOF in 1895, Madagascar in 1896 and the AEF in 1910. A governor or lieutenant-governor presided over individual colonies inside these

federations and in the remaining colonies proper. In the protectorates, a Resident, Resident-General, or sometimes, High Commissioner embodied French authority.

The duties and powers of these officials were broad. They headed
the administration in the colonies, represented the French state
in relations with settlers, indigenes and foreign powers, worked
out budgets, issued decrees, advised the government in Paris,
presided over the privy council (*conseil privé*) – which, although
only a consultative body, was the sole representative institution
in many territories – and controlled public works, justice, polic-
ing and almost everything else. Governors also had the right to
decree states of emergency. Governors were appointed by the
French government and responsible only to the government. The
rights of indigenous governments, in theory, curbed the powers
of French administrators in the protectorates, but in practice,
residents generally ruled much as governors. In short, governors
were potentates in their realms.

Below the governor came an array of public servants, more numerous in the larger colonies, rare in smaller ones. Colonial bureaucrats directed specific government services from departments
of indigenous affairs to departments of roads and public works.
Most administrators congregated in the capital cities of colonies.
But the foot soldiers of the administration were the *commandants
de cercle* (the equivalent of 'district agents' in the British colonial
system) and *chefs de subdivision* (heads of regions) who ruled over
the numerous administrative divisions – there were 118 *cercles* in
the AOF – in the colonies. Often young men, district agents exercised almost sole authority over vast areas and large populations,
assisted only by a handful of assistants, or just a local interpreter-
cum-secretary. Although directly responsible to superiors in colonial capitals, and ultimately to Paris, *commandants de cercle* largely
were on their own in running day-to-day affairs. Even with their
best efforts, large tracts of the empire remained under-adminis-
tered; the governor-general of the AEF admitted in 1914 that he
and his subordinates had real control of only a quarter of the
territory under nominal French administration.

At the apex of the colonial bureaucracy were various ministries
and other government bodies in Paris. Under Napoleon III's Second
Empire, the government briefly included a Minister for Algeria
and the Colonies, but the Minister for the Navy and Colonies
usually held titular authority for overseas possessions. In 1881,

the government first appointed a *Sous-Secrétaire d'Etat aux Colonies* (under-secretary, or junior minister, for the colonies); in 1894, it created a fully fledged Colonial Ministry. At no time, however, did all of France's possessions legally come under the aegis of the Minister for Colonies (although suggestions were made, especially in the 1930s, to create a great Ministry for the Empire). Algeria was included in the portfolio of the Ministry for the Interior, while the protectorates were the responsibility of the Minister of Foreign Affairs (since they technically were independent states under French protection). Other ministries, notably the Ministry of War (or Defence) and ministries concerned with economic affairs, had a large say in determining colonial policy as well.

The Colonial Ministry had an imposing building in the Rue Oudinot in Paris, but it hardly ranked among the largest or most prestigious ministries. In 1894, it counted only 133 employees; in 1935, at the zenith of empire, only 129 staff. From 1890 to 1940, 44 ministers held the portfolio of colonial affairs, a particularly rapid turnover. Among them were distinguished figures who later moved to higher-ranking ministries or became prime ministers or presidents – Théophile Delcassé, Gaston Doumergue, Albert Sarraut, Eugène Daladier. Many, however, were relatively minor politicians with little lasting interest in the empire and little abiding impact on colonial policy.

According to a Senate ruling (*sénatus-consulte*) of 1854, the French Senate enjoyed the right to make legislation for the colonies, although the Chamber of Deputies, especially during the Third and Fourth Republics, often – and loudly – debated colonial legislation. By its powers to pass bills, appropriate funds and approve budgets, call ministers to account and bring down governments, parliament could regularly intervene in colonial administration. Nevertheless in practice most of the regulations under which the empire was governed were decrees issued by the colonial minister or governors. The arcane and complex division of powers among various officials and departments preoccupied constitutional experts and administrative purists, but left the colonies under the benign or arbitrary rule of resident officials.

The administrators' wide powers created discontent among colonists, especially the growing number of settlers in Algeria and New Caledonia. They baulked at intervention by governors often serving only short terms, inexperienced junior administrators, and

ministers appointed almost at random from the ranks of victorious politicians in Paris. Settlers demanded devolution of power,
some measure of autonomy and representation in parliament and
local assemblies. But the French political system, which placed a
premium on standardisation of laws and institutions throughout
the country and centralisation of power in Paris, was not congenial
to British-style self-government.

Indeed, the concept which governed French colonial policy
through the late nineteenth century was 'assimilation', a policy
'directed at removing all differences between colonies and the
metropole by endowing them with the same administrative, fiscal,
judicial, social and other regimes as the metropole and at giving
their inhabitants full civic rights and obliging them to the same
duties' as citizens in France itself.[13] (Rights, though perhaps not
duties, applied only to Europeans and a few other French citizens
in the colonies, not the indigeneous masses.) The policy aimed,
in bureaucratic terms, to make colonies little overseas Frances
and perhaps, in the fullness of time, to turn Africans, Asians and
islanders into French men and women of a different colour.

Officials, and almost everyone else, discovered that such a policy
could not be fully implemented given the distances of colonies
from France, the particular problems administrators faced on the
ground, the small number of European residents, the extraordinary differences between French and indigenous cultures, and
the manifest impossibility of transforming vast regions of foreign
continents into French provinces. By the early 1900s, 'association'
replaced 'assimilation', allowing greater flexibility for administrative, legal and financial policy, foreshadowing a less dramatic replacement of indigenous institutions and attitudes by French ones,
projecting a slower (and perhaps less complete) *francisation* of
colonised people. But 'association', even more than 'assimilation',
remained a general principle rather than a detailed programme.[14]

The government largely left colonial development to private
initiative in the years from the 1880s to the First World War,
although Paris provided encouragement and·some subsidies for
entrepreneurs and settlers, and undertook important public works
projects, notably the construction of railways. The government
felt its main duties were conquest, pacification and administration, not large-scale settlement (except transportation of prisoners to penal colonies) or the establishment of public companies
for agriculture and commerce.

Government hesitation to become more completely involved in colonial activities reinforced the role of the colonial lobby and private interests ranging from business to the church. Promoters, entrepreneurs and settlers repeated with almost tedious regularity, in fact, that the government did too little for them. The business community complained about discriminatory tariff policy and restrictions on trade between colonies and countries other than France, as well as government unwillingness to provide more funding for infrastructural development and aid in locating labour. The church protested that some governors were avowedly anti-clerical, that the state was not willing to provide subsidies for their missionaries' education and health work, and that settlers, through ungodly personal habits and exploitation of local populations, corrupted indigenes. Settlers, in turn, cried that both government and church were trying to restrict their acquisition of land and labour (all the while arguing among themselves about such issues as free trade versus protectionism). Such lack of accord among those active in the colonies provided further indication that colonialism was not the unified, monolithic enterprise it sometimes appeared.

Anti-colonialism, 1880s–1920

The work of the colonial lobby, expansion of overseas territories, and increasing government enthusiasm did not silence anti-colonialists.[15] Indifference to empire itself represented a passive sort of anti-colonialism, roundly combated by the colonial lobby. Opponents of expansion advanced arguments to counter the basic tenets of expansion. Further takeovers seemed to many a dangerous over-extension of French power and brought into the empire territories of uncertain value. If colonialists cheered each additional square kilometre brought under French control, anti-colonialists wondered about the uses of remote deserts and jungles. The Voulet–Chanoine *affaire* in 1898 seemed to exemplify the madness of unbridled conquest. Even some colonialists favoured withdrawal from certain regions in order to bolster French presence in others. Elisée Reclus, a pro-colonial member of the Paris Geographical Society, in 1911 published an audacious book whose title summarised its argument: *Lâchons l'Asie, prenons l'Afrique* ('Let go of Asia and take Africa'); Reclus argued that Indochina was too distant to bring many advantages to France, and should be exchanged for greater holdings in Africa.

The *mission civilisatrice* evoked the least opposition from Europeans who, except for a few isolated voices, thought France was indeed carrying out a praiseworthy humanitarian effort in the empire. However, colonial scandals made some wonder if France did dispense civilisation. The Gaud–Touqué scandal of 1904 – in which two French administrators were brought to trial (although only given suspended sentences) for particular brutality in the recruitment of porters in Oubangui-Chari – was only one of a number of abuses revealed to the French public which fuelled anti-colonialism. At a 'protest meeting against colonial barbarity' in 1906, the prominent intellectual and novelist Anatole France thundered: 'Whites do not communicate with blacks or yellow people except to enserf or massacre them. The people whom we call barbarians know us only through our own crimes. Certainly we do not believe that more crimes are committed on this wretched African earth under our flag than under the banners of various [other] realms and empires. But it is our responsibility as Frenchmen to denounce the crimes committed in our name.'[16]

A few critics went further than denunciations of abuses to question the moral right of Europeans to impose foreign civilisation on non-Western peoples. Jean Jaurès, leader of the Socialist party and one of the most articulate French politicians at the turn of the century, commented in parliament after the acquisition of Morocco in 1912:

> I have never painted an idyllic picture of the Muslim populations, and I am well aware of the disorder and oligarchic exploitation by mighty chiefs which takes place. But, Sirs, if you look deeply into the matter, there existed [before French takeover] a Moroccan civilisation capable of the necessary transformation, capable of evolution and progress, a civilisation both ancient and modern. . . . There was a seed for the future, a hope. And let me say that I cannot pardon those who have crushed this hope for pacific and human progress – African civilisation – by all sorts of ruses and by the brutalities of conquest.[17]

Anti-colonialists expressed grave doubts that the empire could serve as an outlet for national energies and a source of national rejuvenation. Georges Clemenceau, a Radical politician and future prime minister, argued to the Chamber of Deputies in 1885, the year of Ferry's defence of colonialism:

> My patriotism lies in France. . . . While you are lost in your colonial dreams, there are at your feet men, Frenchmen, who call for useful and beneficial efforts to develop French genius. . . . Do you not think that [the social question] provides a sufficient domain for human ambition, and that the idea of increasing knowledge and enlightenment in our country, of developing our well-being, increasing the exercise of liberty, the right to organise a struggle against ignorance, vice, misery, to organise a better use for our social forces – do you not think that is enough to occupy the activities of a politician or a party?

A journalist, referring to the needs of France compared to efforts spent on the empire, succinctly said, 'We should colonise France – the Crau [a poor region in the Midi] rather than Dahomey, put the French from France . . . ahead of the Malagasy, Dahomeans and Tonkinese'.[18]

The economics of expansion created much discussion and criticism. As the colonial budget tripled from 1885 to 1902, economists questioned the returns from such expenditures, and many were sceptical about just who pocketed the profits. Socialists took particular aim at arguments that economic benefits from colonialism accrued to the nation as a whole. Extending the Marxist analysis of economics to the colonies, they argued that the empire only provided further profit opportunities for the bourgeoisie. The bourgeois monopolised capital and controlled industry and trade; they exploited natives overseas just as they exploited proletarians at home. Neither the indigenous peoples in the colonies nor the French working class could hope to reap benefits from colonial business, since its rewards would go to European capitalists. In the views of Socialist leaders such as Jules Guesde, the most outspoken anti-colonialist of the late 1800s, and his successor Jaurès, capitalists were prime movers behind expansion, finding in the empire chances for profits over and beyond the usual returns they banked. Colonies allowed them to do business with even less regard for labour conditions, humanitarian concerns and the welfare of workers than they showed in France.[19]

Critics of colonialism from the political left encounted predictable hostility to their views of expansion and general arguments

about European economy, society and government. Colonial promoters accused them of condemning France to small-power status, falling behind its economic, political and military rivals.
Although they published widely, held countless meetings and elected
increasing numbers of members of parliament, Socialists failed
to capture political power in France until the late 1930s. Their
opponents – conservatives, centrists and non-socialist Radicals –
who held control adhered ever more strongly to belief in the
merits of expansion. Anti-colonialists advanced strong critiques
but were incapable of influencing opinion strongly enough to
defeat the expansionists.

Colonialism and Anti-colonialism, 1920–1939

In the interwar years the French empire reached its greatest extent. France, Britain, the United States and Japan – as well as the
Netherlands, Portugal and Spain, whose possessions largely pre-
dated the 'new imperialism' of the nineteenth century – were
victors in the First World War and the colonial masters of the
world. Although Italy and Japan made moves to increase their
imperial domains, and Germany hoped to regain its colonies, the
colonial 'scrambles' of the pre-1914 period seemed to have ended.
The period from 1918 to 1940 was the 'golden age' of French
colonial empire.[20]

   The attention of the colonial lobby and colonial authorities –
an increasingly incestuous group – turned from conquest to development. Promoters no longer expended their energies drumming
up support for conquest, even though French public opinion never
stood solidly behind the empire; one of the leading colonialists,
Albert Sarraut, lamented in 1935 that most of the French remained
indifferent about colonies. Promoters now emphasised the need
for government investment in the possessions, development of
infrastructure, concessions on trade and tariffs, recruitment of
settlers and contract labourers, greater political autonomy for local
colonial governments under the control of French settlers. Such
demands were not new, but they had earlier taken a back seat to
calls for expansion and pacification. Now they became the *raison
d'être* of the colonial lobby and the preoccupation of colonial
officials.

   A major change of the war years and the period immediately

following was the rallying of Socialists to colonialism. Before the foundation in 1905 of a unified Socialist party (the *Section Française de l'Internationale Ouvrière*, SFIO), socialism was a rapidly growing movement fragmented by doctrinal dispute and factional rivalry. Jaurès' dynamic leadership made the SFIO into a powerful political opposition and Jaurès (who was assassinated in 1914) remained a firm opponent of expansion. When the conquest of an empire had become a *fait accompli*, however, the Socialists altered their view. Léon Blum, a new Socialist leader, stated in 1925: 'We are too imbued with love of our country to disavow the expansion of French thought and French civilisation'. He added, in words not radically different from those of colonialists a generation earlier, 'We recognise the right and even the duty of superior races to draw unto them those which have not arrived at the same level of culture.'[21] The SFIO henceforth promoted 'modern colonialism', fighting abuses of colonialism rather than the system itself. Increased self-government, economic development, gradual enfranchisement of indigenes, a crackdown on mistreatment of natives, restrictions on exploitative business activity and promotion of education, health care and other benefits for non-Europeans featured as the goals of Socialist colonial policy. Socialists believed that such actions would spread the same ideals and reforms they advocated for Europe to the colonies. Underprivileged European settlers, wretched imported contract labourers and indigenous peoples would all benefit.

Official policy also underwent a transformation. Economics lay at the heart of the new programme announced by Sarrault in the 1920s. Etienne's successor as the colonialists' unofficial leader, Sarrault called for the *mise en valeur* of the colonies, a wholesale plan to develop colonial resources to increase production and stimulate trade between France and the empire. This demanded substantial French investment to improve roads and railways, port facilities and transport links, schools and hospitals.[22]

The archetype of the interwar colonialist was no longer the intrepid explorer hacking his way across a tropical jungle or the brave soldier defeating 'savages' and capturing another outpost for France. The new colonialist was the entrepreneur armed with designs for bridges and schools or figures for imports and exports. The dawn of the age of aviation illustrated the metamorphosis. Planes connected Marseille to Algiers in 1921, Tunis in 1923 and Casablanca in 1924. By the mid-1930s there were commercial flights from France to Dakar and Antananarivo, with connections *en route* to Brazzaville and Bamako. A route to Beirut, opened in 1929, was extended to Saigon in 1931 and Hanoi four years later. By 1939, French colonial air routes covered 41 000 kilometres and carried 7000 passengers. Flights were long by latter day standards – it took four-and-a-half days to reach Bamako, five-and-a-half-days to get to Hanoi in propeller-driven aircraft in the 1930s – but distances between metropole and empire had been effectively and figuratively shortened. The aeroplane seemed a fitting symbol for the colonialists' new aspirations and initiatives.[23]

Policy-makers hoped their undertakings would bring prosperity to the metropole and French settlers overseas, and they also intended such projects to improve the situation of indigenes. Old racist stereotypes of non-Europeans persisted, but a benign, if condescending, paternalism gradually became more accepted than the blind fears and outright race hatred of the period of conquest. The service of colonial soldiers during the war suggested even to hardened racialists that non-Westerners might have meritorious qualities. The policy of 'association' abandoned the effort to transform overseas outposts into clones of France. Missionaries and teachers were more numerous in the empire than ever before, and most of their work targeted indigenous populations. Post-First World War colonialism portrayed itself as modernising, entrepreneurial and humane.

All, however, was not quiet on the colonial front. Revolts in Morocco and Syria in the mid-1920s pointed to the failure of total pacification. The organisation of Asian, African and islander cultural movements and political parties, both in the colonies and among expatriates in Paris, signalled the birth of a new anti-colonial nationalism. While the Socialists seemed reconciled to the empire, French Communists – leftists heartened by the success of the Bolshevik Revolution of 1917 who broke away from the SFIO to found the French Communist Party (*Parti Communiste Français*, PCF) in 1920 – maintained the anti-colonialist rage. At the congress which led to the divorce between Socialists and Communists, the future Communists supported affiliation with the Moscow-dominated Third International with a motion 'to denounce colonial imperialism and to give active support to peoples subjugated by European capitalism in their struggle against oppression in all its forms'. Among members of the new Communist Party was Nguyên Ai Quôc, a young Vietnamese living in France who later led the Indochinese war of independence under the name Ho Chi Minh. Ho and nationalists elsewhere set up Marxist-inspired colonial parties which garnered support from the PCF and the Third International.

In 1924, in helping to set up the Committee Against the Rif Wars – the first formal anti-colonialist association – the PCF threw its weight behind Abd el-Krim, who led a rebellion against the Spanish and French in the Rif mountains of Morocco. The PCF called for immediate cessation of hostilities, the withdrawal of French troops from the protectorate and all other colonies, and recognition of an independent Rif republic. Even more contentiously, the PCF leader, Jacques Doriot, shocked colleagues in the Chamber of Deputies with calls for French soldiers to desert and fraternise with the rebels. The parliamentary chamber erupted in chaos as Doriot declared: 'Today, Abd el-Krim is fighting for peace, he desires peace. In the name of my party, I declare that we recognise Parisian workers' right to insurrection, and we recognise the right of indigenes to rise up against the colonisers.' A *député* from Algeria fired back: 'You are pushing them towards revolt. You are provoking revolt. That is a crime.' To clamours on the back benches, Doriot continued: 'The strength and union of workers, peasants, soldiers and colonial peoples will impose on the capitalists of France and Spain the evacuation of Morocco and the other colonies.' Another *député* cried: 'This is a veritable provocation to desertion. . . . It is an outrage that such language can be used in the French parliament.' (The parliamentary record notes 'strong applause from a number of members; commotion on Communist Party benches'.) Doriot concluded: 'Withdraw from Morocco! May French, Spanish and Arab soldiers fraternise! Long live independent Morocco!' The PCF translated Doriot's speech into Arabic and published it in Morocco. The party organised a strike in Paris; demonstrations against French suppression of the uprisings in Morocco and Syria drew close to a million participants throughout France. Violent clashes punctuated the protests, and Doriot was briefly placed under arrest.[24] Over the next few years, Communists frequently and loudly denounced European colonialism, as Communist journals, public meetings and party congresses became focal points for anti-colonialism. Yet Communist voters and supporters remained a small minority of the French electorate, marginalised by their opponents (generally including their former partners, the Socialists).

Not all opposition to colonialism came from the Communist left. Dissidents within the Catholic and Protestant churches expressed doubts about the colonial venture, and the pope warned missionaries that they were agents of Christ not of politicians. Various anti-colonial organisations were set up, including such international bodies as the League Against Colonial Oppression and Imperialism, founded in Brussels in 1927 under the honorary presidency of Albert Einstein; when it folded in 1932, the French members formed a new anti-colonialist organisation, but it too remained small. More effective in developing anti-colonial sentiment were journalists and writers such as Anatole France, Romain Rolland, Henri Barbusse, André Gide, Albert Londres and a number of *avant-garde* authors (such as the surrealists). But the well-organised colonial lobby, drawing support from government and funds from large memberships, was easily a match for anti-colonialists.

The mid-1930s brought economic depression to France and the colonies – prices of tropical commodities and other primary products fell, colonial businesses went bankrupt, heavily-indebted settlers lost their properties and savings. Many colonial development projects were indefinitely filed away before being implemented. Yet, as international trade conditions worsened and tariff walls climbed higher, France came to rely increasingly on colonies as a source of raw materials and a market for manufactured goods; economic links between metropole and empire had never been so strong as during the Depression.[25]

Economic crisis in France debilitated centrist governments; hence the left – both the SFIO and the PCF – and a new reactionary right gathered strength. In 1936, the Popular Front, a coalition of Socialists and Radicals with support from Communists, won election under the leadership of Léon Blum; Marius Moutet served as colonial minister for the two-year life of the government. Blum's government intended great reforms for the empire, and he announced a plan to 'put into place a programme of action which conforms to both the legitimate wishes of the indigenous masses and the generous intentions of the government and the capacities of the metropole'. One of Blum's colleagues added that 'the Republic's colonial policy has a duty to . . . undertake the great enterprise of renovation of the French colonial system in the direction of a general amelioration in the conditions of political and social life for the overseas populations'. The government appointed a 42-member commission, consisting of administrators, intellectuals (such as the novelist André Gide and the historian Charles-André Julien) and representatives of labour and business, to investigate colonial conditions. It received numerous submissions and amassed considerable documentation but its planned trips to the colonies were abandoned when the French Senate, controlled by opponents of the Popular Front, severely reduced the commission's budget; the commission resigned in protest, and no report was ever prepared.[26]

Opposition from colonists and conservative opponents thwarted another initiative of the Blum government. The Popular Front endorsed a proposal of Maurice Viollette to extend the vote to 25 000 Algerian *évolués* (a term used for those who generally spoke French, held a European-style job and were otherwise 'Frenchified'), although Blum made the tactical mistake of submitting the measure to parliament rather than simply proclaiming enfranchisement by decree. Colonists and their supporters treated the move as little less than treason, especially in light of rising nationalist sentiment among Algerians. One of the largest nationalist movements in Algeria, the *Etoile Nord-Africaine*, also rejected the measure – arguing that it simply pulled the indigenous bourgeoisie into the French orbit – and demanded Algerian independence; the government dissolved the organisation and arrested its leaders. But nothing could save Violette's proposal.

Blum and Moutet had more success in promoting economic development, especially the expansion of agricultural production, even if plans to set up a colonial investment fund failed. Calls for commercial development won favour with the business community, as did the government's opposition to colonial industrialisation. Moutet argued that the metropolitan and colonial economies should complement each other. Metropolitan entrepreneurs feared competition and shrinking markets, while the Socialists wanted to avoid the creation of an industrial proletariat in the empire. Moutet was able to pass the first labour legislation designed to protect indigenes' rights, and he ordered an end to transportation of prisoners to Guyane (although the penal colony did not close until after the Second World War). Yet the Popular Front's tenure was too short, and opposition too great, for it to fulfil the expectations of reform which accompanied Blum's election.

Towards the 1940s

The year 1938 brought the fall of the Popular Front and saw the European powers give in to Hitler's expansionism through German annexation of the Sudetenland. Colonialists in France, just as on the eve of the First World War, proclaimed that – as one slogan put it – France would find 'salvation in the empire' with its wealth, force of soldiers, territory, and prestige. Anti-colonialists disagreed, and even commentators far from the ranks of anti-colonialists expressed caution. After all, Germany, Italy and Japan coveted French possessions and were gathering the strength which might allow them to attack the empire. The French Ministry of War admitted that France had only 75 000 colonial soldiers, and over half were stationed outside France itself. French men and women who read the rare reports about the empire in the mainsteam press learned about nationalist movements, demonstrations and rebellions which occurred in the late 1930s all the way from Morocco to Vietnam. Promoters of *francisation* were well aware that only 2000 Malagasy, 2555 Annamese and 72 000 Africans in the enormous AOF held French citizenship. Economists knew that commercial relations between France and the colonies remained fragile.

In early 1939, 44 per cent of those surveyed in an opinion poll said that they were *not* ready to fight 'rather than cede the least part of our colonial possessions'; 40 per cent said they were prepared to do so, and 16 per cent remained undecided. To the question: 'Do you think that it would be just as painful to cede a piece of the colonial empire as a piece of French territory?', 53 per cent said yes, 43 per cent no, and 4 per cent did not respond. The French had developed, even if only tardily, a strong colonialist feeling, but it had limits; they expected much from the empire but were perhaps not ready to sacrifice their lives for it. The empire, they hoped, could compensate for various French deficiencies, such as lack of sufficient troops or better economic health. Hopes were based more in the myth than the reality of empire.[27] (The myth survived the Second World War.[28])

The first principle of French imperial policy at the end of the 1930s was to safeguard the empire. This meant preserving colonies from indigenous nationalism, insurrection and independence, and defending the empire from foreign attack and conquest. Having spent the years from 1830 to 1912 – or 1919, if the mandated territories are included – acquiring an empire, the French had then spent two decades consolidating their hold, trying to develop colonial economies, implant French settlers and win support from a *francisé* native elite. The French state had provided the legislation, appropriated the money, designed the development plans and adopted the ideology which made conquest and maintenance of empire possible. Groups inside the body politic, notably the colonial lobby, itself a collection of individuals pursuing overlapping objectives, had put forward the arguments, created the images and campaigned for the measures which made the empire. If France as a whole had become colonialist – a debatable proposition – it was thanks to their work.

4 The French Overseas

One aim of expansion has been to find places for colonies of settlement. With European expansion in the nineteenth century, however, this was seldom the most pressing priority. For the French, only Algeria and New Caledonia became true *colonies de peuplement* and, compared with many other populations in Europe, the French were notorious for not migrating. Yet many French men – and a substantial number of French women – spent shorter or longer periods in the empire. Some were famous or infamous; most won neither glory nor fortune. They included explorers and conquerors, soldiers and sailors, traders and farmers, teachers and doctors, priests and nuns, as well as the large corps of administrators who ruled France's imperial domains.

The number of French families whose lives were directly touched by colonial ventures – those whose son, for example, did a colonial tour of duty in the army or whose daughter ministered in a colonial convent or hospital – is undoubtedly substantial. When Algeria became independent in 1962, a million French citizens left North Africa. The size of French communities elsewhere was far smaller, though communities of expatriates lived in Morocco and Tunisia, in the larger African cities such as Dakar and Abidjan, in faraway Indochina and Madagascar, and on far-flung islands over which the French flag flew. Small islands, isolated outposts in the Sahara and posts in the equatorial jungle played home to a French district agent, a *gendarme*, perhaps a priest and teacher, a trader or agriculturalist.

The overseas French formed the personal link between colonies and metropole. To the government in Paris, they represented French interests overseas even when, as was often the case, they

122

appeared a contentious lot demanding greater political autonomy, more generous subsidies, and protection against 'natives'
and foreigners. To the indigenes, the French residents in their
midst were the most obvious embodiment of the foreign state
which controlled their destinies and proclaimed its mission to
civilise them and develop their resources. Several generations of
readers (including schoolchildren) learned about the adventures
of explorers in pith helmets, soldiers in starched uniforms, priests
in white cassocks, and colonists in their coarse working clothes.
Such images were part and parcel of colonialist and anti-colonial
propaganda. For advocates of expansion, settlers stood as living
proof of France's grandeur and achievements; for critics, they
were the most appalling example of French conquest, profiteering
and racist brutality.

French colonials were far from a homogeneous population. Many,
in fact, were not of French parentage, especially in Algeria, to
which Spain, Italy and Malta contributed a large proportion of
settlers. In a number of colonies, imported labourers made up a
substantial part of the population. Moreover, bitter antagonism
divided French expatriates among themselves. Administrators regularly accused colonists of speculation, lack of entrepreneurial effort and mistreatment of indigenes; colonists accused bureaucrats
of tying their hands with unnecessary red tape and regulations.
Missionaries sometimes damned the administration as anticlerical and colonists as immoral, while administrators reacted against
the zeal and self-righteousness of religious congregations. Colonists of one generation did not always welcome younger migrants,
and the emerging colonial elite looked down their collective nose
at more proletarian arrivals. Merchants who favoured free trade
did not see eye to eye with farmers or mine-owners who clamoured for protectionist tariffs. Anti-colonial expatriates denounced
their compatriots for a variety of misdeeds. In short, colonial
societies were no less stratified or fragmented than French society
in the metropole. Factionalism and social cleavages were perhaps
aggravated by the presence of indigenes and foreigners, as well
as by the distance that allowed new ideals, new ambitions and
new pretensions to flourish.

The indigenes allowed, or forced, the French to coalesce for
purposes of defence. Labour provided by local populations, contract workers or foreigners enabled French migrants even from
modest backgrounds to enjoy the benefits of house-servants and

subalterns and to take on bourgeois affectations. The supremacy of the French, of whatever condition, whether beribboned governors or dusty *petits blancs* (poor whites), depended on the enforced legal, political, economic and cultural inferiority of those whom they ruled. White skin and French citizenship gave expatriates unique and, for some years, seemingly uncontestable rights of dominance. The French were the overlords.

Explorers

Explorers preceded colonists and administrators. The celebrated eighteenth-century voyages of discovery in the South Seas, with rugged sailors and hardy captains charting unknown waters, foreshadowed later missions to push back the boundaries of the known world, reach forbidden cities and raise flags over ever more distant countries. With Oceania crisscrossed by the early 1800s, explorers turned to Asia and Africa. More than any other Frenchmen, explorers exemplified the lure of empire.[1]

The Sahara sounded a particularly powerful call, despite (or perhaps because of) its emptiness, difficulties of travel through the vast desert and the rumoured inhospitality of Moorish and Tuareg tribes. The only means of traversing the Sahara until early in the twentieth century was by camel caravan, led by indigenous guides, which generally set out from Tangiers, Tripoli or another Mediterranean port, although occasionally adventurers tried to cross the Sahara from the south. Numerous explorers lost their lives to thirst, disease or attacks. Those who returned to tell their stories enriched geographical knowledge, inspired further expeditions and alerted the government to the need to 'pacify' tribes which refused to submit to foreign domination, robbed or killed traders, or engaged in the slave trade (which Europeans, after the abolition of slavery in their own colonies, tried to eradicate).

German and English explorers preceded the French in the Sahara, but a Frenchman finally braved the desert sands. René Caillié was born in 1799, the son of a butcher. As with many explorers, reading whetted his desire for travel: 'The story of Robinson [Crusoe] set my young head on fire; I was burning to have adventures like him, and already felt a desire welling up in me to distinguish myself by some important discovery.' In 1816, Caillié set sail for Senegal, travelling in the same fleet as the *Méduse*.

Caillié survived shipwreck but fell ill in Saint-Louis and was unable to take part in a Sahara expedition. Undeterred, he returned for a short visit to Africa two years later. In 1824, Caillié resolved to win a prize offered by the Paris Geographical Society to the first Frenchman to visit Tombouctou.

Caillié prepared thoroughly for his trek. He lived with Muslims in Senegal and converted to Islam under the name of Abd Allahi. Lacking capital for his venture, he accepted a job in an indigo factory and accumulated enough savings to set off in 1827. The beginnings of the trip brought fear and discouragement: 'I wanted to die, I prayed to God, in whom I placed my full confidence, not in hope of getting well, but in hope for a happier life after death.' After almost twelve months of travel, Caillié reached Tombouctou on 20 April 1828. Like earlier voyagers he was much disappointed with the fabled city: 'The spectacle which lay before my eyes did not at all correspond with the image of grandeur and wealth which I had held dear; on first sight, the city was only a mass of badly constructed mud houses. In all directions, all one could see were immense plains of blowing yellowish white sand and total aridity. The sky, at the horizon, was a pale red; there was something sad about everything in nature; there was great silence – one heard the song of not a single bird.' Caillié dutifully explored the city for four weeks, then departed in a huge caravan of 1400 camels. Heading north to Morocco, braving thirst and constant fear, he hoped that the French consul in Rabat would help him return to France. The consul, an indigenous Jewish merchant, refused to assist him, arguing that he had no instructions from his superiors to do so. The consul in Tangiers, fortuitously a member of the Paris Geographical Society, proved more accommodating. Soon Caillié was back in Paris to collect the Society's prize. Two years later he published three volumes on his adventures. Exhausted by his voyages, Caillié died in 1838.

Caillié's successor in French exploration of Africa was Henri Duveyrier. Unlike Caillié, he was born into the minor nobility in 1840; rather than getting inspiration from Robinson Crusoe, he was stimulated by the Saint-Simonian doctrines of his father. A precocious child, Duveyrier studied in France and Germany, where he learned both Chinese – his father wanted him to go to Asia – and Arabic. At the age of 17, Duveyrier landed in Algiers; in an oasis in the Algerian hinterland, he made the acquaintance of a Tuareg to whom he gave his pistols. The Tuareg was so delighted

that he offered to present Duveyrier with a camel, a gift the Frenchman declined, although he accepted the Tuareg's offer of a tour
to his native land. The Tuaregs, Saharan nomads, were little-known
tribesmen reputed both for their indigo-dyed clothing and their
pillaging of rival tribes. Duveyrier was not able to take up the
Tuareg's offer, as he was scheduled to return to Europe. He published (in German) an account of his trip and made friends with
a German explorer who became his patron.

Despite fierce opposition from his father, Duveyrier began to
organise his next trip: 'I know very well that the voyage which I
am going to undertake is not without danger, but I feel full of
confidence in my own strength.' At the age of 19, he again set
off for North Africa, armed with a commission from Napoleon
III to research Roman ruins in the Sahara. He journeyed from
the Algerian coast to Touggourt and Biskra, then reached the
oasis of Ghadamès, centre of one of the Tuareg confederations.
Taken to their leader, Duveyrier received a warm welcome, which
led him to beseech the French government not to attempt military action against the Tuaregs. French troops nevertheless soon
began forays into the region. Islamic fundamentalists threatened
Duveyrier, and only the Tuaregs' goodwill saved his life.

In September 1861, Duveyrier returned to Algiers, where he
fell ill from typhoid and malaria. On his recovery, he sailed to
France to collect a medal from the Geographical Society and, in
1862, published the first major study of the Tuaregs. Disenchant-
ment soon set in, as the government refused his advice on African policies, and journalists blamed his favourable impressions
of Tuareg hospitality for the deaths of several later explorers.
Duveyrier continued writing, served on various official commissions, and in 1885 led a government mission to Morocco, where
a rebellion in the Rif mountains staunched plans for a further
expedition. He committed suicide in 1892.

The fate of another explorer was no happier. Camille Douls'
first overseas voyage, in the early 1880s, was to the West Indies,
but his real dream was the Sahara. Douls spent two years in Morocco
learning Arabic and studying Islam; since he intended to pass as
a Muslim, he had himself circumcised. In 1886, aged 22, Douls
left for the Canary Islands where, against all advice, he convinced
fishermen to deposit him on the Atlantic coast of Mauritania,
then one of the least known and supposedly most dangerous regions of Africa. On landing, he exulted:

I was on African soil, in the middle of the desert, alone and isolated in the territory of a barbarous and fanatical people, abandoned on an inhospitable coast where Christians had been massacred.... I was not conscious of the danger to which I was exposing myself; I was young and I trusted in a favourable star.... At most I felt a vague sentiment of the unknown which was increased by the solitude and the savage environment in which I found myself. I sat on the rocks which overhang the sea, facing these two immense domains which most strike the human heart – the ocean and the desert.

Soon Moors captured Douls. He claimed to be a shipwrecked Algerian merchant, a story they did not initially believe. Kept in chains, Douls finally managed to convince their chief, helped by quotations from the Koran, that his tale was true; he even acquitted himself well in an interrogation about Muslim theology. The chief ordered his release. Douls lived with the Moors for five months, the first European accepted in their midst, and took part in raids on other tribes, the violence of which shocked the European. The chief proposed his own daughter as wife for Douls. The explorer said that he must first go to Marrakesh to fetch a dowry of seven camels. Once there Douls identified himself as a European to a visiting English delegation and was thrown into jail by the Moroccans. He made friends with the warder, a Luxembourg native and veteran of the French Foreign Legion. The guard contacted the English, who alerted the French consul, and the Europeans secured Douls' release. Back in Paris, he joined the Geographical Society and won Duveyrier's support for an expedition to Tombouctou. Disguised as a Moroccan pilgrim, in 1888 he left Tangiers, heading towards the desert, and was never seen again.

Caillié, Duveyrier and Douls were the models of the romantic explorer, but by the late 1800s such adventurers were the exceptions rather than the rule. Most explorers were now military officers at the head of battalions of soldiers, who penetrated unknown parts of the Sahara or the equatorial jungle to stake French territorial claims, promote trade, subdue tribes or undertake some government project. Scientific research or exploration provided convenient covers for military campaigns with money and materials supplied by the state. The Foureau–Lamy expedition in 1898, for example, consisted of 263 African troops, 14 French officers and 1000 camels (of which 140 died over a seven-day period). But it was the earlier, lone explorers who paved the way for later imperialists.[2]

Missionaries

Among the most ubiquitous of French groups overseas were missionaries, and even anticlerical governments considered missionaries a useful, or necessary, adjunct to expansion. In the nineteenth century, new orders of priests and nuns organised specifically to proselytise in the colonies. In 1807, Anne-Marie Javouhey founded the Sisters of St Joseph of Cluny, which sent nuns to Senegal and participated in an aborted settlement in Guyane. The 1830s saw the foundation of the Marist Order, whose priests and brothers worked principally in the South Pacific. Two other orders created in the 1840s fused to become the Fathers of the Holy Spirit, who were particularly active in sub-Saharan Africa. In 1868, Father Charles Lavigerie organised the Society of Missionaries; known as the White Fathers, Lavigerie's priests, and an order of White Sisters, became the most important French missionary congregations in Africa.

By the end of the 1800s, several thousand French priests and nuns ministered throughout the empire. Priests performed their ecclesiastical duties, but both they and the sisters opened schools, operated hospitals and sometimes set up farms or trading posts. Most missionaries, like clerics in France, came from a rural background and modest families. Few received extensive training or preparation for the different societies and environments to which they were sent. All, however, were imbued with revivalist faith and thought they were defending Catholicism against the forces of secularism at home and paganism abroad. They regarded themselves as servants of God, the pope and France – masters who did not always share the same goals.

Missionaries played a crucial rule in the acquisition of France's empire. Their presence often pre-dated that of soldiers and administrators, and quarrels involving missionaries provided the justification for several takeovers. French missionaries were present in Vietnam, for instance, for two centuries before French conquest of Cochinchina, and priests created a virtual theocracy in Wallis and Futuna 50 years before France established a protectorate over the islands. Perceived slights to French missionaries provided the rationale for French expansion in Tahiti and Indochina, and Lavigerie's efforts created a beach-head for France in Tunisia.

Lavigerie was the prime example of a missionary imperialist, a prelate able to sway French policy in the Maghreb. Born in 1825, Lavigerie briefly taught at the University of Paris after his ordination. He became director of French schools in the Middle East, journeying to Syria in 1860 just after a massacre of Christians there. Lavigerie was soon elevated to the episcopate as Bishop of Nancy, then in 1866, became Archbishop of Algiers: 'Algeria is the door opened by Providence to a barbaric continent of two hundred million souls.' He realised that conversion of Berbers and Arabs from Islam to Christianity was a difficult cause, but he never failed to see himself as a crusader against Islam: 'Islam ceaselessly makes redoubtable advances among the African populations. It imposes itself on them by violence. . . . The Muslim religion is truly the masterpiece of the spirit of evil. . . . How can we wrest away souls from its empire? Islam cannot perish but of itself, by the excesses which are the consequences of its doctrines.'

With the blessing of the pope, who bestowed on Lavigerie the grand title of Apostolic Delegate to the Sahara, Southern Regions and Equatorial Africa and Archbishop of Carthage, he set up schools and infirmaries, shepherded small congregations and unfalteringly supported French expansion. In particular, Tunisia interested Lavigerie, partly because Carthage had been the home of St Augustine: Lavigerie's long-term aim was to resurrect a Christian empire in North Africa. His lobbying contributed markedly to declaration of a French protectorate over Tunisia in 1881. An Italian newspaper pertinently remarked: 'Cardinal Lavigerie renders to French influence in the Mediterranean greater service than an army corps.' The French statesman Gambetta added: 'That is true, and one must recognise that it costs less.' At Lavigerie's death in 1892, France controlled Algeria and Tunisia, and exercised great influence in Morocco; conversion of Maghrebins to Catholicism proved less successful.[3]

Missionaries encountered more luck in black Africa than in the Maghreb – the 1912 statutes for the protectorate of Morocco, indeed, forbade proselytism. Black Africans practised a number of traditional religions, although Islam was strong in the northern reaches of sub-Saharan Africa (as well as in eastern Africa) and was spreading rapidly. Missionaries made it their goal to stamp out animism and other 'heathen' religions, and combat such practices as 'lewd' dancing and ceremonies, polygamy, sexual promiscuity and other customs contrary to Catholic ideology or French interests. Catholic missionaries (as well as some French Protestant pastors) fanned out from coastal centres and played a role in French colonisation of such territories as the Côte d'Ivoire and Dahomey. Away from the cities, priests and nuns, along with the occasional administrator, were the French men and women Africans most often encountered.[4]

Missionaries in Africa became heroes for parishioners at home, and some gained renown around the world. Charles de Foucauld, born a viscount in 1858, led a dissipated life in the military before becoming a priest. He travelled around Morocco, then settled as a hermit at Tamanrasset in the far south of Algeria. Foucauld compiled a Tuareg dictionary and completed ethnographic work on the nomads, inspired the creation of several religious orders and became a saintly figure for Catholic colonialists, venerated after he was killed by Muslims in 1916. Albert Schweitzer, an Alsatian Protestant born in 1875, was a professor of theology and organist before moving to Africa. Also a medical doctor and specialist on tropical diseases such as leprosy and sleeping sickness, Schweitzer founded a clinic at Lambaréné, in Gabon, in 1913. He operated the hospital until his death in 1965 (by which time Gabon had gained independence), winning the Nobel Peace Prize in 1952 for his humanitarian efforts.

In Indochina, French missionaries competed with Buddhism and Confucianism and came up against local mandarins. Priests saw mandarins, who exercised both political and spiritual authority, as the major obstacle to the spread of both Christianity and French influence. Nevertheless, the number of Catholic missionaries in Indochina rose from 63 in 1874 to 349 in 1901, and 389 in 1913. The ordination of Vietnamese clerics more than compensated for the stagnating number of expatriates; Indochinese priests increased from 44 to 544 in a 40-year span. Missionaries scored their greatest victories in Vietnam, but evangelists worked in Cambodia and Laos as well. The influence missionaries exercised outside the religious milieu sparked criticism from settlers and Indochinese, who accused priests of meddling in government affairs, trying to limit settlers' use of local labour and acquisition of land, and seducing Indochinese away from their culture. On balance, however, most agreed with the comment of one missionary in Annam that 'the more Christians there are in the kingdom, the more friends France has'.[5]

In the South Pacific in the 1800s, Catholic and French were almost the same, as Frenchmen were the main Catholic priests not only in the French colonies but throughout Melanesia and Polynesia. They competed rather successfully with evangelists from various Protestant denominations (most of whom were British, Australian or American). French Protestant pastors also took charge of congregations in the EFO and New Caledonia. The French Oceanic territories, like the *vieilles colonies*, were thoroughly Christianised.

Soldiers and Sailors

French troops played an essential role in colonisation. Naval commanders charted distant oceans and raised the flag over the possessions acquired in the mid-1800s; administration of the colonies was the responsibility of the Navy until the 1880s. Army officers explored the African interior, claiming territory for France as they advanced. The names of such military figures as Marshal Bugeaud, Marshal Lyautey, General Gallieni, General Faidherbe and General Dodds were synonymous with conquest, and later officers prominent in French history, including Marshal Foch, Marshal Pétain and General de Gaulle, had strong links to the colonies. The military subjugated populations which resisted French occupation, quelled insurrections, protected settlers, came to the defence of traders and missionaries, protected the empire against foreign powers and eventually struggled to maintain French control in the face of independence movements. Military figures played a part in the colonial lobby. Thousands of ordinary Frenchmen served overseas as military conscripts or volunteers. Several leading novelists associated with colonial literature, such as Pierre Loti and Victor Segalen, were navy officers. The ethos of colonial life – the idea and practice of conquest, the ceremonial of parades and flags, the virile virtues associated with overseas life – was linked to militarism.

The navy held an especially important place in expansion. Until the age of aeroplanes, colonies were accessible only by sea. Many

colonial acquisitions were chosen to afford the navy good harbours and facilities for provisioning. The navy held credit for French
takeover of Indochina. Captains served as colonial governors, and
admirals such as Chasseloup-Laubat and Rigault de Genouilly
became ministers. The navy provided a lifeline to the outside world
for isolated and remote colonies.[6] In the South Pacific, for
instance, the navy's annual tour of islands, with visits to French
possessions and those of other powers, provided an opportunity
to show the flag, deposit or collect administrators and missionaries,
sort out problems between Europeans and islanders, and render
services to settlers.

Naval officers in the nineteenth century generally came from a
privileged background; many noblemen saw a military career as
an appropriate way to serve their country. After graduation from
the naval academy, they began tours of duty in the Mediterranean,
Atlantic, Pacific or Indian Ocean, for France maintained fleets
around the globe. Responsible to the navy minister in Paris, they
nevertheless had great latitude to undertake actions as they saw
fit, necessary autonomy given the distances at which they often
found themselves from Paris and the unpredictability of situations which they encountered. Some used their powers freely to
interpret vague instructions issued by superiors in order to declare protectorates or annexations. The reports naval officers wrote
about their activities provided a major source of intelligence to
Paris about overseas developments.

Ordinary sailors came from more modest backgrounds than admirals, and many had little formal education and no overseas
experience before they embarked on their first voyages. They paid
the price of cramped quarters, loneliness on long sea journeys,
tropical diseases, warfare, harsh discipline and meagre pay. Such
hardships were the expected lot for those who enlisted in the
navy, but risk and adventure were probably an attraction for many.
The same disparities between commanders and troops existed in
the army as well as the navy, and the life of soldiers serving in
colonial garrisons or traipsing through steaming jungles or fur-
nace-like deserts was no easier than that of sailors. Nor did rewards differ, from home leave to the pleasures of adventure,
camaraderie, drink and sex in exotic outposts.

Soldiers in the empire served under a baffling variety of regi-
mental banners. Some formed part of the regular French army
dispatched to colonies on particular assignments. Others belonged

to the *troupes coloniales*, first created in 1822 under the authority of the navy but transferred to army administration in 1900. (*Marsouins* were infantry units serving with the navy.) In 1914, French forces boasted 60 battalions of colonial troops, which rose to 201 battalions at the end of the First World War. There were, as well, non-European soldiers, usually collectively, if mistakenly, referred to as the *tirailleurs sénégalais*. The *zouaves*, an infantry corps set up in 1830, took part in many subsequent military actions in North Africa and Indochina, as well as the Crimean War. The *spahis* belonged to a cavalry corps officially organised in 1834 and later reserved largely for indigenous troops. The infamous Bataillon d'Afrique, created in 1860 as a disciplinary corps for conscripts with a police record, undertook many engineering and public works projects.

The Foreign Legion

The most legendary, though not the largest, French military force in the empire was composed of soldiers who were not usually French citizens. The Foreign Legion (*Légion Etrangère*) gained fame for its trademark white caps (*képis*), bravado in battle, and an unsavoury reputation as a gang of misfits and criminals fleeing their home countries to enlist anonymously in a mercenary army. The Legion acquired notoriety for arduous training and merciless discipline, both of which contributed to great battle effectiveness and a high rate of desertion. Movies such as *Beau Geste* promoted the swashbuckling image of the Legionnaires, although Laurel and Hardy sent up their reputation in *Beau Hunks*.

The Legion, established in 1831, was plagued in its early years by lack of qualified non-commissioned officers, poor organisation and often wavering support from French authorities and the regular army. It saw its initial overseas action in Algeria in 1832, but in its first four years in North Africa, fully one-quarter of the Legionnaires died from disease or were discharged with ill health. In 1835, France hired out the whole Foreign Legion to the Spanish to defend the Madrid government against rebels.

Later in the decade, the Legion returned to Algeria to extend French control and pacify Berbers and Arabs. Its headquarters were established in Sidi-bel-Abbès, a base it unwillingly quit in 1962. The Legion numbered several thousand soldiers in the mid-nineteenth century, the largest number being Spaniards and Italians.

Their life in the Sahara was tough, and the Legion often served on the front-line in campaigns. The French continued to send Legionnaires around the world. From 1854 to 1856, they participated in the Crimean war; 1600 died there. In the 1860s, they went to Mexico to try to prop up the regime of Emperor Maximilian, put into office by Napoleon III; the anniversary of the battle of Camerone, where a unit of the Legion suffered brave but total defeat, became the Legion's major festival.

Subsequently, the French mostly deployed the Legion in the empire. In the 1880s and 1890s, Legionnaires helped to establish French rule in Tonkin. They went to Dahomey in Western Africa to combat King Béhanzin and enlarge French holdings on the Gulf of Guinea. In 1895, they took part in the expedition to Madagascar, a campaign which killed a third of all Legionnaires who took part. In the early twentieth century, Legionnaires continued to complement the regular army, serving almost everywhere in the empire, recruiting soldiers from near and far. They fought in both world wars, helped to put down Abd-el-Krim's rebellion in Morocco in the 1920s and were among the most active French troops in the Indochinese and Algerian wars. The force, which counted as many as 33 000 men at its strongest, survived the end of the French empire, though in much reduced numbers. The Foreign Legion still plays a role in French defence with bases in French Polynesia, Guyane and Mayotte.[7]

Hubert Lyautey

Among the soldiers responsible for France's empire, few were so accomplished as Hubert Lyautey, who served in Algeria, Indochina and Madagascar, became the first Resident-General of Morocco and organised the Colonial Exhibition of 1931. Lyautey was born in 1854 in Nancy, capital of Lorraine. His father was a well-to-do engineer; his grandfather, a much-decorated general in the Napoleonic wars. Lyautey's mother was a Norman aristocrat, and he adopted many of the principles he associated with the aristocracy – patriotism, belief in the moral and political value of the elite, monarchism and Catholicism.

Upon graduation from the French military academy, Lyautey went for two months' holiday to Algeria in 1878, his first contact with Africa. Enchanted by the warmth and colour of the Maghreb, he returned with favourable impressions of Arabs and Islam. Two years later, after dreary provincial postings, Lyautey received an assignment to North Africa, initially in Algiers, then as leader of military campaigns in the south of Algeria. The stay confirmed his fascination with Africa and his vocation as a colonial officer. One night he wrote home from a desert post:

> With my brigade I am leading the campaign . . .; the moon rose an hour ago, it is a beautiful night, one of those bright and clear nights that you will remember, dear father. . . . What exquisite delight! On the southern route, in front of me, are five horsemen, the pearl white haunches of their small horses glistening in the light; I am letting myself be taken in by all the dreams that can be imagined by a twenty-seven year old lieutenant – soon to be promoted to captain – who is crossing the desert . . . Hosanna! Here is my Africa!

To Lyautey's disappointment, his superiors recalled him to France for a four-year stint. In 1894, he again won a colonial posting, this time to Indochina, where he became a close associate of Gallieni. Lyautey's assignment was to lead troops to the northernmost reaches of Indochina, the frontier along the Chinese border, to subdue local populations and wipe out rebellion (which the French called the 'piracy' of the Black Flags). Lyautey accomplished his mission with merit, then went to set up the colonial administration in Tonkin before serving as head of the military office of the Government-General of Indochina. By the time he left Asia in 1897, he was a lieutenant-colonel and had been decorated with the Legion of Honour.

Lyautey followed Gallieni to Madagascar, where his mentor became governor-general. Lyautey excelled as a commander and administrator on the Indian Ocean island. He pacified northern and western Madagascar, administered a military district of 200 000 inhabitants, began construction of a new provincial capital at Ankazobe and a major roadway which traversed Madagascar. He instigated the planting of rice paddies, persuaded Malagasy to cultivate coffee, tobacco, grain and cotton for export, opened schools and set up textile workshops. In 1900, Lyautey became commander of the entire southern region of Madagascar, which gave him control over an area a third the size of France, populated by 1 million inhabitants; 80 officers and 4000 soldiers served under his command.

Three years later, Lyautey was transferred to Algeria to command a subdivision south of Oran and later the whole Oran district. His primary duty was to protect a new railway line against attacks from Morocco. But Lyautey's sights were set on the conquest of Morocco. Under his orders, French forays gradually established toeholds in the sultan's realm. The 1907 murder of a Frenchman in Casablanca provided justification for troops to cross the border from Algeria and take Oujda. Lyautey then went to Rabat to put further pressure on the sultan. There he became embroiled in a power struggle between the sovereign and his brother, a quarrel which mirrored French and German rivalry over Morocco as each imperial power promoted its candidate for the throne.

In January 1911, General Lyautey returned to France, without enthusiasm, to command forces in Rennes. But in March, the French convinced the sultan of Morocco to accept a protectorate and chose Lyautey as Resident-General. Lyautey ruled Morocco until 1925, although he carefully maintained a deferential stance *vis-à-vis* the sultan. Lyautey extended effective French control throughout Morocco, subduing regions resisting submission; he set up an economic and administrative infrastructure for the protectorate, began a programme of public works and town planning, promoted education and medical care, and commanded troops during the First World War.

In the early 1920s, rebels in the Rif mountains, led by Abd-el-Krim, attacked French troops, and Paris slighted Lyautey by naming General Pétain military commander of 100 000 soldiers sent to put down the insurrection. Feeling bitter and ignored, Lyautey resigned in 1925 and returned to France. He edited his letters, took part in various public events, directed the 1931 colonial exhibition, and assumed the posture of a colonial elder statesman, befitting his rank as Marshal of France and member of the French Academy. At Lyautey's request, his body was buried in Morocco after his death in 1934, although it was repatriated to France in the early 1960s and now lies under the dome of the Invalides, near the sepulchre of Napoleon.

Lyautey's views provide insight into the mentality of the colonialist, although his ideas were not shared by all empire-builders. (Lyautey, for example, opposed settlement of French migrants in Morocco, a programme promoted by many other colonialists.) Proud of belonging to the French elite, Lyautey saw colonial work as a duty owed to his class and nation. He viewed modern currents of thought, including republicanism and socialism, with suspicion. Lyautey thought that the army had a key place in national and colonial life; although he did not spare the army from strident criticism in several controversial articles he published as a young officer, he underlined the social role of the military in regenerating France. Lyautey thereby placed an emphasis on action: 'My ideal has always been the union of politics and action.' He relished power; in Indochina, he confided: 'Here I am like a fish in water, because in great enterprises, the manipulation of things and men is power, everything that I love.' While ruling over southern Madagascar, he wrote to his father: 'I am Louis XIV and that suits me.'

Lyautey imagined that he did not crave power for its own sake. He advocated colonial development, especially the creation of economies which would return profits to France: 'The *raison d'être* of our military operations in the colonies is always, and above all, economic.' This stimulated his interest in building roads, setting up artisan shops, planting new crops. To achieve these ends, Lyautey did not advocate annihilation of local cultures or populations; he pronounced great respect for non-European civilisations and enforced the prohibition on Christian proselytising in Morocco. He borrowed from one of his mentors in Indochina, Governor Lanessan, a formula he thought applicable everywhere in the empire: the French should 'govern with the mandarin and not against the mandarin'. Colonialists must dominate indigenes but not humiliate them, he thought, although he reacted against utopian hopes of 'assimilation' of indigenes. Lyautey preferred the association of local chiefs with French authorities and parallel promotion of both indigenous and French culture. He favoured protectorates over annexation, and the Moroccan post of Resident-General consequently suited him well. In short, Lyautey conceived of the colonies as realms to govern for the good of the local population and the benefit of France.

Personal considerations entered into Lyautey's perspectives. He enjoyed the masculine company of young officers and the camaraderie of colonial camps. He liked hot climates: 'We are colonials, united by a shared hatred of the cold, worshippers of the sun and light.' The colonies provided an escape from frigid France, a new arena for national revival through heroic action and dedicated work. Lyautey's sense of mission sometimes swelled into

megalomania. One of his great disappointments was that he had
taken a relatively minor part in France's political life and the
First World War; he would have happily played the role of national saviour. Lyautey's self-assigned mandate blended an author-
itarian sense of action and accomplishment with an almost mystical
sense of his own vocation and the destiny of France:

> Even supposing that France gains nothing [from the colonies],
> we will have at least been the labourers in a providential effort
> on this globe if we have brought back life, agriculture and man
> into regions given up to banditry and sterility, if we have made
> these rivers the conduits of transport . . . if we have exploited
> these forests and revived these fertile but uncultivated valleys.[8]

Settlers

Explorers, by the nature of their quests, were peripatetic; administrators and military officers, by the terms of their posting, seldom stayed more than several years in any one outpost. A number
of traders lived in a colony only so long as business prospered.
Priests and members of religious orders stayed longer; indeed,
many spent exceptionally long periods in their missions. Settlers
were committed to the colonies, usually for indefinitely extended
periods or for life. Often they gave up the resources they possessed at home, taking to the colonies whatever capital or possessions they could transport. As time passed, they became more
distanced from France, increasingly rooted in their new countries.
They married and had children, and their offspring became more
attached to their birthplaces, more detached from a 'mother
country' which many had never known. Habits, attitudes, dress,
dialects, diets changed over time and space, though few French
men and women overseas lost a primal link with the language,
culture and attitudes of France.

Nineteenth-century France was not a fertile ground for emigrants. Falling birth rates caused worry about depopulation and
reduced the overpopulation which stimulated migration from other
countries such as Germany. A large proportion of the French
enjoyed access to land, and many possessed outright title to properties in a country which remained rural and agricultural; France,
unlike Italy, had no large dispossessed peasantry looking for land

overseas. Industrialisation created an alternative to expatriation, even if the growth of factory cities created new problems. Compared with nations like Ireland, France was a prosperous well-fed country; though dire poverty did exist, famine and misery did not force millions to seek a better life elsewhere. France remained a relatively tolerant country, as well, and no groups suffered the sort of pogroms which forced some eastern Europeans into exile.

Furthermore, French colonies were not entirely hospitable to migrants. Remoteness, tropical diseases and rumours about savage tribes dissuaded all but the adventurous. The smaller outposts were too distant and tiny to support large migrant communities. Guyane's jungles seemed impenetrable. Parts of Africa, with Saharan sands in the north and dense jungle in the centre, could hardly host large numbers of expatriates, and coastal regions were already crowded with Africans. Protectorates, such as Morocco, Tunisia and the mandated territories, seemed uncertain destinations. The *vieilles colonies* of the Antilles and Indian Ocean faced economic difficulties after the abolition of slavery and attracted few migrants; tiny Saint-Pierre and Miquelon were too tiny and cold for large-scale settlement. Such colonies as Madagascar were not securely in French hands until the very end of the nineteenth century. Guyane and New Caledonia suffered from their reputation for penitentiaries.

Yet a number of French men and women did dare a new life overseas, moving to the Maghreb, Indochina or black Africa, and particularly to Algeria and New Caledonia. Promoters vaunted the availability of land, job prospects, salubrious climate, natural beauty and the chance to make a new start of things to readers of colonial propaganda and potential colonists who wrote away for documentation. Paris tried to attract much-needed professional people – lawyers, doctors, engineers, surveyors – to work in the empire. Private institutes advertised financial assistance to would-be migrants, and the government occasionally offered subsidies and designed schemes for military men and public servants to remain in the empire after their retirement.

Paris and the colonial governments also populated the colonies with non-French residents. Migrants from around the Mediterranean poured into Algeria with France's blessing. Of the 162 000 Europeans in Morocco in 1931, 40 per cent were not French; not until the 1930s did French citizens outnumber Italians in Tunisia. Plantation owners imported Indian labourers into the West

Indian colonies and Réunion, while New Caledonian authorities recruited workers from Japan, Indochina and the East Indies, and a Scottish entrepreneur brought Chinese farmworkers to Tahiti. Syrians and Lebanese moved in substantial numbers to Africa (and the Caribbean) even before France won a mandate over the Levantine territories. Indochina already counted a large population of Chinese, who had migrated southwards long before the French took over Vietnam, Cambodia and Laos. Most colonies had a heterogeneous population – a mosaic of ethnic groups in the African colonies, Jews in North Africa, minorities such as Hmong tribes in the hill country of Indochina and the Native Americans in the jungles of Guyane. By the end of the colonial period, therefore, almost all French colonies displayed a complex demographic mixture of indigeneous peoples, French settlers and migrants from elsewhere in Europe and Asia.

Algeria

One of France's greatest twentieth-century authors, Albert Camus, was a European Algerian, or *pied-noir*.[9] An uncompleted but largely autobiographical novel, on which Camus was working at the time of his death in 1960, provides a personal portrait and poignant insight into the life of settlers in North Africa. Jacques Cormery, the main character, is born (like Camus) in 1913, just as his father takes up a position as manager of a rural estate. His paternal family were Alsatian migrants who arrived in Algeria after the Franco-Prussian War; his mother's family, Spaniards from the Balearic Islands. Soon after Jacques' birth, his father dies on the battlefields of the First World War. Jacques and his brother grow up in poverty in Belcourt, a working-class neighbourhood of Algiers. Their small flat accommodates the two boys and their mother in one bedroom, an uncle on a couch in the kitchen and an imperious grandmother in her own room. Both women are illiterate, and Jacques' mother works as a cleaner; his uncle is a semi-literate barrelmaker. The family's plight is so bad that Jacques' grandmother forbids him to play soccer because his shoes will wear out too quickly. The family's staple food is a stew of beef heart and lungs; dessert is a seldom-seen luxury. Misery, heat and hard work are the lot of the poor underclass in the French colony.

Jacques has few diversions. He accompanies his grandmother to silent films, where he must read the dialogue to her, and he

goes hunting with his uncle. He excels at primary school, aided
by a kindly schoolmaster, then wins a scholarship to the *lycée*. At
first, Grandmother refuses to let him accept the offer, for the
family needs a breadwinner not a scholar. Deft intervention by
Jacques' teacher changes her mind.

Algiers in the interwar years is a city recreated in the French
image, with cafés and monumental government buildings, the quarters of the rich separated by a boulevard from the poor neighbourhood of the Cormerys, a jumble of French, Italian, Spanish
and Maltese immigrants. Arabs live in the background, working
for the Europeans, drinking mint tea not anisette, attending the
mosque rather than the cathedral. Jacques rides alongside them
on the tram and, when he can scrape together a few coins, buys
brightly coloured pastries from them outside the cinema. But
Europeans and North Africans lead separate lives. Some of the
Muslims are more prosperous and better educated than poor whites
like Cormery's family, yet Europeans lord it over Maghrebins. They
literally barricade themselves behind locked doors to protect themselves from 'natives',

> this intriguing and disquieting people, close and yet separate,
> that one brushed past during the day; sometimes there was friend-
> ship or camaraderie but, when night fell, they returned to their
> own unknown houses which we never visited, barricaded also
> with their women whom we never saw or, if we saw them in the
> street, we did not know who they were with veils covering half
> their faces and their beautifully soft and sensual eyes above
> the white mask. Though fatalistic and exhausted, they were so
> numerous in the neighbourhoods where they clustered that there
> hovered an invisible threat which you could sniff in the air on
> certain evenings when a fight broke out between a Frenchman
> and an Arab.

The book recollects Jacques' childhood in Algiers as the 40-
year-old Cormery, now a famous author, returns to Algiers to visit
his aged mother and beloved schoolteacher. Cormery is also searching for memories of the father whom he has never known and
about whom it is possible to turn up only bare traces – even his
mother cannot remember details about her husband's life. Jacques
sees his own condition, the fatherless child without a history, as
that of the *pieds-noirs*; the situation is not an exotic mystery but a
desperate plight:

There was only the mystery of poverty which creates beings without names and without a past. . . . The Spaniards of the Sahel,
the Alsatians of the highlands of this immense island cast between sand and sea that an enormous silence was now beginning to cover, that is, the anonymity of bloodlines, of courage,
of work, of instinct, both cruel and compassionate, . . . in this
land of the forgotten in which everyone is the first man . . .
like all the men born in this country who, one by one, tried to
learn to live without roots and without faith, and who all together
today, risk the ultimate anonymity and the loss of the only sacred
traces of their past on this earth.

Camus was writing in the midst of the Algerian war of independence, which pitted North African nationalists against *pieds-
noirs*. His manuscript tries to situate these European exiles in Africa,
seen as heroic pioneers by colonial promoters, as cruel racist
exploiters by the independence-fighters and anti-colonialists, in a
history where they themselves were victims.[10] Here were no dashing explorers, much less fabulously wealthy colonial nabobs, but
the poor of Europe transplanted to harsh colonial realities, un-
loved by the 'natives' whom they dominated, and treated with
disdain by their metropolitan compatriots.

One factual example of French colonisation is the Algerian town
of Annaba. Before the French conquest, Annaba counted a population of around 4000 persons, including Berbers and Arabs, descendants of Moors forced out of Spain at the end of the fifteenth
century, Turkish administrators, Mzabite traders from the Sahara,
black slaves, a large Jewish population and a few Europeans. Among
the last were employees of the *Compagnie d'Afrique*, which had
traded in Annaba since the mid-1700s. The French took Annaba
in 1832, two years after the conquest of Algiers. Most of the local
population fled and only trickled back over the next decade. The
French population was initially composed of soldiers, who requi-
sitioned buildings and renamed the city Bône. In 1833, 750 Europeans lived there; men outnumbered women by seven to one. By
the mid-1840s, when births first exceeded deaths among Europeans, the European population had grown to 5000, and there
were now two Europeans for each Algerian. The French, however, comprised only one-third of the Europeans, being outnumbered by Maltese and Italians.

More foreigners came with the opening of phosphate mines

and exploitation of forests of cork oak in the city's hinterland, the building of a rail line, construction projects and expansion of the bureaucracy. A transient population evolved into a rooted, stable one. By the 1890s, locally born Europeans outnumbered migrants from overseas and, since Jews and many foreigners had been naturalised, French citizens formed a majority. Great social segmentation accompanied the growth of Bône. A small French elite held economic and political power, Maltese specialised in market-gardening, and Italians in construction and fishing; Jews worked in skilled trades and filled lower level white-collar posts, and Mzabites ran textile shops. Almost all Europeans lived in the new city of Bône and its suburbs, while Jews congregated in the *mellah*, or ghetto. The European neighbourhood boasted an elaborate town hall, theatre, shops lining shaded streets, and typically French cafés. Arabs and Berbers, mostly unskilled workmen, lived in the old kasbah or outside the city. Muslims maintained their own social venues, mosques, religious schools, cafés and souks, and were little assimilated into French colonial life.

Bône enjoyed a lively colonial life. Jérôme Bertagna, leader of the colonists and mayor from 1888 to 1903, took credit for building a European-style city, even if almost 30 enquiries investigated him for corruption, graft and misuse of public funds. Bertagna and his clients jostled for control of the municipal council – where Arabs had only 3 representatives, versus 27 for Europeans – against a rival faction; much voting fraud was alleged, and elections were regularly annulled. Political debate revolved around support for or opposition to Bertagna, and a violent anti-Semitic campaign being waged in Algeria and metropolitan France. Uppermost in colonial politics lay settlers' desire to wrest increased autonomy from Paris.

At the beginning of the 1900s, Bône's Europeans indeed won a measure of self-government. Colonists from diverse backgrounds had melded into a settler population who considered themselves at home in Algeria. The Jews, still somewhat apart, had cast their fortunes with the French. Muslims remained on the margins of society, unintegrated, disenfranchised and largely unrewarded for half a century of French colonisation. In 1900, the first meeting of the Muslim Benevolent Society and, nine years later, the founding of the Young Algerians movement, foreshadowed the militant nationalism which eventually forced almost all Europeans to leave Bône in 1962.[11]

The non-Muslim population of Algeria was constituted over a long period by a variety of immigrant groups.[12] In 1839, almost nine years after the French conquered Algiers, the country counted 35 000 Europeans; in 1856, there were 130 000; by 1926, Europeans numbered 833 000 and in 1954, at the start of the Algerian war of independence, there were 984 000 Europeans. Almost four-fifths in the mid-1950s had been born in Algeria, proof of the entrenchment of the migrant populations that had arrived over the past century.

The first French migrants to Algeria were military men who arrived in the wake of the conquest, both modest soldiers and aristocratic officers – known as the 'yellow gloved colonists' (*colons aux gants jaunes*) – who left France after the Revolution of 1830 and the end of the Restoration monarchy. Few had great skill as settlers or farmers, and many left. From 1842 to 1846, 198 000 Europeans arrived, and 118 000 departed. Thousands died from the cholera or malaria that plagued cities and wiped out several new settler villages; cholera killed 12 000 people in Algiers and 14 000 in Constantine (including Algerians) in 1835. After the Revolution of 1848, and particularly after Napoleon III's *coup d'état* and the establishment of the Second Empire in 1852, the government transported as many as 14 000 political prisoners to Algeria; a number remained after their sentences expired. Of 20 000 prisoners and free settlers who landed between 1848 and 1850, 10 000 remained in Algeria; 3000 died and 7000 returned to France. With the Prussian defeat of France in 1871, and the loss of Alsace and Lorraine, emigrants from those provinces fled to North Africa. Recruitment campaigns and land grants also attracted peasants from the south of France and Corsica.

Algeria depended on other countries than France for much of its population increase; in 1886, 219 000 French citizens lived in Algeria, but there were a further 211 000 other Europeans. A population of 35 000 Spaniards in 1849 soared to 160 000 by 1886. Coming from the Spanish mainland and, especially, from the Balearic islands, the Spanish abandoned a poor country with few opportunities. They turned Oran and the western part of the Algerian coast into a virtual Spanish preserve. Italians, who numbered 35 000 in 1886, flocked to Constantine and Bône in eastern Algeria from the overpopulated Mezzogiorno. Malta, a British colony in the Mediterranean, formed a reservoir of migrants to eastern Algeria. Malta was particularly poor, suffering from scarcities of food and space – population density was over eight times higher in Malta than in France – and it benefited from proximity to Algeria and the eagerness of both the French and British governments to promote migration to North Africa. At the end of the 1890s, Constantine counted 11 000 Maltese, a tenth of the city's population.[13]

Algeria thus served as a catchment for migrants from all over the northwest Mediterranean. Vaunted as a new America, a haven for the poverty-stricken masses, Algeria provided refuge to a heterogeneous population held together by the desire to make a new life in better conditions, feelings of superiority to native Algerians and links with France, mother-country for some and protector of all Europeans in the colony. Discord among migrants, however, was common. The French looked down on other migrants, Italians and Spaniards jostled each other for status, and Maltese remained at the bottom of the European hierarchy. Jews, who totalled 35 000 in 1830, were as poor as most of the Arabs and Europeans, but roundly despised by both groups.

France welded these diverse groups into a population that at the time of the Algerian war in the 1950s proudly labelled themselves partisans of *Algérie française*. In 1870, the Crémieux laws automatically granted French citizenship to Algeria's Jews, an action which provoked extreme opposition from Arabs, who could only acquire citizenship by renouncing their traditional Islamic legal status and fulfilling other requirements. The move also discontented some Europeans, and by the end of the 1800s, at the time of the Dreyfus affair in France, anti-Semitism ran rampant in Algeria. In 1889, Paris extended citizenship to Algerian-born children of foreign migrants; this dramatically increased the 'French' population.

By the beginning of the twentieth century, colonialists and colonists proclaimed that France had formed a new race in Algeria, fused together by marriage, schooling, military service, honest work and love of the new homeland. Algerian writers pictured themselves as inheritors of the Crusaders, returning Christianity to the land of Islam, and as pioneers, carving out a prosperous new Europe on the shores of Africa. With land confiscated from Arabs, settlers laboured on farms, tended the vineyards which became the mainstay of the country's export economy, laid rail lines, built French-style cities and elected members to a local assembly and the French parliament. Only with difficulty (or blindness) could they forget that no matter how firmly established they felt in North Africa, settlers lived among millions of Maghrebins and that only the colonial power of France guaranteed their security and position.[14]

New Caledonia

Colonialists trumpeted New Caledonia as an austral France, yet settlement took place only slowly after French conquest in 1853. Few settlers were attracted to the distant colony, said to be inhabited by primitive cannibals and set to become a prison colony. The first prisoners did not land until 1864; they kept arriving until 1897, and the 1901 census, just after the ending of transportation, counted 10 500 convicts in New Caledonia. Most had been sentenced for a variety of minor offences or more serious crimes, including many recidivist offenders. France also transported political prisoners, among them rebels from a Kabyle insurrection in North Africa in 1870, and over 4000 participants in the Paris Commune of 1871. The Communards remained in New Caledonia only until Paris declared an amnesty in the 1880s, but such rebels as Louise Michel, the 'red virgin of the Commune', left an imprint. At a time when Europeans cared little about the indigenous population of New Caledonia, Michel organised classes for Melanesians, collected their folktales and expressed support for a Melanesian rebellion in 1878; most of the other Communards sided with French authorities in the suppression of the revolt.

Regulations obliged convicts sent to New Caledonia with relatively brief sentences to remain in the colony for a period equal to their sentences; those with longer sentences were required to stay for the remainder of their lives. This policy aimed both at populating the colony and rehabilitating offenders. The origins of New Caledonia's European settlement thus lay in the prison population and the large number of emancipists obliged to remain in the Pacific. Some received grants of land from the government, since colonial officials bought or confiscated nine-tenths of the land on the New Caledonian mainland in hopes of turning New Caledonia into a booming agricultural and pastoral economy. But former convicts, largely from an urban and artisanal background, had neither training nor interest in farming. Some found jobs in the nickel mines which produced New Caledonia's main export. Many, however, wandered the country, uneducated and untrained, feared and hated by free colonists, trying to find odd jobs or earn money selling alcohol to Melanesians.[15]

Efforts to attract free settlers met with little success, although small contingents arrived from Alsace and Lorraine after 1871, and from the north of France after the First World War. The cessation of transportation cut off the only source of migrants on which New Caledonia had been able to rely. Scarcity of labour forced entrepreneurs to recruit Japanese, Vietnamese and Javanese contract labourers from the 1890s onwards; many stayed on (although the Japanese were expelled during the Second World War). In the 1920s, Asians outnumbered Europeans in New Caledonia, but subsequent French migration reduced Asians to a minority; foreign settlement and Melanesian depopulation turned the indigenous islanders into a minority as well.

Europeans concentrated in the west and south of the mainland, where rolling plains provided land for farming. Nouméa, the colony's capital, became a largely European city. Free settlers, as well as some descendants of convicts, formed the elite of New Caledonia, earning wealth from nickel-mining and import-export businesses. Poorer Europeans remained in the bush, eking out a living on livestock stations or small farms. Conflict between free settlers and former convicts (and their heirs), and between Nouméa and the countryside, continued to characterise the history of New Caledonia, although the major clashes which occurred pitted Europeans against Melanesians.

Indochina

Indochina counted few settlers in the early years of French control. In 1864, Saigon had a French population of only 594, and the number had not quite doubled a decade later. In 1873, 1114 long-term settlers were outnumbered by 6469 temporary residents, mostly soldiers, sailors and bureaucrats on three-year postings. By the turn of the century, Saigon played host to 3000 French settlers. Haiphong and Hanoi were the other concentrations of French citizens. In 1888, Haiphong counted approximately 500 French expatriates, only one-fifth of them women. The French population of Hanoi stood at 430; it included 73 women and 30 children. Yet the small French population represented a gamut of professions. Hanoi boasted 123 colonial bureaucrats, four lawyers, eight manufacturers, nine cloth-merchants, five butchers, four bakers, four watch-makers and jewellers, two booksellers, four hairdressers, two pharmacists, three tailors, two cobblers, a plumber, four café owners, 39 businessmen, 32 clerks and 15 employees of the opium monopoly – a varied civilian community vastly outnumbered by 12 000 soldiers. At the end of the century, the civilian population had grown to 1088, while the military population had declined. In addition to government officials and the military, missionaries represented one of the largest French groups. In 1904, there were 4 French Catholic bishops, 105 priests and 35 nuns in Tonkin and Annam, 3 bishops, 150 priests and 90 nuns in Cochinchina, and one bishop, 33 priests and 83 nuns in Cambodia.

In Cambodia, in 1883 there were perhaps 100–150 French residents, and the census reported 825 Europeans in 1904, a minuscule expatriate group in a total population of over 1.2 million. Two-thirds lived in Phnom-Penh. Four-fifths were military personnel or bureaucrats (including no fewer than 100 customs agents), but there were 12 teachers, 25 postal clerks and 7 judges, as well as traders and artisans. The number of French residents in Laos was even smaller. In 1900, the French community consisted of several dozen employees and technicians working in the main trading and shipping company and other enterprises. Only 14 Frenchmen worked in the colonial government's headquarters in Vientiane.

The European population of Indochina temporarily swelled because of military activities. In 1888, several years after France expanded into Annam and Tonkin, 12 500 French soldiers were stationed in Tonkin and 2300 in Annam, as well as 2000 in Cochinchina and 600 in Cambodia. The French population of Vietnam grew in the twentieth century with the arrival of larger numbers of bureaucrats, traders who worked in the busy ports of Haiphong and Saigon, workers on the rail line from Haiphong to southern China and planters who developed the rubber industry. In Vietnam, just as in Cambodia and Laos, Indochinese nevertheless overwhelmingly outnumbered Europeans.[16]

Senegal

The French in Senegal were generally slave-traders (until the early 1800s) or buyers of groundnuts or other tropical products. Most congregated in Saint-Louis until the establishment of Dakar in the 1850s, although some lived on Gorée and in Rufisque, and there were a few traders in the interior. French businessmen, mostly from Bordeaux, dominated the heights of commerce, although Lebanese and Syrians worked as middlemen or shopkeepers. When Dakar became the capital of the AOF in 1902, and thus the administrative and commercial hub of French black Africa, the number of bureaucrats and other Europeans swelled; over half the Europeans in the AOF lived in Dakar in the 1930s.

The French population of Senegal grew steadily from just over 4000 in 1909 to 8400 in 1935, then increased even more dramatically after the Second World War to reach 38 000 at the time of Senegalese independence in 1960. This represented only a small proportion of the country's total population of 3.1 million, but the privileged political and economic positions of the Europeans gave them status and influence far outweighing their number. Since few of the French were settlers dispossessed of their assets or fearful for their future in an independent Senegal, the country did not experience large-scale emigration of Europeans after decolonisation; ten years after independence, 29 000 French citizens still lived there.[17]

Administrators

Public servants overseas presented the official face of France's imperial presence. Administrators exercised the manifold powers of the French state, implementing decrees sent from Paris and deciding on local regulations. They served as the bureaucratic and legal link between France and both settlers and indigenes. They held responsibility for law and order, kept colonial accounts, collected taxes and oversaw spending, promoted economic development, supervised public works projects, arbitrated between traders, missionaries and other interest groups, came to the assistance of settlers, promoted education and cultural activities and, in their starched uniforms and gold braid, embodied the power and grandeur of France.[18]

Throughout much of the nineteenth century, colonial administrators came from the ranks of the military. As France embraced the idea of expansion and the empire expanded, administration became more complex and colonists voiced criticism of military officers; colonists resented the often high-handed style of navy officers appointed as governors, whom they termed *gaillards d'arrière*, practitioners of 'quarter-deck government'. The government subsequently appointed civilian administrators for all levels of the bureaucracy. Finding good administrators posed great problems, even though a career in the public service promised respectability and job security, an attractive salary and relatively easy promotion. The very prestige of the public service, in part, made the colonies less attractive than the ministries and government departments of the metropole for aspiring public servants. The colonies might offer exoticism, escape from the routine of Europe, or the hope for a young administrator to exercise almost royal control over his district. Nevertheless, colonies were distant, and many posts were isolated in the bush or on outer islands. Tropical heat, lengthy absence from family and friends, the possibility of violent attacks by hostile groups and, especially, disease kept all but the hardy (or foolhardy) from requesting colonial assignments. The high death rate of administrators – 16 per cent of French bureaucrats in sub-Saharan Africa died from disease from 1887 to 1912 – stood as a warning about the potentially fatal rigours of colonial service.

Until the 1890s, the quality of civilian administrators, by general admission, was mediocre. The government hired colonial administrators wherever it found them, for example, among former soldiers and metropolitan bureaucrats. Few had specific training, and a large number had relatively little formal education at all; before 1900, only half the French administrators in Africa possessed a *baccalauréat*, the French secondary school diploma. Dubious backgrounds tainted a few administrators, and superiors often charged subalterns with excessive brutality in treatment of indigenes, regular failure to follow regulations and simple incompetence. On occasion, senior officials proved little better, and constant changes in personnel handicapped the upper echelons of the administration. Paris rarely kept governors in place long enough for them to learn about the territories they administered, and changes were so frequent in some colonies that observers quipped 'about the waltz of governors'.

In an effort to provide more and better quality bureaucrats, the government created a colonial administration corps in 1887. Until 1960 the 4000 public servants who belonged to the corps formed the backbone of French colonial rule in Africa (and were occasionally posted elsewhere). Yet from 1887 to 1900, only several dozen entered the corps annually (and figures fell to single digits in several years); in only four years from 1900 to 1914 did the number of new recruits exceed 70. The numbers help to explain a continued scarcity of administrators and the very low ratio of bureaucrats to the size of the territories they governed and the number of indigenes whom they ruled. In 1912, for example, when the African population of the AOF and AEF numbered approximately 15 million, there were only 341 civilian administrators for the whole of the AOF; the number increased only marginally, to 385, by 1937, and actually declined, from 398 to 366, in the AEF over the same period. (Moreover, at any one moment a substantial number were absent in France or in transit between metropole and empire.)

Training for administrators received a boost with the establishment of the Colonial School (*Ecole Coloniale*), also in 1887, although only about 15 per cent of colonial administrators before the First World War were graduates. The school had no entrance requirements other than a *baccalauréat* until 1896 and was thus much less selective (and less prestigious) than other tertiary institutions; easy admission, however, failed to attract large numbers of candidates. The colonial school included separate sections for future African and Indochinese administrators. The curriculum emphasised the study of law; indeed, most students were obliged to enrol for a law degree concurrently with their two years at the *Ecole Coloniale*. Coursework involved such esoteric topics as Roman law, as well as French administration and colonial policies, history and literature. Only after the turn of the century did the school institute permanent courses on ethnology and anthropology. Language training was minimal and sometimes of limited value. The requirement that future African administrators study literary Arabic hardly prepared them for communicating with indigenes in most parts of Africa, and those destined for Indochina learned classical rather than demotic Vietnamese and Cambodian. Practical training in accountancy, engineering and other fields which might have been of use to future officials was rudimentary. Critics concluded that the *Ecole Coloniale*, despite its merits, hardly provided the training necessary for the colonial field.

The education of administrators improved greatly in the twentieth century. From 1912 onwards, all new members of the colonial administration corps had to be graduates of the *Ecole Coloniale*. The school's directors introduced more rigid selection criteria and significantly revised the curriculum. Especially under Georges Hardy, director of French education in the AOF and Morocco before his appointment as head in 1926, the school became a more demanding training institute and attracted better quality students and teachers (including several renowned ethnologists). Robert Delavignette, appointed in 1937, pursued further reforms; a war veteran who had studied briefly at the school, then worked in Upper Volta and Niger as well as in the Colonial Ministry in Paris, Delavignette was also an award-winning novelist.

The background of students and colonial administrators had changed dramatically since the late nineteenth century. By the 1930s, a third of all students were the sons of senior bureaucrats; most others, the children of professional men or white-collar employees. Only a very small number had a peasant or proletarian background. A sizeable proportion came from colonial settler families or were West Indians of mixed European and African ancestry. Almost none were women.

After graduation new administrators were dispatched to Africa, Madagascar or Indochina. They usually began their career in a remote district. Men in their twenties, as *commandants de cercle* (district commanders), consequently administered extensive regions and large populations almost immediately. Meritorious performance gained them promotion to richer, strategically more important or more populous districts or moves to colonial capitals. Later advancement included appointment to the central administration in Paris – although many administrators, attracted to colonial life, felt repatriation, and the desk job that accompanied it, undesirable. A particularly successful administrator hoped to terminate his career as a governor or even governor-general.[19]

Some administrators were undistinguished, and most of those at the lower levels of the hierarchy were known only to colleagues and colonists. A few, such as Paul Doumer and Albert Sarraut, gained fame in their lifetimes. One of the most honoured, although his life was cut short by war, was Joost Van Vollenhoven. Born in 1877 in the Netherlands, Van Vollenhoven moved with his parents to Algeria in 1886. After earning a law degree in Algiers, he studied at the *Ecole Coloniale* and completed a doctorate in law. Van Vollenhoven taught at the *Ecole Coloniale* and worked on the staff of the Minister for Colonies, where he quickly rose to become secretary-general of the ministry in 1903 and director of colonial finances two years later. He then moved to Africa as

secretary-general to the government of the AEF; after a brief return to the minister's staff, he became secretary-general of Indochina
and, briefly, acting governor-general. At the exceptionally young
age of 28, Van Vollenhoven was appointed governor of Guinea;
soon he was governor-general of the AOF. At the beginning of
the First World War, Van Vollenhoven enlisted as a lowly sergeant in the French forces, declining the first-class passage back
to France to which his position entitled him: 'It is not the governor
who returns to France, but Sergeant Van Vollenhoven going to
join the army', he said. After being wounded in 1915, he was
offered a position with the chief of staff of the French military;
Van Vollenhoven refused and returned to the front. Early in 1918
he resigned as titular governor-general in protest against the nomi-
nation of a commissioner of French troops in black Africa, who
was given the rank of governor-general – Van Vollenhoven argued that the governor-generalship could not be divided between
himself and another man. The prime minister refused his resignation. Van Vollenhoven, now a captain, assumed command of a
Moroccan infantry company on the front lines, where he was killed
in July 1918.[20]

The memoirs of administrators provide valuable accounts of
their duties and attitudes. A number spent their retirement writing such reminiscences; some are largely self-aggrandising mono-
logues with little literary or historical merit, while others are fine
eyewitness records of colonial society. They recall how their curi-
osity about Africa or Asia was awakened by colonial novels, illustrated newspapers or the exploits of explorers. The empire loomed
as an alternative to a humdrum existence in France, a way of
serving the mother-country, and a career with potentially rapid
advancement. For many, the initial preparation in the metropole,
or even stays in colonial cities, were a way of marking time until
they could reach the distant postings they craved. In remote outposts, they became 'the true chiefs of the empire' (in Robert
Delavignette's phrase) and 'kings of the bush' (as Hubert
Deschamps described them). Alone and still largely inexperienced,
they relished the challenges of administration and the power that
went with it. They necessarily became jacks-of-all-trades, taking
care of administrative paperwork, going for tours of their districts, resolving personal problems, entertaining visitors. Their
memoirs underline the extraordinary variety of their duties and
responsibilities, a source of contentment and disappointment. They

had to develop competence in domains ranging from accountancy to engineering, agronomy to transport, and they had to master
the intricacies of colonial law and administrative procedures. Their
staffs were small, instructions from Paris often vague, and coun-
sel lacking. They needed a deft touch to work with bureaucratic
superiors, colonists and indigenous leaders, and they required
the determination to enforce compliance with their decisions. Many
made a concerted effort to learn local languages and inform themselves about the cultures of the people in their charge, and all
seem to have developed a great attachment to the countries where
they lived. The rewards for their work were often illness, fatigue
and frustration, but satisfaction at projects accomplished, the company of their colleagues (and often the comfort of local women)
and a sense of fulfilling the *mission civilisatrice* provided compensation. All were imbued with the ideals of empire, but many were
also aware of its anomalies and ironies.[21]

Women in the Colonies

'Colonising was an essentially masculine act', according to two
historians of women in the French empire. The very acts of colonisation – exploration, conquest, development of natural resources,
pacification of indigenes, the governance of new domains – were
associated in nineteenth- and early twentieth-century thought with
the male gender. Most official agents of expansion, army and navy
troops and government bureaucrats, were men, as were priests
and almost all traders. Women remained largely absent in exploration and conquest and rare in the early years of occupation.
The military and administration did not encourage men to take
their wives or families to the colonies; until the early 1900s, the
Banque de l'Indochine, among other colonial businesses, did not
allow its employees (all of whom were men) to be married. In
remote outposts and zones considered dangerous, European women
were not to be seen. By the end of the nineteenth century, only
the larger concentrations of Europeans in Algeria, Indochina, New
Caledonia and some of the bigger black African cities had a significant female component.

The women who lived in the colonies in the late 1800s and
early 1900s, with the exception of Algeria, were generally wives
of higher-ranking administrators or businessmen, nuns or an ex-

ceptionally small number of professional women, usually nurses or teachers. Among transported prisoners, women were also rare: Cayenne in 1866, for instance, counted only 240 women prisoners compared to 16 800 men, while only 400 women convicts numbered among the thousands of prisoners sent to New Caledonia in the 15 years after 1870. Attempts by the government to round up orphan girls for the colonies met with almost no success, and other attempts to recruit women migrants fared little better. In 1897, a French Society for the Emigration of Women to the Colonies was established and within a year claimed to have found 400 to 500 candidates for settlement, but only a dozen actually migrated. Yet in 1900, a book on *La Femme aux colonies* assured interested women that the empire would provide a hospitable home: 'A woman who arrives in Tonkin with a trade is sure of success. . . . There are no [European] women in Tonkin who fail to marry.' The sex ratio between men and women was heavily weighted in favour of men – there were about 20 European women for 200 European men in Gabon in the early part of the twentieth century – and this imbalance seemed to offer partners for women migrants intending marriage. Few were interested in trying their chances alone in the empire, even if colonialists promised professional advancement, husbands and happiness. Heterosexual men in the colonies, themselves often only short-term residents, might yearn for European wives but most made do with indigenous concubines or prostitutes who haunted military camps.

Indeed tropical life was difficult for women, subject to the many exotic diseases which men could catch and threatened by other health problems as well. Some women recorded that hot climates disturbed their menstrual cycles; women risked great danger in childbirth because of the scarcity of doctors and medicines, at least until better care arrived in the last decades of empire. Women suffered from lack of companionship in isolated postings or absence from husbands gone away on tours of duty. Many women found their status ambiguous, especially in Islamic societies where women were generally veiled and cloistered. By contrast, in Polynesia, French women may have seemed curiously prim and proper compared with local women.

Women professionals usually received less pay than men for equal work; although the Faculty of Medicine in Algiers awarded a degree to a woman as early as 1895, even decades later women physicians earned three to four times less than their male colleagues. Women undoubtedly faced other overt or subtle forms of personal and professional discrimination as well. Nevertheless, women professionals achieved distinction. Dr Françoise Legey, for instance, directed an infirmary in Algiers which handled 20 000 consultations with local patients a year in the first decade of the twentieth century. Legey later moved to Morocco, where her clinic in Marrakesh saw 60 000 patients annually. Other women set up workshops or carried out humanitarian activities. In settler colonies, women worked as labourers on farms and vineyards alongside their husbands. Some women found employment in traditionally 'feminine' occupations as seamstresses, librarians, music teachers or midwives; there were also women shopkeepers. A particularly large cohort were missionaries, and Catholic nuns were a familiar presence throughout the colonies. Several female congregations were created primarily for colonial service, such as Mother Javouhey's religious order and Lavigerie's 'White Sisters'. Nuns worked both in large cities and in remote areas, generally specialising in education and medical care. In sub-Saharan Africa, Indochina and the islands, they recruited numerous local women for religious orders.

These independent professional women, and the wives who accompanied husbands to the colonies, were supposed to be dutiful auxiliaries in the colonial effort. They enjoyed few legal or political rights, but then women in metropolitan France did not gain the suffrage until 1945. They faced numerous obligations, and were expected to be guardians of morality, loyal spouses and mothers, the keepers of hearth and home, and informal social workers. Few had training for their work and they were often ill-prepared for the colonies. Some were undoubtedly spoiled by the presence of domestic servants and the prestige they enjoyed simply by being French and white. Most, at least until the post-Second World War period, lived within the confines of their assigned roles, seldom enjoying the independence or opportunities afforded to men.[22]

Isabelle Eberhardt

The single best known woman in the French empire was probably Isabelle Eberhardt, born in 1877 in Geneva. Her mother was of German and Russian background; her father, either the aristo-

cratic Russian general who wed her mother or a former Ortho-
dox priest, amateur anarchist philosopher and tutor to the couple's
children who ran off to Switzerland with her. He taught her
French, Russian and a smattering of Arabic, which along with
Pierre Loti's *Le Roman d'un spahi* awakened her fascination with
the Levant. She made friends with a Turkish diplomat in Switzerland, and through a newspaper advertisement found a pen-pal in
North Africa, a French officer. Her interest in the Muslim world
grew stronger when one of her brothers joined the French Foreign
Legion.

Shortly before her twentieth birthday, Eberhardt and her mother
travelled to Bône, so Eberhardt could be nearer her brother and
her correspondent. Both women converted to Islam. Although
Eberhardt's mother died soon afterwards, she stayed in Africa.
Dressed as a man, Eberhardt journeyed south to the Sahara under
the name Si Mahmoud. Although Maghrebins saw through her
disguise, she found a warm welcome thanks to her knowledge of
Arabic and the Koran. Eberhardt was soon initiated into one of
the semi-secret Muslim confraternities which wielded great influence, and rivalled each other for power in the desert.

The next few years saw Eberhardt travelling in Algeria and Tunisia, making trips to Geneva to attend to family affairs, and sailing to France to see her ex-Legionnaire brother. Thought to be
wealthy, Eberhardt was in fact penurious, beseeching patrons for
money, contracting loans and welcoming small sums sent from
Russia by her mother's husband or given to her by friends in
French literary circles. When in North Africa, she continued her
study of Muslim culture, started writing stories and sketches of
Arabic life, indulged in hashish and anisette liquor and began a
romance with an Algerian sergeant in the French *spahi* corps.

On one trip to the desert, as Eberhardt was received by the
leader of a Muslim sect, a North African man tried to kill her.
She escaped with several wounds, recovered in a French hospital
and left on another voyage. The trial of her assailant forced
Eberhardt to return to the scene of the crime, where she experienced a spiritual episode which she said turned her into a mys-
tic. Although she pleaded for mercy for her attacker, he was
sentenced to hard labour for life. Rumours circulated that the
head of Eberhardt's own confraternity had set up the attack in
order to besmirch its rivals, or that French officials had masterminded a plot against her. Outspoken sympathy for Arabs,

conversion to Islam, her practice of wearing men's clothes, and legendary smoking, drinking and swearing hardly endeared Eberhardt to the French. At the trial, authorities informed Eberhardt – still a Russian citizen – that she was to be expelled from French North Africa.

Eberhardt's Algerian lover joined her in France, where they married. Since his rank gave the Algerian French citizenship, and marriage extended citizenship to Eberhardt, she now had the right to return to North Africa. The couple settled in a small Algerian town, where Eberhardt's husband worked as communal secretary. She became a journalist, and her articles earned the antipathy of French residents; she condemned the 'imbecile Europeans who poison the country with their presence ... indiscreet, arrogant beings who imagine they have the right to make everything resemble their own ugly effigy'. She continued work on a novel and a collection of stories. Whenever possible, she went into the desert.

Eberhardt found herself on the border between Algeria and Morocco in 1903. At Colomb-Béchar, she met Lyautey, who took a liking to the non-conformist Russian-French-Muslim writer; she warmed to the aristocratic officer who displayed such interest in Islam and North Africa. Lyautey informally employed Eberhardt for intelligence missions. She soon became entangled with a Moroccan religious confraternity which either offered her hospitality or held her hostage. Suffering from malaria, she managed to reach a hospital in Algeria. She remained in Aïn Sefra, joined by her husband, but within months drowned in a freak flood in 1904, at the age of 27. Lyautey chose her tombstone.[23]

Colonial Life

Few women or men in the empire had a life as colourful as that of Eberhardt.[24] Only a few of the overseas French made great fortunes or lived in luxury. Disease took a huge toll on Europeans who fell victim to malaria, yellow fever, dengue fever, sleeping sickness and leprosy, as well as other illnesses.[25] Warfare, attacks by hostile peoples and frequent accidents in deserts, jungles or coral-reefed islands often spelled death. Medical care was often inadequate, and incapacitation could end a colonial career.[26]

Working conditions were harsh. Most settlers in the 1800s and early 1900s had to build and maintain their own houses, clear forests or bushland for farms, and set up their own shops or offices. Drought, floods, plagues of locusts and other natural disasters destroyed crops. Saturation of markets and volatile prices for primary products limited sales and could bring bankruptcy, a fate many suffered in the 1930s. Entrepreneurs found capital and regular labour difficult to procure. Many colonists were deeply indebted to traders or bankers. Until well into the twentieth century, colonists collected no social security benefits – family allowances, pensions, superannuation – and even when a welfare system was set up in metropolitan France, benefits did not always extend to the empire. Subsidies for passage to the colonies or materials for farming or business were quickly exhausted.

Social life was limited in most colonies, though cities such as Saigon and Algiers provided activities similar to those of French provincial centres. The cultural life of theatres, art galleries, concert-halls and, later, cinemas, even in bigger colonial towns, was slim. In more remote outposts, French expatriates might spend weeks or months without sight of another European, and not all enjoyed such isolation and solitude. Returning to France was a seldom-experienced pleasure and entailed a lengthy journey – in the late 1800s, journey by steamship from France to colonies in Asia or the Pacific required six or seven weeks of travel. Mail arrived infrequently, and letters and newspapers were out of date. Settlers knew they were viewed with, at best, suspicion by the indigenous populations among whom they lived, and generally regarded with condescension by residents of the metropole. Many expatriates took refuge in alcohol, opium or hashish, or simply gave in to lethargy and torpor.

A few colonists earned a great deal of money and had the material benefits to show for it. An upper class of business people, officials, military officers and professionals lived in the larger colonial settlements. Algiers and Hanoi played home to big bankers, wealthy traders, powerful lawyers, distinguished professors and other notables. There were rubber planters in Indochina, large landowners in Algeria and proprietors of sugar plantations in the Antilles; some fitted the stereotype of the rich colonist dressed in immaculate white suit, shaded by the veranda of his mansion, planning his next business venture, dinner party or trip to France, with wife and concubine, employees and staff at his beck and call. Such exemplars of colonial success were not so numerous as the public liked to believe.

The rich and the less well-to-do did enjoy benefits of colonial life. Colonists attracted by adventure, exotic locales and faraway places flourished, providing they possessed the mettle to confront their new situations. Poor migrants sometimes acquired the land, money and social status they lacked in France. Settlers of modest means could afford servants, including cleaners, cooks, child-minders and the ever-present 'boy' who served as the factotum of colonial households. Even the poorest migrants felt superior to the 'savages' and 'primitives' surrounding them, and they lorded over the natives with power and privilege which they could never have enjoyed in France. By the early twentieth century, better medical care, more rapid transport, the growth of cities and the development of infrastructures had reduced hardships of the past. By the 1950s, prosperous European neighbourhoods of many colonial cities differed little from similar suburbs in France. Such French domains as Morocco, with fine scenery, plentiful jobs, and proximity to France, provided agreeable habitats for expatriates.[27]

Big-game hunting and fishing, treks through the bush, membership in clubs, gatherings at cafés, official ceremonies and the passage of visitors provided recreation. Those with cultural inclinations became amateur or professional writers or painters. The magnificent landscapes which brought tourists to Africa, Asia and the islands lay at the colonists' door. Sport occupied much leisure time. Horse races took place in Algeria soon after the French conquest, yacht and canoe clubs existed in North Africa as early as the 1860s, cycle racing and boxing were popular for participants and spectators, soccer teams were organised in colonies such as Algeria and New Caledonia by 1910.[28]

The empire also presented sexual opportunities.[29] European and indigenous prostitutes set up casual brothels outside military camps and followed soldiers on campaigns. Rape of local women undoubtedly occurred. Colonial cities had *quartiers réservés* of whorehouses and cabarets, and certain streets of the kasbah were congregation spots for prostitutes. Many single Frenchmen had affairs, of shorter or longer duration, with indigenous women. *Mariage à la mode du pays* – recognised liaisons between white men and black women – had been common in Africa since the 1600s, though by later centuries not so openly celebrated or publicly enjoyed as in earlier periods. The scarcity of European women in Africa during the 'new imperialism' led many men to look to African women for sexual companionship, and a number of Europeans probably took particular pleasure in relations with exotic women. In Indochina, European men often kept a concubine (*congaï*), who sometimes lived in an outbuilding on the European's property. Men of homosexual orientation were able to find sexual partners among local populations as well.

Colonial officials took a tolerant view of Frenchmen's sexual dalliances, seeing opportunities for relations as a release for expatriates' sexual desires, a way to keep men satisfied in the colonies. Indeed some authorities viewed interethnic sexual relations as a subtle way of courting favour among non-European populations and socialising indigenes to European ways. Missionaries, however, bemoaned lax tropical morals, and doctors worried about the high incidence of venereal disease. The arrival of larger numbers of women, including settlers' and administrators' wives, curbed some of the sexual licence, although brothels and informal liaisons continued to flourish.

A major by-product of sexual partnerships between European men and indigenous women were *métis*, or 'mixed-breed', children. Several prominent colonialists, such as General Alfred Dodds, a *métis* from Senegal who established French outposts on the Gulf of Guinea, were of mixed parentage; Governor Faidherbe recognised the son he had with an African woman. Recognition of a *métis* by the French father, through legal marriage or declaration of parentage, gave the child French citizenship (and, before the abolition of slavery, freed him or her from servitude). The *métis* in some colonies emerged as a powerful intermediate class between Europeans and indigenes. *Métis* dominated the professional classes in the Antilles and Réunion, where they won election to local assemblies and the French parliament. The *métis* of French Polynesia (called *demis*, or 'halves') increasingly dominated economic and political life. French education was more easily available to *métis* than to 'full-blooded' indigenes, and the administration gave them preference in employment over non-Europeans.

Not all *métis* enjoyed a happy life. Illegitimate or unrecognised *métis* children in Africa or Asia, like other indigenes, lacked citizenship and the vote until after the Second World War. *Métis* were sometimes treated as outcasts by both the French and their mothers' compatriots. Some felt torn between two cultures, at home in neither. Nationalists suspected *métis* of collaboration with the French, while the French feared their support for pro-independence movements. *Métis* were the butt of jokes and the object of cruel caricatures in colonial literature. Racists clamoured about degeneration in French blood because of sexual unions with inferior foreigners and saw *métis* as a diabolical and dangerous hybrid. Discrimination caused some *métis* to deny their African or Asian heritage and 'pass' as European, or to flee their home villages or countries. By their mixed bloodlines and cultures *métis* embodied the legacy of the colonial epoch.[30] When other French residents departed at the conclusion of their tours of duty, or when their fortunes had been made (or lost), or when independence arrived, the *métis* remained as a permanent reminder of the French presence overseas.

5 The Uses of Empire

One of the principles of colonialism was that the empire should be of use to France. Colonialists ardently believed that colonies must return profits. Colonies should provide commercial advantages as sources of raw materials, markets for exports and destinations for investments. French technological and industrial expertise should find a chance to undertake great projects in the colonies, and business should find opportunities for trade. Some of the colonies should provide land for settlement; colonies might also offer a place of exile and rehabilitation for wrongdoers. The colonies should serve as a reservoir of labour for enterprises throughout the empire (or even at home) and soldiers for the military. The colonies should be strategic outposts for the armed forces. The colonies should increase the prestige and power of France, maintaining its position in the first rank of the world's nations and giving it leverage over rivals both in Europe and the wider world.

If the colonies failed to provide such benefits naturally, the government must ensure that they became profitable through a concerted policy of economic development, regulations on tariffs and trade, pacification of rebellious populations and support for settlers. If a colony showed little return in the present, perhaps it held potential for the future: colonies were long-term investments. As a last resort, however, colonialists admitted that a truly unprofitable colony might be sold or traded for a more promising possession. In short, each colony was intended to present some economic, political or strategic advantage to France either now or in the future.

It is extremely difficult, if not impossible, to draw up a general balance sheet to prove if, and when, a particular colony, or the whole empire, was of benefit to France. In some cases, colonies manifestly did not provide much monetary reward. Uninhabited islands, such as Clipperton and the sub-Antarctic islands, produced no appreciable economic profit for France, and the small volume of raw materials or exports credited to several others (such as the tiny amount of copra harvested in Wallis and Futuna) were trivial in any general accounting. Yet the very places which brought no gain to business sometimes held interest for other reasons; geopoliticians and military strategists stressed the significance of sub-Antarctic islands, and missionaries pointed proudly to the conversion of Wallisians and Futunans.

Outposts largely devoid of interest at the time of takeover later developed into more useful possessions. Guyane, where a punishing tropical climate and endemic diseases condemned settlement for over two centuries after France's first occupation in the 1600s, excited gold-rush fever for a brief period in the 1800s. Dry and inhospitable Djibouti, with little attraction when France obtained Obock in the 1870s, developed as an important Red Sea port and terminus for the rail line from Ethiopia. Makatéa, a relatively distant island even from Tahiti, became a profitable source of phosphate 60 years after France raised the flag there.

Size was no guarantee of worth. In the *ancien régime*, small sugar islands in the Caribbean were more valuable than the cold plains of Canada. By contrast, the expanses of the Sahara and Sahel held few resources of interest to France and presented formidable obstacles to exploitation; nomadic tribes were largely exempted from military service and so did not even provide manpower for the army. Madagascar, an island larger than France itself, never returned the profits which colonial promoters anticipated, and efforts to develop the Congo met with long-term failure. Guyane and Terre Adélie, which remain French possessions, continue to prove resistant to development.

Imports, Exports, Investments

In economic terms, colonies held particular significance as producers of raw materials which did not exist in France but which were in demand by French manufacturers or consumers. Tropical goods comprised the first category of such products. The search

for these commodities had motivated the 'spice trade' – a mis-
leading term for trade in a variety of materials from culinary spices
to rare woods, perfume essences, gums, resins and much else –
of an earlier age, and they continued to attract commercial interest.
Many were foodstuffs which could not be grown in France (or
only in limited zones and restricted quantities), but which were
readily available in warmer climates. For instance, France had been
a major European consumer of coffee since the end of the 1600s,
and planters attempted to grow coffee in such widely-separated
colonies as the Antilles, Réunion and New Caledonia. But western Africa, especially the Côte d'Ivoire, became the major exporter of coffee to France by the late nineteenth century. Cocoa,
a critical raw material in France's confectionery industry, represented another major import from sub-Saharan Africa. Spices, such
as vanilla from Madagascar and Tahiti, remained sought-after items.
Sugar reigned as the quintessential tropical commodity in the
ancien régime, although beet sugar later competed with cane sugar,
sugar from Martinique, Guadeloupe and Réunion still supplied
the French market. Rice, which the French consumed in increasing quantities and introduced as a basic foodstuff throughout the
empire, arrived from Madagascar and Indochina. The French prized
such tropical fruits as bananas and coconuts – rare and expensive delicacies in the 1800s. The perishability of fruits limited large-
scale transport until the development of refrigerated cargo ships.
But colonies near France, such as Morocco, provided citrus fruits,
and western Africa and the Caribbean islands produced bananas;
even more exotic mangoes, papayas and pineapples came from
North Africa or the West Indies. Raw materials from the tropics
entered into the manufacture of other foodstuffs. A prime example
was margarine, developed as a substitute for butter during the
Franco-Prussian War; colonial supplies of peanut oil (from west
Africa) and coconut oil (often from the South Pacific) were necessary to the manufacture of margarine. France acquired foodstuffs
from the waters surrounding its colonies as well; the single export from Saint-Pierre and Miquelon was codfish, a staple for black
populations of the West Indies. In a special category was colonial
alcohol. Rum made from cane in the West Indies and Réunion
supplied the bulk of French consumption. Although metropolitan France was a major producer of wine, the North African colonies
provided a cheaper *vin ordinaire*; wine accounted for four-fifths
of Algeria's export earnings.

Other agricultural products had industrial uses, demand for which increased with industrialisation in the 1800s. Cotton was important for textiles; although the colonies never became a prime source, attempts were made in Tahiti to grow cotton in the 1860s. Copra (the dried meat of coconuts) and groundnuts were important sources of oils used as machine lubricants and soap (as well as in food production); in the 1800s, France was Europe's premier importer of copra. Groundnuts were the major export of parts of west Africa, copra the leading product of several islands. Rubber achieved great importance at the end of the nineteenth century for bicycle and automobile tyres and products ranging from linings for machine parts to condoms. Some rubber came from central Africa, and rubber production became the major economic activity in Indochina.

Minerals were extremely valuable colonial products. Precious metals, other than gold in Guyane and a little silver in North Africa, were in short supply in French colonies, but other minerals counted among major colonial exports. Nickel came from New Caledonia. Used as an alloy in steel and vital in the construction of ships and armaments, nickel's value increased dramatically with the second industrial revolution of the last quarter of the nineteenth century, the invention of steamships and the growing militarisation of Europe. New Caledonia possesses one of the world's largest deposits of nickel and was the world's greatest exporter at the end of the 1800s. Phosphate was crucial in production of artificial fertilisers; in Tunisia, Morocco and Makatéa, France had large and accessible deposits of ore. The African colonies supplied iron, lead, bauxite and tin, and tin came from Indochina, too.

Many other raw materials – such as hardwoods from Gabon and perfume essences from the Comoros Islands – figured on lists of colonial exports. In certain cases, colonial production supplied most of French needs; in other cases, it supplemented supplies from France itself or areas outside the empire. Colonial commodities were not always of the highest quality, the most easily available or least expensive by comparison with those of other suppliers. Coffee from Central and South America, for instance, competed with coffee from the empire, and some traders and consumers preferred Latin American blends. Furthermore, substantial intercolonial rivalry existed: different colonies in French western and equatorial Africa, as well as islands in the Caribbean and the Indian and Pacific Oceans, competed to ship coffee to France. Colonial and metropolitan products occasionally competed directly, as occurred with sugar.

Colonies lacked the infrastructure to produce manufactured goods. French officials generally felt that colonies ought not to develop a manufacturing sector except for specific food-processing industries (such as beer-making) and the production of some goods for local consumption. Not until the 1920s did policy-makers seriously debate the merits of colonial industrialisation, and opinion remained divided. Only rare manufactured products, chief among them 'native handicrafts', usually artisan crafts, penetrated the French market, and imports of factory-made goods seldom if ever theatened French producers.

By contrast, France exported enormous quantities of manufactured goods to the colonies. Simple articles, such as woven textiles, baubles and beads, mirrors and metal instruments such as knives and scissors had filled the coffers of early explorers and conquerors, who exchanged the items for tropical goods and the labour of indigenous peoples. Modest wares and even trinkets had purchased men and women during the slave trade. As French imperial control expanded, so did the introduction of European products. This 'marketing' created a demand for manufactured goods, which could be sold to indigenes for whom machine-made items and metal goods were as exotic as were tropical products to Europeans. Every area of French conquest boasted a network of trading posts, from urban emporia to tiny general stores in the bush where Africans, Asians and islanders purchased French goods of enormous variety: clothing and fabrics, leather shoes (a new item of apparel for many), hats, watches and jewellery, cigarettes and matches, furniture and housewares, work tools and farming, fishing and cooking utensils, glassware and metal goods, paper products and almost everything else. Novelties which later conquered markets included radios and bicycles. Many European commodities had great practical use, while others – such as the European suit of clothes, shoes, hat and watch – symbolised the prestige of foreign luxury and Western modernity.

European settlers formed a substantial market for manufactured goods, especially in colonies where Europeans were numerous. Expatriates yearned for goods from 'home', wares which they either bought from local traders or purchased directly from the mail-order catalogues of metropolitan department stores. Sales of tropical requisites ranging from pith helmets and mosquito netting to consumer durables thrived. Employees posted to the empire arrived with heavy trunks packed with goods they considered indispensable for colonial life. Settlers and, to a lesser extent, indigenous populations developed a taste for newfangled devices, such as automobiles, though few non-Europeans had the means to buy motorcars. One special category of export was weapons for arming both settlers and local populations often engaged in warfare with each other.

Colonial businesses purchased large quantities of French exports. Planters needed seed, chemicals and farming utensils. Miners required tools with which to extract minerals and refine them for export. Almost all the equipment used to develop local economies came from France. Public works programmes necessitated vast amounts of imported goods for the construction and furnishing of schools and hospitals, offices, barracks and private dwellings. Governors' palaces, city halls and cathedrals could not be built without at least some French materials. The construction of harbour facilities and roadways similarly demanded French machinery. A great railway building programme required even more materials from France – machinery to level ground and cut through forests, rails and cross-tyres, materials for bridges and tunnels, locomotives and carriages, signalling equipment, furnishings for train stations and ticket-offices, uniforms for employees. Colonial development thus not only responded to a desire to market local resources but itself provided a major market for French exports.

Metropolitan sales to the colonies included 'invisible exports', a host of services ranging from technical expertise, so important in public works projects, and agronomy, to insurance, shipping and banking. Among the major French enterprises involved in the colonies were shippers such as the Messageries Maritimes, which served Asia and the South Pacific, and the Compagnie Transatlantique, which sent ships to the Americas and West Indies. Although neither restricted its business to the French empire, colonial service helped to make the companies two of the world's largest shipping firms. Capital was a prime French export, invested in trade, public works programmes, farming or mining, or lent directly to private settlers or colonial governments. Each colony had banks which shifted funds from the metropole to the empire, provided private accounts, and financed local projects. The tertiary sector, such as shipping and banking, gave jobs to settlers, employees sent from the metropole, and some indigenes.

Colonial Economic Policy

In order to make the greatest profit from the empire, programmes designed to make the best possible use of local resources were needed. During most of the nineteenth century, the government had little in the way of a coherent and coordinated programme of development. The colonial lobby regularly agitated for public and private investment to develop possessions, improve economic infrastructure, locate adequate labour, and favour settlement of French men and women with the appropriate technical expertise, business acumen and moral fibre.

The government expressed support for such objectives but initially did relatively little to stimulate colonial economies. Politicians indeed were adverse to spending large sums on development, and parliament in 1900 passed a law requiring, in principle, that colonies should foot the bills for their expenses from their own revenues. Profit-making was left largely to private business, while the government busied itself with the considerable task of extending empire, subduing territories already conquered, and putting in place colonial administration.

Yet the central government could not shun responsibility for such areas as monetary and tariff policies. Promoters demanded that French trade and tariff systems be designed in order to protect colonial production from foreign competition and secure colonial products access – and preferably privileged access – to metropolitan markets. French purchasers were not always so willing to accommodate colonial products, either because they competed with commodities produced domestically or because other suppliers provided similar materials at better prices. Colonial tariff policy was a continual tug-of-war between defenders of free trade and advocates of protection. France had entered a period of free trade in the 1860s, but the economic difficulties of the late 1870s and 1880s led to the erection of high tariff barriers. France nonetheless set up a customs union with Algeria in 1884 and with Indochina three years later.

Under a comprehensive system instituted in 1892, Algeria, Indochina, Tunisia, Madagascar, Gabon and the *vieilles colonies* were assimilated into the French tariff zone; products could circulate freely between these possessions and the metropole. The 'special regime non-assimilated' colonies – the AOF except for Dahomey and the Côte d'Ivoire, Saint-Pierre and Miquelon, New Caledonia and the EFO – admitted French products without tariffs; but their exports to France were taxed at the same rate as 'most favoured nation' foreign goods. The 'open-door colonies' – Morocco, the AEF except Gabon, and other outposts – had low levels of tariffs on all imports and exports (although there were complicated exceptions). French colonies, in general, could trade with each other without tariff liability. The system sparked ire among producers of certain colonial commodities; New Caledonian settlers were particularly angered that their exports were assessed duty in France. Campaigns for tariff revision met with some success.

Officials in the colonies and in Paris, as well as private entrepreneurs, promoted endless projects to develop colonial resources and make money. Individual businessmen were often the first Frenchmen in distant outposts and spearheaded the establishment of protectorates or annexation. The two Lamberts in Djibouti and the Comoros and James Higginson in the New Hebrides, through their trading and pastoral activities, almost single-handedly represented French interests and lobbied for takeover of these outposts. Merchants, planters, wine-growers, pastoralists, miners, shippers and bankers formed a powerful and vocal segment of the expatriate community, even when their interests clashed. Despite criticism of businessmen for alleged rapacity and exploitation of indigenous labour (and in other cases, for their supposed lethargy), most colonialists saw businessmen as crucial to the imperial effort.

Metropolitan business had a major stake in the empire. The business community in port cities and in some manufacturing centres played a large role in promoting expansion and reaped many of the rewards of conquest. Traders from La Rochelle, Nantes and Bordeaux had gained their fortunes from the slave trade and commerce between Europe and the Americas; they maintained interest in the *vieilles colonies* and often expanded into Africa. Businessmen in Marseille avidly promoted expansion in Africa, and Marseille became France's largest port partly on account of trade with the Maghreb and sub-Saharan Africa. The Marseille Chamber of Commerce, which included businessmen involved in colonial endeavours, was a powerful institution in Marseille and in the colonial lobby. The Chamber of Commerce of Lyon, a major textile centre, promoted colonialism in Indochina. Companies throughout France which needed raw materials from the colonies or which saw the empire as a promising market for manufactured goods pressured for expansion.

A few metropolitan companies became almost totally dependent on the empire for supplies or sales, but a larger number got involved in colonial business simply because of the profit-making opportunities the colonies afforded. More than 400 French companies formed the French Colonial Union (*Union Coloniale Française*) in 1893, the peak organisation of businesses involved in the empire. The union, with its fortnightly colonial journal, large research library, monthly meetings, and annual banquet attended by top political and commercial leaders, stood as one of the most active of all colonial interest groups.

The government maintained close links with the Colonial Union and with businesses. Paris intervened continually if erratically in colonial economies, sometimes against the wishes of colonial and metropolitan businessmen, but often at their behest. Despite emphasis on private enterprise, it was becoming increasingly evident in the early decades of the twentieth century that the state was the motor behind colonial economies. The state determined financial policy. Paris provided funds necessary to colonial governments which, despite the principle that they should earn their own keep, seldom paid their own way. The state represented the largest overseas investor in the empire. Garrisons and the bureaucracy provided an essential market for European exports. Public works undertaken and financed by the government proved the most dynamic economic activity in many colonies and a necessary auxiliary to private business everywhere. During economic crises, only the government was able to bail out businesses or settlers on the edge of ruin, and various subsidies – passage for migrants, tax incentives for companies, government contracts – were vital. The government's land policy determined conditions by which properties could be acquired for plantations, mines or other activities. The government's policy on indigenous populations and contract workers regulated the labour market.

By the 1920s, realisation that the government could not cling to *laissez-faire* principles and allow the free hand of the market to develop colonies led to a more interventionist economic policy.

The new approach targeted the *mise en valeur* of the empire; a phrase with no exact equivalent in English, *mise en valeur* aimed at the wholesale development of the natural and human resources of the colonies. It was the brainchild of Albert Sarraut, who served at various times in both houses of the French parliament, was six times Minister for the Colonies and twice held the post of governor-general of Indochina; Sarraut was also briefly prime minister on two occasions. In a programme presented to parliament in 1921, developed in more detail in a 675-page book published in 1922, *La Mise en valeur des colonies françaises*, Sarraut argued that a concerted effort was needed to provide colonies with the necessary infrastructure to realise their potential: 'The moment has come to substitute general and precise action for isolated and uncertain directions.' Colony by colony, Sarraut listed the great resources the empire possessed. Equally long lists enumerated the requirements of colonies: port facilities and improved shipping, roadways and railways, electrification and better sources of energy, more schools and hospitals. The realisation of such projects, Sarraut said, was the direct political and financial responsibility of the state. Neither private enterprise not local colonial governments could bear the weight of large-scale developments; yet without them, the empire would not provide the profits which colonialists expected.

Sarraut's proposals were never entirely implemented. Some policy-makers thought them too expensive, others believed France had more pressing priorities than colonial investment, still others disliked the interventionist government action they mandated. His ideas nevertheless exercised considerable influence in colonialist milieux and led to the assumption of a greater economic role by the state in the interwar years. They also fed into the debate on the merits or hazards of colonial industrialisation. The Depression, then the Second World War, however, made the sorts of projects Sarraut considered vital more difficult. Colonial leaders revived many of his ideas in a new *mise en valeur* after 1945. Ironically, many of Sarraut's projects were realised only in the last years before decolonisation.

Colonial Projects

Great projects for colonial development litter the history of overseas expansion. Promoters and entrepreneurs dreamed of establishing prosperous plantations, booming trade entrepôts and busy mines almost everywhere. Even grander designs tempted some colonialists. One of the wildest envisaged the creation of an inland sea in North Africa. Near the Tunisian coast French explorers had discovered several saline depressions (*chotts*) which seemed to lie below sea level. Surveys suggested that they were the remains of an ancient inland sea covering thousands of square kilometres. A canal from the seacoast at Gabès, Captain François Roudaire argued in the 1870s, could link these lakes with the Mediterranean and recreate the inland sea. Evaporation would then increase precipitation, transforming the arid climate of Tunisia and Algeria. The lakes would afford sites for new settlements and ports and provide striking proof of French technological prowess. The government appropriated funds and constituted commissions to investigate Roudaire's studies. But scientists were dubious about whether the *chotts* were below sea level and feared that the great lake might totally evaporate. Most considered the project a folly, and the proposal disappeared into filing cabinets.[1]

The construction of rail lines won more serious attention. Railway-building was a nineteenth-century passion; the train symbolised the triumph of the industrial age. Building railways represented enormous capital investments and potentially large profits; it provided employment for construction and operation of the lines. Rail networks tied together national and international markets as a vital medium for transport of materials to factories and ports. The train speeded up travel for passengers as well, making movement of workers, tourists and troops quicker, cheaper and more efficient. From the 1840s to the end of the century, a network of train lines spread over France. Not suprisingly, colonialists wanted to extend the railway throughout overseas possessions. Short rail links – for example, in the West Indies, Réunion and New Caledonia – served to transport sugar or nickel ore to ports. Projects covering hundreds or thousands of kilometres, however, seemed more exciting for the *mise en valeur* of Indochina and Africa.

The most ambitious rail line, though it was never built, was the Trans-Saharan Railway. Explorers in the mid-nineteenth century had suggested a link between Algeria and France's trading posts in sub-Saharan Africa. In 1875, a young engineer published a prospectus for a rail line which caught the attention of the Minister for Public Works. It argued that a line across the Sahara would open the desert to commerce, complete pacification of Algeria, give prestige to France and aid to eliminate slavery among Africans. Paris commissioned three studies of northern and western Africa and the Sahara. The first two proved inconclusive: the third mission, led by Paul-Xavier Flatters, came to grief when Tuaregs killed many of its members, including Flatters, in 1881. The government suspended further studies.

The 1890s saw the project resurrected, thanks to the growing influence of the colonial lobby and increasing Franco-British rivalry in Africa. Promoters suggested a great rail line stretching from the coast – Algerian politicians squabbled over whether Algiers, Oran or Bône should be the terminus – southwards into the desert. A station at Colomb-Béchar, 450 kilometres inland, would make the mineral deposits of the interior accessible and turn the town into an industrial centre. The line would then continue southwards to In-tassit, in the heart of the Sahara 1871 kilometres from the Mediterranean, before bifurcating with one trunk line heading towards Ségou and Bamako and possibly on towards Senegal, the other to Niamey or Ouagadougou and towards the Congo, or alternatively to Dahomey and the Gulf of Guinea. The AOF and AEF would thus be linked by train with Algeria. An even more ambitious promoter argued as well for the construction of a line from the central Sahara across eastern Africa to Djibouti, joining the Atlantic and the Red Sea.

The more modest project won approval, and Paris dispatched the Foureau–Lamy mission in 1898 to survey possibilities for the Trans-Saharan line. Its reports, as well as pacification of the Tuaregs, encouraged hopes for construction. Businessmen organised committees and the government commissioned further studies for the 10 000-kilometre line. Undertaking work proved more difficult, and little was achieved before the First World War brought efforts to a halt. In 1923, the government again gave the green light to the project although capital was lacking. Four years later, a new Trans-Saharan committee grouped together those interested in the project, though one official remarked acidly, 'I know no better example of the slowness with which we [French] move from an idea to its implementation than the Trans-Saharan railway'. Not until 1931, confirming such criticism, did a law lay out the line's precise route and the statutes of the operating company; the money would come from German post-war reparations payments. Critics of the Trans-Saharan still referred to it as a 'mirage', a project 'built on sand'. The Depression soon made it impossible to pursue plans for the railway.

In the late 1930s, then under the wartime Vichy government, during the reconstruction period of the late 1940s, and in 1957, with the creation of an Organisation of Saharan Regions in the dying years of the empire, promoters and policy-makers repeatedly discussed the Trans-Saharan, a project emblematic of imperial dreams which never became realities. Even after the independence of the sub-Saharan African possessions and Algeria, railway enthusiasts dug up plans for the Trans-Saharan, though to no avail.[2]

Another railway project, this one actually completed, although with great loss of life, was the Congo–Ocean line in the AEF. Colonialists argued that the *mise en valeur* of equatorial Africa necessitated a rail link between the territory's capital, Brazzaville, on the Congo River, and the Atlantic Ocean, 400 kilometres away. A river connection from the coast, via the Kouilou and Niari rivers, had proved unsatisfactory since neither river joined the Congo or could be navigated as far as Brazzaville, and shipment of products between the coast and the interior demanded long and costly porterage by human carriers. At the end of the nineteenth century, the Belgian government spent large sums building a rail-way from Léopoldville, capital of the Congo Free State, across the river from Brazzaville, to the Atlantic; the French used the Belgian line, but considered reliance on a foreign railway unacceptable.

From the mid-1890s, French teams considered building an equatorial railway and tried to select a route; after much discussion, authorities decided on a link between the port of Pointe-Noire and Brazzaville. Not until 1909 did parliament authorise the government to raise a loan to build the line, and sufficient funding was not available until 1914 – a most unpropitious year. After the First World War, Paris revived the idea for a Congo–Ocean link, new discussions took place, and in 1920 the president signed another decree authorising the railway. Work finally began early in 1921 on the first 20 kilometres of the track westwards from Brazzaville. The following year, work started at the western terminus at Pointe-Noire.

The rail line did not open until 1934. The company which won the contract encountered technical difficulties in laying tracks, especially in the central section: less than 50 kilometres of rail through hilly landscape required no fewer than 36 major viaducts and bridges, 63 smaller bridges, 12 retaining walls and 6 tunnels. Outweighing technical problems was the difficulty in finding labour, particularly in the sparsely populated western Congo. Gross over-estimates of the population had given entrepreneurs hopes of finding workers easily, but the first recruitment campaigns proved that labour was scarce. The builders, in cooperation with the colonial government, set out to find men further afield. The conditions in which they worked, and the high death toll they suffered, turned the Congo–Ocean into a blood-soaked scandal.

Railway builders looked for workers throughout the AEF, hired some from the Belgian Congo and tried importing labourers from China. Most came from the interior of the AEF as far north as Oubangui-Chari. Recruiters promised steady work and salaries, but strong-arm pressure and probably outright terror accompanied the recruitment drive. Some Africans resisted by rebellion, others escaped convoys bound for the work-sites, still others were declared unfit by doctors, and disease carried off many; a third of those initially recruited never worked on the rail. Africans opposed employment for personal and family reasons. Long journeys to the construction sites – several months of travel through dense jungles from Oubangui-Chari – and absence from home, generally for 13 to 18 months, wreaked disastrous effects on community life and subsistence farming. In the work camps, hired men found poor housing, hard labour and a dearth of food.

From 1921 to 1932, some 127 250 men worked on the Congo–Ocean railway, about one in ten men in the AEF. Approximately 16 000 died on the job. At the coastal end of the line, where work was hardest and labourers came from furthest away, a fifth of all workers died. Doctors blamed pulmonary infections, dysentery and malnutrition. Overwork and mistreatment also played a role, as did lack of medical care – until the beginning of 1926, in one camp, there was a single doctor for several thousand workers. By that time metropolitan journalists and anti-colonialists had revealed the extent of the carnage, charging (with exaggeration) that one African was killed for every railway crosstyre laid. Conditions improved somewhat during the last years of construction; by 1932, more than twenty infirmaries cared for African labourers, as well as two dispensaries reserved for the vastly smaller number of European employees.

Forty years after the first studies of a railway for the AEF, the Congo–Ocean line opened. The construction company had paid well over a billion francs for a rail line that roughly paralleled the Belgian line, which had been functioning perfectly well before the French began work. The rail failed to effect an economic revolution in the southern AEF. The Congo, living under the shadow of the failure of concessionary companies to which its development had been entrusted and the high cost of the rail, remained one of the poorer French domains.[3]

Colonial authorities pursued great rail projects elsewhere, notably the costly line from Haiphong to Yunnan, in southern China,[4] but the rail was not the only object of hopes for development and profit-making. Colonists, for instance, had great expectations for agriculture. Particular hope was invested in Morocco, where fertile coastal plains promised good terrain for crops which could be easily transported to nearby French markets. Regular droughts posed the major problem, but colonial shakers and movers predicted that Morocco would become a wheat granary for France, much as they imagined (not altogether rightly) that it had been for ancient Rome. During his tenure as French Resident-General, Lyautey, otherwise sceptical about settlement of expatriates, granted land from the public domain – properties usually expropriated from Moroccans – to French agriculturalists. Succeeding administrators encouraged settlement as well.

Over the 25 years after 1917, the government set up 1583 settlers in Morocco, adding at least 10 000 additional hectares to cultivation each year. By 1931 a quarter of a million hectares were newly tilled by sponsored colonists. A half million hectares were also settled by 1500 private colonists. The area planted in cereals rose from 1.9 million to 3 million hectares in two decades. Low yields persisted – in the best years, a hectare produced less than half the crop of a comparable area in metropolitan France – and overhead costs were high. But tariff-free exports to France absorbed the crop. Colonial wheat-farming seemed to lessen France's reliance on foreign wheat and, at the same time, advance colonisation of North Africa.

At the beginning of the 1930s, disaster struck with a plague of locusts, which destroyed 860 000 hectares. A severe drought followed, and exports fell dramatically. Wheat production could not

satisfy Moroccan demand (notwithstanding which export continued), and famine spread. Shipments of wheat met hostility from
French farmers also suffering hardship. In 1932, the government
agreed to curtail further extension of wheat-farming and to space
out exports to France to offset competition to domestic French
wheat-growers. Nevertheless, better weather produced a large surplus
of grain, which found no buyers in Morocco or in France, despite dramatically reduced prices. The dream of turning Morocco
into a granary came to an end.

Agriculturalists had meanwhile tried to solve the problem of
water shortages. Experts decided that water from the Atlas mountains could provide irrigation – 'not a drop of water should reach
the sea', a popular catch-phrase argued. In 1926, the first modern dam opened in Morocco, and technicians busily prepared
schemes for a network of dams and canals to harness the country's
water supplies. Inspiration came from a 'California model' of irrigation. Teams sent to the United States found that California,
a region of similar size, latitude and climate to Morocco, enjoyed
good fortune with production of citrus crops. Fruit became the
replacement for wheat, a new miracle crop for Morocco. The
colonial government established an agency to promote citrus crops,
published a specialised journal on fruit trees, and sent students
to study agronomy in California universities. Only 1470 hectares
were planted in commercial citrus groves, primarily orange trees,
from 1912 to 1928; by 1956, at the end of the protectorate, groves
covered 46 280 hectares. Exports of citrus fruit increased from
5000 tons in the late 1930s to 127 000 tons in the mid-1950s.

Success in fruit production led to projections of bringing 1
million new hectares under cultivation by the year 2000, an aim
which drove economic policy in Morocco over the decades before independence. Programmes undertook cultivation of previously
unused land, consolidation and redistribution of properties into
more efficient holdings, construction of dams and irrigation works,
and increased use of machinery. The creation of an Irrigation
Office symbolised the technocratic spirit of economic development which was supposed to bring prosperity and modernity to
Morocco. Large land-owners, mostly French colonists, reaped the
profits of agricultural expansion and land speculation, and Moroccan peasants paid the cost in land expropriation, flooding of
land and competition. In the zone of government-sponsored irrigation, a quarter of the land was owned by French settlers, who

accounted for 0.5 per cent of Morocco's landowners. Achievements fell short of goals in the agricultural revolution, yet the large-scale introduction of citrus crops and irrigation projects left an important agrarian legacy for independent Morocco.[5]

Doing Business in the Colonies

The government, which designed such projects as colonial railway networks, settlers such as the wheat-farmers and citrus-growers of Morocco, and private firms – such as mining, trading and shipping companies – all played a role in the economic development of the empire.[6]

The Banque de l'Indochine

One of the most powerful colonial enterprises was the Banque de l'Indochine, known as the French bank in Asia. At its zenith in the 1920s, the bank had 20 branch offices and credits of 3.5 billion francs. The official note-issuing bank for Indochina, the *comptoirs* in India and the South Pacific colonies, the bank was the major (or only) French deposit and credit institution in these possessions. It was, as well, the most important French bank in China.

The Banque de l'Indochine was one of a number of specifically colonial banks, although larger and richer than most. The government established the first colonial banks in Martinique, Guadeloupe and Réunion in 1853, and in Guyane and Senegal in 1855; their brief was to issue currency and provide credit to planters for workers' salaries after the emancipation of slaves. The new colony of Cochinchina played host to several French and British banks. Metropolitan financiers, businessmen and government officials, however, wanted a French bank able to stimulate the local economy and manage currency for the colony. In 1875, a consortium of banks founded the Banque de l'Indochine in Paris. Almost two-thirds of the capital came from three banks (the CNEP, Paribas and CIC), which also controlled the bank's board of directors. Prominent businessmen predominated among other stock-holders. The government neither invested in the bank nor had representation on its board (although it maintained a permanent commissioner at the bank). The government granted the bank rights to issue currency, a lucrative contract which made the Banque de l'Indochine the architect of colonial monetary policy. The bank could also accept deposits, make loans and engage in discounting and currency exchange.

The bank immediately opened the office in Saigon that remained the centre of its activities, and in 1876 issued the first French piastres, the colony's currency. The bank was required to hold metal piastres worth at least a third of the value of paper currency which it issued. The silver piastres in circulation (often Mexican coins) differed in value because of varying silver content, which gave wide latitude to the bank to negotiate currency rates. (The bank hired indigenous workers skilled at 'jingling piastres', judging the coins' silver content by the sound they made when dropped.) Currency transactions and note-issuing initially comprised the bulk of the bank's activity, with deposit banking a secondary concern – the Saigon office paid no interest on deposit accounts (except those of the Catholic mission in Hong Kong and the syndicate of opium-farmers).

The bank quickly became the major lender in Indochina. Some clients were European settlers, even though they remained few in number in the late 1800s. Paris encouraged loans to settlers in order to build the colonial economy; the government guaranteed repayment of loans to rice-farmers in return for a 3 per cent commission on the interest rate of 15 per cent which the bank charged. The bank lent to Chinese and Vietnamese in Indochina through the intermediary of a Chinese comprador employed by the bank. The comprador arranged loans and assured repayments in return for a salary and commission, which gave him extraordinary economic leverage and was alleged to be an opportunity for corruption. The bank also lent to French businesses, showing a clear preference for large firms and for companies in which the bank itself owned stock. These included the licensed liquor distiller, various coal companies, rail and maritime transport firms and manufacturers of such consumer products as matches and paper.

Within a decade after its establishment, the bank in Saigon, joined by a branch in Hanoi in 1886, held immense power. No French farmer, trader or industrialist could do business without recourse to its services. Meanwhile, the Pondichéry office, founded in 1877, failed to return substantial profits, although the creation of a railway between the French outpost and surrounding

British India, combined with plantations of groundnuts, foreshadowed a brighter future. By the end of the century, the bank had expanded rapidly and earned handsome profits from all its branches. From 1885 to 1898, the Banque de l'Indochine set up offices in Haiphong, Hanoi, Tourane and Phnom Penh in Indochina, Nouméa in New Caledonia and, outside the empire, in Hong Kong, Bangkok and Shanghai.

The Shanghai branch, established in 1898 at the request of the French Ministry of Foreign Affairs, was especially promising. Shanghai was the major centre for Chinese international trade; seven-eighths of China's silk exports and one-third of its tea passed through the Shanghai port. France enjoyed a large concession in the city, as did Britain, America and Japan; the Messageries Maritimes served the port; 112 French companies established offices there by 1912. In 1905 China accounted for a third of the bank's business. The Banque de l'Indochine had become the second largest foreign bank in China, although only half the size of its chief rival, the Hong Kong and Shanghai Bank. It lent to French businesses and invested heavily in real estate companies, the French firm which operated Shanghai's trams and electric lighting, and a shipping company. The bank financed a number of projects elsewhere in China and took a major role in the consortium which funded the Haiphong to Yunnan rail.

After 1900, the bank's fortunes continued to improve. New branches opened in Battambang (Cambodia), Papeete, Singapore, Djibouti, Vladivostok and Guangzhouwan. The volume of business it transacted increased seven times over from 1898 to 1924, dividends paid on its stock soared sixfold from 1905 to 1928, and its own stock portfolio diversified to incorporate almost fifty companies in Indochina. The bank became the major financier of the *mise en valeur* of French Asian and Oceanic colonies in the 1920s, including the dramatic growth in rice and rubber plantations in Indochina. It also continued to finance public works projects, such as the Trans-Indochinese railway from Hanoi to Saigon completed in 1936.

Such dynamism provoked criticism as well as praise. Small businessmen and settlers charged that the bank was less willing to finance their activities than to collaborate with big businesses which guaranteed high profits. They said the bank was too financially conservative, too lax in taking advantage of possibilities for expansion. (No office was opened in Laos, they pointed out, until

1953.) Others were concerned about the cosy relationship between the bank and the government. Almost all commentators felt that the bank was more interested in its own profits than in the overall welfare of the colonies. In short, the Banque de l'Indochine seemed the symbol of a successful, if rather monopolistic, link between finance, industry and government at the apex of imperialism.

Criticism increased during the Depression. As prices fell and many settlers abandoned their properties, the bank acted ruthlessly in Indochina, refusing to renegotiate loans and, despite the depreciation of the piastre, insisting that the nominal value of loans be repaid. As individuals and companies went bankrupt, the bank assessed the value of the holdings they were forced to put up for sale, and often purchased land, buildings and firms owned by ruined colonists. The bank bought half of the buildings forcibly sold to pay off its clients' debts, acquiring the sites at advantageous prices because of lack of other bidders with access to credit. The bank obtained stock-holdings in 27 new companies during the Depression as well. Accusations of exploitation were ignored, and plans by the government in the late 1930s to end the bank's note-issuing privileges were thwarted. The Depression, so disastrous for colonists, was good business for the bank.

During the Second World War, when pro-Vichy governors ruled Indochina, the bank carried on business as usual. Management at head office in Paris divided between collaborationists and *Résistants*, but a close relationship with the Vichy government and German occupation forces tarnished its reputation. After the war, the bank tried to reclaim its old position, but the colonial war in Indochina endangered its status in the Far East. The victory of Mao Zedong's Communist revolution led to closure of the bank's offices in China. In the early 1950s, scandal erupted when the bank was accused of trafficking in piastres, working with shady money-traders who profited from the disparity between the official conversion rate (fixed at 17 piastres to the franc in 1945) and the unofficial rate (between 8 and 10 piastres) current in Indochina and Hong Kong. Partly in response to such allegations, the government abolished the bank's note-issuing privilege in Indochina in 1953; this was of little worry to the bank since most of its profits came from loans and investments. By the early 1950s, the bank apparently realised that France would never be able to re-establish control over Indochina. It began to withdraw its investments and opened offices in two more promising locations, Saudi Arabia and South Africa. The new branches, and expanded operations in metropolitan France, absorbed capital transferred from Indochina. Within five years after the French withdrawal from Vietnam in 1954, the company had amortised its losses.

The Banque de l'Indochine continued its activities in South Vietnam (under the name of the Banque Française de l'Asie) until the Communist victory there in 1975, and it exercised note-issuing rights in the French territories in Oceania until 1967. At that date only 5 per cent of its business came from Indochina, 4 per cent from the Pacific islands; two-thirds of its business was transacted in Europe. The bank had made a successful transition from being colonial to becoming a metropolitan bank, although one which maintained considerable overseas stakes and retained an aura of exoticism inherited from the past. The Banque de l'Indochine fell on hard times and in the mid-1970s was absorbed by the *Compagnie Française de Suez* into an institution bearing the name of Indosuez. As a postscript to its retreat from the empire, the bank withdrew from the French Pacific territories in the late 1980s.[7]

The CFAO

Another grand colonial business was the French West African Company (*Compagnie française de l'Afrique occidentale*, CFAO). The ancestor of what became the major French trader in west Africa was a small company established by Charles-Auguste Verminck in 1845. With branches in Senegal, Sierra Leone, Liberia, the Côte d'Ivoire and Nigeria, Verminck's operations flourished. In 1881, he transformed the enterprise into a joint stock company with capital of 15 million francs. He counted 80 European and 300 African employees. Times changed with a recession, which forced Verminck's company to undertake complete reorganisation. With loans from several Marseille banks, the company, now managed by Frédéric Bohn, re-established itself in 1887, took the name CFAO and moved its headquarters from Paris to Marseille.

The next years brought great growth to the CFAO, which increased its trading posts from 46 in 1887 to 145 in 1911; the European staff in Africa swelled to 255 men. From its initial bases, the CFAO expanded throughout western Africa – in both French and British colonies, as well as Portuguese Guinea – from Senegal south to Nigeria. The CFAO bought tropical commodities from African producers, particularly groundnuts, palm oil and palm nuts, and rounded out its cargo with items such as birdfeathers and leather.

But the CFAO's main activity was selling rather than buying. The CFAO became the 'general store' for both European expatriates and indigenes in west Africa, selling food products and alcohol, ammunition, furniture, metalwares and, especially, textiles. By the late 1800s, African populations had developed Westernised consumer habits and, because of labour provided to Europeans, enjoyed increased purchasing power; Africans consequently bought larger quantities of European fabrics, utensils and household products.

At each of its trading posts the CFAO constructed a large building with a ground-floor general store; the company's agent (and other European employees) lived on the first floor, and outbuildings contained strorage areas. Agents were young Europeans recruited directly by the company and employed for renewable three-year stints. The CFAO also hired Syrians and Lebanese, who began to migrate to west Africa in the 1890s and gravitated towards shop-keeping, as well as Africans, employed as manual labourers and intermediaries in trade between coastal areas and the interior.

CFAO directors upheld three principles in their dealings – precepts which often demarcated them from other traders. First, the company opposed exchange of African products as payment in kind for European goods; in the CFAO's system, monetary payments regulated sales and purchases. This insistence on using currency contributed greatly to the monetisation of the west African economy. Secondly, the company avoided extending credit to its clients (although it sometimes lent to European administrators whose good offices it sought). This meant that Africans needed to possess hard currency for their purchases, though it kept them from becoming overly indebted to shop-keepers. Thirdly, the company prided itself on setting prices for the wares it sold at a 'normal' European level, rather than with the exorbitant markups added by many traders, and (it claimed) on paying the highest possible price for African goods.

Like all colonial companies, the CFAO encountered obstacles. Directors complained of difficulties in recruiting competent Europeans to work in Africa. Bad living conditions and disease handicapped its employees. Competition from British, German and other

French companies was intense – in 1907, several former CFAO employees helped establish a rival company (the *Société commerciale de l'Ouest africain*, SCOA). Trading cycles created slumps, although the geographical spread of the CFAO's posts made it easier to close unprofitable outlets. This flexibility, added to determination to maintain high turnover of stock, assured profits. By the early twentieth century, the company's trade boomed, and it paid healthy dividends to stock-holders. The company also diversified; it purchased a few small ships, invested in a colonial bank, acquired a stock portfolio and arranged several informal cartels in west Africa. The CFAO, however, never showed great interest in creating vertical or horizontal monopolies; it remained, as it began, a trading company.

The CFAO did not restrict trading to the metropole and French possessions. Much of the cloth it sold came from Britain, purchased through branches in Manchester and Liverpool, and its other European purchases were almost evenly divided between French and British suppliers. But it participated in various colonial organisations in France, such as the Colonial Union, and established links with influential members of the colonial lobby; occasionally it contributed modest sums to politicians' electoral coffers. Nevertheless, the CFAO's business activity, rather than lobbying and colonial chauvinism, assured it the major role it played in French Africa. Indeed, while the CFAO supported the French administration on such projects as the construction of railways and port facilities, it sometimes clashed with French officials or settlers. It resolutely supported free trade and opposed protectionism; it avowed opposition to forced labour, imposition of high taxes on Africans, the privileges given to 'concessionary companies' in equatorial Africa, and wartime recruitment of Africans for the French army.

The company foresaw long-term advantages from such 'pro-African' policies. Bohn wrote in 1899: 'It is not just an obligation based on humanity and justice which we have to fulfill *vis-à-vis* the populations which have accepted, or which have had to submit to, our protection. It is moreover an act of good practical policy, because the future of the economy, here and elsewhere, depends largely on the size of the population, that is to say, on the number of producers, consumers and tax-payers. All the expense, all the effort, devoted to favour an increase in the population and to improve its well-being will contribute to enrich and bring prosperity to our great colony of west Africa.' 'Progressive' attitudes hardly endeared it to more rapacious profiteers, who complained that the CFAO was trying to achieve a stranglehold over west African trade.

The CFAO weathered the First World War without great difficulty, but staffing problems and competition continued to plague it in the interwar years. One chief executive resigned in the 1920s to join the SCOA, and younger employees chafed at paternalistic company policy which required them to dine together in common halls in trading outposts and forbade them to marry during the first six years of their contracts. The company hired increasing numbers of Africans, both as labourers and as stock-takers, secretaries and accountants. The interwar years saw expansion in the CFAO's domain of activity with its entry into the AEF and particular efforts at improving business in Nigeria. By 1939, the CFAO boasted 421 trading establishments in 17 colonies; the Gold Coast (Ghana) and Senegal took pride of price. Fierce rivalry – 33 large trading companies, and 78 smaller ones, existed in the Côte d'Ivoire in the late 1930s – provided an incentive to consolidate markets and, in some cases, arrange market-sharing agreements. Another strategy was to set up subsidiary activities: the CFAO established a metropolitan company to promote African products in France, invested in a groundnut-oil refinery in Senegal, furnished capital for a banana company in Guinea, and launched a transport company in the Soudan. Such moves departed from the company's pre-war reticence to expand beyond trade.

A boom in certain sectors occurred in these years; exports of Senegalese groundnuts almost doubled in the two decades after 1910 and, following a drop during the Depression, stood at more than three times the 1910 value by 1937. Others areas fared less well, especially during the economic crisis, and west Africa sought substitute products for traditional exports in bananas, sisal, tea, cotton and hardwoods. The CFAO exported old and new goods from Africa but still earned its profits mostly from sales: textiles, always the most important commodity, a variety of products listed in the manifests of its 'fancy shop' (sugar, alcohol, clothing, kerosene and petrol, watches, utensils, etc.) and, increasingly, heavy equipment (construction materials, motors, machinery ranging from sewing-machines to combustion engines). The company pioneered the import of automobiles into west Africa – the number of motorcars and motorcycles in the AOF soared from only 16 in 1913 to

10 000 twenty years later. Sales, like purchases, dropped during the Depression but recovered by the late 1930s. The same held true for profits; despite somersaults in the market, the CFAO stood in good financial straits on the eve of the Second World War.

In the war years, the CFAO headquarters, in Vichy-controlled France, was cut off from the company's operations in Africa. Until the Liberation the Liverpool branch of the CFAO directed most of the company's African trade, although local managers enjoyed great autonomy. Scarcities of export products, lack of transport and the impossibility of replacing European employees made the early 1940s difficult.

During the remainder of the colonial period, until the independence of the sub-Saharan possessions in 1960, the CFAO retained its position as *the* French company in black Africa. The company chose to rely on its traditional sphere of influence rather than becoming embroiled in post-war reconstruction and development in Europe. It studiously avoided involvement in political activities which could compromise its future in Africa. While remaining loyal to French interests, the company pursued greater 'Africanisation' of its labour force; in 1953, expatriate Europeans accounted for only 7 per cent of its 12 300 employees in Africa. Company leaders maintained a liberal policy towards local workers, gradually extending welfare provisions and promotions to higher levels of the managerial hierarchy.

The company reoriented its sales strategy in the 1950s to concentrate on machinery, construction goods and electric wares, rather than articles for personal consumption. Buyers, more often than before, were other companies, colonial governments, agricultural cooperatives or subcontractors involved in public works projects. Old-style emporia gave way to newer style department stores, often branches of French firms franchised to the CFAO. As the company steadily reduced its purchases of African primary products, more than ever, the CFAO was a vendor of foreign wares to Africa. At the time of its centenary in 1987, 60 per cent of the CFAO's staff worked in Africa, and 48 per cent of its business came from Africa. Despite investment in the remaining French outposts (primarily Réunion) and other islands in the Indian Ocean and Pacific, the bulk of the CFAO's other business came from Europe.[8]

The CFAO was the model of a colonial import-export company. Supporters underlined its geographical and market diversification, level-headed financial and employment policies, and liberal attitudes towards Africans. Detractors accused it of paternalism towards both African and European staff, failure to invest in a lasting infrastructure which would have brought long-term benefit to Africa, and perpetuation of the asymmetrical exchange of European manufactured goods for African primary products. But, like the Banque de l'Indochine, the CFAO did business in the empire for the good of the company's shareholders and, it argued, advantages to France and to its overseas domains.

Colonial Economies

Each of France's colonies has its own economic history: the human and natural resource endowment of the country, traditional patterns of production and exchange, construction of a European-style infrastructure, efforts to develop real or imagined local potential, attempts to locate capital, labour and markets, exchange of commodities between the metropole and the particular outpost, cycles of growth and decline.[9] Indochina and the AEF provide case studies.

Indochina

With the possible exception of possessions in the Maghreb, Indochina was France's most precious colony. Indochina contained valuable mineral resources and provided fertile soil for plantations; tropical climate enabled the cultivation of crops which could not grow in France. The Banque de l'Indochine provided finance. The large population supplied a labour force. Saigon and Hanoi became major colonial cities. Indochina was well situated to act as a base for French trade with China, Southeast Asia, Australasia and Oceania.

The French did not immediately take advantage of their assets in Indochina when Saigon fell in 1862 and Cambodia accepted a protectorate the following year. In the 1870s, Franco-Indochinese trade, mostly of rice, only amounted to the small sum of 4 million francs. The Banque de l'Indochine led the way among new companies, but it took time for other firms to get established: a river navigation line in 1881, a coal supplier in 1888, a tram operator in 1890, a cement firm in 1899, a cotton company in 1900. By the time of the First World War, large businesses dealt in such products as rubber, electricity, rice, tin and alcohol. The number of settlers, not surprisingly, was small in the first years of colonisation, but their ranks soon swelled. From the early years of the twentieth century to the Great Depression of the 1930s, thanks to settlers, entrepreneurship, government effort and the action of the Banque de l'Indochine, the economy of Indochina thrived.

Agriculture formed the basis of Indochina's wealth and employed the vast majority of the local population. Settlers acquired plantations from the government, generally from land which entered the public domain on the annexation of Cochinchina or was acquired from indigenous proprietors by purchase or dispossession elsewhere. French irrigation and drainage work and extension of plantations to previously fallow land increased crop yield, although farming remained labour-intensive and technology-poor – animal and human waste continued to provide the major source of fertiliser. Rice was Indochina's chief crop, accounting for two-thirds of the colony's exports through the 1920s. From 1900 to 1928, the area planted in rice doubled, and production grew from 4.3 million tons to 7 million tons. Most rice went to Hong Kong and China, especially to the less fertile southern provinces neighbouring Indochina; some was exported to Europe, although French consumers preferred large-grain Chinese rice to the small uneven grains of Indochina.

Maize also proved profitable. The Vietnamese had produced small amounts of corn as a foodstuff, but at the beginning of the twentieth century exports averaged only 170 tons a year. Growing demand in France encouraged more extensive plantings; by 1913, annual export soared to 88 000 tons and reached a maximum of 575 000 tons in 1937. Production of other agricultural products increased at impressive rates. Exports of copra, for example, rose from 3800 tons in the 1899–1903 period to 9400 tons 30 years later. Pepper, kapok and lacquer exports tripled during the same years, while sales of aniseed grew ten times over. Tea exports shot up from an annual average of 160 tons in 1899–1903 to 2000 tons by the late 1930s. Some commodities, however, did not fare so well – silk exports actually dropped, and coffee never really took off – but agriculture generally registered a high level of success.

Rubber formed an economic sector to itself. The first rubber trees arrived in Indochina in 1897, imported by a Navy pharmacist. Several years passed before the first plantations were established, and growers waited another six or seven years for the trees to produce latex. Exports of rubber amounted to an average of 160 tons in the 1909–13 period and climbed to 520 tons in the 1914–18 span. Rubber production then increased dramatically to 20 000 tons in 1934 and 59 450 tons in 1938. The 1920s saw the most rapid extension of rubber cultivation: already in 1921, 29 000 hectares were planted in rubber; by 1927, 127 000 hectares were covered in rubber trees (98 000 in Cochinchina, 27 000 in Cambodia – where there had been only 18 hectares in 1921 – and 1700 in Annam). Rubber emerged as a quintessential colonial primary product destined for metropolitan markets, produced by native labourers working in harsh conditions on plantations owned by Europeans in a pattern of proprietorship showing distinct traits of monopoly control. A third of the 1005 plantations totalled more than 40 hectares and represented 94 per cent of the total area planted in rubber; 27 companies owned over two-thirds of total hectarage planted in rubber. Rubber accounted for the bulk of Indochina's exports in the 1930s; most went to France.

Indochina also provided minerals. Tonkin, in particular, contained large coal and tin mines, and smaller deposits of zinc, antimony, manganese, gold, phosphate and graphite. Mining of anthracite and bituminous coal held pride of place. The French opened numerous mines in Tonkin in the early twentieth century, and prospectors tried to develop mineral resources elsewhere. The number of government-issued prospecting permits soared from 125 in 1914 to 17 685 in 1930. Mining provided a major source of employment; in 1913, 12 000 Indochinese worked in the mines. Monopolistic tendencies were as obvious in mining as in rubber production; in the late 1930s, a single company, the Charbonnages du Tonkin, produced 71 per cent of Indochina's coal and employed 25 000 labourers. Its production, combined with that of one other company, accounted for fully 92 per cent of Indochinese coal. The second most important mineral was tin. Production stood at 44 tons in 1913, 410 tons a decade later; after the opening of tin mines in Laos, production climbed to 1602 tons in 1937. In that year, mining employed 271 Europeans and 49 200 Asians. Yet working conditions were so bad in the major coal mine that it was called 'the hell of Hong Gay', and the Nam Patène mines were known as 'death valley'.

Creation of a modern economic infrastructure represented big business in Indochina. The French dug 1300 kilometres of canals. French steamers sailed navigable portions of the Mekong and Red rivers and operated coastal services. Authorities improved the road system for the transport of goods and use by private drivers, usually European – the number of automobiles in Indochina grew from 350 in 1913 to 17 800 in 1933. Railway-building was a mania in Indochina as elsewhere. Indochina counted only 178 kilometres of train track in 1898, but 2908 kilometres 40 years later. The height of railway construction, from 1898 to 1913, saw the commencement of most major trunk lines; at one point, 60 000 Vietnamese laboured on a single line. The pride and joy of rail builders were the links between Haiphong, Hanoi, Laokay on the Chinese border and Kunming, capital of the Chinese province of Yunnan, and the Trans-Indochinese rail connecting Hanoi with Saigon. The train transformed transport; twice as much merchandise travelled by rail in 1937 as in 1913.

Industry was not well developed in Indochina, and many colonialists hoped that it never would be because they feared competition to manufacturers at home. Nevertheless, a number of plants opened in Indochina; cloth-making was particularly prosperous. Local industries processed raw materials, as was the case with mills which husked and bleached paddy rice, and the factories which transformed latex into sheet rubber. Other concerns produced materials for local markets. The major cement company represented share capital of 43 million francs in the mid-1940s, and firms making paper, matches and distilled alcohol figured on the list of large enterprises.

Notwithstanding the unequal distribution of profits and the social cost paid by indigenous workers, Indochina's trade prospered until the Depression of the early 1930s, fell with the economic crisis, then recovered rapidly. Indochina traded with neighbouring countries, but France took an increasingly larger share of the trade. From 1911 to 1930, France purchased a fifth of Indochina's exports; that proportion stood at 53 per cent in 1938. Over the same period, the French share of imports into Indochina swelled from 30 to 57 per cent. Two-thirds of exports from France were composed of textiles (despite the growth of local industries) and metallurgical products, followed by other manufactured articles and foodstuffs. By the mid-1930s, France purchased 41 per cent of Indochina's rice, most of its corn (which satisfied 80 per cent of French demand) and almost all of its rubber (which, however, fell short of fulfilling French demand). Indochina also traded with other French colonies; in particular, Indochinese rice went to sub-Saharan Africa. Indochina bought cigarettes and wine from Algeria, and fabrics and yarn from French India. Furthermore, Indochina provided several thousands of workers for the nickel mines of New Caledonia.[10]

Not all enterprises in French Indochina scored successes, and the Depression ruined many settlers. But Indochina (or at least the more prosperous Vietnamese part of it) was a model colony. It produced a wealth of useful raw materials and purchased French exports. It provided a profitable destination for French investments. It supported 42 345 Europeans (and others assimilated to that category) by 1937. Tax and other revenues – including the especially important tax collected on opium – covered the bill for Indochina's administration and defence. Except for a few disturbances, an uprising in 1930 and the agitation of the Communist Party, pacification seemed accomplished. The 23 million Indochinese (including 326 000 ethnic Chinese) might have just cause to feel ambivalent about the French presence, but promoters in the metropole saw Indochina as a crowning achievement of French expansion. The era of prosperity, however, did not last long; war and Japanese occupation came in the 1940s, then a war of independence forced French evacuation in 1954.

The AEF

While Indochina was one of France's most successful colonies, French Equatorial Africa proved one of the most disappointing and controversial. The AEF was a huge and completely undeveloped territory, at least in its usefulness to European business, when Brazza established control in the 1880s. The first years after French takeover saw little activity other than episodic and un-regulated trading. By the end of the nineteenth century, the government decided that the only way to speed development and avoid anarchy was to parcel out Gabon, the Moyen-Congo and Oubangui-Chari – territories later joined with Chad to form the AEF – to private companies. In 1899, 40 'concessionary companies' won control over 700 000 square kilometres (of the 900 000 represented by the AEF). Concessions ranged from 1200 to 140 000 square kilometres. In return for a bond, nominal annual rent, 15 per cent of profits and supplementary contributions to the cost of setting up customs posts and telegraph lines, the companies ob-

tained a monopoly on ivory and rubber trading and a free hand
to exploit their land for 30 years. After the end of the period,
the companies would receive legal title to lands which they had
effectively developed. Promises of final settlement were particularly generous – a company could hope to get 100 hectares of
land, for instance, for having domesticated a single elephant.

The policy of issuing patents to concessionary companies signi-
fied the government's own inability or unwillingness to create a
modern economy in the AEF. The project also harked back to
the charter companies which had developed colonies in the 1600s.
Furthermore, the strategy paralleled plans by Britain and Germany to use private companies in eastern Africa. Major French
firms, however, showed little interest in investing in equatorial
Africa and were notably absent among concessionary companies
set up for the AEF. Capital came mostly from colonists and medium-
sized trading companies already involved in the region; foreign
capital, especially from Belgium, was significant. Investors hoped
for handsome profits, especially after the much vaunted Congo–
Ocean railway opened.

High hopes were not realised. A decade after the companies
were founded, only seven paid dividends to shareholders. Ten
disappeared completely by 1904, and at the end of the 30-year
concession period, only eight remained. Delays in building the
railway, the costs and distances involved in porterage, unhealthy
conditions in tropical forests, difficulties in finding labour, and
the international economic climate stifled development. European
traders and entrepreneurs were slow in coming to the AEF; the
European population grew from 800 in 1900 to just over 2000 a
decade later. Production of ivory, previously a profitable export,
declined from 210 tons in 1905 to 97 tons 15 years later. Rubber
production stagnated from the turn of the twentieth century to
the First World War. The only bright spot was production of tropical
hardwoods, particularly mahogany, which rocketed from 2000 tons
in 1898 to 150 000 in 1913; commercial forestry was confined
largely to Gabon, which consequently became a more valuable
possession than the Moyen-Congo or Oubangui-Chari.

Labour posed a big problem for the concessionary companies,
as for the railway builders. Most companies hired employees only
by agreement with local sultans, who provided workers in exchange
for a commission. To aid companies to secure labour and help
defray administrative costs, the government instituted a head-tax

on the African population and imposed fines for non-payment;
chiefs found employment as tax-farmers, and peasants found themselves obliged to search for employment to pay taxes. Abuses of
labour were commonplace, and companies generally honoured
work regulations in the breach.

Scandalous treatment of Africans horrified at least some sectors of French opinion. One of the worst single incidents was the
locking up of 45 women in Lobaye in 1905 to force them and
their menfolk to work for a concessionary company; most of the
women died. At M'Poko, the murder of at least a thousand African workers led to indictments of 236 persons; most got off, and
the affair was hushed up. Workers were regularly coerced into
labour, and beaten with chains and whips to ensure their obedience and productivity. At the beginning of the twentieth century,
an African had to work for several months to pay the head-tax,
and wages were not always paid in money – in 1910 a day of
back-breaking porterage earned a spoonful of beads. By the First
World War, the economy of the AEF thus was little monetised. In
fact, traders opposed paying workers with money, which would
have permitted Africans to bargain with different traders more
easily. Commerce in the AEF remained an exchange of guinea
cloth, hardware, foodstuffs, alcohol and firearms – 20 000 of which
were imported into the Congo each year – for ivory, rubber or
labour. Individual traders earned good profits though investors
did not; coastal wholesalers added 40 per cent to the cost of the
items they offered for sale, and a similar amount was added again
by traders in the interior. Most traders, incidentally, were not
French, and the largest trading company, with 39 outlets, was
British; the cloth it sold came from Britain, the utensils from
Germany.

The concessionary regime was manifestly a failure. In the interwar years, journalists and travellers, such as André Gide, revealed
mistreatment of indigenes. An official report in 1925 stated that
the concessionary companies had left the AEF as poor as they
had found it. By the 1930s, ivory reserves were thoroughly depleted. In some regions of the AEF, supplies of rubber, a prime
export, had been exhausted. The Depression caused a crash in
the price and demand for rubber; in any case, Southeast Asian
rubber provided unbeatable competition for African producers.
Efforts to export palm oil, coffee, cocoa and cotton met with no
appreciable success. A modern economic infrastructure was still

lacking, and Africans had not been turned into Western-style workers.

Forestry remained the big economic activity of Gabon. Some 12 000–15 000 Gabonese harvested mahogany, ebony and acajou; almost all Gabonese men at some time in their lives worked in lumbering. Workers lived in camps and received cash wages; bad conditions and overcrowding led to high death rates and the spread of venereal disease and malaria. Nevertheless, business boomed. Prices for a ton of exotic hardwood soared from 30–60 francs in 1916 to 800 francs at the height of the wood boom in the 1920s, then fell back to 250 francs in the 1930s. Gabon's economy, unique in the AEF, had indeed experienced take-off, which created links between Gabon, the metropole which purchased the wood, and other French colonies which provided food for the labourers – dried fish from Mauritania, maize from Dahomey, peanuts from Senegal, rice from Indochina.

The economy of the AEF showed limited diversification. The standard of living for the African population probably declined during the concessionary regime. The companies' actions in the first years of the system have been characterised as an 'economy of pillage' marked by human exploitation and environmental depredation. Only by the late 1920s and early 1930s, as concessions expired and government capital replaced private funds, the logging industry stabilised, and the volume of exports and imports grew, did the AEF really develop a 'proper' imperialistic economy capable of expansion and profit-making.[11]

The Value of Empire

Various individuals and firms made money from the colonies, but general questions have long nagged economic historians: How important was the empire for the overall French economy? When all the sums were done, did France make money from the colonies? Was the empire essential to France's economic growth or did it hinder modernisation and hold back growth? Not until the 1980s did students of French colonial history have a comprehensive study of the economy of French colonialism. Jacques Marseille's analysis of the empire and French capitalism challenged many assertions about the monetary value of expansion. Although contested by some historians, his hypotheses provide the most considered view available of the commercial balance-sheet of colonialism.[12]

Marseille cautions that it is difficult to judge definitively whether the empire produced an overall profit or loss for France. It is impossible fully to calculate the quantitative and qualitative gains or losses of empire, to include fully the multiplier effects which expansion produced, or to factor in such benefits as prestige and international power or discount such disadvantages as international conflict and war. Simple statistics, however, indicate that in some years before the First World War, the empire was France's second most important commercial partner. Yet in 1913, the colonies supplied only 9.4 per cent of French imports and purchased only 13 per cent of its exports; the empire thereby accounted for 10 per cent of France's foreign trade. As for foreign investment, the empire remained in third place for French overseas holdings, far behind Russia and Latin America.

Marseille argues that general figures, which seem to indicate that the colonies occupied a relatively minor place in France's economy, hardly tell the full story. A breakdown of trade statistics reveals surprises. Exports of jewellery to the empire were twice as important as sales of machine tools, for instance, and France sold a larger proportion of its candles than of its locomotives to the colonies. For sales of certain French-made products, the colonial market was vital: the empire bought 86 per cent of bleached cotton textiles, 80 per cent of iron and steel construction materials, 76 per cent of beer, 56 per cent of rails and 54 per cent of shoes – to take examples of industries which relied on the colonial market for substantial sales. As for imports, France purchased from the colonies 95 per cent of its rice, 90 per cent of its cane sugar, 88 per cent of *vin ordinaire*, 81 per cent of its olive oil, 79 per cent of its phosphate, 72 per cent of its groundnuts and 21 per cent of its rubber. The empire thus provided the bulk of certain products in demand in France, as well as a supplementary supply of many other commodities.

Furthermore, Marseille suggests that the commercial importance of the empire increased dramatically as time passed, especially after the First World War. From 1928 until 1960, the empire formed France's premier trading partner. (The colonies nevertheless accounted for only 12.7 per cent of total French imports and 17.3 per cent of exports in 1928.) With the 1930s Depression, France relied ever more heavily on the empire. Algeria alone took 45 per cent of France's exports and furnished 40 per cent of its imports during the economic crisis of the interwar years. During the Depression, the empire held particular importance as a larder of raw materials – it furnished nearly all of France's imports of agricultural products – and absorbed most of its textile exports. After the Second World War, the trend towards greater trade between metropole and colonies continued. The year 1952, when the empire absorbed 42 per cent of France's exports, represented the apogee of post-war trade between France and the colonies. Similarly, the empire captured a steadily growing proportion of French overseas investment, as much as 30 to 40 per cent at the end of the 1920s. After 1918, the empire became the leading destination for French investments (partially by default because of the Bolshevik Revolution in Russia and the fragmentation of the Ottoman Empire). France spent more money on the colonies than ever after the Second World War; from 1947 to 1958, more public money was expended in the empire than for the entire period since the 1880s. Ironically, the years immediately preceding decolonisation were the time when the empire had finally proven its commercial value. Yet, Marseille adds, there existed strong economic arguments in favour of decolonisation, and the loss of empire did not plunge the French economy into crisis. Indeed, France felt few deleterious commercial or financial effects from imperial divestment.

Despite the demonstrated value of the empire to French trade and investment, Marseille remains dubious about claims that the empire was necessary to French economic growth and modernisation. He finds that the larger, more dynamic and more innovative industries were more often attracted to other external markets (for instance, in Europe and the Americas) than to colonial ones. New industries, such as electrical, chemicals and metals industries developed in the late nineteenth century, found useful markets in the colonies in the early years of their technological development and market formation, but colonial markets then declined in importance. Smaller, less dynamic, even declining firms and sectors found more hospitable markets in the protected colonial world; without sheltered markets, some such firms would not have survived. The empire continued to buy products for which the global market was shrinking rather than expanding. Marseille concludes that the empire did not play a large role in the modernisation of French economic infrastructure; by contrast, the reliability of colonial markets (supported by tariffs) favoured the persistence of small concerns, old-fashioned business practices and traditional marketing methods. In structural terms, Marseille suggests that, for all its worth, the empire indeed acted as brake rather than accelerator in French economic growth.

The Marseille thesis contradicts the traditional argument, expressed by Lenin, that colonial expansion was a necessary and inevitable stage in the history of European capitalism. Marseille speaks of a 'divorce' between the economic transformation of the colonies and that of the metropolitan economy. More vibrant sectors in French capitalism found ample outlets for expansion domestically, elsewhere in western Europe or, in the years before 1914, in Russia, the Ottoman Empire and Latin America. These areas held more interest for French business than all but a few of the colonies, such as Algeria and Indochina. Many colonies – including, somewhat surprisingly, the black African possessions which had excited such hopes, as well as most of the smaller outposts – were of relatively marginal economic utility except for specific commodities, such as the nickel of New Caledonia or the hardwood of Gabon.

The empire was by no means of negligible commercial value. In the years before the First World War, the empire, much of which had been only recently acquired, provided a field for a number of companies to earn good profits. After the war, economic policy-makers made a conscious decision to increase France's economic exchanges with the empire, even at the expense of trade and investment with other parts of the world. In the economically hard Depression years, the empire represented a fallback position for French trade and investment. After the Second World War, as France pumped money into the colonies for development projects, export-oriented agriculture and mining, and a variety of import-substitution industries, the colonies gained marked economic stature. Throughout modern colonial history, the empire contributed to French growth even if it did not lead it or propel the French economy more rapidly towards structural transformation. The empire, moreover, remained an area of great hopes for commercial benefit, even if the potential was not always realised.

6 The French and the 'Natives'

No issue is more emotive in the history of overseas expansion than relations between Europeans and the populations of the countries which they invaded, conquered and settled: relations between the colonisers and the colonised. Colonialists proclaimed that Europeans replaced savagery with civilisation, backwardness with modernity; the creation of economic infrastructures, the opening of schools and infirmaries, and the establishment of modern law codes and institutions immensely improved the lives of Africans, Asians and islanders. Anti-colonialists presented evidence that the slavery, warfare, violence, taxation, exploitation of labour and destruction of local cultures which accompanied European expansion wreaked brutal and irreparable damage on non-European societies.

No one denied that the indigenous populations bore the brunt of the changes wrought by colonialism, whether for better or worse, and that these changes were dramatic. A distinguished historian of Africa wrote in the early 1960s:

> A century ago, the peoples of Dahomey for the most part still went about naked or dressed only in a vulgar loincloth, they were armed with bows and arrows, and their farming equipment consisted of rudimentary hoes. Now they are dressed, they travel by automobile, they use the telephone and take aeroplanes; transistor radios broadcast the latest news to the deepest bushland.... They have gone from the iron age to the twentieth century. The material and technical circumstances of this mutation are worth considering.[1]

The human costs of that transformation also merit reflection.

Several straightforward points on the effects of European expansion seem evident. First, in taking over foreign possessions, Europeans encountered cultures which they seldom if ever understood and often dismissed; certainty of European cultural superiority and racial supremacy lay at the base of imperialism. Secondly, Europeans established domination by force of arms; weapons were used when necessary or expedient, but brandished always. European firepower eventually bested indigenous armaments in wars of conquest. Coercion, economic pressure and deals worked out among rival European colonisers were supplementary tools of power used against those brought under foreign flags. Soldiers, judges and police preserved colonial control. Thirdly, few of the Europeans who ventured overseas were entirely either the heroic bearers of liberation and civilisation whom colonialists praised or the sadistic, rapacious profiteers whom anti-colonialists damned, although examples of both stereotypes could be found. Even if most of the French involved in colonial activities did not fit neatly into either paradigm, the nature of colonial domination nevertheless institutionalised unequal relations between Europeans and non-Europeans and promoted social, economic and cultural abuses of indigenous peoples. Colonised peoples suffered deprivation of political rights, land spoliation, appropriation of labour, pillage of resources, cultural alienation and outright violence. However, Africans, Asians and islanders were not impotent in the face of European incursions. They could and did respond with various types of resistance during the period of conquest, throughout the colonial era and in a revival of nationalism which contributed mightily to decolonisation. But a number of colonised people, individually and collectively, collaborated with foreign administrators, European businessmen and missionaries to secure advantages from their conquerors. Resistance and collaboration[2] form leitmotifs of African, Asian and island reaction to European colonialism.

Racism and Cultural Superiority

Attitudes towards non-European cultures and ethnic groups formed the intellectual context which allowed conquest and colonialism, but theorists also devised arguments about European racial and cultural superiority precisely in order to justify naked conquest.[3]

Almost from the beginnings of Western history, Europeans imagined themselves superior to other peoples, although they were not the sole cultural group convinced of its superiority. Drawing on Biblical tales, European writers, for instance, decided that Europeans and Africans descended from different sons of the patriarch Noah; the damnation of Ham, ancestor of Africans, condemned his lineage. The Crusades to free the Christian holy lands from Muslims reinforced European prejudices that Arabs were fierce and immoral warriors who had usurped legitimate European rights and destroyed Graeco-Roman achievements in the Middle East (and North Africa). At the time of Europeans' first contacts with Native Americans in the 1500s, learned theologians argued whether 'Indians' were animal or human, if they had a soul and were capable of Christian salvation or were soulless and irredeemable. European discovery of the South Pacific islands in the 1700s prompted further discussions about 'primitive' peoples, although for some commentators, Polynesians fared well in cross-cultural comparisons, and their very lack of 'civilisation' was a blessing.

Deprecation of non-European cultures continued in the nineteenth century. Explorers returned with stories of barbarism. Accounts of cannibalism and human sacrifice – practices travellers grossly exaggerated, misunderstood and ripped from their socio-cultural contexts – were guaranteed to send a shiver of fear up European spines but also, more significantly, to convince Europeans of their own superiority to the horrible people who engaged in such unspeakable acts. Reports of culturally sanctioned practices which Europeans (and undoubtedly some non-Europeans) found shocking, ranging from Chinese foot-binding and Polynesian tattooing to African scarification and circumcision, seemed to cry out for a *mission civilisatrice*. Accounts of the harem stimulated European lust but underlined the perceived lubricity of Muslims, and writers hinted at 'unnatural' practices – sodomy, bizarre sexual initiations, transvestism, castration – supposedly widespread outside Europe.

Miscellaneous observations coalesced into canonical stereotypes. In most European views, for instance, Indochinese were physically weak, sickly and deficient in virility: 'Poor folk, physical strength is lacking in them, just as are many other qualities', lamented a writer in 1879. Moreover, Indochinese were ugly; an 1886 visitor to Vietnam observed: 'The common man . . . is quite simply hideous.

The bestial face of such a man is always immobile, inert and seems petrified in idiocy.' Indochinese were unclean: 'of disgusting dirtiness, devoured by vermin and eaten away by skin diseases, covered in stinking rags,... [the Indochinese] sweats filth and ignoble wretchedness through his very pores', according to an author in 1882. Even women, who usually had some redeeming qualities in the eyes of male Europeans, initially received unflattering reviews – 'The women are truly horrible', wrote a soldier who took part in French campaigns in the 1860s and complained in particular about the stained teeth of women who chewed betel-nuts. Moral vices complemented physical defects; Europeans characterised Indochinese as lazy, inconstant, lacking in foresight, addicted to gambling and opium, vain, given to bragging and cruel.[4]

Opinions about black Africans were even less positive. The physical strength of Africans, in seeming contrast to the debilitated state of Asians, impressed Europeans but made Africans seem more like animals than humans. Rumours about Africans' supposed sexual prowess provided further 'proof' of base animality. Few nineteenth-century reports about Africa failed to reduce Africans to beasts, often using comparisons with monkeys or chimpanzees. A work by one Virey, first published in 1801 and often reprinted, said that Africans were 'a bit like orang-outangs'; their nose, hair and lips 'truly show a tendency towards similar forms, and if this physical similarity is unmistakable, it is also noticeable in their morals. The black man is a born mimic, like the monkey; he recognises the intellectual superiority of the white, easily enough accepts slavery and is insouciant and lazy.' Virey added that blacks had smaller brains than whites, as well as different nervous systems with 'an extreme disposition towards nervous sensations and excitement, signs of a greater animality than that of the white'. For good measure, he reported that some thought African blood and semen were black – an example of the extraordinary errors perpetrated about Africans. (As late as the 1850s, a 'specialist' lectured the very respectable Paris Geographical Society on the African 'Niam-Niam' people, whose sole article of furniture was a bench with a hole drilled through the seat to accommodate their tails.[5])

Attitudes changed somewhat during the nineteenth century thanks to abolitionist literature and more reliable eyewitness reports from Africa. But stereotypes remained. An 1843 article in a prestigious journal bore the title 'The Negro is an Intellectual

Monstrosity'. One writer noted in 1889 that Africans constituted 'thousands of gorillas swarming and vegetating on land which is nevertheless rich in resources'. The very colour of African skin – always simply 'black' in the European gaze – functioned as a symbol for their status: black was the colour of night, darkness, evil. In the early nineteenth century, blacks were seen as fit only for slavery; in the late 1800s they were thought capable only of manual labour or other tasks requiring little intelligence.

New theories overlaid views of non-Europeans. The nineteenth century gave birth to systematic and 'scientific' doctrines of race and culture. Theorists of 'degeneration' discussed the cultural and biological decline of Asian civilisation, while they argued that whatever little might exist of value in North African culture was a degenerated vestige of ancient Roman occupation of the Maghreb. Scientists and social scientists busied themselves with discussions about skin colour, race and the origin of humanity: Did all humans emerge from the same stock and one family ('monogenism') or from several ('polygenism')? Had black Africans always been black or had early migrants south of the Sahara turned black? (This question was debated as late as 1883.) Were 'yellow' Asians a separate race? Were nomadic Tuaregs and Moors white or black? Were Berbers and Arabs the same or different races? Were west African Peuls or east African Nubians survivors of 'white' presence in Africa? Were Africans and Pacific islanders leftovers of the stone age? Researchers conducted experiments on somatotypes, cranial size, and other physical and intellectual capacities to create categories of different 'races', often neatly arranged in hierarchies. Arthur Gobineau stood in the forefront of speculation, and his *Essay on the Inequality of Races*, published in the 1850s, provided an authoritative statement of new racial theories. (Gobineau himself opposed colonialism, however, fearing that interbreeding between Europeans and foreigners would contaminate and degenerate European blood.) A misreading of Darwin's theory of evolution, and the ideas of anthropologists, ethnologists and linguists, contributed to conclusions about the innate racial inferiority of those whom Europeans conquered (or wanted to conquer).

The grace of God or the work of nature, therefore, gave Europeans a mandate to annex foreign countries and civilise lesser races. Dressed in different fashion over the years, this idea persisted through much of colonial history. 'Equality', a sacrosanct principle of the French Revolution, would not extend to non-Europeans until and unless they 'assimilated' into European civilisation – a dubious prospect in the view of most colonialists. Even liberal humanitarians seldom disagreed with the argument that Europeans should dispense civilisation to the savages. Not until the middle of the twentieth century did more than isolated voices demand liberty and equality for colonised peoples. Old stereotypes, outmoded 'scientific' theories and incomprehension of foreign cultures have not disappeared in the post-colonial age.

Resistance to French Rule

In most cases, the initial reaction of non-European peoples to colonisation was resistance. Algerians fought a sustained war against French conquest for two decades after 1830, with Abd el-Khader as leader of the struggle to preserve Algerian independence. Tahitians waged war on the French after the declaration of a protectorate over the Society Islands in 1842. The first French attempts to take Tonkin in the 1870s and 1880s, like efforts to conquer Madagascar in the 1880s, failed in the face of resistance. Formidable political and military leaders – El Hadj Omar, Béhanzin, Lat Dior, Samory Touré – fought against French takeover of sub-Saharan Africa. Sultans Adbelaziz and Moulay Hafid held out against takeover of Morocco. Queen Ranavalona in Madagascar and Queen Pomaré in Tahiti tried unsuccessfully to forestall French occupation. Tuaregs battled the French all the way from Mauritania to Niger. Although a few possessions were secured by simple flag-raising, France acquired many of its colonies, often only after a number of years and at great cost, by defeat of local leaders and their supporters.

Resistance did not end with French victory. Many more years passed before 'pacification' – a euphemistic term that really meant defeat of resistance movements and subjugation of colonised populations – and it was seldom complete. France did not pacify parts of Morocco and Mauritania, for instance, until the 1930s, only a quarter-century before these countries regained independence. New resistance groups surfaced almost everywhere after French takeover and mounted campaigns to evict foreigners. Often dismissed by authorities as 'rebellions', 'uprisings', 'insurrections' or cases of 'insurgency', many constituted cohesive, well-organised and articulate efforts to overthrow French rule. The 'Black Flags' action in Tonkin in the late 1880s, the 'red scarves' rebellion in Madagascar, demonstrations and attacks on the French during the First World War, Abd el-Krim's movement in the Rif mountains of Morocco in the 1920s, and the Yen Bay incident in Vietnam in 1930 represent only a small sample of attempts to end French rule. Although some responded to particular situations – rebellions during the First World War were, in part, reactions against recruitment of troops for the French army – most exemplified anti-colonialism and nationalism.

Tactics for resistance varied. Early resistance movements fought with traditional weapons as well as whatever European arms they could procure. Tactical alliances between local leaders, or sometimes with France's imperial rivals, marshalled support and reinforced troop strength. Deft negotiation could produce better terms when defeat threatened or had been suffered. Traditional tribal, clan or ethnic groupings formed rallying-points for resistance, and new figures rose to lead campaigns. Continued adherence to customary religions, the revival and spread of Islam, even Christian doctrines contributed to ideologies of resistance. New cultural movements – such as *négritude*, the ideas of black writers who re-evaluated African culture in more positive terms in the early twentieth century – gave stimulus to political action. By the early 1900s, Western-style political parties promoted welfare and demanded redresses of the grievances of colonised peoples. Petitions, meetings, demonstrations, the publication of newspapers and books (when these were not forbidden by French authorities) all served in the struggle against foreign overlordship. Elections for local assemblies and the French parliament, although instituted in most colonies only after the Second World War, provided a new avenue of protest.[6]

Two cases of post-conquest rebellion, one in the South Pacific, one in the Middle East, illustrate the diversity of resistance. They differed in tactics and organisation, but the goal of each was to win back independence. Both were unsuccessful, although each contributed to later anti-colonialist movements.

The 1878 Rebellion in New Caledonia

By the mid-1870s, two decades after French annexation and ten years after the first convicts arrived, New Caledonia was a small but burgeoning European settlement in Oceania. Mining of nickel, destined to become the territory's major commercial activity, had already begun, and settlers held high hopes for development of pastoralism and agriculture. Nouméa was a bustling little port, and European villages had sprung up around the Grande Terre, the New Caledonian mainland. Colonial promoters praised the merits of a colony which they hoped would become a prosperous 'austral France'.

The indigenous Melanesians lived on the fringes of European society. In any hierarchy of races devised by nineteenth-century theorists, Melanesians came close to the bottom. Early explorers found the dark-skinned islanders physically unattractive and some-times inhospitable. Reputation for fierce tribal warfare and can-nibalism underlined their alleged savagery. Closer contacts rein-forced racist feelings that Melanesians were a primitive relic of prehistoric times. Starting with such assumptions, and lacking serious ethnological work to correct such misunderstandings, most French observers decided that Melanesians had no organised sys-tem of government, a rudimentary economic system, superstitions legends which passed for culture, and only elementary forms of architecture and craftsmanship. Just a few Europeans appreciated the functional utility and aesthetic beauty of Melanesian houses and gardens, masks and ceremonial clubs, and fewer still under-stood the complex structures of Melanesian kinship and geneal-ogy, divisions of political authority, and rich oral literature.

The French were dubious about civilising Melanesians. The Melanesian population dropped markedly after Europeans arrived on the islands because of foreign diseases, the spread of alcohol and warfare. Some thought that Melanesians were a dying breed and would, quite literally, become an extinct species. In the mean-time, Melanesians seemed to have little to offer Europeans. Sup-plies of sandalwood which Europeans had bought in the islands were being gradually depleted, and New Caledonia contained no exotic goods, such as ivory, gold, or spices, with which to whet traders' appetites. Businessmen considered Melanesians such an unwilling and unreliable labour force that they imported mine-workers from Asia. Tax revenues collected from indigenes, though substantial, did not cover the colonial budget. Missionaries – Prot-estants on the Loyalty islands north of the mainland, both Prot-estants and Catholics on the Grande Terre – were succeeding in converting many Melanesians, but neither church nor state made great efforts to open schools, teach French or provide vocational training. Melanesians, divided into over 30 language groups and 200 'tribes' (a word inappropriately attached to Melanesian clans), even seemed incapable of resisting French advances.

The most important Melanesian resource which the French coveted was land. Melanesians were farmers, growing yams, taro and other tropical products in carefully tended fields. They did not raise livestock, however, as the only mammals in pre-contact New Caledonia were bats and rodents. Land provided a livelihood for Melanesians but also held profound cultural significance. Melanesians traced their ancestry to certain totems, often associated with a particular site. Even when they had migrated around the island in pre-European times, as was common, Melanesians identified with a specific locale where their clan had originated. Many legends and religious beliefs attached to the land. Land, therefore, was a key part of Melanesian identity.

The French wanted land for settlement and cultivation; the western plains of the Grande Terre attracted interest as prime real estate for cattle-raising and farming. A series of government decrees, the first proclaimed shortly after European takeover, transferred Melanesian land to European hands. Nominal payments, expropriation and claims on what seemed to Europeans unoccupied property provided the mechanisms for dispossession of Melanesians, gradually pushed off more fertile land and left with less arable and mountainous pockets. As planned, Europeans imported livestock and established farms, often near remaining Melanesian properties, for example, in the European settlement at La Foa. In the absence of fencing, European cattle frequently strayed into Melanesian fields, destroying crops. This aggravated Melanesian resentment at European occupation.

Intermittent violence had targeted the French since 1853, but in 1878 a spark ignited rebellion. Near La Foa lived a pardoned French convict and his Melanesian concubine. The couple had sheltered another Melanesian woman, possibly because she did not wish to marry the husband chosen for her by her family and clan. On 18 June 1878, men from her clan killed the couple who had given her refuge and their children. Several days later, Melanesians attacked the police station at La Foa, killing four *gendarmes* and a servant, then ambushed settlers.

Telegraph reports informed Nouméa of the incidents, and the governor immediately dispatched a gunboat. Before it arrived,

Melanesians had attacked a police station at Bouloupari, another European centre. Insurrection soon spread throughout the central region of the Grande Terre. The leader of the movement, which seemed surprisingly well coordinated given the terrain of New Caledonia and divisions among different Melanesian groups, was a chief named Atai. Although friendly with various French residents, he had given voice to Melanesian hostility to land spoliation. On meeting the governor, he was reported to have held out one hand, in which he held a clump of earth. 'This is what we had before you came', he said, before showing his other, empty hand, and adding, 'And this is what we have now'.

Rebels contracted alliances with each other; some Melanesians offered assistance to French forces, who played on traditional clan rivalries to recruit support. To combat the rebels, the French used military troops, convicts and political prisoners transported to New Caledonia after the Paris Commune of 1871. Fierce fighting continued around La Foa and Bouloupari until August, when Atai was ambushed and defeated. He was killed and beheaded; the French sent his head to an anthropology museum in Paris. Yet the uprising spread further afield on the Grande Terre. Melanesians raided more European farms, and the French burned Melanesian villages in reprisal. European armaments and soldiers finally overcame the Melanesians, largely quelling the insurrection by October 1878 although the government-declared state of siege in several communities lasted until June of the next year.

The insurrection left 200 Europeans and 1200 Melanesians dead. The French restored law and order and continued settlement. Colonists, frightened by the prospects of another rebellion, felt even less generous towards Melanesians than before the uprising. A French general sent to investigate the revolt wrote a report highly critical of French settlers and government authorities. Melanesian activists later found in Atai the ancestor of contemporary nationalist movements.[7]

The Druze Uprising

Under the terms of the League of Nations mandate which consigned Syria and Lebanon to French administration after the First World War, Paris did not enjoy sovereignty over these regions of the former Ottoman empire. But the French High Commissioner in Beirut effectively exercised a free hand in ruling them. In 1920 and 1921 the French divided Syria and Lebanon into four states, including a separate one, the Jabal (or Djebel) Druze, for the Druze minority. The Druzes were a breakaway sect of the Ismaili branch of Islam, characterised by strong communal ties, rites of initiation and prohibition on conversion of outsiders. A Druze attack on Maronite Christians in 1860 had prompted Paris briefly to station troops in the region to protect Christians, and the Druzes still harboured resentment against the French. In the 1920s, Lebanon gained separate administration, now as 'greater' Lebanon after the merger of the Christian highlands, the largely Muslim cities of Tripoli, Sidon and Tyre, the Islamic Bekaa Valley, and Beirut, which had almost even numbers of Christians and Muslims; this satisfied the expansionist hopes of some Lebanese but resulted in virtual demographic parity between Muslims and Christians. Governors administered all four Middle Eastern states under the watchful eye of French delegates; the question of whether governors should be indigenous people or Frenchmen remained contested.

Nationalist Syrian leaders organised an embryonic political movement in the 1920s and demanded unification of the four states and independence. The French refused to consider such changes in the immediate future. Dissent was especially strong in the Jabal Druze, where 43 000 of 50 000 inhabitants belonged to the Druze sect. The French worked effectively with the first governor of the Jabal Druze, Selim Al-Atrash, patriarch of the dominant family. Riots broke out in 1922, however, when the French plundered and shelled the house of Sultân Al-Atrash, a powerful relative of Governor Selim, after Sultân had organised a commando raid to rescue a dissident leader arrested for allegedly conspiring to assassinate the French High Commissioner. The revolt did not escalate, but Selim's death the following year led to a deterioration in relations between the French and the Druzes.

The new governor was a French colonel, Gabriel Carbillet. Inspired by ideas of colonial development current in the interwar period, Carbillet avidly undertook public works projects; the Druzes were hardly enthusiastic about the roadways, irrigation and sanitation systems, and schools which he promoted. They particularly objected to forced labour instituted for work on the projects. Carbillet also attacked the privileges of land-owning families by offering land rights to peasants. Conservative and fearful of their masters, peasants showed little interest, and the plan backfired.

The Druze elite, not surprisingly, was angered by the land programme and by Carbillet's fiscal policy, which removed tax collection from village leaders (who had earned a commission on
the revenue they raised) and made taxes payable directly to central authorities. In 20 months in office, Carbillet thereby earned
the antipathy of Druze leaders and masses. He pursued an increasingly harsh policy which included imprisonment of several
hundred Druzes, the imposition of collective and individual fines,
and general rough handling of the local population. The High
Commissioner, receiving reports of widespread discontent, ordered
Carbillet to take a leave of absence in mid-1925.

This concession did not satisfy Druze notables, led by Sultân
Al-Atrash. In July 1925, the Druze assembly voted overwhelmingly
against Carbillet's return, while mass demonstrations against French
policies took place in Suwayda, the Druze capital. On 11 July,
French authorities summoned several Druze leaders to Damascus
for an audience with the High Commissioner; during the night
before the meeting was scheduled to take place, however, police
arrested the leaders and deported them to remote Palmyra. Sultân
Al-Atrash, rightly fearing a French ploy, had refused to go to Damascus so escaped arrest. He proceeded to call for insurrection,
marshalled an army of 8000–10 000 men – a fifth of the population of the Druze state – and on 20 July occupied the second
largest Druze city, Salkhad (which French soldiers had precipi-
tately abandoned). Buoyed by victory over a French military detachment, half of whom were killed, the next day, rebels successfully
drove northwards and besieged Suwayda. Druzes and French troops
waged pitched battles, with French superiority in weapons matched
by Druze manpower and tenacity. The Druzes won a signal victory in early August.

Rebellion spread. Nationalist leaders in Damascus issued a call
to arms and again demanded unification of Syria as an independent
state, the constitution of a popularly supported government and
withdrawal of foreign forces. Taking a cue from the French Revolution, they affirmed commitment to the principles of liberty,
equality and fraternity and denied that they wanted complete French
eviction from Syria and Lebanon. The rebels' manifestos, which
spoke of Syrian nationalism and pan-Arabism, attracted support
across the spectrum of Muslims, from landowners and merchants
to peasants and nomads. Only several small Muslim groups (notably the Alawites) remained untouched by rebellion. Christians,

terrified of Muslim attacks, cast their lot with the French, and the French used Circassian and Armenian troops against rebels, highlighting ethnic and religious aspects of the struggle.

As insurrection broke out in Damascus and provincial centres such as Homs, the Druze revolt turned into a nationalist revolution against the French mandate. Political meetings debated the ideological goals of rebels. Guerrilla actions, including attacks on police posts, transport lines and official headquarters, as well as pillage and sabotage, paralleled battles throughout August and September 1925. The French responded by outlawing nationalist parties, arresting rebel leaders, bringing in 15 000 troop reinforcements from North Africa and carrying out aerial bombardments. Particularly punishing was a 48-hour bombardment of Damascus in October, which killed 1400 people and wreaked considerable damage on the city's architecture and archaeological sites; the action provoked widespread condemnation in France and abroad.

Firepower began to turn the tables to French advantage. Early in 1926, the rebellion began to peter out because of French strength, attrition of rebel ranks (and factional rivalry) and the more conciliatory attitude of a new French representative in Damascus. With deft manoeuvres, Henry de Jouvenel offered the Syrians amnesties and greater participation in government, a strategy designed to win support, backed up with further air raids and punitive expeditions. By the spring of 1926, Jouvenel's diplomatic and military counter-offensive won the day. French forces captured Suwayda in April, although soldiers continued to attack pockets of resistance over the next few months. Jouvenel appointed a local leader to head the Syrian government, although curbing powers and soon dismissing nationalist members of his cabinet. Jouvenel's successor continued the conciliatory approach to the extent of working out a constitution allowing for full Syrian self-government. This went too far for Paris, and the Ministry of Foreign Affairs, which held responsibility for Syria, rejected the constitution, replaced the High Commissioner and suspended the Syrian assembly.

The rebellion cost French forces 2500 lives; perhaps 10 000 Syrians and Lebanese died. The insurrection failed, but it showed the strength of opposition to colonial rule – even in the attenuated form of a League of Nations mandate – and proved how both French policies of 'divide and rule' and the supposedly enlightened approach of colonial development and modernisation provoked discontent. Finally, it emphasised that only by military repression and deft collaboration with segments of local populations could France impose its will on distant domains.[8]

Indigenous Peoples and the Colonial System

Citizenship, Law and Political Representation

Law provided a way of establishing and preserving French control over the countries and peoples it conquered. The government in Paris was the source of colonial law, and its representatives in the colonies were the executors and enforcers of law. Populations brought under French administration lacked a say in the formulation of law codes; indeed colonialists would have thought it odd to consult 'primitive' tribes in Africa and the Pacific on legal questions, and French legislation could overturn statutes in the more 'civilised' protectorates and colonies of the Maghreb and Asia. Law-making was reserved for French citizens, yet even French settlers had little influence on legislative debate.

Indigenes, in general, were not French citizens but only subjects. Only after 1848 in the *vieilles colonies* (Martinique, Guadeloupe, Guyane and Réunion), in the four communes of Senegal (Saint-Louis, Dakar, Gorée and Rufisque), and later in the former realm of the Pomaré dynasty in the EFO (Tahiti and neighbouring islands) were natives of the colonies automatically French citizens. Others could gain citizenship by marriage or, in the case of children born to a Frenchman, formal recognition by the father.

Indigenes could petition for naturalisation, but various obstacles stood in the way. In general, to be naturalised, an indigene was required to be at least 21 years of age and to have served for three years in the French military or public service. In many colonies, other requirements included knowledge of French, justification of good character, meritorious service to France (perhaps attested by a decoration) and justification of sufficient material means of existence. Acquisition of citizenship generally entailed renunciation of customary status in local society, for instance, a Muslim's status according to Islamic law codes in Africa or traditional 'customary' law in the Pacific islands. Many were reluctant to take such a major step, for giving up traditional status could cut them off from their own communities and had a price – for example, Muslim men could henceforth have only the one wife allowed by French law rather than the multiple wives permitted under Islamic law. Furthermore, it meant that in civil cases, indigenes would be liable to French jurisdiction rather than traditional law codes; in societies where such questions as land use and inheritance were decided on the bases of customs and procedures foreign to French law, as was usually the case, a change in status held material and cultural repercussions. The trade-off, for most, was unacceptable, since French citizenship did not carry with it the vote, concessions on taxes, exemption from military service or many other immediately appreciable benefits.

Without citizenship indigenes were subject to an arbitrary system of law, the *code de l'indigénat* (the indigene or native code). A body of various regulations in many colonies, rather than a systematic law code, the *indigénat* gave police and judicial power to administrators. Without recourse to the usual process of arrest, indictment and trial, administrators in colonies where the *indigénat* was in force could summarily impose punishments for a host of offences. Fines, imprisonment, or both, could be levied on individuals and, collectively, on villages or other communities; indigenes could also have their property confiscated, be forced to provide free labour to the administration, or submit to corporal punishment. The list of punishable offences was lengthy; under an Algerian law of 1888, over 20 offences included: statements made against France or its government, disrespect or offensive conduct to a representative of colonial authority, refusal to take part in patrol duties or to furnish (for a price set by French officials) transport, food, water or fuel to administrators, negligence in payment of taxes or tax avoidance, detaining stray animals or giving refuge to vagabonds, travelling without a permit, not registering a weapon, brawling or other disorders, holding public meetings without authorisation or opening schools without a permit. Indigenes had only a *pro forma* right of appeal (and, in Algeria, only after 1890).

Codes de l'indigénat came into effect in Algeria from as early as 1834 and, although considered temporary, were regularly renewed. Use of the code was far from exceptional; in 1903–4, for instance, officials pronounced 22 407 convictions on the basis of the *indigénat* in Algeria. Regulations in Algeria provided a model for similar systems in Cochinchina in 1881, New Caledonia and Senegal in 1887, Tahiti in 1897, Cambodia the following year, and Madagascar in 1901; authorities applied the code elsewhere in Indochina and in sub-Saharan Africa, too. In some areas the list of punishable offences was even longer than in Algeria. In New Caledonia, for instance, natives could also be punished for littering, lighting a fire without proper precautions, cutting wood without authorisation, failing to declare births and deaths to local officials or not informing health authorities of illnesses from contagious diseases. The Indochinese were prohibited from buying alcohol and umbrellas.

Not all indigenous people were subject to the code. French citizens were exempt, so naturalisation brought immunity. Indigenous judges and those appointed to government posts, retired military officers and holders of military medals or the Legion of Honour could not be sentenced under the *indigénat*. The French thus used the *indigénat* as an easy means to control what they considered rebellious, dangerous, lazy or insolent individuals. Policy-makers saw the *indigénat* as a way to mete out swift, simple and efficient punishment. General Gallieni argued in 1905 that 'in a country where our sovereignty and our power must be affirmed by the maintenance of order and morality,... the delays and reservations inseparable from the application of justice, even in a simplified form, sometimes present serious inconveniences'.

For colonised peoples no greater proof of the inequity of foreign control existed than the *indigénat*. French officials, including those of subaltern rank, could arbitrarily impose token or severe punishments on individuals or groups for behaviour which, in some cases (such as offering hospitality to vagabonds) conformed to local customs, or for misdeeds (like failing to follow French standards of hygiene and dress) which had no cultural relevance. Any attack on France or its representatives, or failure to obey their orders, could be punished. The very latitude implicit in the list of offences, and the discretionary way the punishments could be pronounced, hardly discouraged abuses. Despite mounting protests, however, the *code de l'indigénat* was not abolished until 1928 in Algeria and 1946 elsewhere in the empire.[9]

The French also used more formal judicial procedures to punish criminal offences and political actions. Most of the nationalist leaders who emerged in the years after the 1920s were at some time subjected to arrest, conviction and incarceration for subversive acts or similar offences. Some were executed. The government used its powers to ban newspapers, censure publications, disband political parties and trade unions, prohibit demonstrations and forbid 'dangerous' individuals from residing in the colonies. Exile, whether imposed by administrative, judicial or military procedures, was an especially strong action against rebels; in the early years of colonisation, the French sent Abd el-Khader to Syria, Béhanzin to Martinique, Queen Ranavalona to Réunion and el-Mokrani's supporters to New Caledonia. Law was always on the French side.

Indigenes throughout the empire lacked political representation. Only after 1848 in the *vieilles colonies* and after 1915 in the 'four communes' of Senegal did all French citizens in the colonies have the right to vote in local and national elections. Algeria, divided (like the metropole) into *départements*, also had representation in the French National Assembly; since only French citizens voted, European settlers held control of the ballot box. French citizens selected delegates to the Superior Colonial Council (*Conseil Supérieur des Colonies*) established in 1883, but it enjoyed only consultative status and, in practice, exercised little influence. Europeans in the colonies, even when few in number, monopolised power in local assemblies (where they existed), city councils and other consultative bodies. Administrators, such as officials in the Arab Departments (*Bureaux Arabes*) which existed in Algeria from 1833 to 1914, made decisions about indigenous affairs. Only indigenous leaders appointed to government positions – for example, as *caïds* in North Africa and *petits chefs* and *grands chefs* in New Caledonia – held any institutionalised role in the colonies proper. In the protectorates, French authorities easily rejected or ignored resolutions and decrees of officially established local assemblies and titular rulers.

Only after 1946, and the constitution of the Fourth Republic, did France establish local assemblies throughout the empire. In most colonies, however, Europeans and indigenes constituted separate electoral colleges. Representatives of the Europeans were far more numerous than warranted by their proportion in total populations and, in any case, the assemblies' powers were strictly limited in a political system which eschewed colonial self-government. With the passage of new legislation in 1956, local governments gained real – but still restricted – powers, but the constitution of the Fifth Republic, adopted in 1958, again reduced those powers.

Land

While the French gave indigenous peoples little legal or political benefit from their rule, the colonial government imposed a number of obligations and extracted a variety of benefits from them. One of the most important was land. After conquest, the French needed land for government offices, forts and military barracks, shops and churches, houses and other accommodation. Larger amounts of land were required for public works projects, such as port facilities and rail lines, and still more property for settlers and their enterprises – the vineyards of Algeria, wheatfields and citrus orchards of Morocco, coffee plantations of West Africa, rice paddies and rubber plantations of Indochina, and livestock ranches of New Caledonia. The opening of mines – tin in Tonkin, phosphate in Tunisia, nickel in New Caledonia – meant claims on subsoil resources and sites for excavation. The French also wanted to exploit the forest resources of equatorial Africa.

The different societies which France colonised had a variety of written and non-written regulations concerning acquisition, use and disposal of property; few paralleled French law on land titles. Monarchs, such as the sultan of Morocco, emperor of Annam, dey of Tunis and the chiefs of some African regions, owned much of the land in their realms. In some areas, religious establishments held land as well. Families, 'tribes', villages, clans and individuals all owned land. Communal rights, ceremonial usages, usufruct rather than title, rotating use of land on the basis of collective decisions and many other patterns of land use obtained. In some parts of the empire, 'ownership' in the European sense was a foreign concept.

Conquest and occupation, jurists argued, gave France the right to take over properties, redistribute land and institute new land title regulations. Indeed the intellectual arguments justifying conquest provided an imperative to do so. The author of one legal tome put it simply in 1910:

A people or a race does not have the right to place itself outside the universal community of nations. The logic of things demands, furthermore, that a race which is hardly civilised must not retain a territory where more numerous populations from a more advanced civilisation could find great resources. We cannot recognise the indigenes' right to be the sole possessors of the riches of the soil and to deprive the rest of humanity of them through their ignorance, laziness or incapacity.

The French Civil Code, he argued, stated that vacant lands and lands without owners – the term *maîtres* (literally, 'masters') could mean those simply using land as well as holding legally recognised title – were part of the public domain. The author added:

It seems natural that indigenes can lose their right of sovereignty following a *prise de possession* by a more civilised nation, so long as this takeover conforms to the regulations of international law and falls into one of the categories of means recognised as legitimate, such as cession by the indigenous sovereign, conquest or pure and simple occupation when it is a question of new countries, which are often uninhabited or endowed solely with rudimentary political organisation.[10]

France thus assumed power to dispose of land as it saw fit. The legal niceties varied from colony to colony, but the end result was usually that the government and settlers could obtain land they wanted through dispossession of the original owners, with or without compensation. France considered itself the inheritor of public property of regimes it replaced, and passed legislation allowing the acquisition of private property. Authorities affirmed, in most colonies, that they would respect the rights of indigenous proprietors; such promises were not always kept.

Acquisition of land was most important in colonies of settlement. As French troops advanced in Algeria, the government took over land abandoned by fleeing Algerians and confiscated the lands of tribes which took up arms against the French. An 1843 decree added lands owned by religious foundations (*habous*) and the lands of the former bey of Algiers (*beylik*) to the public domain. A decree the following year allowed the *habous*, previously declared inalienable, to be subdivided and sold to colonists. It gave any owner of uninhabited and uncultivated land three months to put forward a claim; since many Algerians, unaware of the regulation, did not do so, more land entered French hands. In 1851, Paris declared all Algerian forests state property, a measure which permitted the arrest of Algerians who violated restrictions on hunting or other use of forests. The law recognised a difference between collective property (*arch*) and individual holdings (*melk*), although many Algerian property-holding arrangements did not fit precisely into either category. The state could expropriate collective holdings for settlement. The government, furthermore, implemented a policy of *cantonnement*, in which lands which Algerian communities were considered not to need were forcibly taken over by the state; Algerians were concentrated in reservations, generally on less valuable land. The head of the Constantine land bureau judged that it was usually sufficient to allow Arabs to keep a quarter to a half of the property they claimed, but some communities lost as much as 85 per cent of their holdings.

Widespread spoliation caused criticism in France; even Napoleon III argued that Algeria was an Arab kingdom (under his rule), where indigenous rights ought to be preserved. An 1863 law confirmed Algerians' rights to lands which they occupied or to which they had traditional claims; possibilities of expropriating *melk* and *arch* land were to be limited. Settlers protested vigorously, and the measure was never widely applied. By the end of the 1860s, one-third of the Algerian land which had been surveyed had been taken over by the state, much of it redistributed to colonists. The defeat of el-Mokrani's rebellion in 1871 provided an opportunity to confiscate 450 000 more hectares of land. Over the next decade, the government freely handed out 30 000–40 000 hectares a year to new settlers, and migrants also purchased properties.

An 1895 enquiry estimated that since 1830, Algerians had lost the use of 5 million hectares of land; by 1936, the total rose to 7.7 million hectares, which represented about 40 per cent of the land possessed by indigenous Algerians before French conquest. Dispossession was even more dramatic than that figure indicated because of the rapid growth rate of the Algerian population – which almost doubled between 1914 and 1954; moreover, much land remaining in Algerian hands was of inferior quality. The result was pauperisation of Algerians, increasing possibilities for settlers to enrich themselves, and rising hatred of the French.[11]

In New Caledonia, trumpeted as France's other *colonie de peuplement*, spoliation proceeded in similar fashion. In 1855, the government declared that Melanesians ought to enjoy rights to the lands they actually cultivated but not to vacant lands. The differentiation took no account of Melanesian understanding of land ownership and use, but the law allowed the sale at public auction of land lots deemed unoccupied. Subsequent decrees made it easier for colonists to obtain land outside the public domain and to acquire free concessions from the government. Between 1860 and 1880 settlers' land thereby rose from 1000 hectares to 230 000 hectares, including small holdings and veritable latifundia owned by Nouméa businessmen.

Authorities pursued *cantonnement* in New Caledonia just as in Algeria. A decree of 1868 established native reservations (*réserves*) under tribal control. The fact that 'tribes' were not real indigenous units and that the land set aside was not always the same territory as particular clans claimed did not trouble the authorities. The decree declared *réserves* inalienable. As more settlers arrived, however, the government in 1876 allowed the redrawing of *réserve* boundaries. In 1897, yet another decree let the government resettle Melanesians if their land (including *réserves*) was 'needed' by Europeans; within five years, Melanesian *réserves* on the Grande Terre shrank from 320 000 to 120 000 hectares. At the end of the century, Melanesians retained control of only one-tenth of the land on the New Caledonian mainland.[12]

Colonists obtained much land elsewhere in the empire. In Indochina decrees by the French government and, under French pressure, the Annamese emperor, permitted large-scale expropriation and redistribution of properties. By 1930, the French had acquired 104 000 hectares in Tonkin, 168 400 in Annam and 606 500 in Cochinchina. Before French conquest, most Vietnamese enjoyed effective control of their own land. By the middle of the twentieth century, over half the Tonkinese and Annamese were landless and in Cochinchina, where French settlers concentrated, only a quarter of the Vietnamese owned land.[13] In the AEF, the government granted monopolistic use (though not actual title) of most land to concessionary companies set up in the 1890s. In the AOF, a small number of settlers owned an outsize amount of land in both towns and the rural areas. In the New Hebrides, one French settler purchased nominal title to a third of all land. Much of the land remaining outside French hands – the Sahara, tropical jungles in Guyane and the AEF, and tiny islands – was ill-suited, in any case, for profit-making.

Taxation and Labour

Europeans expropriated land and appropriated indigenes' labour and earnings as well. The French collected a variety of taxes, including taxes on land, imported goods, tobacco, alcohol and opium.

Indigenous men (though often not women), except those exempt because they were French citizens or fell into certain narrow categories of employment, also paid a head-tax (*capitation*). The rationale was that public works programmes and other French efforts benefited indigenous populations as well as Europeans in the colonies, and indigenous populations should help fund such undertakings; in particular, authorities said that the *capitation* helped to pay for medical services provided to indigenes.

Many Africans, Indochinese and islanders, however, lived in a subsistence economy which remained only partially monetised. They had to obtain waged employment or sell commodities they produced to obtain cash for the *capitation*. This state of affairs fitted into French plans for the development of salaried employment. Wage labour, it was thought, accustomed colonised peoples to European labour systems and stimulated productivity; in addition, the incomes people earned would increase their purchasing power, aiding European trade. Fines levied for non-payment of taxes produced further revenue for colonial treasuries.

The government, as well, obliged indigenes to contribute labour, without remuneration, to the administration. This much resented *corvée* usually required men, and sometimes women, to provide free labour for a certain number of days per year – in principle, no more than ten – generally to public works projects, such as the maintenance of roadways. Abuses of the *corvée* were common and sometimes led to veritable forced labour.

The collectors of the *capitation* (usually exempted from the *corvée*) were indigenous officials appointed by the administration. Their backgrounds, titles and duties varied widely from colony to colony. These intermediaries between the foreign colonisers and the indigenous masses became an elite in local populations, wielded significant power, and, in relative terms, received substantial pay – and, sometimes, such honorary attributes as uniforms and decorations.

Most indigenes in the empire worked as manual labourers: forestry-workers in the AEF, mine-workers in Tunisia and New Caledonia, workers on vineyards in Algeria, harvesters of groundnuts, coffee, cocoa and other tropical products in the AOF and Madagascar, rubber-gatherers in Indochina. Everywhere in the empire, they held jobs at ports and construction sites, and the building of railways and canals employed enormous numbers of Africans and Asians. Perhaps the most back-breaking labour – and most criticised employment – was the use of porters in equatorial Africa. Explorers, traders and planters hired men and women to serve as human beasts of burden in dense tropical jungles, carrying on their backs or heads enormous loads, trekking between settlements or between navigable portions of waterways or rail lines. Porters, like many other labourers, received only derisory wages, and thousands died from overwork.

Manual labour performed by indigenes was physically hard and often dangerous. It demanded little training and presented almost no possibilities for advancement. Employers enforced harsh discipline, reinforced with corporal punishment of malefactors or shirkers. Absences from work were not tolerated, even for reasons of sickness, family responsibilities or attendance at ceremonies and festivals. Indigenes, however, had no alternative to work, as they had to earn money for taxes and wanted an income for imported goods. Trade unions for indigenous workers did not exist in most colonies until after the Second World War, and the government often banned them as subversive. Industrial action was not especially fruitful, as employers could often find replacement labourers and troops could end demonstrations. Administrators wielded the *code de l'indigénat* against 'wrongdoers'. Only revelations by anti-colonialist journalists of horrific conditions drew attention to the plight of colonial labour.

A significant number of indigenes found slightly better jobs as domestic servants – cooks, cleaners, drivers, attendants, housekeepers, nannies, waiters. The administration, businesses and wealthy settlers employed retinues of retainers, and even colonists of relatively modest means hired a cook, housekeeper and *boy* (the English term was used), whom expatriates considered an indispensable servant. Memoirs of colonists devote warm pages to the domestic staff whom they employed, although accounts are usually coloured with reminiscences of occasions when servants, unaware of European customs, did silly things – for instance, wearing garnish intended for trays of food. Often, too, they contain asides about what Europeans saw as dishonesty, duplicity and stupidity.

The industrial sector, little developed in the colonies, provided jobs for workers in bottling and canning plants, factories which refined raw materials for export (such as mineral refineries), and small establishments making textiles, furniture and other goods for local consumers. Other indigenes worked in the service sector of the economy, as employees in hotels, shop assistants, hospital orderlies, garage mechanics, lower-level technicians in manufacturing, printers, telegraphers, subaltern white-collar employees in offices. Especially in cities, a large demand existed for employees in the tertiary sector, from butchers and bakers to secretaries and clerks. Although such jobs were not necessarily highly paid, nor were service workers always well treated, conditions were less arduous than for manual labourers.

The churches provided employment as well. Thousands of Africans, Asians and islanders became priests, friars or nuns in the Catholic church, and pastors and deacons in the French Protestant church or other Protestant denominations. Churches were eager to develop vocations among parishioners in order to provide necessary staff and further entrench Christianity. Training for an ecclesiastical position or acceptance into a religious congregation provided some education, food, clothing and lodging, and a certain status in both European and indigenous eyes. The price was abandonment of traditional religious beliefs, obedience to church regulations and, for Catholics, celibacy.

White-collar jobs represented career opportunities and possibilities of upward mobility for local populations. Few Africans, Asians and islanders possessed the skills necessary for office work – at a minimum, literacy in French and numeracy – in the late 1800s and early 1900s, but those who did usually gained status in their own communities and became essential auxiliaries to the French. By the 1930s and 1940s, and certainly after the Second World War, more and more were able to procure white-collar jobs, and both the administration and some private enterprises made a conscious effort to 'indigenise' their staffs. The so-called *évolués* ('evolved ones'), who spoke French and had European-style work, were seen as proof of French success in the *mission civilisatrice* and as leaders of the reconstructed empire. But the ranks of *évolués* also provided most of the nationalist leaders who campaigned for independence from France.

Some categories of employees who held office jobs or similar employment played a particularly vital role in the colonies. Interpreters, for instance, served as links between the French, who seldom learned local languages well, and the bulk of the indigeneous populations, most of whom did not have the opportunity to learn French. The administration had an interest in paying interpreters well and seeing that they worked in relatively agreeable conditions. Though few in number – there were 248 official interpreters in the AOF and 49 in the AEF in 1913 – interpreters joined the Europeanised elite among colonised peoples. Indigenes, as well, found work in the increasing number of post offices – there were 262 post offices in the AOF on the eve of the First World War. The postal service offered steady work, reasonable salaries and distinct chances of promotion, as did the indigenous police forces. The AOF counted 3658 African policemen in 1911, the AEF 2331 constables.[14]

The military was one of the largest employers of men in the empire. Indigenes served in various units, but by far the most famous were the *tirailleurs sénégalais*, the misleadingly called Senegalese gunners. Governor Faidherbe created a corps of 500 Senegalese troops in 1857, although the French had used African soldiers earlier. By the turn of the century, the *tirailleurs sénégalais* numbered 8400; in the 1920s, 48 000. Despite the name of the corps, soldiers came from throughout sub-Saharan Africa, the largest contingents from Soudan and Upper Volta. Volunteers generally issued from the African masses rather than the elite – the typical soldier was a physically fit peasant in his twenties – and agreed to serve for five or six years. From 1912 onwards, the French recruited conscripts as well as volunteers. The *tirailleurs sénégalais* received a salary (in 1910) that was only half of the daily wages of a labourer, and a quarter of their earnings were withheld until their discharge; promotion past the rank of lieutenant was rare. (In 1928, there were only 40 African sergeants.) Volunteers sometimes received a bonus, however, and *tirailleurs sénégalais* gained exemption from the *capitation* and *corvée*; they received a half-pension after 15 years, a full pension after 25 years of service.

The *tirailleurs sénégalais* served throughout the empire. They took part in the conquest of Tonkin in the 1880s, and composed 15 per cent of the French army which occupied Morocco in 1911–12. During the First World War, 171 000 soldiers from the AOF and AEF fought for France and suffered high casualty rates. The heroism of the *tirailleurs sénégalais* during the war helped change stereotypes of Africans, the jungle savage replaced by the smiling, brave soldier willing to sacrifice his life for France. In the Second World War, 160 000 *tirailleurs sénégalais* served in French forces, and during the Indochinese war for independence, 56 000 black African troops fought on the French side.

Service as *tirailleurs sénégalais* left a strong mark on African men. The mortality rate of African soldiers was three times that of

European troops; over 33 000 black Africans died in the First World War, and many other indigenes suffered injuries which left them incapacitated. For survivors their tours of duty had provided a chance for distant travel, social promotion and a certain education and vocational training. On discharge, some returned to their home villages. A large number clustered in larger towns in Africa, where the administration gave returned soldiers preference for such jobs as policemen, forest guards, postmen, male nurses and chauffeurs. On the eve of independence, France's black African colonies counted 96 000 veterans of the *tirailleurs sénégalais*.[15]

Education and Health

Colonialists took great pride in France's establishment of schools and hospitals throughout the empire. The colonial world had boasted various systems of education before falling under European rule: Islamic *medersas* in the Maghreb and part of black Africa, Buddhist and Confucian education in Indochina, traditional forms of education everywhere, Christian missionary schools in a number of locales. The French brought a European system of education to Africa, Asia and the islands. Many schools were established by religious congregations, whose members were teachers. Colonial authorities gradually set up state schools as well, particularly when anticlericalism gathered strength in France, leading to the separation of church and state in the metropole in the early years of the twentieth century.

Whether under church or state control, most schools concentrated on the basics: reading and writing French, arithmetic and introductory courses in science, history, geography and other disciplines. Whether the curriculum should be especially adapted for the colonies or adhere to standard courses and examinations set in France created heated debate. Educational theorists in France generally considered that most indigenes had little need for advanced education and would seldom get past elementary classes. Tailored diplomas, such as a special colonial school certificate (*brevet de capacité coloniale*) awarded by secondary schools, seemed appropriate, even if not equivalent to French diplomas (like the *baccalauréat*). Others dismissed such certificates as second-class and demanded that the metropolitan curriculum and degree structure be fully instituted overseas.

Textbooks shipped from France were written for a metropolitan audience and often had little direct resonance in the colonies. African and Indochinese students learned about 'our ancestors the Gauls' (as a well-known history text began), memorised lists of French provincial capitals and major events in European history, and studied the flora and fauna of temperate and Alpine regions far away. Until well into the twentieth century, teachers and texts paid at best cursory attention to the history, geography and culture of Africa, Asia or the islands. The study of French was all important, for acquisition of French, teachers and politicians claimed, provided access to further knowledge, an opening to the outside world and career possibilities. Mastery of the complex rules of French grammar, proper articulation of French speech and familiarity with the classics of French literature formed the crowning achievement of education in the empire and further evidence to colonialists of the success of the *mission civilisatrice.*

The aim of education, more or less openly admitted, was to produce cadres for the lower levels of the administration and professionals. Indeed French authorities had no intention of producing a large highly educated class for whom possibilities of employment would be few and among whom nationalist or anticolonial sentiments might develop. French expatriates constituted the majority of students at universities established in Algiers, Hanoi, Dakar and other cities, as well as the few secondary schools which existed – there were only two secondary schools (*lycées*) in the AOF.

Indigenes predominated in specialised vocational and professional schools. Medical schools founded in Antananarivo (in 1897), Hanoi (in 1901) and Dakar (in 1918) trained indigenous medical doctors over a five-year period of study. Numbers, however, remained small. The Vietnamese school admitted an average of 25 students a year, the AOF school a dozen; 400 indigenous doctors graduated from the Dakar school from 1918 to 1937. Schools in Hanoi and Fès provided training in agronomy. The Ecole William-Ponty, established in Senegal in 1903, the most famous French school in black Africa, educated schoolteachers, bureaucrats and military personnel; in 40 years, it graduated 2200 students.

Despite the achievements of such institutions, only a minuscule proportion of colonised people received a French education. At the end of the nineteenth century, 2500 pupils studied in primary schools in the AOF, with a similar number enrolled in the AEF. Rapid growth followed; in 1935, primary schools counted 62 300 pupils in the AOF, 15 877 in the AEF, 12 514 in Cameroon and 10,018 in Togo. These figures represented less than 0.5 per cent of the population in the AOF and AEF, 0.66 per cent in Cameroon and 1.33 in Togo. Almost all pupils were in the first years of elementary school. Only 930 pupils in 1934–5 had reached the final years of primary school (*écoles primaires supérieures*) in the AOF, ten in the newly-opened *école primaire supérieure* in Brazzaville, the sole such school in the AEF.[16]

Results did not differ dramatically elsewhere in the empire. In 1939, in Algeria, of 1.25 million children aged six to fourteen, only 110 000 were enrolled in schools; in 1954–5, just over 15 per cent of school-age students attended classes, and there were only 6260 non-European students in secondary schools (of whom more than a fifth were non-Muslims). Only one in seven Muslims spoke French and one in eighteen or twenty was able to read and write French; among Muslim women, only one in 150 read and wrote French. In Indochina, 200 000 out of over 2 million school-aged children were enrolled in 1925; even in the regions best endowed with schools, only one in twelve boys and one in a hundred girls were enrolled. Only 10 per cent completed five years of schooling. There were only three *écoles primaires supérieures* in Tonkin, and four each in Annan and Cochinchina. The smaller, more remote and more 'primitive' colonies were less well served; not until the late 1960s, for instance, did the first Melanesian earn a *baccalauréat*. Conditions did improve after the Second World War. For instance, in Madagascar, there were 185 000 primary school students in 1930, but the number had grown to 321 000 in 1958, by which time just under half of school-age children attended classes, and four-fifths of *lycée* students were Malagasy.[17]

The French were proud of their achievements in health care as well as education. The colonial medical corps, established in 1890, employed 5000 doctors, pharmacists, nurses and other personnel over the next 70 years. The French created 41 general hospitals, almost 600 smaller hospitals, 2000 dispensaries, 6000 maternity units, 6 medical schools, 21 institutions for training doctors' assistants and nurses and 14 medical research centres (*Instituts Pasteur*) in the empire. Statistics record impressive achievements – for instance, doctors administered 20 million smallpox vaccines from 1948 to 1954 alone. There were also great advances in medical care; the number of public clinics (including hospitals) grew in the AEF from 53 in 1925 to 209 in 1939 and 393 in 1956; in the

AOF the number of medical practitioners grew ten times over during the interwar years, as did the number of hospital beds. French medical care reduced the incidence of epidemic disease: the mortality rate for victims of smallpox in the AOF fell from 16 to 4 per cent in the 15 years after 1935, and the number of children in Dakar carrying traces of malaria in their blood plummeted from 47 per cent in 1938 to 1 per cent in 1954.

Different statistics put some of these achievements into perspective, underlining the tireless work done by medical personnel but pointing as well to the inadequacy of health care. The AOF might well boast 30 000 hospital beds in the mid-1950s, but the total population of French West Africa then stood at 18.7 million.[18] In Indochina in the early 1940s, there was one medical doctor for every 157 000 people, and one nurse for each 15 000 inhabitants; as many as 90 per cent of Vietnamese villagers suffered from tuberculosis, malaria or trachoma.[19]

Culture and Identity

European presence had an immense impact on the cultures and national identities of colonised people. Colonialists claimed many accomplishments: Europeans abolished slavery, ended cannibalism and human sacrifice, reduced the arbitrary and tyrannical power of traditional rulers, provided greater opportunities for labour, dispensed health care and education, and brought scientific and technical modernity to Africa, Asia and the islands; missionaries added that they had brought the true faith of Christianity to the heathen. Anti-colonialists, including many nationalists in the colonies, however, claimed that Europeans had systematically tried to destroy pre-contact culture, outlawing ceremonies, demeaning indigenous art, music and literature, disrupting social relations, replacing religious beliefs, displacing social orders established over centuries or millennia. Commentators such as Frantz Fanon argued that by forcing people to behave like Europeans and only rewarding those who did so, the colonial system had turned indigenes against themselves, breeding self-hatred, scorn for inherited traditions and values, feelings of inferiority and futile attempts to mock European attitudes and behaviour.[20]

Certainly, even when they admired certain aspects of non-Western cultures, Europeans always broadcast the message that European civilisation was superior not only for themselves but for those they conquered. Europeanisation was modern; African, Asian and island cultures were, by and large, backward or degenerate. 'Natives' who jettisoned their old cultures (or at least their most 'primitive' aspects) and adopted French ways had a better chance of success in the new world of science, technology, industry, international trade – and European overlordship. The irony was that opportunities to take advantage of modern European culture through education and jobs with real potential for training and advancement were severely limited.

Colonised people lived under a double burden of trying to fulfil traditional familial, communal and cultural responsibilities and, at the same time, coming under increased pressure to westernise. Some wholeheartedly adopted European ways, essentially becoming more French than the French, although they often experienced a rude shock on realisation that the French themselves seldom saw them as true equals. Others clung tenaciously to non-European beliefs and behaviour, even if such efforts became increasingly difficult in the face of obligatory labour, taxation, military service and propaganda. Still others developed syncretic belief systems combining Western and indigenous traditions.

Most indigenous people found some compromise between the traditions which they revered and the colonialism they were forced to accept. Local chiefs tried to maintain a degree of authority under French auspices. Non-Christian beliefs could be quietly incorporated into Christianity, overlaid by Catholic or Protestant nomenclature, doctrines or ceremonies. The French language could provide a vehicle for preserving or reviving local cultures – Léopold Sedar Senghor was both the first black African to pass the highest French state examination (*agrégation*) and leader of the *négritude* movement. Political ideas imported from Europe, whether French constitutionalism or Marxist revolutionary theories, inspired national independence movements, the leaders of which issued from European-educated colonial elites. Even in daily life, European food, clothing and building materials supplemented but did not entirely replace traditional materials. Such compromise with colonialism, whether unwilling, reluctant or enthusiastic, proved the strength and resiliency of Africans, Asians and islanders in the face of European domination.

Colonised Women

The status of women in societies which France conquered varied greatly. Traditional society in the Comoros Islands, for instance, was matrilineal and matrilocal, while in most other cultures it was patrilineal and patrilocal. In many Islamic countries, religious and legal authorities permitted polygamy, although this was not allowed in some other cultures. In much of the non-European world, great emphasis was placed on the pre-marital virginity of women, but this was less the case, for example, in Polynesia. In general, outside Europe just as in European societies, women had an inferior position to men, seldom enjoying equal access to political power, economic opportunities or culture. Gender roles were usually different and clearly marked, although women laboured along-side men in agriculture and other economic activities while also being responsible for child-rearing and housework. Furthermore, in most societies, special ceremonies, initiation rites or art forms were reserved for women.

The effects of colonialism on African, Asian and islander women were great. Some colonial theorists thought that women provided the key to European control: if indigenous women could be con-verted to Christianity, convinced to send their children to Euro-pean schools, or given European employment, they would pass on Western habits and beliefs to their offspring and other mem-bers of the family. Writers also promoted campaigns to eradicate what they saw as the mistreatment of indigenous women by their menfolk and the subordinate position of women in 'native' societies – preaching however, that was not always put into practice.

Missionaries and other expatriates tried to stamp out what they considered obscene behaviour, sexual licence and nudity among women. In Oceania, they encouraged (or sometimes forced) women who had previously worn clothing which did not cover their breasts or legs to wear *robes mission* ('mission dresses'), demure loose-fitting frocks which covered them from the neck to below the knees. Paradoxically, in Islamic societies, where women were veiled, the French sometimes obliged women to remove scarves and veils, which they regarded as part of antiquated Muslim fanaticism. Prudery, however, did not keep Europeans from being sexually obsessed with non-European women.

Europeans provided various types of employment to indigenous women. Some, voluntarily or by economic necessity, became

prostitutes or concubines of European men. Others joined religious orders. Many found work as domestics, generally performing duties – house-keeping, child-minding, cooking – considered
appropriate for women. Women also worked on sugar and rubber plantations; they harvested tropical products, worked in offices and, in central Africa, did back-breaking porterage. Only a
very few women found highly skilled jobs, largely because they
lacked opportunities for education; although a school for Muslim girls opened in Algiers as early as 1845, and many schools
elsewhere accepted girl students, numbers remained extremely
low. Nevertheless, by the twentieth century, indigenous women
had trained as teachers and nurses. Women who did achieve great
wealth, political power or European culture – for example, various indigenous monarchs or chiefs, and a dynamic circle of West
Indian literary women active both in the Antilles and in Paris –
were the exception rather than the rule. In any case, the French
often limited (or eliminated) their authority – Queen Pomaré of
Tahiti and Queen Ranavalona of Madagascar were both forced
to submit to French overlordship.

The French undertook particular campaigns to disseminate better
health care for pregnant women and infants, although results were
sometimes disappointing. They tried to introduce indigenous
women to European innovations, such as the sewing machine,
ostensibly intending to liberate them from some of the more arduous chores but also hoping to create new commercial activities
and train labourers. Certain colonialists hoped to transform African, Asian and islander women into European-style housewives
and employees, but not all women were keen to abandon their
old ways, and some who tried to do so found that they became
outcasts in both European and indigenous society.[21]

The Colonial Landscape

The French had an enormous impact on the natural and built
environments of the countries they conquered, just as on the lives
of the peoples who came under their control.[22] They introduced
new species of plants and animals into various colonies or dramatically extended the area cultivated in particular crops. In the
1600s, they had introduced sugar to the West Indies, and in
the eighteenth century, navigators took breadfruit from Tahiti to

the Antilles. Europeans later took rubber trees to Indochina, cattle to New Caledonia, and sheep to tiny Kerguelen. They greatly expanded vineyards in North Africa, coffee plantations in West Africa and coconut plantations in the New Hebrides. They also planted market gardens of European fruits and vegetables to satisfy expatriates' taste.

Economic development and public works projects transformed natural resources. Canals, dykes and dams changed the flow of rivers, and irrigation works channelled water to areas brought under cultivation. Loggers felled forests of tropical hardwood, while miners excavating nickel, phosphate and other ores left gaping holes where open-cut mining had been practised. Engineers ordered the clearing of land for roadways and railway lines, and settlers cleared land for houses. In settler colonies, whole towns and villages sprang up in previously virgin territory. Artificial fertilisers changed the composition of the soil. Expatriates and tourists on safari killed elephants, lions and other big game animals for sport, leaving some species in dangerously reduced numbers.

Environmental degradation was not solely the fault of the foreigners, nor was it unique to colonised areas. Much of it occurred before campaigns for nature conservation attracted public opinion. Yet programmes of reafforestation, repair of the environment after mining, and efforts to preserve flora and fauna from extinction were relatively rare. Colonists treated the natural world as a sometimes agreeable, often dangerous terrain to be conquered, mastered and exploited. Driven by the aim of colonial development, they saw the natural milieu of the empire as an inexhaustible storehouse of resources for their use. Areas which were immediately or potentially of use had to be brought under control, and would become the subjects of countless development studies and often unrealised projects. New uses could be found for even the most unpromising regions, as when France began setting off nuclear explosions in the far reaches of the Sahara in the early 1960s, then transferred the testing site to a remote atoll in Polynesia after Algerian independence; few policy-makers expressed concern about radioactive pollution from atmospheric or underground tests.

The way colonial places looked metamorphosed dramatically. French construction materials provided new building-blocks, from iron rails to concrete and glass buildings. French schools, churches and train stations dotted the landscape. Tin roofs replaced thatch,

European-style houses replaced indigenous dwellings, 'modern conveniences' replaced non-European kitchens, toilets and bathrooms (at least for the richest inhabitants). New sources of energy arrived with electricity and the internal combustion engine. Even the sounds of Africa, Asia and the islands changed with the roar of automobiles, trains and aeroplanes, the sound of European machinery, the music from radios.

Such changes were magnified in colonial cities. Indeed large cities constituted one of the most remarkable legacies left by colonists. The French founded a number of cities, such as Dakar, which became one of the largest African metropolises. The French were proud that, under their control, Saigon became the 'Paris of the Orient', complete with wide boulevards, municipal buildings and bustling cafés. They made Algiers resemble a French provincial capital and constructed new European cities (usually called *villes nouvelles*) on the outskirts of pre-existing indigenous cities. Larger cities from Hanoi to Antananarivo, Abidjan to Brazzaville, even such backwaters as Nouméa and Papeete drew migrants from their hinterlands and overseas. The establishment of commercial entrepôts, administrative centres and military garrisons produced a new kind of urbanisation. The colonial world increasingly became dominated by cities, and colonised populations moved towards becoming city-dwellers.[23]

The new activities and growing population of cities created a need for urban planning, and French designers largely created colonial cities in the French image. Building programmes and renovation projects left an indelible imprint on colonial landscapes. Cities housed massive constructions meant to show off French power. Governors' palaces spoke of the might of the French administration, while public buildings, such as post offices, testified to French modernity and the benefits of colonial rule. Theatres and opera-houses – the French built Asia's biggest theatre in Hanoi – were showpieces for French culture, although patronised only by a few expatriates and a minuscule local elite. Broad streets and great squares, similar to those of Paris, provided axes to connect buildings and, not coincidentally, avenues for the movement of troops.

Architectural styles mirrored colonial policy. In the late 1800s, French buildings embodied the idea of colonial assimilation. In Indochina, for instance, grand edifices in resolutely French style showed no influence from the Vietnamese or other local archi-

THE FRENCH AND THE 'NATIVES'

tectural traditions. Greek columns and a neo-classical façade decorated the governor's palace in Saigon. The city hall, complete
with arches and a clocktower, was a gaudy pastiche of the Hôtel-
de-Ville in Paris, its wedding-cake pretentiousness provoking criticism even from Saigon's European settlers. The central train station
in Hanoi could just as easily have graced a French provincial city
as the capital of Tonkin; the Pont Doumer over the Red River in
Hanoi – proclaimed the longest bridge in Asia, although it had
only one lane for traffic – would have looked at home spanning
the Seine; and the towers of Hanoi's cathedral seemed to come
from a medieval illumination.

After the turn of the century, as the idea of association replaced assimilation, architectural styles also adapted. Newer buildings in Vietnam sported upturned roofs, verandas and cupolas
that looked indigenous, even if they were a mixture of various
Vietnamese, Cambodian and Laotian styles. Lyautey's desire to
protect Morocco's cultural patrimony inspired an eclectic blend
of Western and North African motifs in an 'Arabising' style. Architects employed white stucco walls, ornamented columns and
porcelain or tile mosaics, incorporated Muslim wooden screens
and prayer niches, and added horseshoe arches and vaulted
corbelling. Buildings like the central post office in Casablanca,
built in 1920, or the sultan's palace in Casablanca, looked North
African from outside, although their spatial orientation, disposition of rooms and use revealed French inspiration. Nevertheless,
Lyautey's hybrid architecture and urban planning, particularly in
Casablanca and Rabat, created a design which attempted to mate
the Maghrebin and the French, a fitting symbol of the French
impact on indigenous civilisations in the colonial world.[24]

7 Colonial Culture in France

Colonial expansion and the affairs of empire seldom became the preoccupation of the French. Most were more concerned with economic development and conditions of employment, political campaigns and ideological quarrels in local politics, and the ever-changing state of European conflicts, than with the affairs of remote outposts. Only the exploits of swashbuckling explorers, the dangers of 'native' revolt or occasional rumours of war with an imperial rival captured front-page attention, at least until the Indochinese and Algerian wars awakened the French to the hazards of colonial involvement.

Nevertheless, a substantial number of people displayed great interest in the empire, and the lives of most French citizens were at some time touched by colonial activities. Schoolchildren read about colonies in textbooks, spectators attended colonial fairs, soldiers joined colonial regiments, churchgoers donated to missions, residents of port cities witnessed ships arriving with cargoes of exotic goods, collectors bought colonial paraphernalia – masks and statues from Africa, coffee-pots, copper trays and djellabas from North Africa, silk robes and opium pipes from Asia, or maybe colonial stamps and medals.[1] Almost everyone ate bananas and drank coffee grown in the colonies. The average French person was perhaps not fanatically interested in Greater France, but few did not in some way come into contact with colonial concerns.

For some, the colonies were a hobby, a passion, even an obsession. They joined colonial associations and subscribed to colonial newspapers, read colonial novels and frequented colonial exhibitions. They were the creators and consumers of a colonial culture or, perhaps, subculture. Just as others had their own particular subcultures – professional, political, religious, sexual – so certain individuals spent much time and energy immersed in the empire. Many were only armchair colonialists with little intention of actually becoming involved in the colonial adventure through trade, military service, missionary work or settlement. But a general public nourished by the cultural manifestations of colonialism provided the seedbed for the growth of colonial vocations. The culture of empire also provided the ground for anti-colonialism. Public meetings, travelogues, novels, manifestos and associations spread opposition to overseas expansion just as promotion of conquest. Anti-colonialist leaders took as passionate an interest in empire as did their opponents, even though their points of view differed radically. Furthermore, many initially attracted to the *outre-mer*, including notable writers and social scientists, then discovered the dark side of colonialism; colonial experiences thereby bred anti-colonialism.

If the empire was seldom in the foreground of French life or culture, it often lay in the background. Edward Said has pointed out how imperial expansion permeated European culture, either directly or indirectly, for instance in the many works of literature with colonial settings or in which significant turns in the plot depend on colonial events, even when the link is not clearly drawn.[2] Some of France's finest writers and artists – and countless mediocre ones – integrated imperial themes into their works, and the influence of empire ranged from the most unashamedly propagandistic colonialist books and paintings to the the most anti-colonialist, from the most unadventurous old-fashioned styles to the most avant-garde innovations.

The cultural influences of empire were exceptionally wide-ranging, from esoteric scientific research to poster art and advertisements. Colonial influences can be identified in music: such vaudeville songs as 'Ma Belle Tonkinoise' (about a Frenchman's Vietnamese concubine), as well as orchestral works by composers like Maurice Ravel and Darius Milhaud. The colonies suggested new fashion – women's clothing at the beginning of the twentieth century, with Oriental silks, mock Levantine frocks and a more natural look than was common in the nineteenth century, owed much to exoticism.[3] The colonies provided a new destination for holidays; ever increasing numbers of tourists took ocean cruises to Africa and Asia, visited the temples of Angkor Wat and the *casbah* of Marrakesh, or went on African safaris and Saharan treks.

Fans of automobile racing and aviation followed the exploits of
drivers and pilots, just as their ancestors had charted camel trips
across the African interior. The first automobile crossing of Africa, from Algeria to South Africa, organised by André Citroën
in 1924–5, riveted public attention, and the documentary on the
Croisière noire packed cinemas. The pioneering flights from France
to Africa undertaken by Antoine de Saint-Exupéry, and the accounts in his own books (*Courrier du Sud* and *Vol de Nuit*), similarly excited a large audience. Saint-Exupéry, an aristocrat, creator
of one of the most beloved characters in modern French literature, *Le Petit Prince*, and heroic aviator – he almost died after his
plane crashed into the Libyan desert on a flight from Paris to
Saigon in 1935 – became the model of a new explorer.[4]

A large measure of the cultural influence of colonies simply
prolonged earlier European fascination with far-away places – the
French of the *ancien régime* indulged in fantasies about Oriental
harems, devoured the narratives of explorers in the South Pacific, decorated their houses with *chinoiseries* and *japonaiseries*.[5]
Starting in the mid-nineteenth century, France's arbiters of culture discovered new domains where they could respond to the
call of the exotic, and the expansion of empire provided an opportunity to do so.

Literature

With the expansion of the reading public in the nineteenth century, thanks to increasing literacy and wider dissemination of books,
the written word served as a key medium for the spread of ideas,
and misapprehensions, about the world overseas. Academic careers, colonial vocations, and general interest in distant places
owed much to reading, and novels exercised a particularly strong
attraction. Works of fiction made the empire more familiar to
the French, romanticised colourful and distant places, served as
propaganda for colonialist ideas or, in some cases, for anti-colonialism.[6]

Exoticism was present in many works of nineteenth-century literature. Jules Verne, the father of science fiction, created fantastic
locations in his tales, whose publication (beginning in the 1860s)
gave readers a taste for travel and adventure. Earlier in the century, the Romantic novelist François-René de Châteaubriand set

Atala (1801) and *René* (1802) among the Indian tribes of North America. Alphonse de Lamartine, Gérard de Nerval and Théophile Gautier wrote about travels in the Levant; Eugène Fromentin, a lesser literary craftsman but an author popular with the public, made his reputation with books about Africa (*Un Eté dans le Sahara*, 1857, *Un Eté dans le Sahel*, 1859). Gustave Flaubert, the leading novelist of the mid-1800s, set out for Egypt in 1849, and his letters and notes describe hospitals and mosques, bazaars and bordellos.[7] Flaubert set *Salammbô* (1862) in Carthage (Tunisia), and chose exotic locations for several stories. Guy de Maupassant visited Algeria and Tunisia in the 1850s and returned with newspaper articles and short stories. Arthur Rimbaud, *enfant terrible* of French letters, did the travellers one better by giving up his career as a poet and settling as a trader in Djibouti.

These writers' works showed no unanimity of opinion about the colonial world except for the seduction of things exotically different, the strange customs of indigenes, the brightness of colours and the pungency of odours overseas, the wild lure of the desert and the sensuality which seemed to pervade Africa – belly-dancers, brothels, the harem, and Oriental 'vices'. While Maghrebins or black Africans were sometimes portrayed as one-dimensional characters, foreigners did not escape untarnished. Maupassant, whose writings are among the most sensitive accounts of North Africa, centred several stories on sexual adventures and underlined the primitive 'otherness' of North Africa. But he hardly spared his compatriots: 'We are the ones who seem barbarian in the middle of these barbarians – brutes to be sure, but who are in their own land, and whom the centuries have taught customs which we do not yet seem to have understood. . . . We have remained brutal conquerors, maladroit, infatuated with preconceived ideas.' In addition to dictatorial chieftains, duplicitous women and fierce warriors among the 'natives', Maupassant wrote about cruel army officers, impoverished settlers, and petty administrators in the ranks of the French.[8]

Two works stand out in the late 1800s because they were so widely read and because the pictures they paint of the new colonies in the Maghreb and sub-Saharan Africa are so rich in colour. One is an adventure, indeed a satire, the other a sentimental tragedy. Both contain truculent criticism of colonialist misperceptions, but they must be categorised as colonialist novels as they make the empire a terrain of adventure for the hardy, a place where individuals and the nation can find outlets from the constraints of life at home.

In 1872 Alphonse Daudet published *Tartarin de Tarascon*, the first of his satirical novels about a silly but endearing braggart from the small southern town of Tarascon. The novel begins with an evocation of Tartarin's fascination with exotic places. His bookshelves contain the works of Captain Cook and African explorers, his garden miniature palms, baobabs and banana trees. Tartarin is a great hunter, but since game is scarce around Tarascon, hunters show their prowess by shooting at caps thrown into the air. Without ever having set foot outside his province, Tartarin pretends to be an adventurer. His drinking buddies call his bluff, and he leaves for North Africa, after outfitting himself with safari gear, and donning 'harem pants' and fez even before boarding the ship at Marseille. Misadventures start on arrival in Algiers, when Tartarin calls the ship's crew to arms when he mistakes porters for pirates. Tartarin finds, to his amazement, that cafés and hotels, train station and theatre, officious bureaucrats and snooty women make Algiers look more like a city in the French Midi than the gateway to Africa.

Tartarin meets up with hunters, only to discover that they shoot birds and rabbits rather than lions. He pals around with a Montenegrin prince, and cavorts with an Arabic woman. Longing for adventure rouses Tartarin, and off he goes to the Sahara, aboard a camel and accompanied by the prince. Deception follows; the prince robs him, and the only lion he finds is an old blind beast kept as a pet. After unsuccessfully stalking lesser prey, Tartarin by mistake shoots the pet lion and must sell all his possessions to pay a fine for killing the animal. He mails the pelt back to Tarascon. Tartarin heads back to Algiers (to discover that his 'Arabic' love was an imposter), then takes a ship for Marseille – his trusty camel refuses to be abandoned and swims out to the ship. Tartarin and camel return to Tarascon, where his townsmen greet the tatty big-game hunter as a hero.

Tartarin de Tarascon is a burlesque which became a bestseller. The novel contained a few insights into colonial life – Daudet's description of the social hierarchy points out: 'At the top, they said, there is "Massa" Governor, who takes everything out on his chief of staff; the chief of staff, in revenge, takes everything out on the soldier, the soldier, in turn, on the settler, the settler on the Arab, the Arab on the black, the black on the Jew, and the

Jew on the donkey; the poor little donkey, having no one to beat up, straightens his back and bears his burden.' Such comments, however, are buried in the exotic scenes of Tartarin's adventures – souks and minarets, absinthe-scented cafés and burning deserts, veiled women and half-naked servants, administrators in pith-helmets and soldiers in *képis*. The novel reduces Algeria and its population to a comic-book background for Tartarin's bumbling. Arabic women are alluring, Africans untrustworthy, officials boorish, 'natives' innocently 'primitive', the colonies a dangerous playground, African society a set-piece for comedy.

The most prolific author of novels about foreign parts filled with rip-roaring adventure, tear-jerking romance and tragic destiny was Pierre Loti, the *nom de plume* of Julien Viaud. Born in the port of Rochefort in 1850, Viaud was the son of a municipal official. When Julien was eight years old, his beloved older brother, a navy doctor, left for a tour of duty in Tahiti. The reports Gustave sent back sparked Julien's interest in the wider world, and Gustave's death at sea in 1865 left a permanent scar on him. Julien decided to follow in his brother's footsteps, and in 1867 entered the French naval academy; his first voyage took him to the Mediterranean, Brazil and North America. In 1872, Viaud went to Polynesia, where he searched for traces of his brother, and like him, had an affair with a Tahitian woman; Viaud also began writing adventure stories. The next years saw Viaud, now an officer, on voyages to Senegal and Turkey.

In 1879, Loti published his first novel, *Azyadé*, set in Constantinople, a romance of the exoticism and eroticism of the harem and the mystery of a stereotypical Levant. In the following year came *Le Mariage de Loti*, based on his and his brother's sojourns in Tahiti, replete with luxuriant vegetation and nubile women; the novel made Loti one of France's most popular writers. His most famous book, *Le Roman d'un spahi*, appeared in 1881. It was the best known, and probably most influential, novel about the colonies in its day, and the memoirs of later travellers (such as Isabelle Eberhardt), administrators and colonial promoters cited Loti's work as the inspiration for their fascination with empire. *Le Roman d'un spahi* is a panorama of colonial life written in overwrought prose and packed with adventure, danger, sex and 'local colour'.

The novel is the story of Jean Peyral, born to poor peasant parents in the Cévennes. After an uneventful childhood – he is an indifferent student and a bit of a larrikin – Peyral is conscripted into the French army for five years. Feeling the 'mysterious attraction of the unknown', he chooses to serve as a *spahi*, a colonial cavalry-soldier. The robust, 'extremely handsome' and rather naïve Peyral hopes to find in the colonies an outlet for his youthful energy. His first taste of the colonies is Saint-Louis and a liaison with an older mixed-blood Réunionnaise; momentary guilt when he receives letters from his childhood sweetheart back in France gives way to gratification. After surviving tropical fever and getting jettisoned for another lover by his lady friend, Peyral plunges into the nightlife of the army outpost, drinking, womanising and picking fights with fellow officers before leaving for a desert posting. In the second part of the novel, three years later, Peyral is living in a remote camp with Fatou-gaye, his African concubine, happy despite remonstrances from family and fiancée in France. As his tour of duty in the bush draws to a close, Peyral dreads a transfer to Algiers. At the last moment, he swaps postings with a mate and goes to an even more isolated outpost in Guinea to take part in the 'pacification' of rebellious tribes. Fatou-gaye accompanies him, but they soon quarrel, and Peyral begins to beat his lover, especially after she sells his most treasured possession, his father's watch; the couple break up. By the third part of the novel, Peyral, now 26, calls Senegal home, although a letter announcing that his French girlfriend intends to marry a different man causes him remorse. He moves on to another remote post, where he comes upon Fatou-gaye, with the infant child he has fathered. After a short and sweet reunion, Peyral charges into combat. Stabbed by African rebels, he dies on the battlefield. In the novel's closing scenes, Fatou-gaye finds his body and, distraught, kills their child.

Le Roman d'un spahi presents a vivid picture of the life of action possible in the colonies. Loti repeatedly describes Peyral as a good-looking, macho man long on stamina and short on emotions and intellect, drawn to the rough life, sensual pleasures and fighting spirit of the empire, the type perfectly suited for the rigours of foreign service. Descriptions of the beauty of deserts and jungles alternate with scenes of tropical torpor, laziness and hot monotony. Sexual contacts are easy, the pay good, battles heroic, comrades jovial and loyal.

Loti reserved his most extended descriptions for Africa and the Africans – the novel even includes a pedantic 'digression on music and story-tellers'. Peyral's first image of Africans is negative: 'In the first moments after his arrival, [he] looked with disgust on this black population; in his eyes, they all looked alike; for him, they all wore a simian mask.' The most frequently voiced description of Africans is how they resemble monkeys – 'Pretty little monkey', one of Peyral's friends calls Fatou-gaye, and he is repulsed by the light-coloured palms of her hands, 'which, in spite of himself, gave him a bad impression of the paws of a monkey ... something not human which was frightening'. Fatou-gaye is little more than an animal: 'Indeed he considered her as an inferior being, more or less the equal of his yellow mongrel dog.' Sensuousness and debauchery mark African culture: 'These chants and this negro gaiety had something heavily voluptuous and sensually bestial in it.' Heat, tropical surroundings, and pagan dancing fuse: '*Animalis fobil!*, screaming of unbridled desire, – of black sap overheated by the sun and torrid hysteria, an alleluia of negro love, a hymn of seduction sung by nature, by the very air, the ground, the plants, the scents.'

Such evocations – whether Loti's or only Peyral's sentiments – mirrored European attitudes about the animal nature of Africans, their unrestrained sexual desire, the lasciviousness of their songs and dance. *Le Roman d'un spahi* sent a shiver of excitment through readers tantalised by escape from the humdrum existence of late nineteenth-century France. Though the colonies meant expatriation, separation from friends and family, illness and possible death, they promised adventure, virile action and sex. 'All of this gives off the odour of a land of exile, so far away from the motherland; the least details and the smallest things are strange. But there is such a magic in tropical sunrises, such limpidity in the morning air, such well-being in the dawn freshness.' Peyral, like other adventurers in the colonies (or just armchair travellers), is seduced: 'Alas! He loved Senegal, poor fellow; he realised it now; he was attached to it by a host of intimate and mysterious ties.' Several passages of *Le Roman d'un spahi* warn against false expectations: 'Take these sailors, these *spahis* – abandoned, these young men spend their lives far away on the sea or in countries of exile, living in the crudest and the most abnormal conditions.' But such caveats hardly dissuaded readers caught up by the heady excitement of Peyral's escapades.

Loti fell prey to his own fantasies. Almost everywhere he went, from Iceland to Japan, he gathered material for the novels which won him election to the Académie Française. He pursued liaisons with women (and probably men as well) in many of the ports in which he called. He decorated his house in La Rochelle with Turkish rugs, North African copper, black African statues and a miscellaneous assortment of souvenirs. Loti spent 42 years in the navy, though not without clashes with his superiors because of his eccentricities and his denunciation of the French takeover of Tonkin in the 1880s; he nevertheless retired with high rank. He returned to service during the First World War and was accorded a state funeral on his death in 1923.[9]

By the end of the nineteenth century, some authors took exception to the romanticism of Loti's novels and their critique (however muted) of certain aspects of colonialism. In Algeria, a small circle of authors prided themselves on writing about reality rather than fantasy. Chief among them was Louis Bertrand, whose *Le Sang des races* (1899) and *La Cina* (1901) embody 'Algerianism', the literary current of the *pieds-noirs*. Bertrand said of *La Cina*: 'I only repeated, in literary form, what I had heard said around me.' If that is the case, his laudatory story of a heroic woman settler is a perfect example of unreconstructed colonialism and racism. An archbishop in the novel affirms: 'I want to form a single block of all these populations which have arrived from France, Spain and Italy and pit them against the common enemy, the Muslim, whom we have had the idiocy to allow to survive, although he ought to have been pitilessly exterminated.' The book denies that there was anything legitimately African in Algeria: Roman ruins and the history of European intervention from St Louis to modern times, as well as olive groves and vineyards, 'proved' that North Africa rightfully belonged to Europeans and that the Arabs were intruders. Bertrand's novels, marked by praise for settlers, disdain for Arabs and bitter anti-Semitism, earned applause from colonialists, and Bertrand won election to the Académie Française in 1925.

Other 'Algerianist' authors followed the same line. For example, Ernest Psichari, who also lived for a time in Mauritania, saw the French conquest of Africa as a new crusade, a mystical mission. A heavenly voice in one of his novels, the hero of which is a Frank crusader, proclaims: 'This land of Africa is mine, and I will leave it to my children. It does not belong to these miserable people, these shepherds and camel-herders.' Novels by the conservative Melchior de Vogüé heralded the valour of military conquerors, while those of the socialist Paul Adam saw imperial expansion as liberation of enserfed races. The very titles of Robert Randau's works – *Les Colons* (1907), *Les Explorateurs* (1909) – reveal their themes; an apologia for colonialism is their brief.

The first decades of the twentieth century saw more works in this vein, but also novels which denounced expansion. Anatole France's *Sur la terre blanche* (1905) contained an uncompromising indictment of colonialism, which had brought few benefits to France and even fewer to conquered peoples. *Les Immémoriaux* (1907), by Victor Segalen (like Loti, a navy doctor) painted a bleak picture of the destruction of Polynesian culture through European conquest.

By the 1920s, the French intelligentsia had a more subtle picture of Africa than ever before, thanks to exposés of colonial conditions, the influence of African art on avant-garde painters and sculptors and – to the few who knew them – such works as Guillaume Apollinaire's writings on African sculpture or Blaise Cendras' collection of African stories, legends and songs, *Anthologie nègre* (1921). A wider audience was familiar with jazz, which the French identified as having African roots.

Most innovative among dissident novels was René Maran's *Batouala*, published in 1921. Maran was a black Frenchman, a Guyanese descendant of Africans transported to the new world; he was an administrator in the colony of Oubangui-Chari, in the AEF. *Batouala*, set in central Africa, tells the story of an aged chief and the rivalry of a handsome younger man for his principal wife. There are scenes of the chief's daily life, a grand ceremony of male circumcision and female excision, and a great hunt. The book, recounted from the perspective of Chief Batouala, incorporates African tales and songs and paints a portrait of local customs, food, clothing and habitat, as well as the tensions within traditional society. *Batouala* was the first black novel in French literature; it created a literary sensation, especially after winning the Prix Goncourt, France's most prestigious literary award.

Batouala also sparked controversy, not just because its theme was so different from most French literature. In writing *Batouala*, a colonial bureaucrat damned French colonialism, and his critique enraged colonialists. Maran's preface sounds the charge: 'Civilization, civilization, pride of the Europeans, and the burying-ground for innocents. . . . You build your kingdom on corpses. Whatever you may want, whatever you may do, you act with deceit. At your sight, gushing tears and screaming pain. You are the might which exceeds right. You aren't a torch, but an inferno. Everything you touch, you consume.' Chief Batouala continues: 'Men of white skin. What had they come to look for, so far from their homes, in the land of the Blacks? How much better they would all do to go back to their lands, never to leave again!' The novel particularly damns porterage, common in the AEF: 'Everybody knows that the whites, saying that they are "collecting taxes", force all blacks of a marriageable age to carry voluminous packages from when the sun rises to when it sets. These trips last two, three, five days. Little matter to them the weight of these packages. . . . They don't sink under the burden. Rain, sun, cold? They don't suffer.'

Europeans in the novel include crooked traders eager for profit, and a haughty district officer interested only in building bridges where none are necessary and in collecting rubber for export. He exacts fines for the dancing at Batouala's celebrations and shows indifference when the wounded chief faces death. White priests and doctors are compared, unfavourably, with African sorcerers and healers. In the eyes of Europeans, Batouala laments, 'We are only taxable flesh. We are only beasts of burden. Beasts? Not even that. Dogs? They feed them, and they care for their horses. Us? We are for them less than those animals.'

By contrast with invaders trying to strip the indigenes of resources, labour and culture, Africans are the guardians of a proud heritage of poetry, music and philosophy. Polygamy, ritual circumcision, 'lascivious' dancing and funerary customs are shown to have cogency and dignity within the context of African culture. The characters portrayed – the wise but protective chief, his strong-minded and passionate wife, her handsome and daring suitor – are endowed with qualities which make them different to the savages of colonialist literature. In bringing Africans to the foreground of a novel and making them, rather than game-hunters or soldiers, the heroes, Maran achieved a literary breakthrough and issued a defiant attack on colonialism. His was one of the first thoroughly anti-colonial novels to achieve wide attention.[10]

The next decades witnessed a decline in the romanticised images of Loti and the colonial chauvinism of a Randau or a Bertrand – or, at least, such views were not stated so openly. Novelists continued to write works about the colonies; though many had little lasting literary value, they found a ready audience among readers enamoured of exotic tales. Greater writers turned their attention to the colonies as well. André Malraux, a future French Minister of Culture, made his literary name with a novel set in Asia, *La Condition humaine* (1933).[11] A key episode in Louis-Ferdinand Céline's *Voyage au bout de la nuit* (1932), another major novel of the interwar period, is set in black Africa. Some of the works of Albert Camus are set in Algeria. *L'Etranger* (1942), considered the quintessential existentialist novel, takes for its point of departure the murder of an Arab by a French settler, and *La Peste* (1947) is a portrayal of a North African city besieged by the plague.

Other *genres* than novels regularly drew on colonial locales and topics. Travelogues – Henri de Monfreid's accounts of hashish-smuggling in the Red Sea, Paul Morand's adventures in east Asia, writings on the Mauritanian desert by Odette du Puigaudeau – had steady sales.[12] Autobiographies and writings by participants in colonial life, like Gallieni's and Lyautey's memoirs of Tonkin and Madagascar, provided eyewitness views of conquest, pacification and administration. Exposés of colonial horrors, such as André Gide's investigations on the Congo, and Albert Londres's accounts of the penal colony in Guyane and labour conditions in equatorial Africa, buttressed anti-colonialism. Even poetry, from Baudelaire's verses about his Mauritian lover in the nineteenth century to Saint-John Perse's mid-twentieth-century poems inflected with images and rhythms of Guadeloupe, his birthplace, contained links to France's former or remaining overseas domains.

Poetry was one of the main *genres* of a group of West Indian and African writers who studied in Paris in the interwar years and pioneered the concept of *négritude*. Aimé Césaire, later to serve for over 40 years as a French *député* and mayor of Fort-de-France, was a young student from Martinique; Léopold Sedar Senghor, who became the first president of Senegal, a West African; Léon-Gontran Damas, a Guyanese. They and others participated in a new literary movement influenced by Pan-Africanism and the writings of Anglophone West Indians and African-Americans. The aim was to attack colonialism, but, even more importantly, to re-evaluate and legitimise African culture. *Négritude* was the rediscovery of African art, music and customs which had long been denigrated as primitive, savage and uncivilised. The works of Césaire, Senghor and Damas constituted some of the most remarkable French writings of the 1930s and 1940s; they elevated African culture to a new level of respect and called on those of

African descent to reclaim their cultural heritage. Césaire's *Cahiers d'un retour au pays natal*, for instance, recounted a return to the Antilles by a student shocked to see the material and cultural poverty of the islands, where descendants of slaves had been robbed of their African culture and deprived of access to French culture; the rhythms of African drums and dances, the beauty of African men and women, the vibrancy of African life haunt Césaire's lines.

By the middle of the twentieth century, therefore, 'colonial' literature had journeyed far from the adventure stories of the late 1800s or the colonialist apologias or maudlin romances of 'local colour' novelists in the colonies. Major writers had cast a critical eye on France's colonial actions. The colonies had produced several outstanding writers – Camus and Saint-John Perse received Nobel Prizes. Black writers from French Africa and the West Indies had initiated a new school of literature, and authors from the Maghreb and Indochina were making their literary presence felt.

Scientific Research

The colonies were a huge laboratory for research in the natural and social sciences; they suggested theories to test in the lecture rooms of French universities and provided 'artefacts' for display cases in metropolitan museums. Research carried out in the empire enriched most academic disciplines, and particular branches developed specifically for study of the colonies. For instance, colonial law emerged as a specialty in jurisprudence, as legal experts wrote learned treatises on colonial civil and criminal codes, land titles, the status of indigenous populations and the role of colonies in international relations.[13]

The natural sciences benefited greatly from opportunities to do research overseas. Deserts and tropical jungles, including areas hit by natural diasasters (such as the eruption of Mont Pelée in Martinique in 1902), provided perfect sites for research in meteorology, geology, geodesy, seismology and other earth sciences. Meteorology gained particular importance in the age of aviation. Meteorological stations in the minor colonies or remote areas, such as Tamanrasset in the Algerian desert, relayed information to larger weather-forecasting centres, like the one in Algiers where

Camus worked as a research assistant in the 1930s. Another field which benefited was astronomy, as the French built large observatories in Algeria, Madagascar, Indochina and elsewhere. French Jesuit priests were leaders in astronomy, both in the colonies and at an observatory in Shanghai; with the observatory, the neighbouring Aurora University (also run by Jesuits) and physics laboratories, the French maintained in Shanghai the largest foreign scientific complex in eastern Asia.[14]

Study of foreign societies, not surprisingly, received a big boost from French conquests. Ethnographers, anthropologists, linguists and specialists in non-European art flocked to the colonies: students of Islam went to the Maghreb, those interested in Asian history and culture studied Indochina, and the growing number of researchers on 'primitive' societies did work in sub-Saharan Africa and the Pacific islands. Pioneering French ethnographers of Africa such as Paul Rivet, Lucien Lévy-Bruhl, Marcel Griaule and Michel Leiris did fieldwork in French Africa either individually or as part of group expeditions. One of the most famous groups, headed by Griaule, left in 1931 to spend three years travelling from Senegal eastwards to Djibouti. Participants shipped artefacts back to Paris and wrote numerous scholarly monographs – Griaule's work on Dogon masks was the first detailed monograph on African art.[15] Research on and in the colonies was conducted under the auspices of various bodies. In 1839, King Louis-Philippe established a museum to collect colonial 'curiosities', and colonial exhibitions later in the century enriched its vaults. Renamed the Ethnography Museum, then the Museum of Man (*Musée de l'Homme*), it holds huge collections of the art, clothing, household utensils and almost everything else produced by non-European societies, as well as records of scientific expeditions; the museum has sponsored much research and a wide-ranging series of publications. The Museum of Natural History in Paris – which counted among its early acquisitions items brought to France by the eighteenth-century explorers of the South Pacific – began giving courses for explorers and colonial scientists in 1893; in the 1920s, it established three chairs in colonial studies. A prestigious centre for postgraduate teaching, the *Ecole Pratique des Hautes Etudes*, hosted a colonial studies centre as early as 1902. In addition to the *Ecole Coloniale*, there were schools of colonial agronomy and colonial medicine. The Pasteur Institute, specialising in medical research, set up branches in Indochina in 1890, in sub-Saharan

Africa in 1902 and Madagascar in 1910. The French geological services established research stations in Indochina in 1895, West Africa in 1923 and Equatorial Africa in 1929.

More general research came under the aegis of the French Far Eastern School (*Ecole Française d'Extrême-Orient*), established in 1900, one of the most famous colonial research institutes. Similar centres included the Malagasy Academy opened in 1902, the Institute for Advanced Moroccan Studies and the Sherifian Scientific Institute established by Lyautey in the early 1920s, the French Institute of Black Africa, founded in 1936, and an institute for research on Oceania opened just after the Second World War. Smaller research units proliferated; Algeria alone hosted more than 20 botanical gardens and botanical research stations.

Universities were also set up in the colonies. The Jesuits' private St Joseph's University in Beirut by the 1880s won official recognition from the French government. The French created a tertiary institution in Algiers in 1879; in 1909 it became a full-fledged state university, the first in the empire. A university began giving classes in Hanoi in 1907, but authorities closed it after only a year because of fear that it would breed nationalist dissent; the Indochinese government nevertheless reopened a larger and more ambitious university in 1918.

So significant had colonial research become that in 1912 an Association of Colonial Scientists was organised; its successor, the *Association Colonies-Science*, published some 3500 pages just of summaries of scientific works from 1925 to 1940. A giant Congress of Colonial Scientific Research was one of numerous meetings held during the 1931 Colonial Exhibition. To reorganise research in the empire, the Vichy government set up the Organisation for Colonial Scientific Research in 1943. The body survived the war but its changing names – it became the Organisation for Overseas Scientific and Technical Research (ORSTOM) in the late 1940s, then the French Research Institute for Development through Cooperation in the 1970s – symbolised the evolution of policy and politics.

The relationship between the colonial enterprise of the state and research was ambiguous. The government directly or indirectly provided funding and sponsorship for overseas research, and administrators and military officers did much to facilitate it. Navigators carried naturalists on board ship, naval and army missions collected specimens, and colonialists hailed the scientific value of French expeditions. At least during the early colonial era, few doubted that science had a duty other than pure research. The author of *Le Savant colonial* (1930), Edouard de Martonne – himself an army officer, head of the geographical service in the AOF and an accomplished surveyor – said straightforwardly: 'Colonial scientists are agents for the propagation of French culture.' Marius Moutet, Minister for Colonies, told a conference in 1937: 'Scientific work in the colonies is an urgent necessity; it is a condition for [colonial] economic development, but it is also our civilised duty, an example to give, a beacon to shine.' Another commentator added: 'It is through reliance on science, through the creation of laboratories and research stations, that the colonies will be able to know their resources better and to develop them in a rational manner.' In short, political leaders and many scientists saw research as a useful (indeed necessary) auxiliary to colonialism.[16] The brief of colonial universities was to educate the children of settlers and train loyal French-speaking indigenes for administrative, teaching or medical posts. Research in agronomy, earth sciences, mining and engineering aimed to exploit the profit-earning potential of colonies. Present-day ethnologists judge that their predecessors often had simplistic views about native societies which veered from romanticised idealism to outright racist views of 'primitivism'; the conclusions of ostensibly objective and scientific researchers provided grounds for great misapprehension of non-European cultures and brutal treatment of non-Western peoples. Some respectable theories of one generation – for instance, theories of race – were rejected by later specialists as little more than pseudo-scientific propaganda.[17]

It would be unfair to castigate all colonial scientists as lackeys of expansionism; the research of many *savants* won legitimate acclaim from the international scientific community according to the prevailing standards of the day. Moreover, certain researchers were at odds with colonialists. French settlers and administrators in New Caledonia considered Maurice Leenhardt, the leading specialist on Melanesia in the early twentieth century, too sympathetic to islanders. Leenhardt, a Protestant pastor and path-breaking writer on Melanesian culture, incurred the wrath of colonists, who accused him (wrongly) of abetting a rebellion in 1917 and later pressured him to leave the territory.[18] The work of such ethnographers, by showing the complexities of local societies and the

ways they had been affected by land spoliation, forced labour,
Christian proselytism and Westernisation, contributed to the growth
of nationalism. A number of leading social scientists took an active role in anti-colonialist movements after the Second World
War. Researchers also earned tributes from the populations they
studied; when Marcel Griaule died in 1956, he was the first European honoured with a traditional Dogon funeral.

'Colonial' Influences in French Art

Since the discovery of the New World, foreign motifs have been
common in European art. Baroque frescoes included rather fan-
ciful, if seldom realistic, portrayals of American Indians, sometimes joined by Africans and Asians in representations of the
different continents known to Europeans. The eighteenth century saw a vogue for Chinese porcelain and Oriental themes, as
well as designs influenced by the Islamic Middle East, in everything from painting to wallpaper. Exploration of the South Seas,
and particularly European discovery of Tahiti, offered further
inspiration for portrayal of 'good savages', lush vegetation and
the imagined bliss of Oceania.

Proliferation of voyages of exploration and conquest renewed
the fashion for exoticism and gave artists increased chances to
travel and work overseas. Government missions and expeditions
employed artists to draw maps, inventory foreign art treasures
and record impressions of countries visited, whether in sketches,
paintings, or later, photographs. Artists accompanying soldiers
and explorers did work on site or drew on their experiences
when they returned to studios at home. Artists who never ventured overseas also found inspiration in events connected with
colonialism.

One of the most important works painted in early nineteenth-
century France, for instance, related a colonial drama. Théodore
Géricault's 'Le Radeau de la *Méduse*' ('The Raft of the *Méduse*')
pictured survivors of a shipwreck. In 1816 Paris dispatched Colonel Julien Schmaltz, accompanied by his family, staff, soldiers,
bureaucrats and the crews of four ships – totalling 400 passengers – to retake possession of Senegal, returned to France by Britain
at the end of the Napoleonic Wars. One of the ships, the *Méduse*,
sank off the coast of Mauritania. Some voyagers were rescued from

lifeboats, but 147 managed only to climb aboard a 20 x 7 metre raft. At the end of their ordeal, which lasted 13 days without food or water, only 13 remained alive. Géricault's dramatic canvas portrays the shipwrecked passengers on their makeshift vessel: an aged father cradles the body of his son, someone signals for help, others despair. The painting of agonising figures packed aboard a fragile raft captures the dangers of overseas voyages.

Géricault's painting might well have dissuaded intending adventurers, but other works underlined the exotic attraction of colonies. Eugène Delacroix was already an established painter when he won appointment to an official delegation to Morocco in 1832. The Frenchmen visited Tangiers, called on foreign consuls, toured the countryside and journeyed to Meknès for an audience with the sultan, to whom they presented a letter from the French king: the purpose of the embassy was to extend France's influence in the sultan's realm. Throughout the trip, Delacroix made sketches, although he once narrowly escaped being assaulted by Moroccan men angered that he was drawing pictures of their wives. Delacroix returned to France with a horse presented to him by the Moroccan government, cases of souvenirs – sandals, burnouses, swords and pottery – a carefully noted travelogue and sketchbooks filled with drawings which became the basis for full-scale paintings. The stay in Morocco influenced Delacroix's work over the next several decades and made him the foremost painter of 'Oriental' themes in his day.

The sketches picture the landscape and fauna of Morocco – horses and camels fascinated Delacroix – as well as mosques, the kasbah and other cityscapes. Delacroix carefully rendered such everyday objects as caftans and teapots, as well as architectural details of keystone arches and dark passageways. His drawings study the varied population of Morocco, including Berber officials, Negro musicians and a Jewish bride, daughter of a French consular official. Scenes of the Hebrew wedding, the slaughtering of sheep in preparation for feasts to welcome the Frenchmen, and the serving of mint tea by a mulatto slave evoke a strange and enticing land. Pictures of lions, and a magnificent tableau of a lion attacking a horse, conjure up the excitement of the African countryside. A drawing of a lion tearing open the chest of an Arab victim, usually reprinted in red ink to heighten the effect, conveys the dangers of Africa and the bravery of those who ventured into the desert wilderness.

Delacroix's drawings illustrated French magazines, and some were reproduced as lithographs, publicising not only the artist but also North Africa in the years immediately after the French conquest of Algiers. His works were not propaganda, but they broadcast the exoticism of Africa, the picturesqueness of a region which beckoned explorers and traders. Such works helped stimulate interest in the world overseas.

Only four years after Delacroix went to Morocco, Théodore Chassériau visited Algeria. Although a lesser talent than Delacroix, Chassériau would win popularity as an academic painter of Biblical, mythological and Shakespearean themes with appeal to conservative and romantic tastes; he also painted a considerable number of tableaux of North African subjects with themes repeated by later 'Orientalists'. Battles regularly appeared, rendered as colourful jousts with horses rearing, caftans flowing, swords brandished. Combats of Arabs or Kabyles against French troops pitted the West against the Levant, dashing French soldiers against half-savage Muslims. One painting of Arabs recovering their dead from the battlefield, however, left no doubt as to which force was the victor. Chassériau painted Arab chiefs with a certain dignity, whether in battle, visiting vassals or tending horses. But the image of the Maghreb was a country of fierce warriors who must be subdued by hardy conquerors.

Another theme apparent in Chassériau's work – a counterpart to the virility of soldiers – was the seductiveness of Arab women. He painted lithe Moorish dancers, elegant Jewesses resting on a balcony, a naked Arab woman (in reality, a European model in the artist's employ) emerging from a bath in the seraglio. Here was the legend of the pleasures and voluptuousness of a sultan's harem. Other women appeared as passive, tender and agreeable, whether a girl cradling a gazelle or a mother feeding her child. Such views of the seductress or the dutiful wife became stock-in-trade for later painters and contributed to stereotypical views of indigenous women.[19]

Later in the nineteenth century a group of 'Orientalist' and 'Africanist' artists emerged, satisfying growing demand for renditions of Levantine harems and souks, African villages and jungles, temples in Indochina and native life throughout the empire. Colonial associations offered scholarships and prizes to artists. Art academies in the colonies trained painters, and many French men and women who lived overseas tried their hand at leisure-time painting or drawing. In 1894, the first group exhibition of Orientalist paintings opened in Paris and for some years was an annual show. In 1908, the Society of Colonial Artists was organised, and by the 1920s there were identifiable 'schools' of colonial art in Algiers and Tunis. If relatively few works were first-class paintings, they nevertheless entered metropolitan museums and attracted collectors.

Colonial paintings usually emphasised the exoticism and picturesque 'otherness' of foreign life. They portrayed a largely unchanging, traditional Africa or Asia – perpetrating ideas about the timelessness of 'native' life – rather than the effects of European occupation. One of the most commonly recurring themes was the nubile woman, whether black African, Maghrebin, West Indian or Polynesian. Sexual excitement underlies much colonial art, with the attractive and usually half-dressed or entirely naked woman portrayed as the seductive object of male sexual interest. Paintings and sketches ranging from sentimental kitsch to outright pornography showed women as temptresses or concubines.

Most 'Orientalist' painters were not technically innovative. But avant-garde artists submitted to the seduction of the colonies just as did academic painters. The most famous was Paul Gauguin. His childhood in Peru and a brief stay in Martinique whetted Gauguin's interest for the exotic, and a period in Brittany honed his talents as an innovative colourist and painter of the human figure. Gauguin's personal life was not altogether happy; he was estranged from his Danish wife and discontented with French society. In 1891, Gauguin sailed for Tahiti, determined to spend his days among the 'primitive' people of the South Seas. He spent the rest of his life in Polynesia, except for one trip back to France, although he found Tahiti too Westernised and finally settled in the Marquesas islands, where he died in 1903. Oceania did not tame Gauguin's high spirits; he quarrelled with French settlers and railed against the administration, drank excessively and had affairs with ever younger Polynesian women.

Gauguin's works combine various non-European influences (those of ancient Egyptian and Javanese friezes are especially evident), and he completed superior works with various decors. The paintings and sculptures inspired by the sojourn in Oceania are among his best. Gauguin made wooden carvings based on Tahitian and Marquesan sculptures and war clubs and statues from Easter Island; his drawings document his interest in tattooing. The brilliant hues of the paintings reflect the tropical vegetation, rainbow flowers, dark hair and copper skin of Polynesians, and the bright *pareus* they wore as garments. Gauguin's subjects combine different cultural themes. 'Ia Orana Maria' ('Hail, Mary'), with its Tahitian title based on a Latin prayer, portrays a Polynesian woman and child as the Madonna and infant Jesus. Two bare-breasted attendants fold their hands in prayer; a table bears offerings of bananas and breadfruit. Other religious works depict the crucified Christ in a pattern of Oceanic symbols.

Gauguin's paintings show islanders caught between two cultures. 'Tehamana Has Many Parents' is a portrait of a young girl, wearing a European 'mission dress' but with flowers tucked behind her ears; she stands against a panel with a hieratic figure and an undecipherable script. 'Where Do We Come From? Who Are We? Where are We Going?' is a large rendition of the ages of man – or more properly, since the figures are female, the ages of woman – but the work reflects as well on the destiny of colonised Oceanic cultures.[20]

Gauguin's paintings present a melancholy, eroticised vision of the South Pacific as both paradise and paradise lost, and this is part of their abiding appeal. Another of France's greatest artists, Henri Matisse, also found inspiration in Oceania. Towards the end of his life, in the 1940s and 1950s, Matisse created large paper cut-outs sparked by memories of a trip to Tahiti in 1930; 'Oceania: Sky' and 'Oceania: Sea' are panoramas of white shapes against a blue background suggested by the stars and sealife of the Pacific.

Much earlier, Matisse had travelled in Morocco, and the North African journeys inspired his work for several years. Twice in 1912 and early in 1913 – just as France established a protectorate over Morocco – Matisse and his wife visited North Africa. Matisse, like Gauguin a brilliant colourist, found in the sunshine and primary shades of landscapes, buildings and clothing a perfect palette for his brush. Matisse's works were far removed from nineteenth-century Orientalism. He was interested not in painting battles or action-packed adventure but in distilling the essence of scenes from ordinary life into swathes of extraordinary reds, blues and greens and almost abstract shapes. The 'Moroccan Café', for instance, evokes the architecture of a coffee-house through the simple outlines of keyhole arches in the background and four men – lacking even the details of their faces – lounging on the floor, while in the foreground two turbaned figures contemplate a fishbowl and a vase of flowers. In 'The Moroccans' the dome of an Islamic shrine rises behind a terrace with a vase of flowers, in the left foreground is a pile of what seem to be melons, and on the right the outline of a male figure with his back to the viewer.

One of Matisse's paintings is a figure of a sturdy Riffian, a bearded young man with golden skull-cap and brilliant green robe, decorated with embroidery, seated against a blue and green backdrop. Present-day viewers are apt to see the work as a stylised portrait and experiment in form and colour; Matisse's contemporaries sometimes had a different reading. Marcel Sembat, who often commissioned work from Matisse, wrote of a similar painting, 'The Standing Riffian': 'Isn't he marvelous, this great devil of a Riffian, with his angular face and his ferocious build? How can you look at this splendid barbarian without thinking of the warriors of days gone by? Such a fierce expression – just like that of the hero of *The Song of Roland*.' Sembat thus repeated the imperialists' caricature of the savage Mahgrebin warrior yet, by likening him to the hero of a medieval French epic, endowed him with a more refined, and perhaps more 'pacified', status; which interpretation was intended by Matisse is open to question. The meaning of such a painting indeed lay in the eye of the beholder.[21]

Art from Africa and Oceania profoundly influenced avant-garde artists in Paris and other cultural capitals, including Matisse. In the decade before the First World War Parisian artists came into contact with African art, primarily *bois nègres*, wooden sculptures or masks. As early as 1905, a number of collectors, both professional and amateur, showed their African acquisitions to artists, who also visited the Paris ethnography museum. Matisse, Maurice de Vlaminck, André Derain, André Lhote, Jacques Lipschitz, Alberto Giacometti, Constantine Brancusi, Georges Braque and Pablo Picasso, among other prominent artists, became acquainted with, admired and sometimes purchased African art, as did such well-known writers in avant-garde circles as the poet and critic Guillaume Apollinaire (who, with Paul Guillaume, in 1917 published *Sculptures nègres*, the first work on African art in French). They studied African works and shared them with each other – Max Jacob recalled that one evening Matisse showed a small African statue to Picasso, who was so entranced with it that he fondled it for hours, then spent part of the night making drawings of it.

Artists admired African works for their representation of the human body which broke with the Hellenic standards which

dominated the European canon. They liked the angularities, geo-
metrical shapes and purity of form of African pieces, the use of
different textures and incorporation of extraneous materials (like
metal and beads), their earthy or, sometimes, monochrome colours.
Artists were not immune to the 'primitive' exoticism of such works,
so at odds with European norms.

Fauvists (such as Matisse) and Cubists, in particular, borrowed
from African art. Picasso's 'Guitar' (1912), one of the first Cubist
sculptures, took inspiration from a Grebo mask which he owned;
the shape of the mask, with protruding eyes and prominent ant-
lers, metamorphoses into a deconstructed guitar. Art historians
discern the influence of masks from the New Hebrides, Côte-
d'Ivoire, and Congo in 'Les Demoiselles d'Avignon' (1907), one
of Picasso's most famous (and more controversial) paintings; 'Nude
with Raised Arms' (The Dancer of Avignon) resembles a Kota
reliquary figure from Gabon or the Congo. Picasso's large collection of sculptures and masks from sub-Saharan Africa and Oceania
exercised extraordinary influence on his work, especially in the
years preceding the First World War.[22]

Works produced from 1905 through the 1920s show the continuing import of African art: angular figures, faces shaped like
African masks, a vision of beauty which departs from European
classical archetypes.[23] 'Primitivism' continued to pervade European
work. A major exhibition of African art in 1919 coincided with a
'fête nègre' performance of African and pseudo-African music and
dance. In 1923, 'The Creation of the World', a performance inspired by African culture, included decor and costumes by the
Cubist artist Fernand Léger, scenario by Blaise Cendras and music by Darius Milhaud. The Surrealists of the 1920s expressed great
interest in Oceanic art. They joined others drawn to the vogue
for things African and African-American, including the performances of the black American singer and dancer Josephine Baker.

Borrowings from non-Western culture were limited and eclectic,
and few artists, composers or performers took much note of the
sociocultural context of the African art (for instance, its religious
or ceremonial significance). Artists were not necessarily supporters
of colonialism. Some were apolitical, others opponents of expansion. Picasso, for instance, was a lifelong member of the Communist Party and hardly a colonialist. The milieux most receptive to
the still controversial 'modern art' in the early twentieth century
were by no means the same as the colonial lobby.

Photography and Cinema

Photographs provided a new medium through which to view the colonies. In 1839, the Paris Academy of Sciences heard the first French presentation about the new process of photography, and already in 1856, a professional photographer had gone to Algeria to take pictures. *Le Tour du monde*, a newspaper founded in 1860 which focused on voyages of exploration and discovery, and *L'Illustration*, as its name implies, a publication featuring paintings, drawings and photographs, became showcases for exotic illustrations. Amateurs and professionals took pictures: scenes of flora and fauna, tourist shots of holidaymakers, family portraits of colonists and, especially, pictures of overseas landscapes, architecture and people. Photographers also took pictures of military actions – the conquest of Morocco was the first to be photographed comprehensively.[24]

Not surprisingly, preferred subjects for photographs included exotic highlights of a foreign posting or tour. In Indochina, for instance, photographers liked shooting the Along Bay with its myriad of islands, the Mekong River and Angkor Wat temples, rice paddies, ornamented temples and thatched huts on stilts. Buddhist monks in saffron vestments, mandarins in silk robes, peasants in more modest attire, and nubile ladies in as little clothing as possible attracted the photographers' gaze. Curious details excited special attention, such as the fabulously long fingernails of upper class Vietnamese (worn to show that they did not engage in manual labour), or the hideously bound feet of Chinese women. Settlers and tourists wielded their cameras to show French colonial life – crowds in the café outside the Grand Hôtel in Saigon, young folk playing tennis or touring the countryside, dashing officers in uniforms and pith-helmets squiring elegant ladies, big-game hunters with their kill.[25]

Portraits of indigenes were popular throughout the empire, notwithstanding the fear or opposition of some non-Europeans to being photographed. Photographs afforded possibilities for voyeuristic obsession with black and yellow bodies, mysterious Muslim women behind veils and scantily-clad Tahitians, warriors on horseback and 'cannibals' with spears. The fact that few photographs were otherwise labelled than 'native woman', 'local chief' or 'scene of daily life' – almost never was the name of the person indicated – gives a clue as to the way photographers regarded colonised peoples. Photographers, in general, wanted 'typical' scenes of exotic places and no less exotic people, shots which emphasised what was different, attractive, bizarre or even horrifying.[26]

These images were reproduced in books and newspapers and on postcards. Indeed the invention of the postcard (in 1869) offered new commercial and artistic opportunities. Sub-Saharan Africa inspired the creation of some 50 000 postcards from 1900 to 1960; in Senegal alone, printers of postcards produced 5000 designs before 1914. Postcards provided little scenes of foreign life posted by French men or women to relatives, friends, neighbours and colleagues, suitably emblazoned with curious postmarks and stamps – stamps were another minor form of colonial art. Postcards were among the most ubiquitous and widely distributed images of colonial life, guaranteed to send a thrill of excitement through the recipient at the view of a luxuriant tropical forest, imposing monument, languid colonial club, or fetching 'native'.

An extremely popular theme for postcards was the *Mauresque*, the Maghrebin woman. Hundreds of postcards portrayed the North African woman in an erotically half-clothed pose (or naked), or more demurely drinking coffee, smoking, sitting with friends, or engaged in some 'typical' activity. The women are usually beautiful, the appointments of their houses rich, their poses inviting. What the senders or receivers of the postcards did not realise was that many of the Moorish women were actually models, women from the lower orders of society or prostitutes, artfully dressed and carefully posed by the photographer. Despite the beauty and veracity of some views, scenes are sometimes fudged. For example, women often wear far more jewellery than would be common, even for the wealthy, because this made a good pictorial effect. The same model might represent different people – one Algerian woman was described on different postcards (and in different garb) as a 'young Bedouin woman', 'a young woman from the south' and 'a young Kabyle woman'. Postcards of Algeria frequently show men or women smoking a water-pipe, an archetypal Levantine symbol, although it was little used in the country. Photographers wanted to pack as much detail into each postcard as possible; the seemingly 'objective' photograph created a fantasy of Oriental luxuriance.[27]

Moving pictures provided an even newer lens for looking at colonies. The empire did not enjoy pride of place in French cinema – only 85 of 1300 features in the 1930s had colonial settings

– but several significant colonial films arrived on French screens. The most famous was *Pépé le Moko* (1936), about an African, but there were also films about explorers and the Foreign Legion, romances set in the colonies and comedies. The images were usually stereotypical, and African or Asian actors received little credit for their work. Audiences could see countless documentaries, shorts and newsreels – a chronicle of the colonial exhibition of 1931, a three-and-a-half minute film on the proposed Trans-Saharan railway, a short on 'The Work Accomplished by France in its Imperial Domains' or 'France is a Country of 100 Million People', to take examples from the interwar period. Most were unabashed propaganda. In another vein, Jean Rouch pioneered ethnographic cinema, documentaries about non-Western societies completed by social scientists-cum-cinematographers, with *Moi, un noir* in 1957.

Colonies made frequent appearances in advertising, both in illustrated magazines and newspapers, and on posters and handbills. Advertisements touted colonial companies – banks, shipping firms, mining enterprises, and railways. Other companies simply drew on colonial images as a marketing strategy, especially to sell products made with colonial materials. The most famous, and certainly one of the best-known advertisements ever used in France, was publicity for Banania, a sweet powdered beverage made from bananas, sugar and spices which, when mixed with milk, made a popular and, so its producers claimed, nutritious, breakfast food for children and adults. The easily recognised yellow box of Banania featured a smiling African sporting bouffant trousers and a fez with the caption 'Y a bon, Banania' ('Good stuff, Banania'). The picture of the toothy black man changed over the years – after the First World War he became a *tirailleur sénégalais* – but the pidgin caption reinforced a stereotype of the black man as a good-hearted and friendly fellow, if not intellectually gifted. Advertisements featuring young women, such as the lithe West Indians who ornamented publicity for rum, had more or less direct sexual allusions. Smiling black faces often decorated packets of chocolate, cocoa and coffee, as well as soap products – with the implication that the soap or detergent was strong enough even to clean blacks (whom Europeans usually considered innately dirty). Even more racist advertisements jokingly made reference to cannibalism.[28]

Posters aiming to raise money, recruit soldiers or solicit support for colonialism were blatantly propagandistic. One poster for a North African bank pictured native stevedores busily loading goods onto boats in a bustling harbour dominated by a loading crane constructed thanks to French technology and capital. A poster for an organisation promoting imperial commerce showed a ship ploughing through ocean waters with the caption: 'To maintain the past and secure the future, follow in the wake of the French Maritime and Colonial League.' A poster for the Colonial Exhibition of 1931 featured four faces (Arab, black African, Indochinese and Polynesian) silhouetted against several buildings constructed for the fair and a title promising 'A Tour of the World in a Single Day'. Recruiting posters showing tropical posts and heroic soldiers invited young men to join the colonial army. 'The Empire Awaits You', read one such poster. Another promised: 'If you want to go on exotic trips and learn a trade, sign up! You can count on good wages, bonuses and superannuation'; the poster pictured a bare-chested black woman holding pineapples and bananas while a crowd of friendly Africans waited to meet the recruit at the dockside. A Vichy poster had a pith-helmeted scientist at his microscope: 'The Empire needs men from the elite, scientists and technicians'. Pasted onto walls and advertising pillars in the street, displayed in government buildings, schools and post offices, such posters were a colourful and visible reminder of France's imperial destiny.[29]

The Colonial Exhibition of 1931

In addition to literature and visual arts which displayed colonial (though not necessarily colonialist) themes or motifs, exhibitions brought the empire to France. The world fairs of 1878, 1889 and 1900 included colonial sections. In 1906, 1916 and 1922, Marseille, the port city through which two-thirds of France's trade with the empire passed, hosted specifically colonial exhibitions with displays of produce, information booths, performances by dancers and singers from Africa, Asia and the islands, and conferences for academics, business people and colonial promoters. In 1927, the government decided to hold an even grander colonial exhibition in Paris in 1931. As commissioner of the fair, the government appointed Marshal Lyautey.

Lyautey and the government's plan was to create an extravagant display of the variety and riches of France's overseas domains. The exhibition would entertain and inform a populace whose support for the colonial effort had not always been whole-hearted. The fair would show off to the world France's colonial prowess, the extent of its territories, the wisdom of projects for their development, the muscle of a military force strengthened by indigenous troops. The organisers invited foreign nations to mount exhibits in order to demonstrate that expansion was a noble and necessary action undertaken by all civilised nations. The exhibition should spark concrete interest in the empire as well. The visitors' guide told industrialists and traders that they would find presented 'as complete an inventory as possible of the resources offered to your enterprise'; artists would discover 'new methods, new colours, new harmonies'; workers would feel great solidarity with fellow labourers across the seas; France's youth would perhaps be inspired with colonial vocations.

The exhibition, held when French colonialism reached its apogee, was an unprecedented celebration of Greater France and the civilising mission of France. The visitors' guide recalled:

Our protection, you must understand, delivered millions of men, women and children from the nightmare of slavery and death. Do not forget that before we came, on the African continent the stronger dominated the weaker, a woman was but a beast and a child counted for little. There where we found the vestiges of an old civilisation with outdated beliefs . . . how much work we have accomplished! Justice was venal, a state of war endemic, populations decimated by famine and disease, commerce limited to trivial barter, administration xenophobic and pedestrian, the fate of youth lamentable. Today the life of these peoples is closer to your own than you imagine. Examine their work. Look at their reactions. Listen to their songs and their music, and taste their national dishes, which will be available for a reasonable price.

The exhibition represented a great propaganda piece for the empire, designed to spark pride and commitment. The introduction to the visitors' guide quoted Lyautey's olympian injunction: 'You must find in this exhibition, along with the lessons of the past, the lessons of the present and above all lessons for the future. You must leave the exhibition resolved always to do better, grander, broader and more versatile feats for Greater France.'

The site for the exhibition was the Vincennes park in the east of Paris, which visitors could reach by an extension to the Métro

line completed for the occasion. The national government and
the city of Paris spent some 318 million francs on displays and
accommodation. From May to November 1931, 8 million visitors
– 4 million from the Paris region, 3 million from the provinces
and 1 million from overseas – streamed through the gates of what
was officially called the International Exhibition of Colonies and
Overseas Countries. So successful was the exhibition that, even
to the organisers' surprise, it returned a profit of 33 million francs.

Passing under a triumphal arch, past a gilded statue of France
as colonial genius, visitors began their tour at the information
centre, where specialised counters provided documentation on
colonial businesses, tours, and a host of other projects and activities. Fairgoers then promenaded down the Avenue des Colonies.
First they saw pavilions of France's smaller colonies, Djibouti, the
Indian *comptoirs*, the EFO, New Caledonia and the *vieilles colonies*
of Réunion, Guyane, Martinique and Guadeloupe. (A fisherman's
hut further along on the shore of Lake Daumesnil showcased
Saint-Pierre and Miquelon.) Two large exhibitions, one Catholic,
one Protestant, exalted missionary work.

Visitors next reached the highpoint of the fair, the exhibition
devoted to Indochina. Here was a lifesize, detailed reconstruction of the famous Cambodian temples of Angkor Wat. Considered
one of the masterpieces of world architecture, the temple complex had been the object of French study and renovation since
the 1870s. The model in Paris, rising 55 metres into the sky and
covering an area large enough to contain 80 dioramas, was so
popular that organisers had to restrict entry on weekends. Those
who crowded into the mock temple saw displays of rice-planting,
silk-making and rubber-collecting; they studied panels on the different populations of Indochina, and on French education and economic initiatives in Vietnam, Cambodia and Laos.

Continuing the visit, fairgoers came upon the twin exhibits of
the AOF and AEF. A reconstruction of the impressive mud-brick
fortress at Djenné represented West Africa; a 'native' village, the
equatorial possessions. Not far away another village represented
Madagascar. Then came France's North African domains. The
Moroccan exhibit enclosed a 3000-square-metre Maghrebin garden and sultan's palace in the syncretic Neo-Moorish style that
Lyautey had popularised in the protectorate. The Tunisian exhibit recreated a busy market-place. The Algerian display eschewed
exoticism to concentrate on the accomplishments of settlers and

the modernity of a territory proclaimed to be an extension of metropolitan France on the far shore of the Mediterranean. Finally, visitors took in displays from the mandated territories, Togo and Cameroon, Syria and Lebanon: organisers were determined that no significant French outpost would be omitted.

Having toured the French empire and looked at mosques and markets, temples and artisan workshops, visitors continued on to the empires of other countries. Belgium presented a large display on the Congo, the largest colony in Africa; Italy, smallest of the European colonial powers, had reconstructed a Roman basilica from Libya in a display on Cyrenaica and Tripolitania complemented by exhibitions on Eritrea and Somalia; Holland showed off the alluring world of the East Indies. Portugal hosted pavilions on its African colonies, and Denmark offered an exhibition on Greenland. The United States had a pavilion on Alaska, Hawaii, the Panama Canal and other American possessions. The only imperial country missing was Britain, an ironic absence since Britain's empire was the world's largest. Despite repeated overtures by Lyautey and the government, London declined to participate, pleading financial difficulties and the expenses incurred in putting on Britain's own colonial exhibition in 1924.

Tireless fairgoers saw more specialised pavilions on colonial forests, aviation, fine arts and agriculture. They looked at wild beasts in a zoo created for the exhibition (which remains a permanent installation in the Vincennes park). They also stared at 'natives' of the colonies. Several thousand colonial soldiers served as ceremonial guards and participants in parades, and indigenous people from around the empire were brought to France to demonstrate their skills in 'authentic' villages, artisan shops and shows. Especially recommended to give a shudder was the New Caledonian pavilion, where half-naked Melanesians posed; a brochure spoke about the alleged cannibalism of such fierce 'savages'.[30] In the only building constructed to last past the closing of the Colonial Exhibition, the future Museum of the Arts of Africa and Oceania, visitors contemplated examples of non-European arts and crafts. On two small islands in Lake Daumesnil they enjoyed an amusement park. They frequented restaurants and cafés featuring foreign delicacies. They made bookings for lectures and conferences held in a central auditorium. They attended performances, parades, sound-and-light shows and special presentations. And they could remain in the fairgrounds after nightfall to marvel at romantic evening views of the towers of Angkor Wat and the fortress of Djenné.

Few could be unaware, if only subliminally, of the propaganda value of the fair. Display panels showing the achievements of the French *mission civilisatrice* housed in the mock Angkor Wat were a pointed lesson in how French genius had supposedly rescued a remote country from ruin. The relative importance of the colonies might also be apparent to those who looked closer; the AEF village paled by comparison with the fortress of the AOF. Specialists might notice artistic liberties – the towers of Djenné were significantly taller in the reconstruction than in the original, and the animal skulls used on burial totems in Madagascar had been replaced by less macabre carvings – but architects and designers had allowed themselves a certain licence to impress fairgoers.

Joined to the exoticism of the exhibition, the aspect which probably drew in most visitors was a direct message about the utility of empire, especially now that France had begun to feel the effects of the economic depression. Advertisements in the fair's 300-page guidebook enumerated businesses active in the empire. There were ads for the Banque de l'Indochine and the Messageries Maritimes shipping company as well as mining companies, other banks and railways. Sellers of such products as colonial wood hawked their wares. The Chamber of Commerce of Marseille, 'the most powerful institution of the greatest colonial port of France', offered the services of its quays and storehouses, while Bordeaux proclaimed that this 'great French port on the Atlantic is also a great colonial port with direct links to all the French colonies'. The Laffly company advertised 'specialised trucks for colonial transport', a company called Coder, reminding readers that 'the prosperity of colonial exploitation depends above all on the rational and economic transport of their products', tried to sell cargo containers. Other companies promoted material for the production of sugar, rice and rubber and the refining of minerals. Gévelot advertised gunshells for hunting and warfare, and the French Rubber Company presented bicycles and rickshaws (complete with a drawing of an elegant French lady riding in a rickshaw pulled by a coolie). The Vichy spa, 'necessary for all colonials', publicised its services for those who needed to recover from the rigours of foreign climates. *L'Illustration* tried to sell a colonial atlas, and the *Editions Géographiques, Maritimes et Coloniales* offered a free catalogue of books. Galleries showcased native art,

and the famous Sèvres porcelain and glassware company advertised its 'collection of ceramic works, vases and sculptures with
colonial motifs'.

Despite enormous success, not all the French were enamoured
of the Colonial Exhibition. Anti-colonialists roundly denounced
it and asked the French and foreigners to boycott the fair. The
Communist Party damned what it saw as a celebration of brutal
imperial domination and exploitation, while the Socialists expressed
reservations about the form and content of the event. A particularly articulate condemnation came from a group of Surrealist
writers, including André Breton, Paul Eluard and Louis Aragon,
who distributed a tract entitled 'Don't Visit the Colonial Exhibition'; their newspaper published articles on colonial scandals and
the emergence of nationalism in the colonies. The Surrealist
pamphlet and the Communist newspaper L'Humanité highlighted
the arrest and expulsion from France, just before the opening of
the exhibition, of a Vietnamese student charged with subversive
political beliefs and membership of the French Communist Party.
In the socialist paper, Léon Blum, who became prime minister
five years later, denounced the massacre of a group of protesters
who had organised a May Day demonstration in Annam: 'Here
[in Paris] we have the reconstruction of the marvellous stairway
of Angkor and are watching sacred dancers, but in Indochina,
they are shooting, deporting and imprisoning.' Such actions, rather
than the displays in Vincennes, thought the Communists, Socialists and Surrealists, showed the true face of colonialism.

To bring home the point, anti-colonialists organised a counter-
exhibition in October 1931. Divided into three sections, the first,
called 'The Truth about the Colonies', documented forced labour
and other abuses of indigenous populations, and presented displays on nationalist movements. The second part championed the
anti-colonial ideas of Marxism-Leninism and the emancipation of
the tsarist empire's subject peoples since the Bolshevik Revolution of 1917. A final display showed artwork from the colonies
and other overseas countries. Far fewer visitors visited the counter-
exhibition than the Vincennes fair, and the propagandistic nature
of the latter was no less subtle than that of the Colonial Exhibition. But the tracts, newspaper articles and anti-colonialist displays provided a counterpoint to the self-congratulation of the
Vincennes fair, where not a single word was raised about the
deleterious effects of European conquest and administration.[31]

8 Colonial Nationalism and Decolonisation

At the beginning of the Second World War, few political figures, and certainly not the supporters of colonialism, foresaw speedy decolonisation of the empire. In 1943, however, the French granted independence to Syria and Lebanon, the first steps in imperial divestment. Only 21 years later, with the independence of Algeria, France had relinquished most of its overseas possessions. The rapid and thorough withdrawal from the colonies remains a remarkable episode in modern French history.

Decolonisation – the word itself did not enter wide circulation until the 1950s – was a product of changing economic, political and military circumstances in France and the wider world, joined to the growth of colonial nationalism and the triumph of independence movements. Only in hindsight was the process ineluctable. From the 1940s until the early 1960s, debates on decolonisation aggravated politics, colonial conflicts caused ministers to resign and the Algerian crisis brought down the Fourth Republic. Constitutional experts tried to revamp the legal and administrative ties between France and its overseas domains, and right until the dying days of colonialism planners and development strategists designed new initiatives to undertake, yet again, the *mise en valeur* of the colonial world.[1]

The Beginnings of Decolonisation

Protests against French domination and the rise of the nationalism which contributed mightily to later independence began early

266

in the history of colonisation. In some sense, resistance to French takeover – Abd el-Khader's struggle in Algeria, the Tahitian wars of the 1840s, the effort to preclude occupation in Madagascar in the 1880s – links directly with renewed nationalism in the twentieth century. Later nationalist leaders saw earlier figures such as Samory, Béhanzin and Atai as their forebears and liked to trace various earlier episodes of resistance to foreign intervention in a direct line to campaigns for independence after the Second World War. Indeed revolts which punctuated the colonial era, such as widespread opposition to conscription during the First World War, indicated the survival of resistance despite decades of 'pacification' and francisation of indigenes; resentment at foreign control often lay just below the surface of acquiescence and obedience.

A new kind of nationalism and anti-colonialism owed much to the First World War and its consequences, despite efforts to marshal support and recruit soldiers for the war effort. Woodrow Wilson, the American president and a powerful spokesman in international affairs, proposed a charter for the post-war world. Among the 'Fourteen Points' was a call for self-determination by subject peoples, such as those of the former Austro-Hungarian empire, about their future status. Wilson almost certainly did not intend self-determination to apply to colonised Africans, Asians or Middle Easterners, but anti-colonialists and colonial nationalists could extend his principle beyond European shores. If European populations could decide their own fate, why should not non-European peoples enjoy the same right? Furthermore, the post-war settlement saw the establishment of an international organisation with a brief to resolve international disputes and preserve the peace. The League of Nations assumed control of colonies taken from defeated Germany, which it assigned to various imperial powers: the origin of French mandates over Togo, Cameroon, Syria and Lebanon. The League's authority internationalised the colonial question and the terms of the mandates foreshadowed eventual self-government for the territories.

A further development which produced a great impact was the Bolshevik Revolution in Russia in 1917, which brought to power Marxists with an explicitly anti-colonial doctrine; Lenin's *Imperialism, the Highest Stage of Capitalism* had constituted an indictment of colonialism. The Bolsheviks claimed that victory in Russia would lead to the worldwide triumph of the proletariat over the bourgeoisie, replacement of capitalism by socialism, and the liberation of European workers and colonised indigenes who suffered under capitalist domination. The Soviet Union took the lead in the anti-colonialist struggle, broadcasting its message through the Third International (Comintern) founded in 1919, and the various Communist parties which split from the Socialist movement and pledged loyalty to Moscow. Communists, including the French party, thereafter displayed a sometimes ambivalent attitude towards colonialism, but upheld the goal of colonial liberation, even if they did not say that it should occur immediately. The French Communist Party chief in the 1930s metaphorically compared colonial emancipation to divorce, but added that the right to divorce did not imply an obligation to divorce.

The Soviet Union (and later Communist China) provided material and moral support for anti-colonial movements, and the doctrine of Marxism exerted great influence. Marxism provided a coherent analysis of capitalist economic and political domination in Europe and the wider world, suggested a path of liberation and mapped a plan for an alternative society. Given the unwillingness of colonial powers to effect major changes in government, particularly to enfranchise 'natives' and grant them a share of power, or to undertake a more equitable distribution of the rewards of an export-oriented economy geared to the profit-making of a European elite, Marxism held great ideological attraction. The tumult of interwar Europe – marked by the rise of the radical right and the effects of the Depression – projected Marxist theory and Communist practice as a legitimate alternative to capitalism, bankrupt Western democracy, fascism and racism.

Other developments contributed to the growth of nationalism in the early 1900s. Sun Yat-Sen's 1910 revolution in China, which overthrew the Manchu dynasty and inaugurated a republic, sent shock waves throughout Asia, and early Vietnamese nationalists drew inspiration from Sun's success. In the Levant and North Africa, the victory of Kemal Ataturk and his 'Young Turks' in the early 1920s, after the dissolution of the Ottoman Empire, provided an example of successful nationalism and modernisation. Protesters, often drawn from the ranks of students, adopted the nomenclature of Kemal's movement to become 'Young Moroccans' and 'Young Tunisians'.

Nationalist Politics in the Interwar Years

The interwar years witnessed various colonial rebellions. A revolt by Abd el-Krim in Spanish Morocco in the early 1920s implicated the French, who joined forces with the Spanish to defeat the North African leader. Support for Abd el-Krim, and denunciation of the imperialists, formed the loudest protest against colonialism yet heard. Meanwhile, the French quelled the Druze uprising in Lebanon and Syria.

Nationalist activism grew stronger elsewhere in the colonies. Tunisian dissidents had already begun publishing a newspaper in 1907. In 1917, two Tunisian sheiks issued (in Switzerland) a strongly-worded 'protest against French despotism' which called for independence for Tunisia and Algeria. A group of intellectuals in Tunisia demanded a written constitution for the protectorate, and in 1920 organised the Destour Party (from the word for constitution). The Destour nationalists, led by 'Abd-el-Azîz Ta'albi, called for the election of a representative assembly (with voting restricted to Tunisians), and ultimately independence. The party provoked strikes and other contestatory activities in the 1920s and early 1930s. Then, in 1934, the party split, and the Néo-Destour party became even more adamant in opposition to French colonialism. It adopted militant tactics to press for independence, organising boycotts of French products, non-payment of taxes and demonstrations. The French cracked down, arresting many of the party's leaders, including a young lawyer who later became the head of the party and Tunisia's first president, Habib Bourguiba. Nevertheless, the Néo-Destour's influence steadily grew until the French outlawed the party in 1938.

A similar movement developed in Morocco with the activities of students, the Young Moroccans, who created nationalist newspapers and associations in the early 1930s. In 1934, they formed a Moroccan Action Committee, whose manifesto called for France to observe strictly the terms of the protectorate and to grant self-government to Moroccans. The programme, which also asked for the creation of chambers of commerce and muncipal governments, was not particularly radical, yet it drew the ire of French authorities, who dissolved the committee in 1937. Moroccan nationalism, however, was not quelled.

Nationalism had seethed in the Algerian elite since the earliest years of the twentieth century under the symbolic leadership of one of Abd el-Khader's grandsons and the Young Algerians. Sheik 'Abdelhamîd Ben Bâdîs became the dissidents' spokesman. In the context of French political and cultural assimilation, and widespread dismissal of Algerian society as only a collection of warring tribes, he issued a powerful statement:

> The Algerian nation was formed and exists just as were formed and exist all nations of the earth. This nation has its history illustrated with countless great events; it has its religious and linguistic unity; it has its own culture, its traditions, its mores .... This Algerian nation is not France: it is not possible for it to be France. It does not want to become France, and even it if so desired, it could not so be. . . . It wants nothing of assimilation.[2]

Another of Ben Bâdîs' statements resounded as a slogan of national identity and political action: 'Islam is my religion. Arabic is my language. Algeria is my country.' Such pronouncements inspired the setting up of political parties, notably Messali Hadj's North African Star (*Etoile Nord-Africaine*) in 1926. The French banned the party several years later, frightened by its nationalist programme with Marxist overtones, as well as its perceived capability for subversion. This did little to curb nationalist sentiment, but lack of unity handicapped a movement divided among those demanding full rights for Algerians as French citizens, those advocating religious revival coupled with reform, and more militant autonomists and advocates of independence.

Nationalist movements arose more quickly in Indochina than anywhere else in the interwar years. The Vietnamese National Party, one of many political parties established in this period, demanded greater rights for indigenous peoples and the unification of the three provinces of Tonkin, Annam and Cochinchina into an independent Vietnamese republic. More radical still was the Revolutionary League of Vietnamese Youth founded in 1925 by Nguyên-Ai-Quôc (Ho Chi Minh).

More than any other individual in the empire, Ho symbolised the anti-colonial struggle against France. Born in Annam sometime between 1890 and 1894, the future Ho – he used many pseudonyms during his early life – was the son of a mandarin official. Ho was educated in a French school; though his formal training did not extend past primary school, he later became well versed in European, Chinese and Vietnamese culture. In 1911, Ho left Vietnam for Europe as an employee of a shipping line, the start of a 40-year exile. He worked on steamers ploughing the North Atlantic and frequently visited London and New York, learning English in the process. At the end of the First World War, Ho lived in France, where he met other Vietnamese dissidents. He participated in the Congress of Tours in 1920, which saw the establishment of the French Communist Party. Ho addressed the party on colonial issues and won election to its colonial committee. In the early 1920s, while earning his living by retouching photographs, Ho edited an anti-colonial newspaper, *Le Paria*, the 'tribune of the colonial proletariat', and wrote an indictment of French colonialism, *Le Procès de la colonisation française* (published in 1926). In 1923, Ho left France for Moscow, at the invitation of the Comintern, where he joined other colonial rebels at a Marxist training institute. Later in the decade, Ho lived in China and Hong Kong (where he was arrested by the British).[3] By this time, he had founded the Revolutionary League.

In 1930, Indochina erupted when a group of Vietnamese soldiers, influenced by the nationalists, mutinied at Yen Bay. Some troops deserted. Bombs exploded in Hanoi. Peasants in Tonkin, probably aided by Ho's party, rebelled. The French responded by bombing villages and arresting and executing the leaders of the revolt. This turned revolutionaries into martyrs and sparked sympathy for the nationalists.

In 1931, Ho's party changed its name to the Vietnamese Communist Party and affiliated with the Comintern. The aims of Ho's party, as expressed in a 1930 manifesto showing the influence of Marxism, were to:

1. Overthrow French imperialism, feudalism and the reactionary bourgeoisie of Vietnam.
2. Win complete independence for Vietnam.
3. Form a government of workers, peasants and soldiers.
4. Confiscate the banks and other imperialist businesses and place them under the control of the government of workers, peasants and soldiers.
5. Confiscate all plantations and other properties belonging to imperialists and reactionary Vietnamese bourgeois and distribute them to poor peasants.
6. Institute an eight-hour [working] day.

7. End forced loans, the head tax and other taxes which af-
flict the poor.
8. Secure democratic liberties for the masses.
9. Dispense education to all.
10. Secure equality between men and women.[4]

Their achievement implied eviction of the French from Indochina,
expropriation of the rubber plantations which formed the basis
of the colonial export economy (as well as takeover of such powerful companies as the Banque de l'Indochine), and the creation
of a new society on a radically different base to Western capitalist
principles. It was not suprising that Ho was soon condemned to
death in absentia by the French, who still considered his movement a small group which they could easily combat.

Few colonies in sub-Saharan Africa or the island possessions
boasted the nationalist parties, spokesmen or episodes of protest
as did Indochina and the Maghreb. Limited Western education,
disunity and distance from European intellectual currents hin-
dered the creation of nationalist movements. But individual voices,
such as those of Senghor, called the French to task, and Communism promised one ideology and organisation for nationalists.
Dissident leaders were usually intellectuals or professional men –
lawyers, doctors, imams – who combined demands for restoration of national independence and unity with economic and political doctrines borrowed from Marxism or French constitutionalism
(or both) and references to the traditional cultures of their
countries. Such rhetoric struck a responsive chord in the small
educated elite and among peasants who formed the majority of
colonised populations. But in the interwar years, the French state
could effectively contain their actions through harassment, arrests
and the outlawing of parties.

International Developments

Several trends in international relations during the later interwar
period caused particular concern in the empire. The Fascist leader
Benito Mussolini, who came to power in 1922, aimed to revitalise
Italy and recreate a Roman empire. Fascists flexed their muscle
in Italy's Northern African colony of Libya, and colonialists made
threatening noises about taking over neighbouring Tunisia, where

a significant Italian population lived; Italy still smarted from the loss of Tunisia to France in 1881. Promoters of Italian expansion even talked of wresting Corsica away from France. Italian forces invaded Ethiopia in 1935 and conquered the country despite the condemnation of a powerless League of Nations. Added to its colonies in Eritrea and Somaliland, Italian occupation of Ethiopia changed the balance of power on the horn of Africa and directly menaced the French outpost of Djibouti, now surrounded by Italian colonial territory. Because the main economic activity of Djibouti was commerce in the city's port and transport on the rail line to Addis Ababa, the Ethiopian capital, the French had to accommodate the Italians. The two colonial powers lived in uncomfortable proximity.

In Asia, Japan pursued its imperial expansion in the 1930s, gaining a League of Nations mandate over most of the islands of Micronesia, consolidating control over Taiwan and Korea and, in 1931, invading Chinese Manchuria. Japanese interest in Indochina for its strategic location and wealth of resources endangered France's Asian domains. Japan also looked covetously at France's Pacific islands; Japan was the major purchaser of New Caledonia's nickel, which seemed a guarantee of good short-term relations but raised concern about possible Japanese designs. Articles expressing alarm at Japanese expansionism in the Asia–Pacific region filled such journals as the bulletin of the Committee for French Oceania.

The rise to power of Adolf Hitler, who became chancellor of Germany in 1933, held possible colonial ramifications. The Nazi Party campaigned to overturn the First World War peace settlement which, among other provisions, had taken away Germany's colonies. Nazi ideologues spoke increasingly about securing new overseas bases for Germany. Hitler's political programme mandated expansion inside Europe to conquer 'living space' for Germany's Aryan population at the expense of Germany's rivals and 'inferior' non-Germanic populations.

In 1939, the European phase of the Second World War began when Hitler invaded and conquered Poland. The next year, German forces moved westwards. In May 1940, Germany penetrated the Maginot Line and, only a month later, dealt a crushing defeat to France. The loss represented military capitulation and indicted French institutions which had proved incapable of withstanding German aggression. The French government considered taking refuge in North Africa, but soon dissolved in chaos in the face of German advance. A newly formed Vichy government (so-called because of the provincial city where it established head-quarters) signed an armistice with Germany, and German forces occupied much of France. A superannuated First World War marshal, Philippe Pétain, who became the Vichy Head of State, agreed to collaborate with Nazi Germany.

Some of the French felt sympathy with the reactionary govern-ments of Hitler's Germany, Mussolini's Italy and Franco's Spain and hoped that Vichy, with its gospel of 'Work, Family and Father-land', would regenerate France. Others simply saw little alterna-tive to sullen cooperation with a victorious Germany which now controlled much of central and western continental Europe. Still others, however, refused to accept capitulation. A leader for the Free French emerged in the person of a young military officer, Charles de Gaulle. Within days of the armistice, de Gaulle, in a radio broadcast from London, urged continued resistance to the Germans inside France and a concerted effort, in conjunction with Britain and other allies, to defeat Germany from without; France had lost a battle, de Gaulle proclaimed in heroic terms, but France had not lost the war.

The Free French did appear to have lost most of the empire. Colonial officials in general cast their lot with the Vichy govern-ment, which cloaked itself in a mantle of legitimacy. Only a few colonies initially opted for de Gaulle. The Resident in the small Anglo-French condominium of the New Hebrides, Henri Sautot, partly under British pressure, joined de Gaulle's side, then sailed to Nouméa, with aid from the Australian Navy, to rally New Cale-donia to the Free French. By the (northern) autumn of 1940, Tahiti, after squabbling between pro- and anti-Vichy figures, had also joined the Free French. In Africa, the governor of Oubangui-Chari, Félix Eboué, alone pledged support for de Gaulle. The major colonies – those of North Africa and the AOF, Madagascar and Indochina – remained in Vichy hands.

The war dislocated the empire. Relations between colonies and the metropole became difficult: transmission of government in-structions and funds encountered delays, shipping to colonial ports ceased, trade plummeted. The Allied powers regarded Vichy-con-trolled governments with suspicion. The Free French forces were hardly in a position to overturn the pro-Vichy administrations or liberate colonies – an attempt to conquer Dakar proved a failure.

In France itself, where the Resistance mounted a clandestine campaign against Germany and its supporters, and in the empire, the French remained divided about the future of the nation. One incident in the colonies pointed up the dilemma, and the effects it produced. In June 1940, just after the German victory, the Allies asked the French naval squadron based in the Algerian port of Mers-el-Kébir to join their side. The commander refused and, fearing that French ships would fall into enemy hands, the British attacked the squadron. Most of the French fleet was destroyed, and 1300 French sailors were killed.

The progress of the war drew French colonies into military activity. The Japanese attack on Pearl Harbor in 1941 (which brought the United States into the war) and Japanese expansion into Papua New Guinea and the Solomon Islands heightened fears of attacks on France's Pacific islands. American forces soon landed (in the company of Australian and New Zealander troops) and set up enormous bases on New Caledonia, Bora-Bora (in the EFO), Wallis and several islands in the New Hebrides. The islands, especially New Caledonia, became important Allied back-up bases in the Pacific theatre. Effects were dramatic, as thousands of American GIs arrived – as many as half a million American soldiers were stationed in New Caledonia at one or another time, and foreign soldiers occasionally outnumbered the total population of tiny Wallis – with all sorts of goods, such as bulldozers, earth-movers and jeeps, which had never been seen in the islands. The Americans speedily constructed airstrips, built accommodation, hospitals and other facilities. American dollars paid for manual labour, food and other services (particularly laundering) and sometimes the company of local women. Islanders saw American largesse as manna; American technological prowess and 'Yankee efficiency' impressed them; the presence of black American soldiers, seemingly paid the same wages and treated as equals by their white colleagues, sparked questions about the racial hierarchies which characterised French colonialism. The French lacked the money and machines of the Americans, and sat sullenly by while Americans 'occupied' several of the French islands. Perhaps not surprisingly, a few residents – both indigenes and French settlers – campaigned for American annexation at the conclusion of the war, while the New Hebrides gave birth to 'cargo-cults', syncretic religious movements which believed that ships would continue to arrive bearing bounty from America.

The Allies had no trouble defending France's Oceanic territories, and other colonies began to rally around de Gaulle. After
much debate between the British and French on strategies to defeat
Germany and the Axis powers in Europe, authorities decided on
an invasion of North Africa, which occurred in 1942. Bitter battles followed (although most took place outside the French domains), and North Africa was liberated. The British invaded
Madagascar, and most of black Africa came under Gaullist control in the same year. De Gaulle established the Free French base
in Algiers, and the empire played a substantial role for the remainder of the war. More than ever before, the colonies seemed
to fulfil their potential as a source of soldiers, supplies and territory.

Not all was quiet on the colonial front during the war years.
Syria and Lebanon demanded attention. The Vichy-aligned administration of the mandated territories established a virtual dic-
tatorship early in the war and did not hide its pro-German
sentiments. The British, who ruled nearby Iraq and Palestine, were
alarmed that Vichy might authorise German use of France's territories as military bases, which would allow the Axis valuable entry
into the Middle East. In 1941, the British invaded Syria, soon
followed by Free French forces under General Catroux, who took
Damascus. To satisfy both the British and Arab nationalists, Catroux
proclaimed Syria and Lebanon independent. Lebanon's independence did not become effective until 1943, and French forces withdrew only three years later. Syrian independence officially came
at the beginning of 1944, but failure of the new government to
establish control led to insurrection and French bombardment
of Damascus the next year; French forces finally evacuated Syria
in 1946.

North Africa had seen military campaigns (such as the battles
of Bir-Hakeim and El-Alamein) and a recrudescence in anti-French
activity. Nazi Germany and Fascist Italy promoted nationalism in
North Africa to undermine French influence, and some nationalists adopted a more sympathetic tone to the Axis than the French,
whether pro- or anti-Vichy, found acceptable.

The situation was particularly tense in Tunisia. In November
1942 German and Italian forces invaded Tunisia from neighbouring
Libya and occupied the protectorate until they were driven out
by American, British and French troops which arrived from Algeria in May 1943. (The recapture of Tunisia was the last battle of
the Second World War fought in North Africa.) Soon after their

invasion, the Germans had freed the nationalist leader Habib Bourguiba, held prisoner in France since 1938, and escorted him to Rome. Bourguiba refused to become a mouthpiece for the Fascist cause or to endorse the French position. With the liberation of Tunisia, the French dismissed the country's nominal ruler, Moncef Bey, ostensibly because of his presence during the Axis occupation but in reality because he had formed a moderately nationalist government. The gesture helped to stimulate nationalist discontent.

The situation in Indochina was the most complicated in the French empire in the war years and immediately thereafter. Even before war broke out in Europe, Japan began to make demands on authorities in Indochina. In 1939, when Japan expanded from mainland China to Hainan island, across the Bay of Tonkin from Hanoi, Tokyo demanded that shipments of armaments on the Yunnan railway should cease; the French, who deployed only 40 000 troops in Indochina and were in no position to fight the Japanese, agreed. Tokyo soon successfully demanded that its agents oversee rail traffic on the Haiphong–Yunnan line. In June 1940, after their defeat in Europe, the French acceded to further Japanese demands regarding rail shipments between Tonkin and China. The new Governor-General, Admiral Decoux, a strong supporter of Vichy ideology, was unlikely to refuse other Japanese commands.

It was not long before orders arrived. In September 1940, Tokyo demanded permission to station 25 000 troops in Indochina. Before Decoux had time to respond to the ultimatum, the Japanese attacked the French base at Langson. When Decoux's reponse, not surprisingly, was affirmative, the Japanese withdrew. Decoux's stepped-up collaboration convinced the Japanese to leave Indochina in French hands, although earlier in the year they had lent some support to Vietnamese nationalists. Decoux instituted a dictatorial regime and attempted to reconstruct Indochinese society – with youth brigades, public celebrations and the cult of Pétain – in the image of Vichy's 'national revolution'. He also propped up the monarchy in Laos, and in 1941 oversaw the coronation of Norodom Sihanouk as king of Cambodia to assure quiet in those countries.

The Free French Forces could do little to counter collaboration in Indochina other than gather intelligence. De Gaulle, though preoccupied with events in Europe, could not overlook the problem of France's Asian colonies. Vietnamese nationalism continued to fester, despite Decoux's merciless repression of a Communist-led rebellion in Annam early in 1941. President Roosevelt of the United States and Marshal Stalin of the Soviet Union let it be known that they opposed French resumption of control over Indochina at the end of the war. On 8 December 1943, the Free French tried to calm both nationalists and foreign governments with a declaration which promised a liberal constitutional statute and greater participation by Indochinese in local government.

After the liberation of mainland France in 1944, de Gaulle decided to maintain Decoux in office temporarily, notwithstanding his record of collaboration with the Axis. De Gaulle's provisional government had little alternative while war still raged in the Pacific. In March 1945, events took a dramatic turn when the Japanese representative in Indochina issued another ultimatum: because of the risk of an American invasion, Decoux must place French troops under Japanese command. Even before the ultimatum expired, the Japanese arrested Decoux and occupied Indochina. Efforts by troops to resist failed, and the American government declined de Gaulle's plea for an air attack.

Japan, claiming to have liberated Indochina from the French, then approved declarations of independence by the Annamese emperor Bao Daï, previously a tame supporter of the French, and the kings of Cambodia and Laos. Nationalists seized the opportunity, and much of the population welcomed the new situation. De Gaulle replied with an ambiguous declaration promising that when Indochina was finally freed from the Japanese, France would proclaim civil liberties and create new administrative arrangements to assure autonomy in the context of a French Union.[5]

The government of Bao Daï lacked credibility and faced opposition from a more militantly nationalist movement, the Viet Minh. Ho Chi Minh, returning to Vietnam after many years' absence, founded the Viet Minh in 1941 in an effort to take advantage of the unsettled state of affairs. A frontal assault on the French and Japanese by nationalists was not possible, so Ho pioneered guerrilla warfare. Guerrillas, setting out on campaigns from Vietnam's dense forests, mounted lightening attacks on the Japanese and won much public support. The Viet Minh stood ready to take over government. (Ho had also made contacts with the Americans – who at the time considered the Viet Minh the most legitimate nationalist group in Indochina – and, secretly and tentatively, with the French.)

Events moved swiftly. After the Japanese occupation on 9 March 1945 and Bao Daï's proclamation of independence two days later, the French responded on 24 March with the announcement of plans for a post-war 'Indochinese Federation'. In July, the Allies, meeting at Potsdam, agreed that, when the Japanese were defeated, Chinese troops should occupy Vietnam north of the sixteenth parallel of latitude, British troops the south of the country. On 6 August, the atomic bomb fell on Hiroshima; on 14 August, Japan capitulated. A power vacuum resulted in Vietnam, and demonstrations against the Japanese and French raged over the next few days. Ho's forces took control of Hanoi and most of Tonkin, and Viet Minh guerrillas operated in Annam and Cochinchina. Manifestly unable to control the situation, Bao Daï abdicated and his government resigned on 23 August. Two days afterwards, his assistants passed the ceremonial symbols of government to the Viet Minh, effectively recognising Ho's hold on Tonkin. Although the Viet Minh lacked control of Saigon and Cochinchina, on 2 September Ho proclaimed the independence of a united Democratic Republic of Vietnam. French ministers stated the obvious – that this was a colonial crisis. Meanwhile, Chinese forces began to occupy northern Vietnam on 9 September, while British troops took over the south on 12 September. Two weeks later, the French, commanded by General Leclerc, arrived in Cochinchina, accompanied by a civilian high commissioner (as the governor-general was renamed), Thierry d'Argenlieu. A special emissary, Jean Sainteny, began talks with Ho and the Viet Minh.

Vietnam was for all practical purposes divided between Ho's Viet Minh in the north and the French in the south, although the nationalists continued guerrilla activity in Cochinchina. On 6 January 1946, elections in the north for a constituent assembly confirmed Ho's popularity. Elsewhere in Indochina, a French battalion had overthrown the Japanese-installed government in Cambodia and had easily re-established control over Laos, whose leaders, in any case, had been hesitant to accept the independence offered by the Japanese.

French reconquest of Tonkin, however, looked most unlikely. The French decided to negotiate a settlement, and de Gaulle hoped to place on the throne, in place of the discredited Bao Daï, a Vietnamese prince who had taken part in a nationalist rebellion in 1917, but had 'redeemed' himself by joining the Free French. His death in a plane crash foiled the plan. On 6 March 1946,

France agreed to a convention with the Ho government in which 'the French government recognises the Republic of Vietnam as a free state having its government, parliament, army and finances, as part of the Indochinese Federation and the French Union', a less clear-cut statement than at first appeared since the exact nature of the Federation and the Union remained unstated. Furthermore, Paris agreed to the unification of Tonkin, Annam and Cochinchina if a referendum approved the measure. France won China's agreement to withdraw its troops, and the French military prepared to land forces at Haiphong. For a brief moment, it looked as if France was well down the road to peaceful decolonisation of Vietnam.

The Fourth Republic and the Union Française

While the accord between French authorities and Ho Chi Minh was settled, policy-makers in Paris were designing a new structure for the post-war empire. Free French leaders had begun to consider the future of the empire after the setting up of de Gaullle's provisional French government in Algiers in 1943. At the beginning of the following year an unprecedented conference of colonial administrators from the Maghreb, sub-Saharan Africa and Madagascar was held in Brazzaville; 'native' political leaders were not invited. Hosted by Félix Eboué, Governor-General of the AEF, and opened by de Gaulle, the conference deliberated on colonial affairs for a week. A final declaration left no doubt as to the intention of France's post-war rulers to maintain their control over the colonies: 'The goals of the work of colonisation accomplished by France ... preclude any idea of autonomy, any possibility of evolution outside the French bloc of the empire; the eventual constitution, even in a distant future, of *self government* [in English in the text] is to be avoided.' Softening this line, however, other declarations spoke of 'necessary administrative decentralisation' and 'the indispensable participation of indigenes in looking after their own affairs'.

The assembly which met in Paris in 1946 to draw up a constitution for the new Fourth Republic counted a number of representatives destined to play a major role in advancing colonial demands and, in some cases, leading their nations to independence. They included the poet and future president of Senegal, Léopold Sedar Senghor, the future president of Algeria, Ferhat

Abbas, the future president of the Côte-d'Ivoire, Félix Houphouët-Boigny, and such other prominent black men as the Martinican writer Aimé Césaire, Sourou-Migan Apithy from Dahomey, Lamine Guèye from Senegal, Prince Douala Manga Bell from Cameroon and Jean-Félix Tchicaya from the Congo. Although these *députés* did not form a party, nor did they share identical views, they were well linked in particular with the French Socialists and the Communist Party (PCF) which, in cooperation with the Christian Socialists, controlled the constituent assembly and government. (The African delegates had decided among themselves to affiliate with the three major parties in order to maximise their influence.)

Several measures adopted in 1946, generally at the instigation of the colonial *députés*, changed the status of indigenes in the empire. A decree of 20 February 1946 ended the much hated *code de l'indigénat*; a decree of 30 April made the French law code applicable throughout the colonies. On 11 April, legislation introduced by Houphouët-Boigny ended forced labour in the colonies. The Lamine Guèye law of 7 May 1946 made all French 'subjects' in the empire French 'citizens' (though without giving them equal rights to metropolitan citizens or French settlers overseas) without depriving them of their traditional civil status. A law introduced by Césaire made the 'old colonies' (Martinique, Guadeloupe, Guyane and Réunion) into *départements*. Legislation set up the Economic and Social Investment and Development Fund (*Fonds d'investissement et de développement économique et social*, FIDES) to channel capital to the colonies, a tacit admission that they could not develop – or benefit France – with only their own financial resources.

The constitution of the Fourth Republic, adopted in October 1946, established the French Union. According to its preamble, 'France intends to lead the peoples for which it has responsibility to the freedom to administer themselves and to direct their own affairs democratically, avoiding any system of colonisation founded on arbitrariness. It forms with the overseas peoples a Union founded on equality of rights and duties, without distinction of race or religion.' The Union was composed 'on the one hand, by the French Republic, which is made up of metropolitan France [and] the overseas *départements* [and] territories and, on the other, by the associated territories and states' – the colonies of the AOF and AEF thereby became overseas territories, Cameroon

and Togo associated territories and, later and briefly, the
Indochinese Federation became an associated state. The new constitution expressed fine sentiments, but the role of the colonised
people had changed less than the words implied: the populations
of France's colonies were not even given the opportunity to vote
on whether on not to accept the constitution. The changes erased
the word 'colony' from French legal terminology; 'governors' and
'governors-general' similarly became 'high commissioners'. But
French domination of the Union remained: the French president
was president of the Union, and the French government was its
government. The Union assembly, separate from the French parliament, enjoyed only consultative rights. Assemblies were set up
in each of the former overseas colonies, but except in the
départements d'outre-mer and the AOF, each was composed of two
electoral 'colleges', one elected by European residents, the other
by indigenous voters. The former held greater authority; lack of
political development in the colonies, the amassing of economic
power in the hands of settler elites and the administration, and
high levels of illiteracy among indigenous people all meant that
'native' participation in government was severely limited. The
overseas regions elected members to the French parliament, but
they were extraordinarily few in number compared to the number
of *députés* from the metropole – to avoid, as one politician inel-
egantly phrased it, the possibility that 'the grandsons of Makoko
could dictate the law in Paris'.

The constitutional provisions were undoubtedly responses to
demands for change, but also represented efforts to nip nationalist movements in the bud and preserve French dominion in a
rapidly changing world. The post-war world was little favourable
to unreconstructed colonialism. The United States, the Soviet
Union, the United Nations and, soon, the People's Republic of
China opposed old-style colonialism. The victorious powers had
deprived defeated Italy and Japan of their colonies, foreshadowing independence in a short period for Italy's former domains,
although placing the Japanese Micronesian territories in an Ameri-
can-administered trusteeship. Within several years of the end of
the Second World War, Syria, Lebanon and Egypt had obtained
full independence, as had British India (divided into India, Paki-
stan and Sri Lanka), Burma, the Dutch East Indies (as Indonesia) and the American colony of the Philippines.

Underlying currents gradually leached away the foundations of colonialism inside France. The colonies no longer exercised the exotic attraction that they had once enjoyed. The colonial lobby lost much of its sway in the corridors of power. The needs of post-war reconstruction and the boom years, from the mid-1940s to the mid-1970s, created business and employment opportunities in France and throughout Europe. French companies could still make money in the colonies, and indeed benefited greatly from new French capital expenditure, but new possibilities for investment, production and marketing beckoned in a Europe undergoing the 'third industrial revolution', the advent of consumer society and an economic shift away from primary commodities. Raymond Cartier, a journalist writing in the late 1950s, developed the argument ('*cartiérisme*') that French expenditures on the colonies were too onerous on the state and tax payers, and that French resources should be concentrated on the metropole.

Public opinion supported the retention of colonies – 81 per cent of those polled in 1949 agreed that France 'had an interest in possessing overseas territories'; 62 per cent thought France had basically done good work in its colonial mission. But one-third admitted that they possessed no information on the colonies, and 19 per cent could not name a single colony; 52 per cent said they were personally 'indifferent' to the empire. After the loss of Indochina in 1954, 45 per cent still affirmed that it was 'very important' for the other colonies to remain associated with France, but in 1956, only 43 per cent believed that in ten years the African possessions (both in North and sub-Saharan Africa) would be French. If the French were 'pro-colonial', support was not unanimous and a growing number were reconciled to decolonisation.

In the years immediately after the war authorities tried to modernise and revitalise the colonies with new institutions and more generous funds. Throughout overseas domains, groups agitating for reform, autonomy or outright independence nevertheless organised – even in faraway New Caledonia and Tahiti, committees of Pacific islanders, phrasing their demands in ever so moderate and Francophile terms, called for greater democratisation of political life. Militant movements elsewhere were less reticent. Several developments made it immediately clear that the job of holding on to the colonies would be arduous and opposition to continued French control ardent: a violent attack by nationalists in Sétif, in eastern Algeria, in mid-1946, preceded by only a few months the outbreak of the Indochinese War, and in the following year insurrection occurred in Madagascar.

The Malagasy Uprising

Although a nationalist movement emerged in Madagascar in the early twentieth century, its leaders threw their support behind France when the Second World War began. With French defeat, Vichy-appointed leaders ruled until ousted by British soldiers in 1942. The Free French assumed control, but demands for autonomy resurfaced at the end of the war, spearheaded by the Democratic Movement for Malagasy Renovation (MDRM). Anger over wartime conditions imposed on the island – requisitions, forced harvesting, commandeered labour, conscription and obligatory loans – had created much opposition to French rule; in particular, the setting up of rice agencies, to which all rice-growers were obliged to deliver their crops, had caused much discontent and promoted black market activities. The political reforms of the Fourth Republic failed to satisfy nationalist claims. Newspapers spread the anti-colonial views which gained currency on the morrow of the war. The return home of 10 000 demobilised soldiers further unsettled the situation.

France took a conciliatory attitude, but rejected autonomy and supported a rival party to the MDRM. In elections to the French parliament in 1945, nationalists won the two seats designated for Madagascar in the lower house, and a nationalist also won election to the Senate. The *députés* demanded that the law annexing Madagascar to France be repealed and that Paris grant self-government. Peaceful demonstrations supported the cause, and the MDRM leader, Jacques Rabemamanjara, won a newly-created third seat as *député* in late 1946. Tensions ran high throughout the island, although the MDRM appealed for calm.

On the night of 29–30 March 1947, violence broke out. In Manakara district, rebels attacked military barracks and police posts, stole arms, then occupied administration headquarters and European business offices. Rebellion spread, and soon about one-sixth of Madagascar was in open insurrection, as between 15 000 and 20 000 hard-core protesters, joined by many sympathisers armed with knives, hatchets, spears and captured French weapons, attacked Europeans, committing pillage, arson, murder and sabotage. Rebels proclaimed provisional governments in regions they held. In July 1947, the tide began to turn in favour of the French. Heavily armed and reinforced French regiments faced off starving and demoralised rebels, and after almost 20 months, the fires of insurrection were finally extinguished in December 1948.

Repression was quick and severe. Courts passed sentences on thousands of rebels, and a dozen were executed. Two of the nationalist *députés* were stripped of their parliamentary immunity and sentenced to death, although they were later pardoned. The Malagasy senator received life imprisonment, and Rabemamanjara was sentenced to forced labour. Although the MDRM had kept its distance from the rebels and the violence they perpetrated, the government dissolved the party. Approximately 550 French men and women lost their lives in the uprising, but a much larger number of Malagasy died in the fighting or in massacres which followed – the French military in 1949 estimated that there had been 89 000 Malagasy victims of the insurrection and repression.

Particular factors sparked the unsuccessful revolt and the reaction which followed. But the underlying reason was simply Malagasy nationalism and opposition to colonialism. In 1947, the *député* Joseph Raseta commented: 'The desire one day to regain the independence we lost in 1895 has never ceased to haunt the spirit and hearts of the Malagasy.' The French High Commissioner in Madagascar added: 'The first conclusion that the revolt has allowed us to make is that the patriotic feeling of the Malagasy is deeply anchored. . . . All of the indigenous population of Madagascar aspires to the total independence of the Malagasy motherland. . . . Whatever may happen, Madagascar will be independent.' The Malagasy waited for 13 years, however, to win that independence.[6]

The Indochinese War

Hopes for a peaceful settlement to the Indochinese conflict ended quickly. After the March 1946 agreement between Ho and French authorities to a vague Vietnamese independence within the French Union, representatives of the two sides failed to make progress in talks the following month. Ho left for France to pursue negotiations but learned, during a stopover, that France had just set up a separate autonomous government in Cochinchina and southern Annam under the titular authority of Bao Daï. Much to Ho's anger, this indicated France's rejection of the unification of Tonkin and Annam with the southern region: geographical as well as ideological divisions were clearly drawn. Ho wanted nothing less than the unification of Vietnam; the French hoped to reconquer the north or at least preserve a friendly regime in the south. After Ho's arrival in France, the fall of the French prime minister delayed talks which might have worked out a compromise. In July, negotiators failed to reach accord on unification, but Ho and the French signed a modus vivendi and planned further discussions at the beginning of 1947.[7]

The French, however, had decided to try to retake the north by force. On 23 November, France issued an ultimatum to the Viet Minh to evacuate Haiphong. On 29 November, French navy vessels intercepted a Chinese boat carrying contraband petrol into the harbour of Haiphong. Vietnamese nationalists, under Ho's control, fired on the French ships. Haiphong became the site of military warfare with attacks by Vietnamese and French forces on each other which led to the deaths of some 6000 people: the battle in Haiphong is usually considered the start of the Vietnamese war of independence. On 19 December, after the blowing-up of a power station in Hanoi, warfare spread to the Tonkinese capital.[8]

War continued for eight years. By 1950, French colonial forces counted 56 000 Frenchmen, 35 000 Vietnamese soldiers, 25 000 North Africans, 18 000 Legionnaires and 15 000 black Africans. The French initially enjoyed the advantage of firepower and sophisticated weaponry. The more numerous Vietnamese knew the terrain better than their adversaries. They won broad support among compatriots and mounted sustained guerrilla warfare. The Viet Minh moved soldiers and arms through the jungles, often on bicycles unable to be detected by aerial reconnaissance. They created networks for intelligence-gathering, including many double agents who ostensibly worked for the French. They carried out surprise attacks on French convoys, military bases and settlements. The victory of Mao Zedong in China in 1949 provided key backing for the Viet Minh. With armaments provided by the Chinese, the rebels rapidly created a modern arsenal and were able to undertake more classical tactics of military attack as well as guerrilla actions which wore away the enemy by attrition.

Handicaps beset the French from all sides. Recruiting new Indochinese soldiers proved difficult, and the foreigners the French employed hardly inspired trust among the Vietnamese. Military commanders failed to score big victories and registered a severe defeat at Cao Bang on the Chinese border. A popular and strong-willed leader considered the real hope for reversing France's fortunes, General Jean de Lattre de Tassigny, indeed restored morale and regrouped forces, but he succumbed to cancer in 1952. French strategists had little notion of how to oppose the guerrilla tactics the Vietnamese so successfully deployed. The government of Cochin-china was manifestly incompetent, and Emperor Bao Daï, returned to his throne, spent most of his time gambling and womanising on the Côte-d'Azur. French public opinion treated Indochina with indifference which gradually turned into hostility, especially after rumours of scandalous currency speculation, allegedly masterminded by the Banque de l'Indochine. Dissidents in France, led by the Communist Party, campaigned for withdrawal, and a number of soldiers and sailors deserted. In one newsworthy incident, a young sailor, Jean Martin, sabotaged a French military action in 1950 out of sympathy with the Viet Minh; police arrested Martin, but supporters – including the existentialist philosopher Jean-Paul Sartre, who wrote a defence of the 'traitor' – pressed for his release. Even various officials, such as former High Commissioner d'Argenlieu, more or less openly stated that France ought to have decolonised Indochina in 1945. By the early 1950s, larger numbers, including several future prime ministers and the future president François Mitterrand, argued that France should relinquish its colonies in Asia in order to preserve its empire in Africa.

The Indochinese War had assumed proportions larger than the struggle for Vietnamese independence. The start of the Korean War in 1950 marked a new phase in the Cold War which pitted Communism against capitalism and the Soviet Union and China against the United States and its allies. The American Truman doctrine demanded 'containment' of Communism, and French governments were in general agreement with Washington. Just as China came to the aid of the Viet Minh, the Americans shifted weight behind the French, though with the stated aim of an independent but pro-Western Vietnam. The United States provided the French, at their request, with millions of dollars of aid and equipment for the war. The struggle against Ho masqueraded not as a war to preserve colonial control but as defence of the 'free world', represented by France and the pro-French government of Cochinchina, against Ho and the revolutionary Viet Minh. Indeed

Paris by the early 1950s was fighting more to secure the victory of a pro-French and anti-Communist government in Vietnam than to defeat independence.

The tide kept washing against the French. By 1953, with military and political morale low, Bao Daï's restive government successfully pressured for complete independence, as did Sihanouk's Cambodia. The situation in Laos, where fighting had spread, remained unsettled. The Korean War came to an end with a stand-off between North and South Korea, and the great powers called a conference in Geneva to discuss the fate of Korea and, the French finally agreed, of Indochina. On the battlefield, the Viet Minh had steadily advanced and controlled almost all of Tonkin. At the end of 1953, the French took refuge in the hilltop village of Dien Bien Phu, which they thought an impregnable fortress. Dien Bien Phu turned out to be their last stand: Ho's forces surrounded the French positions, which were cut off from the outside world; only parachute drops of men and goods provided a link. After five months, on 7 May 1954, the Viet Minh captured Dien Bien Phu, the final defeat of the French in Indochina. Soon the Geneva conference divided Vietnam at the seventeenth parallel. Ho ruled in the north, Bao Daï nominally retained his throne in the South (until he was overthrown the following year). The conference called for elections on the future of both parts of Vietnam, to be held under international supervision within 30 months, a plan never implemented. Cambodia and Laos gained recognition as independent sovereign nations. In 1955, the last French troops withdrew from Indochina. The United States inherited France's mantle as protector of South Vietnam and erstwhile defender of the region against Communism.

The Indochinese War dealt a resounding blow to the French. France lost its empire in southeast Asia and its influence with Ho Chi Minh and the new government in North Vietnam; in the South, and in Cambodia and Laos, Americans displaced the French. Approximately 20 000 French soldiers, as well as 11 000 Legionnaires, 15 000 Africans and 45 000 Indochinese died fighting the Viet Minh, and the total death toll rose to between 400 000 and 500 000. The war sapped the morale of the French army and contributed to political instability during the early 1950s. The French Union, much championed as the reinvigorated and democratic successor to the empire, had failed as a constitutional structure for the metamorphosis of colonies into 'associated states'.

Withdrawal from China, India, Morocco and Tunisia

In the 1940s and 1950s, in addition to to its departure from Syria and Lebanon, and the defeat in Indochina, France quietly withdrew from several smaller outposts. In 1940, the Chinese nationalist army occupied the French concessions in Shanghai, Guangzhou, Tianjin and Hangzhou, and in 1945, France formally returned them to China. France also gave up its leased territory of Guangzhouwan, bringing to an end its occupation of toeholds on Chinese territory which had never lived up to colonialist expectations and were relinquished without undue concern.

France's *comptoirs* in India had rallied to de Gaulle's Free French in 1940 and in 1946 became a *territoire d'outre-mer*. India, which won independence in 1947, demanded that France withdraw from its five possessions, and many residents of the *comptoirs*, including the territory's *député* in Paris, favoured unification with India. In 1949, Indian armies occupied the largest *comptoir*, Chandernagor; France accepted the results of a referendum which ratified its incorporation into India. In 1954, France proceeded to de facto cession of the other *comptoirs*, Pondichéry, Yanaon, Karikal and Mahé (although the official act of cession was not ratified until 1961). Though giving up its minuscule Indian territories, France had negotiated for a substantial number of residents to retain French citizenship and hoped to preserve some influence in India.

Decolonisation of Tunisia and Morocco proved a more protracted and controversial affair. In Tunisia, nationalists demanded the return of the deposed bey and institutional reform. In 1945, the two Destour parties joined other dissident groups to petition for autonomy. The following year Bourguiba and the Néo-Destour Party switched their aim to complete independence. Fearing arrest, Bourguiba spent much of the next three years in Cairo, where in 1950, he issued a seven-point manifesto demanding the restitution of Tunisian sovereignty and election of a national assembly. A conciliatory French government acknowledged the desirability of autonomy, although it warned that this would eventuate only at some unspecified time in the rather distant future; Paris proposed French and Tunisian 'cosovereignty' over the protectorate. An accord signed the next year, which granted increased powers to Tunisian officials, fell short of satisfying nationalists and outraged settlers. New French prime ministers took a harder line and kept Bourguiba under house arrest from 1951 to 1954. A major general strike in 1952 led to violent confr.ontation between the French and Tunisians, including guerrilla attacks by nationalists. Yet another change in French government, the appointment of Pierre Mendès-France as prime minister in 1954, brought a return to gentler approaches. International circumstances – the French disaster in Indochina and growing problems in Algeria – prompted efforts to solve the Tunisian question quickly and peacefully. In a speech in Carthage, Mendès-France solemnly proclaimed the autonomy of the Tunisian government, although France retained control of substantial areas of administration. In 1955, Bourguiba returned to Tunis in triumph. The next year, somewhat anti-climactically, the French revoked the clause of the Treaty of Bardo establishing a protectorate and recognised the complete independence of Tunisia on 20 March, just a few days after granting independence to the other North African protectorate of Morocco.

According to the Treaty of Fès of 1912, Morocco nominally retained its sovereignty, but the protectorate gradually diminished the powers of the sultan's government and made Morocco little more than a colony. In the interwar years, nationalists demanded that France respect the letter of proctectorate law, then in 1943 they founded the Istiqlal ('independence') party; the French arrested its leaders. The party, however, gained influence with Sultan Mohammed ben Youssef who, in a speech in Tangiers in 1947, proclaimed that Morocco should 'recover its rights' and form ties with the newly-established Arab League and other Islamic states. The sultan pointedly did not vaunt the benefits of ties with France, as was expected in such speeches. Following on a bloody fray between French black African troops and Moroccans only three days earlier – sparked by an attack on a Moroccan prostitute – the omission heralded rebellion.

Some French politicians were not opposed to Moroccan independence, so long as as it took place far in the future (one commentator talked about 25 years) and left Morocco in the hands of friendly rulers. The immediate post-war governments in Paris appointed officials who showed due respect for the sultan and tried, unsuccessfully, to undertake modernisation projects. Other policy-makers opposed concessions to the sultan and nationalists, while colonists in Morocco bitterly resented any changes which threatened their privileged position. Paris decided to stand firm, and appointed as new Resident-General in 1947 a soldier, General (later Marshal) Juin, an Algerian *pied-noir* known for strategic acumen. Juin, who initially advocated liberal views, fell under the influence of European settlers and increasingly adopted an unbending position towards ben Youssef. The next few years saw tense struggles for power between the sultan and the French representative. The French meanwhile courted Thami el-Glaoui, the pasha of Marrakesh, a wealthy and powerful figure who was a traditional enemy of ben Youssef.

By the early 1950s, two sides faced off: the sultan and the Istiqlal party versus the French Resident-General and the Glaoui. Mohammed ben Youssef resisted the orders of French administrators and refused to issue more than a very vague disavowal of Istiqlal, which Paris accused of being infiltrated by Communists and terrorists. Succeeding Residents proved incapable of calming the situation. Late in 1952, after a riot in Casablanca following the assassination of a trade unionist, several hundred lay dead. Troubles continued over the next few years, with sabotage and attacks on the French matched by French repression of dissent, arrests and, in several incidents, torture.

French authorities, backed by settlers and the Glaoui, decided to depose the sultan after new demonstrations (and several dozen more deaths). One night in August 1953, French policemen dragged the sultan and his family (still clad in pyjamas) from his palace and whisked them into exile, first in Corsica, then in Madagascar. They engineered the appointment of a puppet sultan, Moulay 'Arafa, who not surprisingly failed to win acceptance from either nationalists or the Moroccan elite. In France, reformers, anticolonialists and intellectuals protested, in vain, about the deposing of the sultan. Rather than resolving the crisis, the French coup had inflamed passions, and violence increased, carried out by both Moroccan nationalists and a settler militia. A Moroccan attack on Europeans in Oued-Zem in late 1955 led to the deaths of over ninety civilians and policemen; in reprisal, French troops killed 700 Moroccans.

Paris changed tactics, realising that it could not master a situation which threatened to deteriorate further. After much debate, the French allowed Mohammed ben Youssef to return to Morocco late in 1955, where he resumed the throne as King Mohammed V. The Glaoui prostrated himself before the king in ritual submission. Mohammed V signed accords with France which resulted in complete independence for Morocco in 1956; he promised protection to expatriate French citizens and agreed to offers of economic cooperation and aid from Paris. A decade of strife had cost hundreds of lives and tarnished France's reputation, but France had avoided the ignominious defeat it had suffered in Indochina and the quagmire into which it was rapidly sinking in Algeria.

The Algerian War of Independence

The most painful and bloody episode of French decolonisation occurred in Algeria, France's oldest 'new' colony of the nineteenth century.[9] By 1954, 1 million Europeans called Algeria home; although many had Spanish, Italian or Maltese rather than French forebears, they proudly proclaimed their intention that Algeria should remain French. Some 8 million Algerian Muslims, by contrast, largely threw their support behind various nationalist groups.

An incident which took place in 1946 foreshadowed future conflict. In Sétif, in eastern Algeria, nationalists planned a demonstration in connection with celebrations to mark the Allied victory over the Axis powers. Flouting regulations, they brandished nationalist banners and placards. Police charged, some of the demonstrators fought back, and soon 40 lay dead. In the surrounding countryside, Kabyle villagers learned of the fray and rose in rebellion; the military sent in 10 000 troops, while planes bombed and strafed Arab and Kabyle communities. The insurrection lasted only a week, but the death toll numbered 100 Europeans and between 1500 and 45 000 Algerian Muslims who lost their lives in the rebellion or the military repression.

Over the next few years, attention transferred to Madagascar and Indochina. The French had successfully quelled the Sétif rising and arrested many nationalist leaders, but they could not extinguish nationalism. Some Algerian activists continued to favour assimilation or a peacefully negotiated solution to the question of Algeria's relationship with France, but others decided that moderate approaches were doomed to failure and that a more muscular effort was needed. Separating themselves from traditionalist parties, young nationalists created the Revolutionary Committee for Unity and Action (*Comité révolutionnaire d'unité et d'action*, CRUA) in 1954, which divided the country into a number of districts (*wilayas*) each with a rebel leader at its head, a well-organised group of activists and whatever armaments could be procured.

On 31 October, a CRUA declaration demanded independence and called Algerians to arms. In the early morning of 1 November, simultaneous insurrections broke out in each *wilaya*; although the French ignored the manifesto and not all of the attacks were successful, the Algerian war of independence had begun. The CRUA transformed itself into the National Liberation Front (*Front de libération nationale*, FLN) and organised a National Liberation Army (*Armée de libération nationale*, ALN). A new French minister for Algeria, who promised to apply economic and political reforms designed in 1947 but never implemented, received a frosty welcome from both nationalists and settlers.

Disturbances continued, and another major attack occurred on 20 August 1956, when nationalists killed 123 settlers at Philippeville. In reprisal, French forces took a high toll: the French admitted 1273 deaths, the Algerians claimed 12 000. The Philippeville massacre confirmed the FLN's determination to use guerrilla violence and its change of policy from prohibitions on killing civilians; the reprisal demonstrated the strength of French firepower and willingness to use it. Despite the death toll, the FLN solidified its position, as wavering moderates joined the front and the FLN set up a virtual parallel administration; its leaders organised support groups, ran arms, collected donations and killed Muslims who refused to cooperate in the struggle for independence. Despite continued disputes within the FLN, nationalists succeeded in promoting independence, mobilising support among compatriots in Algeria and the large Algerian expatriate community in France, and winning international sympathy. So efficient was their action, and so strong the support for the FLN, that French authorities found it impossible to liquidate the movement.

With aid for Algerian nationalists from the Arab League and the inaugural meeting of the world's non-aligned movement (the Bandung Conference) in 1955, agreement by the United Nations to discuss the Algerian issue, and the independence of neighbouring Morocco and Tunisia in 1956, the war became an international issue. Opinions polarised into support either for the French or the Algerian Muslim nationalists, and overtures at negotiation failed. In October 1956, for instance, a group of Algerian nationalists based overseas boarded a plane from Morocco to Tunisia, where they hoped to use the good offices of the new Tunisian president, Habib Bourguiba, to initiate contacts with the French government. The French airforce intercepted the plane, forcing it to land in Oran; the Algerians, including Ahmed Ben Bella, who later became the first president of Algeria, were imprisoned in France for the duration of the war. The National Assembly voted 'special powers' to the government to deal with the Algerian crisis. The government increased troop levels in Algeria from 80 000 men in 1954 to 400 000 two years later. In a policy known as *quadrillage*, the army divided Algeria into small districts, which it virtually occupied. Military action made it certain that a cycle of guerrilla attacks and reprisals would continue. The conflict seemed a magnified rerun of the Indochinese War, but the presence of large numbers of Europeans, bitterly determined not to 'abandon' Algeria, added another dimension to the war.

On 30 September 1956 the Battle of Algiers began, when three FLN women, dressed as students, left a bomb in a trendy café. The explosion killed three Europeans and was followed by numerous acts of terrorism, and counter-measures taken by French troops, which lasted until October 1957. The Battle of Algiers was the ugliest phase of the war, with random FLN terrorist attacks on military and civilian targets, executions and mutilation of cadavers. The French army, under generals Raoul Salan and Jacques Massu, responded with their own terror tactics, forcibly opening shops which had closed during a general strike, herding strikers back to work, summarily shooting resisters or those thought to be FLN sympathisers and systematically practising torture. Beatings, electric shocks applied to the bodies of suspects (especially to their genitals), holding the heads of suspects under water until they confessed or drowned, and psychological torture were all army tactics condoned by the highest level officers. The terrorism of both the FLN and the French forces provoked widespread outrage.

French military might by 1957 reduced the FLN to its lowest ebb in three years. But if the French had won the Battle of Algiers, they had not won the war. Positions hardened still further, as nationalists regrouped and the French consolidated their hold. The French built electrified barriers along Algeria's borders with Morocco and Tunisia, reinforced with barbed wire and minefields – the Morice Line was a North African Berlin Wall. The FLN held the first meeting of the National Council of the Algerian Revolution (*Conseil national de la révolution algérienne*), a government-in-exile based in Cairo. Violence continued in Algeria with the assassination of several nationalist leaders and the arrest of others, persistent terrorist attacks by the FLN, French bombing of Muslim villages and raids on nationalist centres. Government instability in France – the fall of one prime minister after another in the unwieldly multiparty system of the Fourth Republic – posed questions about the capability of Paris to take further action, whatever it might be.

Affairs came to a head on 13 May 1958, in the middle of a metropolitan political crisis. After the FLN had executed three Frenchmen, in reprisal for the French execution of three nationalists, Europeans in Algeria rebelled and set up a Committee of Public Safety, headed by Massu and Salan. The illegal act was a virtual *coup d'état*, directed at metropolitan inaction and the perceived conciliatory attitudes of the current prime minister towards the nationalists. France had not witnessed such a crisis since 1940, and the only man capable of saving the country again seemed Charles de Gaulle, who had retired from active politics in 1946. De Gaulle accepted the plea of the French president to become prime minister on 1 June 1958; four days later he flew to Algiers, where a sphinx-like assertion that 'Je vous ai compris' ('I have understood you') raised hopes among settlers and nationalists alike.

De Gaulle's government recovered the powers usurped by the Committee of Public Safety. De Gaulle wrote a new constitution for the French Fifth Republic, approved by popular referendum, which gave the president enlarged powers, thus avoiding the instability of the previous regime. De Gaulle, as newly elected president, then proclaimed a programme for economic development, investment and land redistribution in Algeria, the Constantine Plan. The FLN rejected it and officially constitued a provisional government. The FLN and French troops continued shooting, but de Gaulle's advisers were also establishing discreet and clandestine contacts with the FLN and non-FLN nationalists. De Gaulle himself may have already accepted the inevitability of decolonisation. In September 1959, he first publicly used the word 'self-determination' to speak of Algeria's future, tacit acknowledgement that '*Algérie française*' might not be eternal.

A new division appeared between the French government, on the one hand, and European settlers and soldiers on the other. The revival of the alliance between colonists and the military, which had underpinned the failed coup of May 1958, led to the 'week of the barricades' in January 1960. Settlers in Algiers erected barricades in their neighbourhoods and fired on French gendarmes;

the regular army, seemingly in sympathy with the *pieds-noirs*, took no action. After a week, de Gaulle rallied the army in a television address, leaving many settlers even more convinced of his willingness to abandon Algeria to the Muslims. The decision to negotiate with the FLN was reiterated when de Gaulle invited the Algerian provisional government to discuss a ceasefire in June 1960. The meetings failed, yet in another speech de Gaulle said that he was willing to pursue the goal of an 'emancipated Algeria', an 'Algerian Algeria'. To the horror of settlers and diehard opponents of decolonisation, in August 1960 he spoke of an 'Algerian Republic'.

Anti-independence settlers now entered into open opposition to the government, organising a French National Front (*Front national français*, FNF) which attracted considerable support in France, and the backing of General Salan and other officers, as well as a former minister for Algeria. In December 1960, government agents uncovered four plots to assassinate de Gaulle during a trip to Algeria. Although welcomed by settlers two and a half years previously, de Gaulle was now roundly heckled by *pieds-noirs*. Nevertheless, the government proceeded with a referendum, held on 8 January 1961, on proposals 'submitted to the French people by the President of the Republic concerning the self-determination of the Algerian population'. Despite the abstention of 40 per cent of the electorate, three-quarters of the votes cast supported de Gaulle's plan for an Algerian vote on independence. Algeria seemed destined for independence, a solution French settlers and a faction of the military found unacceptable. With aid from the Foreign Legion, four officers (generals Challe, Jouhaud, Salan and Zeller) took over key government, telecommunications and police headquarters in Algiers on 21 April 1961. This represented open mutiny by French troops, enthusiastically backed by settlers who viewed de Gaulle as nothing less than a traitor. The bulk of the army refused to follow the generals, and soldiers loyal to de Gaulle arrested the coup leaders who had not gone into hiding. Before the end of the affair, however, those determined to fight to the bitter end set up the Secret Army Organisation (*Organisation armée secrète*, OAS), which promised attacks on the FLN and any of the French willing to 'abandon' Algeria. The crisis continued throughout 1961, both in Algeria, with FLN attacks and French reprisals, and in France itself. In September 1961, de Gaulle narrowly escaped assassination in Paris. The next

month a major police campaign against suspected FLN sympathisers degenerated into a battle between demonstrators and police in Paris with dozens of deaths. The police also reacted violently
to an anti-OAS demonstration at the Charonne Métro station in
February 1962; eight demonstrators died.

De Gaulle's representatives had been negotiating with delegates
from the FLN and, on 18 March 1962, the two sides signed the
Evian Accords for complete Algerian independence. France would
recognise Algerian unity and independence, and the FLN would
form the new government; independent Algeria would protect
French interests and, for a limited period, allow France to use
several military sites in the country. The next months saw last
ditch efforts by the OAS to thwart independence, with murderous attacks on Muslims and yet another attempt to kill de Gaulle;
realising the futility of its campaign, the OAS adopted 'scorched-
earth' tactics, and destroyed buildings and resources of real or
symbolic value (among them the public library in Algiers). Nevertheless, Muslim voters in a referendum almost unanimously accepted the Evian Accords, and on 3 July 1962, France officially
recognised the independence of Algeria. Violent confrontations
between Muslims and Europeans continued for several months,
as almost a million Europeans fled Algeria for France.

The Algerian War caused immense losses on both sides. In 1962,
Paris admitted that 12 000 soldiers fighting for the French (including 9000 Frenchmen, 1200 Legionnaires and 1250 Muslims)
had been killed, as well as 2500 other French sympathisers who
had taken up arms. French authorities estimated the Algerian death
toll at 227 000 soldiers (including those killed by the ALN for
collaboration with the French) and 20 000 civilians; the FLN claimed
that 1 million Algerian Muslims had been killed. More recent estimates have settled on a death toll, including the French and
Algerians, of about half a million.

Almost 2 million French soldiers served in Algeria from 1954
to 1962, most of them conscripts. The posting of drafted soldiers
to Algeria provoked a 'Manifesto of the 121' in 1960, signed by a
group of French intellectuals including such luminaries as Sartre
and Simone de Beauvoir, on the right of soldiers to disobey orders
and refuse to serve in Algeria. Prominent intellectuals, such as
François Mauriac, published anti-colonial works on Algeria; some
sided with the FLN. French authorities arrested a number who
openly supported the FLN. Despite censure and harassment, no-

table French journals, ranging from revolutionary periodicals of the left to moderate Christian publications, condemned the Algerian war and called for French withdrawal. Differences of opinion on the future of Algeria created the sort of bitter disputes which had only previously been seen in the twentieth century during the struggle between supporters of Vichy and Resistants.[10] Violence, police raids and curfews were instituted in Paris. Rumours circulated that military units opposed to Algerian independence might invade mainland France and take over the government. The atrocities committed by the Algerians inflamed French opinion, and reports of torture by French troops, which only the blind could ignore, were a painful throwback to the very policies which the French had fought during the Second World War.[11] In short, the dispute about Algeria poisoned French public life for eight years, absorbing untold amounts of government revenue, causing death and destruction, dividing the body politic and leaving scars which have not yet entirely healed.

The Decolonisation of Black Africa

The black cultural renaissance of the interwar years – affirming African identity and often contesting French rule – continued after 1945. Novels and poems written by Senghor, Birago Diop and Camara Laye in the late 1940s and early 1950s won attention. The year 1947 saw the publication (in Paris) of the first issue of *Présence africaine*, a pioneering journal of African culture, and of an anthology of Francophone African and Malagasy poetry edited by Senghor and prefaced by Sartre. Two West Indian intellectuals wrote scathing critiques of French colonisation of Africa and exploitation in the African diaspora; in 1952, Frantz Fanon published *Peau noire, masques blancs*, and three years later Aimé Césaire published *Discours sur le colonialisme*. At the same time, anthropologists, such as Claude Lévi-Strauss, questioned stereotypes about the 'primitivism' of African societies. Such works advanced anti-colonialism in black Africa, elsewhere in the colonies and in France.

Modern nationalism in the form of political movements, however, did not manifest itself in the 1920s and 1930s in French sub-Saharan Africa. That situation changed after the Second World War, thanks to increasing literacy and education, the militancy of trade unions, and institutional opportunities for political participation afforded by the Fourth Republic.[12] Charismatic Western-educated leaders also began to establish political parties; usually based in cities, they gradually widened their base to the African masses. The parties' major platform was greater access for Africans to political decision-making. The first to win great support was the African Democratic Rally (*Rassemblement démocratique africain*, RDA) organised by Félix Houphouët-Boigny. Its first meeting, in Bamako, Mali, in 1946, attracted 800 delegates, and the RDA lay claim to being the most important nationalist party in French sub-Saharan Africa.

Houphouët – later president of the Côte-d'Ivoire from independence in 1960 until his death in 1993 – became arguably the most significant Francophone black leader. Born in 1904 to a chiefly family, Houphouët worked as a medical practitioner until 1939, then took over his family's prosperous coffee and cocoa plantations. He also served as an administrative official and just after the war was elected a *député* to the French Constituent Assembly and National Assembly. Although Houphouët allied with the French Communist Party and espoused Marxist ideas, he was primarily a nationalist who called for autonomy for the individual African states which made up the AOF and AEF.

Not all African politicians supported the RDA, either because they disagreed with Houphouët's ideology and electoral alliance with the Communists or because they opposed the splitting up of the AEF and AOF into separate countries, and preferred the maintenance of the federations. Chief among the opponents of Houphouët were Apithy and Senghor, supporters of the French Socialist Party who joined other African members of the French parliament in establishing the Overseas Independents' Group (*Groupe des indépendants d'outre-mer*, IOM).

Politicians throughout Francophone black Africa generally allied with one or the other of these groups, sometimes switching loyalties over time. Strong leaders gradually established authority in the different colonies, constituting networks of support, and gaining election to local assemblies and the National Assembly. Some were intellectuals, others – such as Sékou Touré in Guinea – trade union organisers; the major figure in the Congo, Fulbert Youlou, was a priest. Politicians generally used peaceful, parliamentary strategies to press calls for reform, although they (and more radical politicians) sometimes came into conflict with French authorities. Occasional, if relatively infrequent, violent incidents marked protests. The most notable, and deadly, occurred in February 1949 at Treichville, a working-class suburb of Abidjan, Côte-d'Ivoire, where riots were followed by 400 arrests, then demonstrations throughout the country calling for release of the prisoners; the rebellion culminated in a demonstration in Dimbokro, where soldiers shot and killed 20 Africans and wounded 100 more.

A new French government in 1950, with François Mitterrand in charge of African and 'colonial' affairs, calmed the potentially explosive situation. Houphouët decided that his alliance with the Communists, evicted from power in France and, in the context of the Cold War, regarded with suspicion, was a liability. He broke with the PCF in 1951, as did most of his RDA colleagues, and joined a small moderately leftist group in parliament. Subsequently, despite changes of ministries in Paris and African capitals, Houphouët became France's favoured link with black Africa. Symbolic of his position, Houphouët, like Senghor, who had always been in the good graces of the French, became a junior minister in the French government in the mid-1950s. Such cooperation with the authorities provoked dissent among younger, more revolutionary African leaders, such as Touré.

In these years, Togo and Cameroon experienced the most marked change. The major political figure in Togo, officially an 'associated territory', was Sylvanus Olympio, a young intellectual – he had studied at the University of Vienna and the London School of Economics – and businessman who episodically talked about unification of Togo with the Gold Coast (Ghana), the English-ruled home of the pan-Africanist Kwame Nkrumah. When Olympio abandoned this plan, the French allowed his government greater autonomy than in any other African domain. By 1956, the French retained control only of currency, foreign affairs and defence in Togo.

In Cameroon, France's other 'associated territory', a more radical movement came to the fore, led by a young public servant, Ruben Um Nyobé. Um Nyobé refused to follow Houphouët's break with the Communists in 1951, and became increasingly more doctrinaire while he secured political bases throughout Cameroon. In May 1955, one of Um Nyobé's collaborators, who had just returned from China, said at a public meeting that Um Nyobé, like Mao and Ho, had taken to the jungle in order to organise a revolution. Within days, riots broke out in several locations. French forces restored order, with considerable loss of life, and banned Um Nyobé's party. Calm soon returned, and no Maoist style revolution eventuated.

Two years after the defeat at Dien Bien Phu, 1956 saw the French battling nationalists in Algiers, mounting a failed attack (in cooperation with British and Israeli troops) on the Suez Canal, which the Egyptians had just nationalised, and, without great joy, granting independence to Morocco and Tunisia. A new Socialist government appointed in Paris in early 1956, thankful for the relatively quiet situation in black Africa but concerned about the future, decided to introduce legislation to give greater autonomy to the remaining colonies. The result was the Defferre law, named after the Minister for Overseas France, Gaston Defferre (a Marseillais who had once worked in his father's law office in Dakar).

The new *loi-cadre* (enabling legislation which empowered the government to undertake certain institutional reforms by decree), which was passed in June 1956 and came into effect in April of the following year, had three major aspects. It confirmed a decree of November 1955 which extended suffrage to all French citizens throughout the 'empire' and abolished the double electoral colleges; henceforth, with a unified electorate, the small white minority was deprived of its predominant position. Secondly, the law granted local assemblies increased powers to debate and vote on territorial budgets and administrative matters without the necessary approval of French high commissioners. Finally, the Defferre law increased the powers of government councils elected by territorial assemblies. The French high commissioner still served as president of the council, but there was an elected vice-president. Furthermore, the members of the council, given the title of 'minister', held particular portfolios and responsibility for designated matters.

In retrospect, the changes effected by the Defferre laws might not seem so dramatic as they appeared at the time. But the legislation had established electoral equality and ministerial responsibility in territories where European residents formed a tiny minority. By giving black French men and women such rights as the Defferre law did, France went further than any other country in decolonising its African possessions without according them independence. This represented the sort of self-government which the Brazzaville declaration of 1944 had seemed to avoid, and it went a long way towards satisfying moderate African nationalists. In elections in early 1957, the RDA proved the great victor. Black governments took office, and Paris instructed white public servants to cooperate with the new leaders. The evolution of the French territories was soon overshadowed, later in 1957, by the complete independence of Ghana from Britain under Nkrumah, and French African leaders, such as Touré, agitated for a similar outcome. Senghor and the IOM meantime chafed at the fracturing of the AOF and AEF into separate states, and old rivalries resurfaced.

The Defferre law had been in effect for only a year before the Algerian crisis returned de Gaulle to power and brought down the Fourth Republic. The Fifth Republic substantially altered the arrangements of 1956. De Gaulle's plan for the *outre-mer* preserved the different statuses of overseas *département*, territory and associated state, but greatly reduced the powers given to their assemblies and government councils – what had been given in 1956 was taken away in 1958. For the French Union, de Gaulle substituted a new Community (without the adjective 'French'), in which France would nonetheless preserve its dominant role. The Community – in reality, France – would continue to handle foreign affairs, defence, currency, economic and financial policy, justice, higher education, overseas transport and telecommunications. The powers of the Community institutions, including a Senate and a high court, were left vague. The new constitution contained two novel points. Each 'colony' would vote on its future status – whether to remain a territory, be fully integrated into the French Republic as a *département*, or go its own way as an independent state (with or without association with France). Even after the initial choice, a state could accede to independence either through a mutually agreed transfer of government powers or by request of the local assembly, confirmed in a referendum by a majority of the population. The catch, de Gaulle did not hesitate to point out, was that if a state voted to separate from France, it would forego French financial or technical assistance; this provided a powerful incentive for the poor overseas countries to retain affiliation with France.

Campaigning proceeded apace for the referendum, held on 28 September 1958 throughout French Africa and in the Comoros, Djibouti, French Polynesia and New Caledonia. Most politians lobbied for a 'yes' vote for continued territorial status; Sékou Touré in Guinea and Pouvana'a a Oopa, leader of a Polynesian nationalist movement, provided the only strong opposition. Pouvana'a's calls did not convince the electorate of French Polynesia, but Touré's efforts succeeded. Guinea became independent, de Gaulle reiterated French intention to stop aid, and departing French officials spitefully took away almost everything that was movable – even ripping telephones from their sockets – as they left.

The remaining French territories ceremonially celebrated the birth of the Community in Paris on 14 July 1959. De Gaulle gave to each new head of state a French tricolour, its staff surmounted by a symbol of joined hands. Yet the Community was stillborn. In September, the African heads of government asked de Gaulle to transfer complete authority to them, as permitted under the constitution. After discussion, particularly on the future of a federation established among four West African states (the Mali Federation of Senegal, the Soudan (Mali), Dahomey and Upper Volta), the government agreed; by the end of the year, some of the African states had elected their own presidents, and all had sent ambassadors to Paris. In mid-1960, almost as quickly as French officials could fly from one capital to the other for the lowering of flags and appropriate speeches, the former colonies of the AOF – Senegal, Mauritania, Mali, Upper Volta (later renamed Burkina Faso), Niger, the Côte-d'Ivoire, Dahomey (later called Benin) – and the AEF – the Congo, Gabon, the Central African Republic, Chad – as well as Cameroon, Togo and Madagascar, became totally independent. France had decolonised black Africa and the Community disappeared (in reality, if not on constitutional paper). France's vast African possessions, conquered with such difficulty over a long period, invested with great hopes and great disappointments, became a set of sovereign nations. France could barely digest the change in sub-Saharan Africa, as it had to turn its attention back to North Africa for the final two years of the Algerian war.

Decolonisation: The Last Episodes?

With Algerian independence in 1962, many assumed that decolonisation had come to an end. France's remaining colonies were by and large territorially and demographically small; few had active nationalist movements which pressed for independence. Yet three outposts later acceded to independence under provisions of the 1958 constitution.

The Comoros Islands in the Indian Ocean enjoyed self-government under the Fifth Republic. But resentment festered between Mayotte and the remaining islands, especially after the head of the territory moved the capital from Mayotte to Grande Comore island. A pro-independence movement gradually gained support in the late 1960s and early 1970s from both the local population and such international groups as the Organisation of African Unity. Discontent erupted into various incidents, but there existed no mandate for change until the election of a pro-independence politician, Ahmed Abdallah, in 1973. Paris granted various concessions to the new government and agreed to a referendum on the islands' future. In 1974, 95 per cent of voters in three of the islands voted for independence, while the majority of the electorate in Mayotte opposed it. While the French procrastinated, Abdallah unilaterally proclaimed the independence of the Federal Islamic Republic of the Comoros in July 1975. Mayotte, despite the claims of the Comoros Republic on the island, remains a French overseas outpost.

Nationalist sentiment also emerged tardily in French Somaliland (renamed the French Territory of the Afars and Issas) on the horn of Africa. Violent demonstrations greeted de Gaulle when he visited the capital in 1966, although the following year, 60 per cent of the electorate voted for continued attachment to France. Pro-independence groups marshalled support in the early 1970s and kidnapped the French ambassador in 1975. Demonstrations and abductions continued until France convened a conference on the territory's future in 1977. After a referendum, the territory became independent as the Republic of Djibouti.

The situation in the New Hebrides was particularly complex, as the Pacific archipelago was a Franco-British condominium under joint administration (although neither nation held sovereignty over the islands). A nationalist movement developed in the 1970s, spearheaded by English-speaking Protestant leaders, and gained the approval of the British, who were anxious to decolonise. The Francophone Catholic minority, supported by French residents of the New Hebrides and nearby New Caledonia, showed less enthusiasm for independence. Paris and London finally agreed on independence in 1980, although Paris did so only reluctantly. In the dying days of the condominium and the first days of independent Vanuatu, as the new nation was called, the struggle turned into a comic opera on one of the largest islands in the archipelago. On Santo, a movement led by a traditional tribal leader opposed to the national pro-independence leader (whose base lay on another island) garnered support from an assortment of French planters, New Caledonians, a liberterian American foundation, Catholics and other dissidents. With tacit support from the French representative in the capital, Vila, Santo seceded, but the secession movement soon collapsed and Vanuatu was unified; rancour and many divisions remained.

The independence of the Comoros, Djibouti and Vanuatu had few repercussions on French life, though a few French lobbyists criticised the government for withdrawal from each. By the 1970s, such vestiges of empire held little interest for the French. Only in the 1980s, with an independence struggle in New Caledonia marked by a higher level of violence than seen in the decolonisations of the 1970s did the French again become embroiled in a 'colonial' question.[13]

Ending the Empire

The various cases of decolonisation show the importance of nationalist movements in pressing for independence, but also point to gradual reassessment of the merits of clinging to overseas domains. As economic opportunities and full employment beckoned in the 1950s and 1960s, maintaining the empire seemed to incur increased costs and energy. Anti-colonial feeling in France – whether motivated by ideological support for emancipation of colonised peoples or sheer pragmatism – gained strength. Authorities initially, and often adamantly, rejected independence, quashing rebellions with military force, arresting nationalists and resolving to maintain French presence. They also promised political democratisation and economic development. Even with concessions, nationalist movements could not be extinguished, but gathered renewed vigour. Efforts to keep nationalism from spreading failed, as did attempts to find alternatives to independence: neither the French Union of the Fourth Republic nor the Community of the Fifth Republic proved workable compromises for most 'colonies'. The actual granting of full independence became a long-drawn-out process and, in the cases of Indochina and Algeria, was accompanied by murderous warfare. After lowering the flag, France promised financial, technical and military aid to almost all its former colonies and, other than in Algeria, a substantial number of French citizens remained in the newly-independent countries. Except for the traumatic decolonisation of Algeria, howevever, what is remarkable is how few long-lasting effects on France the giving up of empire entailed.

Epilogue: After the Empire

At the beginning of the 1960s, France had lost most of its overseas empire, and the accession to independence of three other territories left France with only ten overseas outposts by the 1980s. Yet the repercussions of the colonial era, links with former possessions and, sometimes, political controversies with roots in the era of expansion provided ample evidence that France had not – perhaps because it could not – severed ties to its colonial past. The economic dependency of many former African colonies on France provoked charges of neo-colonialism, while French administration of its remaining overseas *départements* and territories brought charges of continued colonialism. Large-scale migration to France from the Antilles, the Maghreb and sub-Saharan Africa changed the demographic complexion of the French population and triggered racism and xenophobia. Somewhat ironically, a nostalgic interest in the colonial era, represented in novels and films, occasionally swept France and reminded the French of their imperial heritage.

The DOM-TOMs

One of the most concrete reminders of France's overseas presence is the persistent attachment of ten outposts to France: the islands of Guadeloupe and Martinique in the West Indies and Saint-Pierre and Miquelon off the coast of Newfoundland, Guyane in South America, Réunion and Mayotte in the Indian Ocean, French Polynesia, New Caledonia, and Wallis and Futuna in the South Pacific, and the French Austral and Antarctic Territories

(*Terres australes et antarctiques françaises*, TAAF). These *départements et territoires d'outre-mer* (DOM-TOMs) are home to 1.8 million French citizens and total 120 000 square kilometres of land, in addition to the uninhabited expanses of Terre Adélie, the French region of Antarctica.[1]

The DOM-TOMs are legally part of France, though their precise statutes differ. Since 1945, Martinique, Guadeloupe, Guyane and Réunion have been fully fledged *départements*, the same administrative division (similar to American or Australian states) as in the metropole. Government institutions, the law code, currency, even postage stamps are the same in the overseas *départements* as in the metropole. As overseas *territoires*, French Polynesia, New Caledonia, and Wallis and Futuna have a greater degree of administrative and political autonomy. For instance, three traditional chiefs play an officially recognised role in Wallis and Futuna, and French Polynesia, alone among French overseas outposts, flies its own official flag (although always alongside the French Tricolour). France nevertheless retains firm control of such substantial areas as international relations, law and order, financial policy and immigration. Saint-Pierre and Miquelon and Mayotte are 'territorial collectivities', with a status midway between an overseas *département* and *territoire*. The TAAF, with no permanent population, is the responsibility of an administrator based in Paris. In the overseas territories, a High Commissioner represents the French state, but there is an elected territorial assembly and head of government, whose powers are relatively broad. In the DOMs, a prefect exercises the powers of the state, and an elected 'general council' selects a president. Except for the TAAF, all the DOM-TOMs elect members to both chambers of the French parliament (and vote in elections for the European parliament) on the basis of universal suffrage.

Economics ties the DOM-TOMs to France as firmly as does politics. New Caledonia possesses the greatest natural resource base of all the DOM-TOMs because of large reserves of nickel. Nickel ore, which provides almost all of New Caledonia's exports, is subject to the volatile international commodities market, and sharp downturns in prices create economic and social problems in the territory. French Polynesia's main export is pearls, but exports cover only about a fifth of imports; French Polynesia relies on French transfers attached to government employment, state investment and nuclear testing. Since the mid-1960s, French Polynesia has been the site of nuclear testing facilities (on the atolls of Mururoa and Fangataufa), transferred to Oceania after the independence of Algeria. Before the suspension of testing in 1992, for almost thirty years the programme powered the local economy, providing employment and attracting subsidies and large-scale infrastructural investment. In Guyane, the forests which cover much of the country have remained unexploited, leaving the French space facilities and launching pad in Kourou as the major resource. Exports from the Caribbean islands are largely limited to rum and tropical fruits, but agriculture has suffered perennial crisis in recent decades. The smallest outposts have a reduced commercial resource base, confined to cod-fishing in Saint-Pierre and Miquelon, and perfume essences and spices in Mayotte; Wallis and Futuna has no appreciable exports. Tourism has become a prime activity in Martinique, Guadeloupe, French Polynesia and, to a lesser extent, New Caledonia and Réunion; the other DOM-TOMs lie too distant from major tourist markets or lack infrastructure to entice visitors.

The DOM-TOMs rely increasingly on public service employment, largesse from the extensive French social welfare system, and other forms of government spending. Migration plays an important role in their economies. Residents of the DOM-TOMs enjoy full right of abode in France and in other DOM-TOMs. In addition to large numbers of Antilleans and Réunionnese who migrated to France from the 1950s onwards, French Polynesians and Wallisians and Futunans found work in the nickel mines of New Caledonia – more Wallisians and Futunans live in New Caledonia than in their native islands – and remittances sent home provide a substantial complement to local earnings.

Socially and culturally, the DOM-TOMs vary greatly from metropolitan France. Only Saint-Pierre and Miquelon and Saint-Barthélémy (a tiny island dependency of Guadeloupe) have entirely ethnically European populations; in New Caledonia, about a third of the population descend from transported prisoners or free settlers in the nineteenth century or more recently arrived Europeans. The largest single group in New Caledonia remains indigenous Melanesians, but there are descendants of North African convicts, Vietnamese and Indonesian indentured labourers and Polynesian migrant workers. In Wallis and Futuna and French Polynesia, the population is Polynesian, although in French Polynesia the indigenous population has intermarried with Europeans over several centuries of contact and there is also a Chinese minority. Most West Indians and Guyanese descend from African slaves who worked on the sugar plantations. The indigenous populations of the Antillean islands have disappeared, although Native Americans still live in remote areas of Guyane. The vagaries of history have brought other ethnic groups to these *départements*, including a small group of Europeans, migrants from India, Syrians and Lebanese, even a group of refugees from Laos who found refuge in Guyane in the 1970s. In Réunion (East) Indians are particularly numerous. As in Martinique, Guadeloupe and Guyane, many residents claim mixed ancestry. In Mayotte, by contrast, the population is homogeneously composed of Muslim islanders, themselves of mixed African, Malagasy, Arabic and Persian ancestry.

Politicians of all political persuasions in the DOM-TOMs have pressured France, sometimes successfully, for greater administrative and financial autonomy. In most of the DOM-TOMs, small if vocal dissident groups call for independence and, in Guadeloupe, Réunion and French Polynesia, violent episodes of protest have occurred. New Caledonia witnessed the most dramatic pro-independence surge in the 1980s. Melanesians, disadvantaged in their own country, where almost all political and economic power belonged to a European minority, increasingly demanded redress of grievances about land spoilation, economic disenfranchisement, migration of outsiders into the territory, and French failure to give due recognition to indigenous culture. Melanesians favouring independence formed a National Front for Kanak Socialist Liberation (*Front de Libération Nationale Kanak et Socialiste*, FLNKS) in 1984 and mounted a militant struggle, sometimes with roadblocks, boycotts of elections or attacks on French settlers. Anti-independence loyalists groups responded with counter campaigns and similarly violent attacks on Melanesians. A 1985 proposal by the Paris government to grant New Caledonia 'independence in association' with France provoked outrage among non-Melanesians, who considered the plan little less than treason while it evoked suspicion among Melanesians concerned about neo-colonialism. Matters then came to a head with virtual civil war. Over 30 Melanesians and Europeans died. Massive troop reinforcements flown into the territory failed to restore calm. Only after several years of confrontation and violence which recalled previous clashes in Indochina and Algeria did most of the different factions agree to a settlement in 1988. Division of the territory into three provinces allowed a degree of local self-government for both Europeans and Melanesians. A vote by New Caledonian residents on the future of their territory is scheduled for 1998.[2]

If many residents of the DOM-TOMs gain advantages from affiliation with France, the benefits France enjoys from overseas outposts are not inconsiderable. The nuclear testing site in French Polynesia and the space station in Guyane provide obvious strategic and scientific bases. As promoters of the DOM-TOMs are at pains to emphasise, the DOM-TOMs give France a sovereign and internationally recognised presence in the Caribbean, the Indian and Pacific Oceans and Antarctica. They trumpet the DOM-TOMs as French windows on the world and showcases for French culture. Under the Law of the Sea conventions, which give nations monopolistic rights to maritime resources in an exclusive economic zone (EEZ) of 200 nautical miles off their coastlines, the DOM-TOMs endow France with the third largest exclusive maritime area in the world. Prospectors have discussed the potential of increased fishing as well as less certain possibilities of exploiting deposits of minerals on the continental shelf or in underwater polymetallic nodules. Much as in the colonial age, arguments about eventual profits from overseas resources mark discussion about the future of the DOM-TOMs.

Migration

The 'Rapatriés'

Decolonisation brought a number of expatriate French men and women 'home', although not all opted to move to France. Especially in sub-Saharan Africa, some stayed on after independence; indeed, in the Côte-d'Ivoire, the number of French residents increased after independence. In countries where decolonisation had been less amicable, or where more militantly nationalistic regimes came to power (and occasionally nationalised foreign holdings), most of the French left. Yet the European population which returned from Indochina, Tunisia and Morocco was not large, and rapatriés (repatriated citizens) assimilated into French life with relatively little difficulty.

Decolonisation of Algeria posed a great demographic problem. One million residents of Algeria claimed French citizenship and descent from European settlers. Because of the ferocity of the Algerian War and the intention of the FLN to 'Algerianise' the economy and administration, few *pieds-noirs* wished to remain. Provisions in the Evian Accords for the protection of rights of French citizens in independent Algeria inspired little confidence, and the support given by *pieds-noirs* to the anti-independence movement tainted settlers in the eyes of the new government. The scorched earth tactics of the OAS in the last months of the war promised to make coexistence between Muslims and Europeans difficult. Algeria's Jews, who had lived fairly harmoniously with their Islamic neighbours before French conquest, but then avidly adopted French language and culture and gained naturalisation long before Muslims, also felt unwelcome.

The result was an exodus of Europeans and Jews. Tens of thousands of Jews left Algeria (and, earlier, Morocco and Tunisia) for Israel. Some *pieds-noirs* went to nearby Spain, far-away New Caledonia, Francophone Québec or Argentina, but most chose France. Throughout 1962, convoys of ships tranferred *rapatriés* and whatever belongings they could assemble – often very little – from Algeria to the metropole. For many, arrival in Marseille was the first time they had set foot on the soil of metropolitan France: 'repatriation' was a misnomer.

The *pieds-noirs* faced a hazardous future in France. Most had lost their assets and could not count on speedy French indemnification; families who had lived in Algeria for several generations gave up homesteads, properties and a way of life. The numerous *pieds-noirs* of Italian, Spanish and Maltese extraction had to integrate into a society where they lacked roots and family connections. The *pieds-noirs* felt resentment and hostility in a country which had claimed to defend them but, it appeared to some, had abandoned *Algérie française*. The metropolitan French did not hold the *pieds-noirs* in high esteem; at best, they were an embarrassing relic of a colonial adventure better forgotten.

Half of the *pieds-noirs* settled in the south of France, the Midi, in such cities as Marseille and the towns of Provence, as well as in Corsica; a quarter went to Paris. Despite lingering bitterness, they established themselves remarkably well in business, government and the professions, surprising statisticians and sociologists by the rapidity of their assimilation and upward social mobility. They continued to press for compensation for losses in Algeria, but the wait turned out to be long. In 1970, the government first appropriated money for compensation, sums which *rapatriés* claimed were too little; legislation in 1987 set aside some 30 billion francs to be paid over a 13-year period.

Many *pieds-noirs*, particularly those who had spent much of their life in Algeria, sustained a veritable cult of *Algérie française*, joining *pied-noir* associations, publishing newsletters, setting up study centres, laying wreaths on the anniversary of the 1954 rebellion, and making pilgrimages to shrines containing religious statues brought back from North Africa. Gatherings of *rapatriés* in the early 1990s drew as many as 350 000 participants. They preserved customs and habits from North Africa, enveloped in a nostalgic romanticisation of the 'good old days' in Algiers, Oran or Constantine.[3]

The Harkis

Perhaps the most poignant group of *rapatriés* were Algerian Muslims – generally known as *harkis* (from the Arabic for movement) – who had fought for the French between 1954 and 1962. Various considerations motivated Muslims to support the French rather than their nationalist compatriots. Some genuinely believed in the benefits of the French presence in North Africa. Others opted for France because of family or village disputes or personal rivalries. Still others resented the contributions which the FLN collected and the exactions it inflicted on those who would not pay, perform services for the independence movement or obey FLN regulations. The weakness of the FLN at the outset of the war and at several later stages probably convinced some that France would be the victor. Moreover, French authorities coerced Muslims into support with incentives ranging from money to torture – officials sometimes gave FLN sympathisers a choice between joining the French or enduring further punishment.

By 1960, at least 70 000 Muslims were officially members of quasi-military corps fighting under French command. (Muslims also enlisted in the regular army.) They enjoyed fewer privileges and earned lower pay than French soldiers, although their wages compared favourably with those of Algerian workers. Use of North African troops formed part of an effort to 'Algerianise' the war and reduce pressure on French forces.

At the war's end, the FLN undertook a purge of Algerians who had collaborated with the French (or were suspected of having

done so). Estimates of the number of Muslims executed by the
FLN or massacred by mobs, among them many *harkis*, range from
10 000 to 150 000. The French displayed little enthusiasm to
shoulder responsibility for their comrades-in-arms. Paris eventually agreed to repatriate *harkis*, and 85 000 accepted the offer by
the end of 1962; the total of *harkis* and other pro-French Muslims who moved to France amounted to approximately 140 000.

The *harkis'* situation was not a happy one. Independent Algeria
branded them traitors; France saw them as a burden. Fears lin-
gered that *harkis* retained dangerous links with the OAS or even
the FLN. Most migrants, peasants with no formal education or
vocational training and only rudimentary knowledge of French,
faced significant obstacles to integration. Authorities placed most
harkis in temporary camps, then gradually transferred them to
public housing or to villages in forested areas: officials decided
that forestry work would be appropriate employment for *harkis*.
Politicians promised education and other benefits; few were forth-
coming.

By 1975, the population of *harkis*, including their French-born
children, rose to 200 000–220 000. Material success remained the
exception rather than the rule, and some *harkis* still lived in camps,
ineligible for a range of benefits extended to *pieds-noir*s. For
example, laws which indemnified European *rapatriés* for loss of
property did not apply to *harkis*, unable to provide legal titles to
property and required documentary proof of other assets lost at
the time of Algerian independence. *Harkis* earned a lower income, lived in poorer quality housing and had a higher rate of
unemployment and school failure than the overall French population. Increased racism also affected harkis; most French people
drew little distinction between *rapatriés* and more recently arrived
migrants from the Maghreb.[4]

Migrant Workers

North African *rapatriés* form part of a larger and longer current
of migration. France has been a traditional destination for migrants, from writers and artists who swelled the *avant-garde* at the
turn of the century to factory hands and agricultural labourers
who helped power France's economy from the 1920s onwards.
The traditional source of migration to France was the neighbouring countries of southern Europe. Italians represented the largest

foreign community in France in the late nineteenth and early twentieth century, joined by Spaniards (the largest group by the late 1960s) and Portuguese.

The colonies sent a stream of migrants to the metropole before decolonisation, including students and intellectuals who later led nationalist movements. Other colonials lived temporarily in France while doing military service or working in business or the public service. Mass arrivals came largely from North Africa, mainly for reasons of proximity; in 1954, 5000 Tunisians, 11 000 Moroccans and 212 000 Algerians lived in France. Post-Second World War reconstruction and the economic boom which lasted until the mid-1970s created a great demand for labour, especially as the French birthrate continued to fall. Demand was especially high in lesser skilled jobs, since French workers acquired higher levels of education and training and moved into more specialised and well-paid employment.

In the 1960s, Paris began recruiting workers from overseas. One target was the *départements d'outre-mer*, especially densely-populated Martinique, Guadeloupe and Réunion. A government office set up to encourage migration arranged transport and helped locate jobs for sponsored migrants, and others arrived independently. Working-age males initially dominated, but their families often joined them later. By 1982, 282 300 migrants from the DOM-TOMs lived in the metropole, almost a tenfold increase of the population from these same areas resident in France in 1954.

Migrants from the Antilles and Réunion possessed certain advantages in the metropolitan job market: French citizenship, command of the language, literacy and, for most, primary and some secondary education. The government recruited many for the lower levels of the public service, especially as post office employees, and for the health service, as nurses and hospital orderlies. Such careers seldom provided high earnings, and migrants had to endure poor housing and the psychological effects of displacement. Since almost all were dark-skinned, they encountered some hostility, or outright racism, from metropolitan compatriots. The DOM migrants nevertheless often enjoyed a better material life in France than in the islands of the West Indies and Indian Ocean, where employment opportunities were limited, unemployment levels high, and living conditions sometimes precarious.[5]

France also sought labourers in Africa, where extremely poor standards of living and overpopulation encouraged migration. The old colonies and protectorates of the Maghreb and sub-Saharan Africa (as well as Turkey and parts of Anglophone Africa) provided the major sources, and post-independence governments agreed to continued migration. The North African population in France grew quickly from the 1960s onwards: Algerians almost quadrupled to 800 000 from 1954 to 1982, Moroccans increased to 431 000, and the number of Tunisians rose to 190 000. (The number of Turks expanded from 5000 to 123 000.) Maghrebins thus formed the largest block among the 3.7 million foreigners (8 per cent of the total population) in France in the 1980s, with Algerians the largest single national group.

The immigrant workers (*travailleurs immigrés*) came from both city and countryside in North Africa; most had few vocational skills, other than physical strength, and little, if any, knowledge of French. The majority, at least at the outset, were men in the prime of life. They secured jobs at the bottom of the professional occupations in France, performing work which the French considered too hard, too low-paid or too demeaning. Three-quarters of all foreigners in France at the end of the 1980s worked as unskilled, semi-skilled or skilled (blue-collar) workers or as service personnel. Of male Algerians, 30 per cent laboured in the construction industry or public works, 30 per cent held factory jobs, and 20 per cent worked in service occupations. Moroccans concentrated in roughly the same areas (especially the automobile industry), though 13 per cent were wage labourers in the agricultural sector. The types of employment found by Tunisians were more diversified – a substantial minority became shopkeepers or hotel and restaurant employees.

North Africans settled near the automobile and steel works or the ports and naval yards which provided work. Most consequently became city-dwellers. The Paris region (the Ile-de-France) housed one-third of migrants, the largest concentration, followed by the highly-industrialised Lyon area and the urbanised southern region of Provence–Côte d'Azur (Marseille and the Mediterranean littoral). Migrants clustered in particular neighbourhoods, usually poorer industrial districts in the centre city, and in suburbs where the government had built public housing. Certain neighbourhoods, such as the Goutte d'Or and Barbès *quartier* in northeastern Paris and streets around the Cours Belsunce in Marseille, became virtual Maghrebin enclaves, complete with 'Oriental' pastryshops, restaurants and open-air markets. Such establishments, as well as mosques, provided venues of sociability for the migrants.

The life of North African migrants was often uncomfortable. Earnings were minimal, and many sent remittances to families back home. Work was hard, marked by the monotony and physical labour of factories or construction, or the mundane tasks of street-cleaning and other service employment. Opportunities for promotion, education or professional training were extremely limited. Migrants usually lived in poor quality lodgings, either dilapidated buildings or 'rabbit warren' hostels. Most suffered loneliness and isolation; lack of leisure time and disposable income limited recreation. The celebrated pleasures of French life – food, fashion, culture – remained unavailable to migrants marginalised by religion, language and class.

The situation of black Africans, who also formed a large component of the migrant population, was little different, in terms of employment, salaries and living conditions. In 1982, 138 050 citizens of former French African colonies (including Madagascar) lived in France; the largest numbers came from Senegal (23 000), Cameroon (14 000), Mauritius (a French colony until the end of the Napoleonic Wars) (13 000) and the Côte-d'Ivoire (12 000). Some Africans and Indian Ocean islanders were diplomats, students, business people or spouses of French men or women. But many worked in factories or had subaltern jobs, ranging from steady employment as cleaners and domestics to odd jobs peddling handicrafts or selling fruits and vegetables in the Paris Métro.

France was home to migrants of other former colonies as well. The 1982 census recorded 11 000 Lebanese and 3600 Syrians in France. Journalists reported that 25 000 Pondicherrians had moved to France after the Indian *comptoirs* were returned to India. There was a large Indochinese population, although more were boat people who reached France in the 1970s than migrant workers or *rapatriés*: 37 000 Cambodians, 33 500 Laotians and 22 000 Vietnamese. Many Southeast Asians concentrated in larger cities, sometimes in specific neighbourhoods, such as Chinatown in the thirteenth *arrondissement* of Paris. Unlike Africans, Asians often worked in family businesses as restaurateurs, retail merchants or importers-exporters; their socioeconomic condition was in general better than that of Africans.

The French developed a certain familiarity with migrants – the local Vietnamese restaurant-owner or Tunisian grocer – but some complained about the foreigners. Regular gripes focused on such

aspects of migrants' behaviour as the sound of their music or the
smells of their food which neighbours, especially in dense high-
rise housing, found noisome. There also emerged a far more
insidious, and sometimes violent, reaction against migrants, especially after the economic recession of the 1970s. Public opinion
in some quarters began to accuse migrants of taking jobs from
'real' French men and women. Certain politicians called for withdrawal of social security benefits to migrants, cessation of migration, a limit on family reunification schemes, the expulsion of
illegal residents (estimated at 100 000–200 000), the return home
of legal migrants (perhaps with a bounty to encourage their departure), and legal changes to make it more difficult for migrants
to obtain permanent residency or citizenship. Extremists physically attacked – and occasionally killed – migrants, while the police regularly 'cracked down' with tactics ranging from overly zealous
verification of identity papers to raids on migrant hostels and
squats.

Such reaction generally exempted Asians, thought to be hard-
working and generally good citizens. Migrants from the DOM-
TOMs usually escaped as well. The brunt of the reaction was borne
by black Africans and, more especially, Maghrebins, even though
Muslim migrants make up only 3 per cent of the total French
population. The reactionary National Front, led by Jean-Marie Le
Pen, who served as a paratrooper in Algeria in the 1950s, has
based its programme on an anti-migrant stance since the 1980s.
In language which has made little attempt to mask racist sentiments, the National Front has accused North Africans of robbing
the French of employment, being involved in organised crime,
drug-dealing and prostitution, and practising all sorts of subter-
fuge to acquire family allowances, superannuation and medical
care. Le Pen's rhetoric has seduced many, lumping opposition to
migrants with campaigns against 'socialo-communism', atheism and
other evils; Le Pen has also celebrated the Vichy regime and the
heroism of French colonists in Algeria. Others contradicted the
National Front's assertions, showing, for instance, that migrants
hold jobs which the French are unlikely to seek, and arguing
that the real issues are disparities of income between migrants
and others, limited opportunities for mobility, and both latent
and overt racism in France.

Many North African (and other) migrants have now lived in
France for a lengthy period; men who arrived alone have brought

wives and offspring; couples have given birth to children in France. Indeed the birthrate is twice as high for Algerians in France as for families of European ancestry. One-third, at least, of the North African population in France is now under the age of fifteen. Second-generation migrants find themselves in a different situation from their parents. If born in France, they are fully fledged French citizens once they come of age. Second-generation North Africans, who often call themselves by the slang-term *Beurs*, grow up with both Maghrebin and French cultural influences. Most are more fluent in French than Arabic; their cultural references are often those of their 'native' French peers. Yet parents may expect them to obey certain rules of the Islamic religion or observe various North African traditions. They have more difficulties succeeding at school and finding a job than do those from European milieux; they may encounter landlords who do not want to rent them housing, and they are more frequently the object of police questioning than French citizens with more identifiably European features. Few, however, desire to return to the land of their ancestors.[6]

Relations with the Ex-colonies

Migration has been only one way in which ex-colonies have maintained close relations with France; trade, aid, technical and cultural links, as well as military intervention, have counted among other ties between France and its former empire.[7] Relations between France and newly independent states were not always close or cordial. Radical regimes in Asia or Africa expropriated foreign property, dissuaded foreign investment, espoused a rigid anti-colonialism which targeted such countries as France, and refused military collaboration. France withdrew its military forces from Algeria even before the delays permitted by the independence settlements. Violent protests against the French military presence in Tunisia in 1961 led to evacuation of Bizerte two years later, and a radical swing in Madagascar forced French troops to leave Diego-Suarez in 1973. *Rapprochement* with independent Vietnam took several decades after 1954. Links with Algeria, not surprisingly, remained particularly cool. Not until 1975 did a French president pay an official visit to Algeria, and although France trod delicately in its diplomatic policies, the FLN government reacted testily to several French initiatives (such as the holding of Franco-phone summits). A range of issues – assets of *pieds-noirs*, dual citizenship (including questions of child custody and military service), migrant workers, promotion of French language and education, French interest in prospecting Algeria's natural gas resources, racial tension in France and Islamic fundamentalism in Algeria – continued to make relations between Paris and Algiers uneasy.

Ties with Morocco and Tunisia and the ex-colonies of sub-Saharan Africa, by contrast, have been intimate, so close, in fact, that critics have accused France of 'neo-colonial' hegemony in some states and of supporting corrupt and dictatorial regimes in others. Links with former African colonies have been the linchpin in France's policy towards the 'Third World' – a term, incidentally, invented in 1952 by a French writer. Officials declared their intentions to maintain friendship between France and independent African states, and a government report in 1963 called for disinterested and generous French support for countries in the 'developing' world, particularly Africa.

Such assistance was badly needed by countries which, just as in colonial times, remained prey to environmental problems, endemic diseases, illiteracy and excruciating poverty. Many ex-colonies relied on their former colonial master for aid and trade concessions. France became the major aid donor to most of its former colonies, either through bilateral aid or through multilateral aid given by international agencies. The old colonies swallowed most of France's aid budget; in the mid-1980s, North Africa received 12.4 per cent of French aid and sub-Saharan Africa 55.4 per cent. Over half of the aid was dispensed in technical assistance, including the work of French *coopérants* (engineers, technicians and, especially, teachers sent overseas). Some 17 000 *coopérants*, either volunteers or those doing overseas service in lieu of obligatory French military duty (for men), worked around the world, the largest numbers in Côte-d'Ivoire, Morocco, Algeria and Senegal.

France traded heavily with its old colonies, to which it accorded preferential tariffs under the European Community's Lomé Accords, which lowered protectionist duties between European countries and the poorest countries of the Asia–Caribbean–Pacific (ACP) zones. In some cases (as with purchases of Algerian gas and West African agricultural products) France paid higher than world market prices for imports from its ex-colonies. France remained the largest trading partner of most of its former possessions in the late 1980s, buying nearly half of Madagascar's exports, one-third of Senegal's and a quarter of those of Morocco. France supplied a third of Niger's imports, a fifth of those to Togo and four-fifths of imports into Chad. Trade links in the post-colonial era do not differ markedly from those of the colonial era: exchange of African primary products for French manufactured goods. In the late 1980s, 48 per cent of France's purchases from ex-colonies in sub-Saharan Africa were agricultural and food products, primarily such tropical goods as bananas, coffee and cocoa; a further 29 per cent were energy and fuel products, such as Algerian gas. France acquired a third of its manganese from Gabon, a similar proportion of its chromium from Senegal and over a fifth of its phosphate from Togo. The bulk of French supplies of cobalt, uranium, phosphate, bauxite, manganese and copper came from Africa. France sold to Africa a variety of manufactured commodities, from clothing and construction materials to high-technology telecommunications gear, armaments, aeroplanes and other transport stock. The balance of trade between France and its African trading partners has, in general, favoured France. Migrant remittances from African workers in France, which formed a substantial portion of several countries' earnings, partly balanced asymmetrical trading relations.

Financial links between France and the African countries have been extremely important. French banks have lent money to governments and private enterprises in Africa, and the currency of most of the old African colonies is pegged to the French franc. In 1948 Paris created an African franc (the CFA franc) as the common currency for the AOF and AEF, and it survived decolonisation. The rate was fixed at (by the 1960s) one CFA franc to 0.02 French francs. The financial stability of nations in the franc zone, many of which are heavily indebted, is thus officially linked to the health of the French franc and French maintenance of the value of the CFA. The states of the CFA zone transact currency exchanges on the Paris market and are required to keep two-thirds of their accumulated reserves in French banks. Economists argued throughout the 1970s and 1980s that the CFA was grossly overvalued. In 1993, France halved the value of the CFA vis-à-vis the French franc, despite African protests; this effectively doubled the cost of living for residents of the CFA zone, while it halved the cost of their exports (making them, it was hoped, more competitively priced on world markets). The devaluation illustrates the partial French economic disengagement from sub-Saharan Africa that occurred in the early 1990s.

Thirty years after the independence of the African colonies, France maintained almost 8000 troops at bases in the Central African Republic, Côte-d'Ivoire, Djibouti, Gabon and Senegal (in addition to troops in Mayotte and Réunion), and a further 1200 military advisers held posts in several dozen African countries. Since the 1960s, indeed, French overseas military intervention has concentrated on Africa (although French contingents have also served in Lebanon and ex-Yugoslavia). Since the early 1960s, the French military has intervened some twenty times in Africa, generally after a *pro forma* invitation by an African government and with the ostensible justification of protecting French lives and property. Paris has deployed soldiers on several occasions in the Comoros, Gabon, Chad, Djibouti, Mauritania, the Central African Republic and Togo, as well as in the former Belgian colonies of Zaire and Rwanda. Such actions reaffirmed Paris's perception that Francophone Africa lies within its military sphere of influence. Several French mercenaries – with or without the knowledge and approval of Paris – have been involved in African *coups d'état.*

Cultural connections between France and former colonies form another aspect of France's international presence. Some 100 million people around the world speak French as a mother tongue or a secondary language; ironically, because of growing population and increasing literacy, more people speak, read and write French now than during the colonial period. French intellectuals and policy-makers have made great efforts to promote the use of French and to export French culture, even with charges that this, too, is 'neo-colonial'. In 1959, the government set up the Agency for Cultural and Technical Cooperation (*Agence de Co-opération Culturelle et Technique*, ACCT) to channel aid from wealthier Francophone countries – primarily France, but also Canada and Belgium – to developing ones. The ACCT has provided funds and materials for education to countries where French is an official or a widely used language. Because of the multiplicity of languages in African countries, many newly independent states adopted French as their official language, or one of several officially recognised languages. A few avid Francophones have preserved French in areas of former French domination stretching from Lebanon to Vietnam. A French-based Creole serves as the everyday language in a number of islands in the West Indies and the Indian Ocean.

A movement to sustain ties between Francophone countries began just at the time of French decolonisation of Africa, spearheaded by such leaders as Léopold Sedar Senghor. The Francophone movement has since grown beyond simple cultural and educational links to become something similar to the (British) Commonwealth of Nations. Meetings of Francophone parliamentarians, Francophone athletic games, an organisation of Francophone universities, and regular summit conferences of what are carefully described as 'those nations having in common the use of French' have cemented ties between France, other French-speaking developed countries, and former colonies of France, Belgium and Britain where French is used. The first Francophone government conference, held in Paris in 1986, drew representatives from 40 states.

Relations between France and its ex-colonies are personal as well as institutional. The first generation of political leaders in Francophone Africa were almost all a product of colonial training. Many in the African elite still study at French universities. Middle-class Africans also fly to Paris for shopping and recreation. The French travel to Africa as business people, *coopérants* or soldiers. In 1989, 26 000 French men and women lived in Morocco, 22 000 in the Côte-d'Ivoire, 16 000 in Gabon, 15 000 in Senegal, 15 000 in Madagascar and smaller numbers in most of the other old possessions. Some 19 000 also lived in Algeria, although most fled in the wake of attacks by Muslim fundamentalists from 1993 onwards. Larger numbers of French citizens in search of sun and exoticism crowd resorts in Morocco and Tunisia or venture further southwards to Senegal and other countries in black Africa. Use of French, a tourist market geared to French tastes and easy air connections with Paris reinforce tourist preferences.

Ties with ex-colonies cover many other areas. Sporting contacts remain close, and one of the year's major sporting events in France is the Paris to Dakar car and motorcycle rally; many Africans enthusiastically follow French soccer matches. Shops in Abidjan and Dakar are stocked with French products, and newstands sell French metropolitan papers as well as local periodicals written in French. Television and radio stations programme variety shows, news broadcasts, serials, sports competitions and films 'made in France'. French fashions, consumer goods and foods – notably the *baguette* – have endured in old colonies long after the departure of colonial rulers.

Contemporary Traces of the Empire in France

Few Maghrebins, black Africans or residents of islands within France's sphere of influence can ignore their historical connections with France. Many contemporary French men and women, however, know little about their country's colonial past, except for vague general ideas about explorers in Africa, *pieds-noirs* in Algeria and the seduction of tropical islands. As they stroll around France's capital, few Parisians would probably be able to identify the origins of street names which pay tribute to colonials and colonialists – the rues Dupetit-Thouard and Général Dodds, Leroy-Beaulieu and Caillié. Over 100 streets in Paris bear the names of men (never women) who made their careers largely in the empire. Museumgoers can visit collections of African and Oceanic art in the building in the Vincennes park which housed part of the Colonial Exhibition of 1931; few pay attention to the colonial murals on the building's façade or examine Marshal Lyautey's study in the foyer. Parisians and tourists hardly take notice of the former *Ecole Coloniale* in the Avenue de l'Observatoire or the *Société de Géographie de Paris* in the Boulevard Saint-Germain, nor do they reflect at the Charonne Métro station on the bloody suppression of a demonstration against the Algerian War which took place there.

The empire nevertheless left its imprint on France's landscape in street names and buildings, art collections and sites connected with the colonial epoch. The passing of time has brought a glance back at the colonial era – evidenced by the large number of novels published in the past decade. In 1984, *L'Amant* (*The Lover*), a quasi-autobiographical novel by Marguerite Duras, one of France's most popular authors, recounted a love affair between a young French girl and an older Chinese businessman in interwar Indochina. The novel had enormous success, won the Prix Goncourt and was turned into a film. Four years later, *L'Exposition coloniale* by Erik Orsenna also won the Goncourt; it charts the life and loves of a Frenchman whose career takes him to rubber plantations in Brazil and Vietnam. Other important contemporary French novelists, including Michel Tournier and Jean-Marie Le Clézio, have won praise for their works, several with colonial settings or themes, such as Tournier's novel about a young Maghrebin migrant to France (*La Goutte d'Or*) and Le Clézio's works on the Indian Ocean. Books written in French by writers from the present-

day DOM-TOMs or former colonies have been honoured by readers
and prize committees. Tahar Ben Jelloun, a Moroccan who lives
in France, won the Goncourt in 1987 for *La Nuit sacrée*, a novel
about the quest for emancipation of a young North African girl
whose father rears her as a boy. Patrick Chamoiseau, a leader of
a new school of creole literature in the French West Indies, in
1992 garnered the award for *Texaco*, an epic about the history of
Martinique. The following year the Lebanese writer Amin Maalouf
collected the Goncourt for *Le Rocher de Tanios*, a French-language
novel about imperialism in the nineteenth-century Levant.

The cinema, too, has rediscovered the empire. Recent successful films have included Régis Wargnier's *Indochine*, in which a
French woman struggles to run a Vietnamese rubber plantation,
has an affair with a dashing young colonial army officer and en-
counters the nationalist movement in the person of her adopted
Vietnamese daughter. Claire Denys' *Chocolat* focuses on the friendship between a French girl and the African 'boy' who serves her
father, a colonial administrator, while Brigitte Rouan's *Outremer*
looks at the lives of three *pied-noir* sisters in Algeria.

In other ways, as well, residual links between France and its
former empire endure. France remains a major stage for the performance of 'world music' by black Africans, West Indians and
singers of Algerian *raï*. Fashion designers borrow styles and motifs from 'colonial' areas, like safari khaki. French diners eat North
African, Vietnamese and Caribbean food in 'exotic' restaurants;
North African dishes such as *couscous, paella* (itself an import from
Spain to Algeria) and *merguez*, Vietnamese *nems* and West Indian
rum are appreciated by restaurant-goers with little other interest
in the colonies. The colonial heritage remains in the background
of much of French life. Food and fashion, music and movies may
be vogues, but underlying French ties with the *outre-mer* – economic, political, social and cultural – are not likely to be sundered.

Notes

Introduction: Reading and Writing About the Colonies

1. The term seems to have been first used in 1903 by Jacques Léotard, secretary-general of the *Société de Géographie de Marseille*.
2. R. de Noter, *La Bonne cuisine aux colonies* (Paris, 1931).
3. See Robert Aldrich, 'The New French Colonial History', in F.J. Fornasiero (ed.), *Culture and Ideology in Modern France: Essays in Honour of George Rudé, 1910–1993* (Adelaide, 1994), pp. 41–55, and C. Coquery-Vidrovitch, 'Coloniale (Histoire)', in André Burguière (ed.), *Dictionnaire des sciences historiques* (Paris, 1986), pp. 141–6.
4. Gabriel Hanotaux and Alfred Martineau (eds), *Histoire des colonies françaises*, Vol. I (Paris, 1929), p. 1.
5. Hanotaux, *Histoire des colonies françaises*, Vol. VI (Paris, 1933), pp. 551–67.
6. Nguyên Ai Quôc, *Le Procès de la colonisation française* (Paris, 1925).
7. See John Hargreaves, 'From *Colonisation* to *Avènement*: Henri Brunschwig and the History of *Afrique Noire*', *Journal of African History*, 31 (1990), 347–52.
8. See H.L. Wesseling, 'Towards a History of Decolonization', *Itinerario*, 11:2 (1987), 95–106.
9. William B. Cohen, *The French Encounter with Africans: White Response to Blacks, 1530–1880* (London, 1980), and *Rulers of Empire: The French Colonial Service in Africa* (Stanford, CA, 1971); Raymond F. Betts, *Assimilation and Association in French Colonial Theory, 1890–1914* (New York, 1961); Christopher M. Andrew and A.S. Kanya-Forstner, *France Overseas: The Great War*

326

and the Climax of French Imperial Expansion (London, 1981).

10. E.g. Hubert Deschamps, Histoire de Madagascar (Paris, 1960); Charles-André Julien, Histoire de l'Algérie contemporaine: la conquête et les débuts de la colonisation (1827–1871) (Paris, 1964), and Le Maroc face aux impérialismes, 1415–1956 (Paris, 1978); Robert Cornevin, Histoire de l'Afrique des origines à nos jours (Paris, 1956) and over 20 other works on Africa; Jean-Louis Miège, Le Maroc et l'Europe, 1830–1894 (Paris, 4 vols, 1961–3); Charles-André Julien and Charles-Robert Ageron, Histoire de l'Algérie contemporaine (Paris, 2 vols, 1979).

11. E.g. J. Ganiage, L'Expansion coloniale de la France sous la Troisième République (Paris, 1968), and Jean-Louis Miège, Expansion européenne et décolonisation de 1870 à nos jours (Paris, 1973, revised edn, 1986), as well as the brief overviews of Xavier Yacono, Histoire de la colonisation française (Paris, 1973), and Les Etapes de la décolonisation française (Paris, 1975). The most recent full-scale study in English is Raymond Betts, Tricouleur: The French Overseas Empire (London, 1978).

12. The survey volumes of Denoël's five-volume series are Jean Martin, L'Empire renaissant, 1789–1871 (Paris, 1987); Gilbert Comte, L'Empire triomphant, 1871–1936. Vol. I: Afrique occidentale et equatoriale (Paris, 1990), Vol. II: Maghreb, Indochine, Madagascar, Iles et Comptoirs (Paris, 1990); Paul-Marie de La Gorce, L'Empire écartelé, 1936–1946 (Paris, 1988); and Jean Planchais, L'Empire embrasé, 1946–1962 (Paris, 1990).

13. Jean Meyer, Jean Tarrade, Annie Rey-Goldzeiguer and Jacques Thobie, Histoire de la France coloniale: des origines à 1914 (Paris, 1991), and Jacques Thobie, Gilbert Meynier, Catherine Coquery-Vidrovitch and Charles-Robert Ageron, Histoire de la France coloniale, 1914–1990 (Paris, 1990).

14. Pierre Pluchon, L'Histoire de la colonisation française. Vol. I, Le Premier empire colonial: des origines à la Restauration (Paris, 1991), and Denise Bouche, Vol. II, Flux et reflux (1815–1962) (Paris, 1991).

15. Notably Robert and Marianne Cornevin, La France et les Français outre-mer (Paris, 1990); Guy Pervillé, De l'Empire français à la décolonisation (Paris, 1991); and Jacques Binoche-Guedra, La France d'outre-mer, 1815–1962 (Paris, 1992). See also Marc Ferro, Histoire des colonisations (Paris, 1994).

16. Jean Martin, Lexique de la colonisation française (Paris, 1988).

17. See D.K. Fieldhouse, 'Can Humpty-Dumpty Be Put Together

Again? Imperial History in the 1980s', *Journal of Imperial and Commonwealth History*, 12 (1984), 9–23, and H.L. Wesseling and P.C. Emmer, 'What is Overseas History? Some Reflections on a Colloquium and a Problem', in *Reappraisals in Overseas History* (Leiden, 1979), pp. 3–17.

Prologue: The First Overseas Empire

1. Robert and Marianne Cornevin, *La France et les Français outre-mer* (Paris, 1990).
2. Philip Boucher, *Les Nouvelles Frances: France in America, 1500–1815. An Imperial Perspective* (Providence, RI, 1989); Lucien-René Abenon and John A. Dickinson, *Les Français en Amérique* (Lyon, 1993).
3. Charles Guyotjeannin, *Saint-Pierre et Miquelon* (Paris, 1986).
4. The French also claimed the Falkland (Malvinas) Islands in the South Atlantic from 1764 to 1767.
5. Louis Sala-Molins, *Le Code noir, ou le calvaire de Canaan* (Paris, 1987).
6. François Biarnès, *Les Français en Afrique noire de Richelieu à Mitterrand* (Paris, 1987).
7. Kenneth McPherson, *The Indian Ocean: A History of People and the Sea* (Delhi, 1993).
8. There were brief French attempts to establish outposts elsewhere in the Indian Ocean: in Ceylon for several months in 1672, in the Maldives from 1757 to 1761, and in the Chagos archipelago from the late 1780s onwards.
9. Arthur Annasse, *Les Comptoirs français de l'Inde (1664–1954): trois siècles de présence française* (Paris, 1975).
10. Yves Benot, *La Révolution française et la fin des colonies* (Paris, 1987).
11. Yves Benot, *La Démence coloniale sous Napoléon* (Paris, 1991).
12. Jean-Joël Brégeon, *L'Egypte française au jour le jour, 1798–1801* (Paris, 1991).
13. Alain-Philippe Blérald, *Histoire économique de la Guadeloupe et de la Martinique* (Paris, 1986).
14. Alexander Miles, *Devil's Island: Colony of the Damned* (Berkeley, CA, 1988).
15. Jean-Pierre Biondi, *Saint-Louis du Sénégal: mémoires d'un métissage* (Paris, 1987).

Chapter 1. The Conquest of Empire: Africa and the Indian Ocean

1. Antony Thrall Sullivan, *Thomas-Robert Bugeaud – France and Algeria, 1784–1849: Politics, Power, and the Good Society* (Hamden, CT, 1983).

2. John Ruedy, *Modern Algeria: The Origins and Development of a Nation* (Bloomington, IN, 1992); Charles-Robert Ageron, *Modern Algeria: A History from 1830 to the Present*, trs Michael Brett (London, 1991); Benjamin Stora, *Histoire de l'Algérie coloniale, 1830–1954* (Paris, 1991); Charles-André Julien and Charles-Robert Ageron, *Histoire de l'Algérie contemporaine* (Paris, 1974–9).

3. Jean-François Martin, *Histoire de la Tunisie contemporaine: de Ferry à Bourguiba, 1881–1956* (Paris, 1993).

4. Charles-André Julien, *Le Maroc face aux impérialismes, 1415–1956* (Paris, 1978); Jean-Louis Miège, *Le Maroc et l'Europe, 1830–1894* (Paris, 1961–3).

5. Christian Roche, *Histoire de la Casamance* (Paris, 1985).

6. Odile Goerg, *Commerce et colonisation en Guinée (1850–1913)* (Paris, 1986).

7. Robert Cornevin, *Histoire de Dahomey* (Paris, 1962).

8. A.S. Kanya-Forstner, *The Conquest of the Western Sudan: A Study in French Military Imperialism* (Cambridge, 1969).

9. Daniel Grevoz, *Les Canonnières de Tombouctou: les Français à la conquête de la cité mythique, 1870–1894* (Paris, 1992).

10. David Levering Lewis, *The Race to Fashoda: European Colonialism and African Resistance in the Scramble for Africa* (London, 1988).

11. Finn Fuglestad, *A History of Niger, 1850–1960* (Cambridge, 1983).

12. Francis de Chassey, *Mauritanie, 1900–1975* (Paris, 1984).

13. Dieudonné Oyono, *Colonie ou mandat international? La Politique française au Cameroun de 1919 à 1946* (Paris, 1992).

14. Robert Cornevin, *Le Togo* (Paris, 1973).

15. Pierre Savorgnan de Brazza, *Au Coeur de l'Afrique, 1875–1887* (Paris, 1992). (Brazza's chronicles were first published in 1887–8.)

16. See Elisabeth Rabut, *Brazza Commissaire-Général: le Congo français, 1886–1897* (Paris, 1989).

17. On Brazza's death, and suspicions that he was murdered, see Jean Autin, 'Brazza: Une mort mystérieuse', *Mondes et cultures*, 49:4 (1989), 668–74.

18. Pierre Gentil, *La Conquête du Tchad (1894–1916)* (Paris, 2 vols, 1970).

19. Roger Joint Daguenet, *Aux Origines de l'implantation française en Mer Rouge: vie et mort d'Henri Lambert, consul de France à Aden, 1859* (Paris, 1992); Philipe Oberlé and Pierre Hugot, *Histoire de Djibouti: des origines à la République* (Paris, 1985); Jacques Trampont, *Djibouti Hier: de 1887 à 1939* (Paris, 1990).

20. Stephen Ellis, *The Rising of the Red Shawls: A Revolt in Madagascar, 1895–1899* (Cambridge, 1985); Mervyn Brown, *Madagascar Rediscovered: A History from Early Times to Independence* (London, 1978); Hubert Deschamps, *Histoire de Madagascar* (Paris, 1960).

21. Jean Martin, *Comores: quatre îles entre pirates et planteurs. Vol. II: Razzias malgaches et rivalités internationales (fin XVIIIe siècle – 1975)* (Paris, 1983).

Chapter 2. The Conquest of Empire: Asia, the Pacific and the Austral Regions

1. Robert Aldrich, *The French Presence in the South Pacific, 1842–1940* (London, 1990).

2. On this episode, see Nancy Nichols Barker, *The French Experience in Mexico, 1821–1861: A History of Constant Misunderstanding* (Chapel Hill, NC, 1979).

3. Milton E. Osborne, *The French Presence in Cochinchina and Cambodia: Rule and Response (1859–1905)* (London, 1969).

4. John F. Cady, *The Roots of French Imperialism in Eastern Asia* (Ithaca, NY, 1954, 1967).

5. Bruce Fulton, 'Jules Ferry's Far-Eastern Imperialism, 1883–1885', in Deryck M. Schreuder, *'Imperialisms': Explorations in European Expansion and Empire* (Sydney, 1991), pp. 64–78.

6. Jean Martin, *L'Empire triomphant, 1871–1936. 2. Maghreb, Indochine, Madagascar, Iles et comptoirs* (Paris, 1990).

7. France also controlled Cheikh-Said, a 1620 km^2 territory on the Arabian peninsula bordering the Red Sea, from 1868 to 1936. However, it remained uninhabited and was only briefly used as a coaling station.

8. Jean-Paul Kauffmann, *L'Arche des Kerguelen: voyages aux îles de la Désolation* (Paris, 1993).

9. Mention could also be made of failed efforts by French

adventurers to set up other colonies. A 32-year-old lawyer from Périgueux, Orélie-Antoine de Tounens, in 1859 proclaimed himself King of Patagonia and Araucania, a vast region on the southern tip of Latin America; he hoisted the French flag and mailed a report to a French newspaper about 'New France'. A year later, Chilean police arrested Tounens; in prison, he showed signs of madness and was repatriated to France. He set up a court in exile and invested friends with royal orders he had created. On three occasions before he died in the 1880s, Tounens tried to return to South America, but each time he was sent back to France. (See Bruce Chatwin, *In Patagonia* (London, 1977), chs 7–8.) Another Frenchman, the Marquis de Rays, in 1877 recruited Catholic settlers for yet another New France, called Port-Breton, located in New Ireland, off the coast of Papua New Guinea. Several hundred colonists, having 'bought' land in the island from the marquis, set sail for their new home. A hundred died shortly after arrival; the rest eventually took refuge in Australia. The French government arrested the marquis in 1881, and convicted him of fraud and other crimes.

Chapter 3. Ideas of Empire

1. The most comprehensive studies of attitudes and ideologies are Raoul Girardet, *L'Idée coloniale en France* (Paris, 1972), and Charles-Robert Ageron, *France coloniale ou parti colonial?* (Paris, 1978).
2. See Chapter 6 for further details on views of non-Western peoples.
3. Quoted in Jean Martin, *L'Empire renaissant, 1789–1871* (Paris, 1987), p. 291.
4. Thomas Schoonover, 'France in Central America, 1820s–1920: An Overview', *Revue française d'histoire d'outre-mer*, 79:295 (1992), 161–97.
5. On these important areas of French commercial and financial activity, see René Girault, *Emprunts russes et intérêts français en Russie, 1887–1914* (Paris, 1973), and Jacques Thobie, *Intérêts français dans l'Empire ottoman (1894–1974)* (Paris, 1977).
6. Quoted in Girardet, *L'Idée coloniale*, pp. 82–6, which also contains a commentary on Ferry's doctrine.
7. In addition to sections in general books by Ageron and Girardet, see Henri Brunschwig, *The Myth of French Imperialism* (London,

1961), Stewart Michael Persell, *The French Colonial Lobby, 1889–1938* (Stanford, CA, 1983), and Marc Lagana, *Le Parti colonial français: éléments d'histoire* (Sillery, Québec, 1990). Pioneering work was done by C.M. Andrew and A.S. Kanya-Forstner: 'The French "Colonial Party": Its Composition, Aims and Influence, 1885–1914', *Historical Journal,* 14:1 (1971), 99–128; 'The French Colonial Party and French Colonial War Aims, 1914–1918', *Historical Journal,* 17:1 (1974), 79–106; 'The *Groupe colonial* in the French Chamber of Deputies, 1892–1932', *Historical Journal,* 17:4 (1974), 837–66; 'Le Mouvement colonial français et ses principales personnalités (1890–1914)', *Revue française d'histoire d'outre-mer,* 62:229 (1975), 640–73 (with P. Grupp); and 'French Business and French Colonialists', *Historical Journal,* 12:4 (1976), 981–1000. A different view is L. Abrams and D.J. Miller, 'Who Were the French Colonialists? A Reassessment of the *parti colonial,* 1890–1914', *Historical Journal,* 19:3 (1976), 685–725.

8. Lagana, *Le Parti colonial français,* pp. 51–8.

9. Persell, *French Colonial Lobby,* p. 87.

10. Dominique Lejeune, *Les Sociétés de géographie en France et l'expansion coloniale au XIXe siècle* (Paris, 1993).

11. Jean Martin, *Lexique de la colonisation française* (Paris, 1988), p. 190.

12. This is discussed in more detail in Chapter 6.

13. Martin, *Lexique,* p. 25.

14. Raymond Betts, *Assimilation and Association in French Colonial Theory, 1890–1914* (New York, 1961).

15. The major general works are Charles-Robert Ageron, *L'Anticolonialisme en France de 1871 à 1914* (Paris, 1973), Jean-Pierre Biondi with Gilles Morin, *Les Anticolonialistes (1881–1962)* (Paris, 1992), and Jean Lacouture and Dominique Chagnollard, *Le Désempire* (Paris, 1993).

16. Quoted in Biondi, *Les Anticolonialistes,* p. 74.

17. Quoted in ibid., p. 99.

18. Quoted in ibid., pp. 29, 83.

19. The argument about the 'economic taproots of colonialism' was further developed by J.A. Hobson, although his work was then little known in France. Lenin later argued that imperialism formed the ultimate stage of capitalism, a necessary struggle through exploitation of overseas resources by a moribund capitalism faced with saturated markets in Europe.

20. Jacques Marseille, *L'Age d'or de la France coloniale* (Paris, 1986); Thomas G. August, 'Locating the Age of Imperialism', *Itinerario*, 10 (1986), 85–97.

21. Quoted in Biondi, *Les Anticolonialistes*, pp. 133, 17.

22. Sarraut's programme is discussed in greater detail in Chapter 5.

23. Martin, *Lexique*, p. 28.

24. Biondi, *Les Anticolonialistes*, pp. 135–41. See also David H. Slavin, 'The French Left and the Rif War, 1924–25: Racism and the Limits of Internationalism', *Journal of Contemporary History*, 26 (1991), 5–32.

25. Jacques Marseille, *Empire colonial et capitalisme français: histoire d'un divorce* (Paris, 1984), chs 6–7.

26. Marc Lagana, 'L'Echec de la commission d'enquête coloniale du Front populaire', *Historical Reflections/Réflexions historiques*, 16:1 (1989), 79–97.

27. Charles-Robert Ageron, 'La Perception de la puissance française en 1938–1939: Le Mythe impérial', *Revue française d'histoire d'outre-mer*, 69:254 (1982), 7–22.

28. See Charles-Robert Ageron, 'La Survivance d'un mythe: La Puissance par l'empire colonial (1944–1947)', *Revue française d'histoire d'outre-mer*, 72:269 (1985), pp. 387–403.

Chapter 4. The French Overseas

1. See Numa Broc, 'Les Explorateurs français du XIXe siècle réconsidérés', *Revue française d'histoire d'outre-mer*, 69:256 (1982), 237–73, and 69:257 (1982), 323–59.

2. Jean-Marc Durou, *L'Exploration du Sahara* (Paris, 1993); Douglas Porch, *The Conquest of the Sahara* (London, 1984).

3. J. Dean O'Donnell, Jr, *Lavigerie in Tunisia: The Interplay of Imperialist and Missionary* (Athens, GA, 1979).

4. André Picciola, *Missionnaires en Afrique, 1840–1940* (Paris, 1987).

5. Patrick J.N. Turck, *French Catholic Missionaries and the Politics of Imperialism in Vietnam, 1857–1914: A Documentary Survey* (Liverpool, 1987).

6. Jean-Pierre Gomane, *Les Marins et l'outre-mer* (Paris, 1988).

7. Douglas Porch, *The French Foreign Legion: A Complete History of the Legendary Fighting Force* (New York, 1991).

8. André Le Révérend, *Lyautey* (Paris, 1983); Barnett Singer,

'Lyautey: An Interpretation of the Man and French Imperialism', *Journal of Contemporary History*, 26 (1991), 131–57.

9. The origin of *pied-noir*, literally 'black foot', a term which only came into common usage after the Second World War, is uncertain. It probably started as a reference by Arabs, who usually wore sandals, to the black leather shoes of Europeans.

10. Albert Camus, *Le premier homme* (Paris, 1994), pp. 257–8, 180–1.

11. David Prochaska, *Making Algeria French: Colonialism in Bône, 1870–1920* (Cambridge, 1990).

12. Alain Lardillier, *Le Peuplement français en Algérie de 1830 à 1900* (Versailles, 1992); Marc Baroli, *Algérie, terre d'espérances: colons et immigrants (1830–1914)* (Paris, 1992).

13. Marc Donato, *L'Emigration des Maltais en Algérie au XIX siècle* (Montpellier, 1985).

14. For differing views of the Algerian French, see Pierre Nora, *Les Français d'Algérie* (Paris, 1961), and Joëlle Hureau, *La Mémoire des pieds-noirs* (Paris, 1987).

15. Isabelle Merle, 'La Nouvelle-Calédonie, 1853–1920: Naissance d'une société coloniale' (Doctoral thesis, Ecole des Hautes Etudes en Sciences Sociales, Paris, 1992).

16. Charles Meyer, *La Vie quotidienne des Français en Indochine, 1860–1910* (Paris, 1985).

17. Rita Cruise O'Brien, *White Society in Black Africa: The French of Senegal* (London, 1972).

18. See the essay on French governors in Africa, and biographies of Faidherbe, Gallieni, Binger, Ponty, Eboué and Delavignette in L.H. Gann and Peter Duignan (eds), *African Proconsuls: European Governors in Africa* (New York, 1978).

19. William B. Cohen, *Rulers of Empire: The French Colonial Service in Africa* (Stanford, CA, 1971).

20. Académie des Sciences d'Outre-Mer, *Hommes et destins*, Vol. VIII, *Gouverneurs, administrateurs, magistrats* (Paris, 1988), pp. 736–41.

21. See, for example, Maurice Delauney, *De la Casquette à la jaquette, ou l'administration coloniale à la diplomatie africaine* (Paris, 1982); Raymond Gauthereau, *Journal d'un colonialiste* (Paris, 1986); Jean Clauzel, *Administrateur de la France d'outre-mer* (Paris, 1989); Olivier Colombani, *Mémoires coloniales: la fin de l'empire français d'Afrique vue par les administrateurs coloniaux* (Paris, 1991); and Guy Georgy, *Le Petit soldat de l'Empire* (Paris, 1992). One of the best memoirs is Hubert Deschamps, *Roi de la brousse: mémoires*

d'autres mondes (Paris, 1975). See also the sketches in Pierre Gentil, *Derniers chefs d'un empire* (Paris, 1972).

22. Yvonne Knibiehler and Régine Goutalier, *La Femme au temps des colonies* (Paris, 1985). See also *La Femme dans les sociétés coloniales* (Aix-en-Provence, 1984), and France Renucci, *Souvenirs de femmes au temps des colonies* (Paris, 1988).

23. Cecily Mackworth, *The Destiny of Isabelle Eberhardt* (London, 1951 and 1977).

24. One of the most incisive memoirs is Roger Curel's ironically titled *Eloge de la colonie* (Paris, 1992).

25. Philip D. Curtin, *Death by Migration: Europe's Encounter with the Tropical World in the Nineteenth Century* (Cambridge, 1989).

26. Léon Lapeysonnie, *La Médecine coloniale: mythes et réalités* (Paris, 1988).

27. Yvonne Knibiehler, Geneviève Emmery and Françoise Leguay, *Des Français au Maroc* (Paris, 1992).

28. Centre des archives d'outre-mer, *L'Empire du sport: les sports dans les anciennes colonies françaises* (Aix-en-Provence, 1992).

29. Ronald Hyam, *Empire and Sexuality: The British Experience* (Manchester, 1990), has some comments on the French case.

30. See the memoir of Philippe Franchini, *Métis* (Paris, 1992); and Léon Poliakov (ed.), *Le Couple interdit: entretiens sur le racisme – la dialectique de l'altérité socio-culturelle et la sexualité* (Paris, 1980).

Chapter 5. The Uses of Empire

1. Michael J. Heffernan, 'A French Colonial Controversy: Captain Roudaire and the Saharan Sea, 1872–83', *Maghreb Review*, 13:3–4 (1988), 145–59.

2. Bruno Carrière, 'Le Transsaharien: histoire et géographie d'une entreprise inachevée', *Acta Geographica*, No. 74 (1988), 23–38.

3. Gilles Sautter, 'Notes sur la construction du chemin de fer Congo–Océan (1921–1934)', *Cahiers d'études africaines*, 7 (1967), 219–99.

4. See Robert Lee, *France and the Exploitation of China, 1885–1901: A Study in Economic Imperialism* (Oxford, 1989).

5. Will D. Swearingen, *Moroccan Mirages: Agrarian Dreams and Deceptions, 1912–1986* (Princeton, NJ, 1987).

6. See, for example, Hubert Bonin, 'Le Comptoir national d'es-

compte de Paris, une banque impériale (1848–1940)', *Revue française d'histoire d'outre-mer*, 78 (1991), 477–97.

7. Marc Meuleau, *Des Pionniers en Extrême-Orient: histoire de la Banque de l'Indochine, 1875–1975* (Paris, 1990).

8. Hubert Bonin, *CFAO: cent ans de compétition* (Paris, 1987).

9. See Catherine Coquery-Vidrovitch (ed. with Odile Goerg), *L'Afrique occidentale au temps des Français: colonisateurs et colonisés, c.1860–1960* (Paris, 1992) on the economic history of the AOF, and relevant chapters in general works for overviews of other colonies.

10. Meuleau, *Des Pionniers*; Charles Robequain, *The Economic Development of French Indo-China*, trs Isabel A. Ward (London, 1944); Irene Nørland, 'The French Empire, the colonial state in Vietnam and economic policy: 1885–1940', *Australian Economic History Review*, 31:1 (1991), 72–89; Martin J. Murray, *The Development of Capitalism in Colonial Indochina (1870–1940)* (Berkeley, CA, 1980).

11. Catherine Coquery-Vidrovitch, *Le Congo au temps des grandes compagnies concessionnaires, 1898–1930* (Paris, 1972).

12. Jacques Marseille, *Empire colonial et capitalisme français: histoire d'un divorce* (Paris, 1984). For further discussion and a different view, see Jean Bouvier and René Girault (eds), *L'Impérialisme français d'avant 1914* (Paris, 1976); Jacques Thobie, Jean Bouvier and René Girault, *La France impériale, 1880–1914* (Paris, 1982); and Jean Bouvier, René Girault and Jacques Thobie, *L'Impérialisme à la française, 1914–1960* (Paris, 1986); Bouvier, Girault and Thobie emphasise the changing complementarity between French 'colonialism' (in possessions over which France held sovereignty) and 'imperialism' (in an 'informal' empire where French investments and trade were particularly important, including pre-First World War Russia, the Ottoman Empire and the Iberian peninsula). After 1918, 'colonial' trade and investment supplanted the old 'imperial' commercial relations.

Chapter 6. The French and the 'Natives'

1. Robert Cornevin, *Histoire du Dahomey* (Paris, 1962), p. 458.

2. Some historians reject the terms 'collaboration' and 'collaborator'. According to a Ghanaian scholar: 'I find the term *collaborator* highly objectionable partly because it is inaccurate

and partly because it is Eurocentric and derogatory. . . . A collaborator is surely somebody who sacrifices the interests of his nation for his own selfish ends. But what these African rulers sought to achieve was not their own selfish ends but in fact the very sovereignty of their state, and what they saw themselves as doing was not collaborating but rather allying with the incoming invaders to achieve this national end.' (A. Abu Boahen, *African Perspectives on Colonialism* (Baltimore, MD, 1987), p. 41.)

3. Pierre Guiral and Emile Temime, *L'Idée de race dans la pensée politique française contemporaine* (Paris, 1977).

4. Ibid., pp. 228–9, 232–4

5. William B. Cohen, *The French Encounter with Africans: White Responses to Blacks, 1530–1880* (London, 1980); Léon-François Hoffmann, *Le Nègre romantique: personnage littéraire et obsession collective* (Paris, 1973).

6. Many of these developments are discussed further in Chapter 8.

7. Roselène Dousset-Leenhardt, *Colonialisme et contradictions: Nouvelle-Calédonie, 1878–1978* (Paris, 1978); Apollinaire Anova-Ataba, *D'Ataï à l'indépendance* (Nouméa, 1984), provides a Melanesian perspective.

8. Lenka Bokova, *La Confrontation franco-syrienne à l'époque du mandat, 1925–1927* (Paris, 1990); Philip S. Khoury, *Syria and the French Mandate: The Politics of Arab Nationalism, 1920–1945* (Princeton, NJ, 1987).

9. See P. Dareste, *Traité de droit colonial* (Paris, 1931); Charles Apchié, *De la Condition des indigènes en Algérie, dans les colonies et dans les pays de protectorat* (Paris, 1898); Jacques Aumont-Thiéville, *Du Régime de l'indigénat en Algérie* (Paris, 1906); R. Ruyssen, *Le Code de l'indigénat en Algérie* (Algiers, 1908); François Marneur, *L'Indigénat en Algérie: Considérations sur le régime actuel, critique, projets de réformes* (Paris, 1914).

10. Edouard Bazet, *Etude du régime des terres dans les colonies françaises* (Paris, 1910), pp. 7, 15–17.

11. Bernard Droz, 'Main basse sur les terres', *L'Histoire*, No. 140 (January 1991), 34–44.

12. Joël Dauphiné, *La Spoliation foncière en Nouvelle-Calédonie* (Paris, 1989); Alan Ward, *Land and Politics in New Caledonia* (Canberra, 1982).

13. Ngô Viñh Long, *Before the Revolution: The Vietnamese Peasants under the French* (New York, 1991).

14. Henri Brunschwig, *Noirs et blancs dans l'Afrique noire française* (Paris, 1983).

15. Myron Echenberg, *Colonial Conscripts: The Tirailleurs Sénégalais in French West Africa, 1857–1960* (London, 1991).

16. David E. Gardiner, 'The French Impact on Education in Africa, 1817–1960', in G. Wesley Johnson (ed.), *Double Impact: France and Africa in the Age of Imperialism* (Westport, CT, 1985), pp. 333–4. See also the essays by A.Y. Yansané and Peggy Sabatier in the same volume.

17. Pierre Nora, *Les Français d'Algérie* (Paris, 1961), pp. 217, 162; Long, *Before the Revolution*, pp. 73–5; Hubert Deschamps, *Histoire de Madagascar* (Paris, 1960), pp. 308–9.

18. Léon Lapeyssonnie, *La Médecine coloniale: mythes et réalités* (Paris, 1988).

19. Long, *Before the Revolution*, p. 76.

20. Frantz Fanon, *Peau noire, masques blancs* (Paris, 1952).

21. Yvonne Knibiehler and Régine Goutalier, *La Femme au temps des colonies* (Paris, 1985).

22. See the special issue of the *Revue française d'histoire d'outre-mer*, 80:298 (1993), and A.W. Crosby, *Ecological Imperialism: The Biological Expansion of Europe, 900–1900* (Cambridge, 1986).

23. See Catherine Coquery-Vidrovitch, 'Villes coloniales et histoire des Africains', *XXe siècle: Revue d'histoire*, No. 20 (1988), 49–73; Yves Marguerat, 'La Naissance d'une capitale africaine: Lomé', *Revue française d'histoire d'outre-mer*, 81:302 (1994), 71–95.

24. Gwendolyn Wright, *The Politics of Design in French Colonial Urbanism* (Chicago, 1991). See also Raymond F. Betts, 'Imperial Designs: French Colonial Architecture and Urban Planning in Sub-Saharan Africa', in Johnson, *Double Impact*, pp. 191–207. On French images of Maghrebin cities, see Michael Heffernan, 'Nature, Culture and the Oriental City: The North African City and the European Geographical Imagination', in Thomas Moeller Kristensen et al., *City and Nature: Changing Relations in Time and Space* (Odense, n.d.).

Chapter 7. Colonial Culture in France

1. See the examples of colonial curios in Eric and Gabrielle Deroo and Marie-Cécile de Taillac, *Aux Colonies: où l'on découvre les vestiges d'un empire englouti* (Paris, 1992).

2. Edward W. Said, *Culture and Imperialism* (London, 1993).
3. Irène Frain, 'Le "look" exotique', *L'Histoire*, No. 69 (1984), 30–3.
4. Paul Webster, *Antoine de Saint-Exupéry: The Life and Death of the Little Prince* (London, 1993).
5. See Alain Busine, Norbert Dodille and Claude Duchet (eds), *L'Exotisme* (Paris, 1988).
6. Martine Astier Loutfi, *Littérature et colonialisme: l'expansion coloniale vue dans la littérature romanesque française, 1871–1914* (Paris, 1971), is an excellent analysis.
7. See Francis Steegmuller (ed.), *Flaubert in Egypt* (Chicago, 1979).
8. A useful collection is Guy de Maupassant, *Ecrits sur le Maghreb* (Paris, 1991).
9. See Lesley Blanch, *Pierre Loti: Portrait of an Escapist* (London, 1983).
10. René Maran, *Batouala* (Paris, 1921); trs Barbara Beck and Alexandre Mboukou (London, 1973).
11. Jean Lacouture, *André Malraux*, trs Alan Sheridan (London, 1975).
12. On the last, one of the most important women travel writers in the French empire, see Monique Vérité, *Odette de Puigaudeau: une Bretonne au désert* (Paris, 1992).
13. P. Dareste, *Traité de droit colonial* (Paris, 1931).
14. Lewis Pyenson, *Civilizing Mission: Exact Sciences and French Overseas Expansion, 1830–1940* (Baltimore, MD, 1993).
15. Jean Guiart, 'The Musée de l'Homme, the Arts, and Africa', in Susan Vogel and Francine N'Diaye, *African Masterpieces from the Musée de l'Homme* (New York, 1985).
16. Christophe Bonneuil, *Des Savants pour l'empire: la structuration des recherches scientifiques coloniales au temps de 'la mise en valeur des colonies francaises', 1917–1945* (Paris, 1991).
17. See P. Lucas and J.-C. Vatin, *L'Algérie des anthropologues* (Paris, 1982).
18. See James Clifford, *Person and Myth: Maurice Leenhardt in the Melanesian World* (Berkeley, 1982).
19. Marc Sandoz, *Théodore Chassériau, 1819–1850: catalogue raisonné des peintures et dessins* (Paris, 1974).
20. Kirk Varnedoe, 'Gauguin', in William Rubin, *'Primitivism' in Twentieth Century Art: Affinity of the Tribal and the Modern*, Vol. 1 (New York, 1984).
21. John Cowart et al., *Matisse in Morocco* (Washington, DC, 1990).

22. William Rubin, 'Picasso', in Rubin, ibid., Vol. 1, pp. 241–343.

23. Gérard G. Le Coat, '*Art Nègre* and *Esprit Moderne* in France (1907–1911)', in G. Wesley Johnson (ed.), *Double Impact: France and Africa in the Age of Imperialism* (Westport, CT, 1985).

24. A pioneering work on colonial photography is Raoul Girardet, *Le Temps des colonies* (Paris, 1979).

25. Charles Daney, *Indochine* (Paris, 1992); among other albums, see Guillaume Zuili, *Pondichéry, Chandernagor, Karikal, Mahé, Yanaon: les anciens comptoirs français de l'Inde* (Paris, 1993).

26. See Charles-Henri Favrod, *Etranges Etrangers: photographie et exotisme, 1850/1910* (Paris, 1989).

27. Malek Alloula, *The Colonial Harem*, trs Myrna Godzich and Wlad Goszich (Manchester, 1986).

28. Bibliothèque Forney, *Négripub: l'image des Noirs dans la publicité depuis un siècle* (Paris, 1987).

29. See Pascal Blanchard and Armelle Chatelier (eds), *Images et colonies* (Paris, 1993), and Jacques Marseille, *L'Age d'or de la France coloniale* (Paris, 1986).

30. Stephen Henningham, '"The Best Specimens in All Our Colonial Domain": New Caledonian Melanesians in Europe, 1931–32', *Journal of Pacific History*, 29:2 (1994), 173–87.

31. Catherine Hodeir and Michel Pierre, *L'Exposition coloniale* (Paris, 1991); A. Demaison, *Guide officiel de l'Exposition coloniale internationale* (Paris, 1931).

Chapter 8. Colonial Nationalism and Decolonisation

1. The most recent full-length studies are Charles-Robert Ageron, *La Décolonisation française* (Paris, 1991), Raymond F. Betts, *France and Decolonisation, 1900–1960* (London, 1991), and Anthony Clayton, *The Wars of French Decolonization* (London, 1994).

2. Quoted in Ageron, *La Décolonisation*, p. 28.

3. See Jean Lacouture, *Ho Chi Minh* (Paris, 1967).

4. Quoted in Ageron, *La Décolonisation*, p. 30.

5. See Stein Tønnesson, *1946: Déclenchement de la guerre d'Indochine* (Paris, 1987), and *The Vietnamese Revolution of 1945: Roosevelt, Ho Chi Minh and de Gaulle in a World at War* (Oslo, 1991). See also Martin Shipway, 'Creating an Emergency: Metropolitan Constraints on French Colonial Policy and its Breakdown in Indo-China, 1945–47', *Journal of Imperial and Commonwealth History*, 21:3 (1993), 1–16.

6. Jacques Tronchon, *L'Insurrection malgache de 1947: essai d'interprétation historique* (Paris, 1986).

7. On the Indochinese war, see Jacques Dalloz, *La Guerre d'Indochine, 1945–1954* (Paris, 1987), Alain Ruscio, *La Guerre française d'Indochine* (Paris, 1992), and Jacques Valette, *La Guerre d'Indochine, 1945–1954* (Paris, 1994).

8. There is a controversy over whether the war began with the French action in Haiphong in November or the Viet Minh move in Hanoi in December – a choice of one or the other events also assigns blame for the start of the conflict.

9. The most recent balanced overview in French is Benjamin Stora, *Histoire de la guerre d'Algérie (1954–1962)* (Paris, 1993); the most thorough in English is Alistair Horne, *A Savage War of Peace: Algeria, 1954–1962* (London, 1977). A useful collection of contemporary articles from *Le Monde* is Patrick Eveno and Jean Planchais (eds), *La Guerre d'Algérie* (Paris, 1990).

10. Paul Clay Sorum, *Intellectuals and Decolonization in France* (Chapel Hill, NC, 1977).

11. See Rita Maran, *Torture: The Role of Ideology in the French-Algerian War* (New York, 1989).

12. See Prosser Gifford and William Roger Louis, *The Transfer of Power in Africa: Decolonization, 1940–1960* (New Haven, CT, 1982); Dorothy S. White, *Black Africa and de Gaulle: From the French Empire to Independence* (University Park, MD, 1979).

13. There are no specific works on decolonisation of the Comoros and Djibouti; the most extensive study of the Santo affair and Vanuatu is John Beasant, *The Santo Rebellion: An Imperial Reckoning* (London, 1984).

Epilogue: After the Empire

1. Robert Aldrich and John Connell, *France's Overseas Frontier: Départements et Territoires d'Outre-Mer* (Cambridge, 1992).

2. Robert Aldrich, *France and the South Pacific since 1940* (London, 1993).

3. Joëlle Hureau, *La Mémoire des pieds-noirs* (Paris, 1987).

4. Michel Roux, *Les Harkis: les oubliés de l'histoire, 1954–1991* (Paris, 1991).

5. Alain Anselin, *L'Emigration antillaise en France: la troisième île* (Paris, 1990).

6. Pierre George, *L'Immigration en France: faits et problèmes* (Paris, 1986); Gérard Noiriel, *Le Creuset français: histoire de l'immigration, XIXe–XXe siècles* (Paris, 1988).
7. See the chapters on migrant workers and international relations, France and Africa, France and the Third World, and Francophonie in Robert Aldrich and John Connell (eds), *France in World Politics* (London, 1989).

Bibliographical Essay

The number of books on the history of French colonialism would fill a small library. The following list concentrates on works published in the last two decades – although many older works are still well worth reading – and highlights volumes in English.

The only other recent general history in English is Raymond Betts, *Tricouleur: The French Overseas Empire* (London, 1978). (Mort Rosenblum, *Mission to Civilize: The French Way* (New York, 1986), is a journalist's lively account.) In French, there have been various works. An important overview and interpretation is a collaborative work of three historians: Jean Bouvier and René Girault (eds), *L'Impérialisme français d'avant 1914* (Paris, 1976), Jacques Thobie, Jean Bouvier and René Girault, *La France impériale, 1880–1914* (Paris, 1982), and Jean Bouvier, René Girault and Jacques Thobie, *L'Impérialisme à la française, 1914–1960* (Paris, 1986). A thorough two-volume history published by Armand Colin is Jean Meyer, Jean Tarrade, Annie Rey-Goldzeiguer and Jacques Thobie, *Histoire de la France coloniale: des origines à 1914* (Paris, 1991), and Jacques Thobie, Gilbert Meynier, Catherine Coquery-Vidrovitch and Charles-Robert Ageron, *Histoire de la France coloniale, 1914–1990* (Paris, 1990). Another two-volume set, published by Fayard, is Pierre Pluchon, *L'Histoire de la colonisation française*, Vol. I, *Le Premier empire colonial: des origines à la Restauration* (Paris, 1991), and Denise Bouche, Vol. II, *Flux et reflux (1815–1962)* (Paris, 1991). Still lengthier, and aimed at a more general public, is a five-volume series published by Denoël: Jean Martin, *L'Empire renaissant, 1789/1871* (Paris, 1987); Gilbert Comte, *L'Empire triomphant, 1871/1936: 1. Afrique occidentale et équatoriale* (Paris, 1988); Jean Martin, *L'Empire triomphant, 1871/1936: 2. Maghreb, Indochine, Madagascar,*

Iles et Comptoirs (Paris, 1990); Paul-Marie de la Gorce, *L'Empire écartelé, 1936/1946* (Paris, 1987); and Jean Planchais, *L'Empire embrasé, 1946/1962* (Paris, 1990). More concise general studies are Jacques Binoche-Guedra, *La France d'outre-mer, 1815–1962* (Paris, 1992); Robert and Marianne Cornevin, *La France et les Français outre-mer* (Paris, 1990); and Guy Pervillé, *De l'Empire français à la décolonisation* (Paris, 1991). Briefer still, although older, is Xavier Yacono, *Histoire de la colonisation française* (Paris, 1973).

An essential and excellent reference is Jean Martin, *Lexique de la colonisation française* (Paris, 1988). The quarterly *Revue française d'histoire d'outre-mer* provides scholarly articles and reviews. See also *Ultramarines*, the semi-annual publication of the Archives d' Outre-Mer and the Institut d'Histoire des Pays d'Outre-Mer. Specialised journals such as the *Journal of African History* and the *Cahiers d'études africaines* also contain articles. Bibliographies include John P. Halstead and Serafino Porcari, *Modern European Imperialism: A Bibliography of Books and Articles, 1815–1972*, Vol. 2: *French and Other Empires, Regions* (Boston, 1974), and the relevant sections of the annual *Bibliographie de l'histoire de France*.

Many works written in the era of expansion are irreplaceable testimonies, though they may now seem quaint or offensive. Lucien Prévost-Paradol, *La France nouvelle* (Paris, 1869) and Paul Leroy-Beaulieu, *De la Colonisation chez les peuples modernes* (Paris, 1874), were early arguments about the need for expansion. Albert Sarraut, *La Mise en valeur des colonies françaises* (Paris, 1923), outlined projects for development. Gabriel Hanotaux and Alfred Martineau (eds), *Histoire des colonies françaises* (Paris, 1929–1934) was a six-volume compendium. Louis Archimbaud, *La Plus Grande France* (Paris, 1928) was one of countless general books. Memoirs, letters and reports of such important veterans of empire as Gallieni, Lyautey, Auguste Pavie and Francis Garnier were published; among the most interesting is Pierre Savorgnan de Brazza, *Au Coeur de l'Afrique* (Paris, 1992), originally published in the 1880s.

Older English-language books are filled with interesting, although now dated, information and insights. Stephen H. Roberts, *History of French Colonial Policy, 1870–1925* (2 vols, London, 1929) was a very thorough work; Constant Southworth, *The French Colonial Venture* (London, 1931), a briefer account. Several books by Virginia Thompson and Richard Adloff – such as *French West Africa* and *The French Pacific Islands* (1971) – were comprehensive accounts.

On the French in North America, a very readable overview is

Philip Boucher, *Les Nouvelles Frances: France in America, 1500–1815: An Imperial Perspective* (Providence, RI, 1989). Lucien-René Abenon and John A. Dickinson, *Les Français en Amérique* (Lyon, 1993) covers both North America and the Caribbean.

There are many fine studies of individual colonies. On Algeria, see the works of Charles-Robert Ageron, including *Modern Algeria: A History from 1830 to the Present* (London, 1991); John Ruedy, *Modern Algeria: The Origins and Development of a Nation* (Bloomington, IN, 1992); and Benjamin Stora, *Histoire de l'Algérie coloniale, 1830–1954* (Paris, 1991). A study of the early years of French involvement is Antony Thrall Sullivan, *Thomas-Robert Bugeaud – France and Algeria, 1784–1849: Politics, Power, and the Good Society* (Hamden, CT, 1983). The best survey of Morocco is still Charles-André Julien, *Le Maroc face aux impérialismes, 1415–1956* (Paris, 1978). On Tunisia, Jean-François Martin, *Histoire de la Tunisie contemporaine: de Ferry à Bourguiba, 1881–1956* (Paris, 1993), is a comprehensive volume.

On sub-Saharan Africa, a fine introduction is Patrick Manning, *Francophone Sub-Saharan Africa, 1880–1985* (Cambridge, 1988), as is François Biarnès, *Les Français en Afrique noire de Richelieu à Mitterrand* (Paris, 1987). The most important recent French collection is Catherine Coquery-Vidrovitch (ed. with Odile Goerg), *L'Afrique occidentale au temps des Français: colonisateurs et colonisés, c. 1860–1960* (Paris, 1992). Studies of particular regions abound; among the most useful are Christian Roche, *Histoire de la Casamance* (Paris, 1985), Odile Goerg, *Commerce et colonisation en Guinée (1850–1913)* (Paris, 1986); Finn Fuglestad, *A History of Niger, 1850–1960* (Cambridge, 1983); Francis de Chassey, *Mauritanie, 1900–1975* (Paris, 1984).

Many studies focus on exploration and conquest in Africa, such as A.S. Kanya-Forstner, *The Conquest of the Western Sudan: A Study in French Military Imperialism* (Cambridge, 1969); Pierre Gentil, *La Conquête du Tchad (1894–1916)* (Paris, 2 vols, 1970); and Daniel Grevoz, *Les Canonnières de Tombouctou: les Français à la conquête de la cité mythique, 1870–1894* (Paris, 1992). On the desert, see Douglas Porch, *The Conquest of the Sahara* (London, 1984), and Jean-Marc Durou, *L'Exploration du Sahara* (Paris, 1993). See also David Levering Lewis, *The Race to Fashoda: European Colonialism and African Resistance in the Scramble for Africa* (London, 1988).

The horn of Africa and the Red Sea have been well served: Roger Joint Daguenet, *Aux Origines de l'implantation française en*

Mer Rouge: vie et mort d'Henri Lambert, consul de France à Aden, 1859 (Paris, 1992), and Philippe Oberlé and Pierre Hugot, *Histoire de Djibouti: des origines à la République* (Paris, 1985).

A good survey of the Indian Ocean is Kenneth McPherson, *The Indian Ocean: A History of People and the Sea* (Delhi, 1993). An exhaustive study of the Comoros is Jean Martin, *Comores: quatre îles entre pirates et planteurs* (Paris, 2 vols, 1983). On Madagascar, see Hubert Deschamps, *Histoire de Madagascar* (Paris, 1965).

On the French in Asia, Milton E. Osborne, *The French Presence in Cochinchina and Cambodia: Rule and Response (1859–1905)* (London, 1969), is still a good starting-point; John F. Cady, *The Roots of French Imperialism in Eastern Asia* (Ithaca, NY, 1954, 1967) retains much value. A superb recent overview is Pierre Brocheux and Daniel Hémery, *Indochine: la colonisation ambiguë, 1858–1954* (Paris, 1995).

On the Middle East, the most thorough English-language study is Philip S. Khoury, *Syria and the French Mandate: The Politics of Arab Nationalism, 1920–1945* (Princeton, NJ, 1987).

On the territories which make up the DOM-TOMs, see Robert Aldrich and John Connell, *France's Overseas Frontier: Départements et Territoires d'Outre-Mer* (Cambridge, 1992). Three works by Alain-Philippe Blérald investigate different aspects of West Indian life: *Négritude et politique aux Antilles* (Paris, 1981), *Histoire économique de la Guadeloupe et de la Martinique du XVIIe siècle à nos jours* (Paris, 1986), and *La Question nationale en Guadeloupe et en Martinique* (Paris, 1988). On Guyane, see Serge Mam-Lam-Fouck, *Histoire de la société guyanaise: Les Années cruciales, 1848–1946* (Paris, 1987), and Alexander Miles, *Devil's Island: Colony of the Damned* (Berkeley, CA, 1988); on Réunion, Marcel Leguen, *Histoire de l'Ile de la Réunion* (Paris, 1979). On Oceania, see Robert Aldrich, *The French Presence in the South Pacific, 1842–1940* (London, 1990) and *France and the South Pacific since 1940* (London, 1993). On the EFO, see also Colin Newbury, *Tahiti Nui: Change and Survival in French Polynesia, 1767–1945* (Honolulu, 1980), and Pierre-Yves Toullelan, *Tahiti colonial (1860–1914)* (Paris, 1984); on New Caledonia, John Connell, *From New Caledonia to Kanaky? The Political History of a French Colony* (Canberra, 1987). Two other outposts are covered by Charles Guyotjeannin, *Saint-Pierre et Miquelon* (Paris, 1986), and Jean-Paul Kauffmann, *L'Arche des Kerguelen* (Paris, 1993).

The activities of France outside the formal empire have inspired several case studies, such as Robert Lee, *France and the Exploita-*

tion of China, 1885–1901 (Oxford, 1989); Jacques Thobie, *Intérêts et impérialisme français dans l'Empire ottoman, 1890–1914* (Paris, 1977); and René Girault, *Emprunts russes et intérêts français en Russie, 1887–1914* (Paris, 1973).

Different periods have attracted detailed historical treatment. On the Revolution of 1789, see Yves Benot's works on *La Révolution française et la fin des colonies* (Paris, 1987), and Jean-Pierre Biondi and François Zuccarelli, *16 Pluviôse An II: les colonies de la Révolution* (Paris, 1989). On the Napoleonic period, see Yves Benot, *La Démence coloniale sous Napoléon* (Paris, 1991), and, on the campaign in Egypt, Jean-Joël Brégeon, *L'Egypte française au jour le jour, 1798–1801* (Paris, 1991). On the period after 1870, see J. Ganiage, *L'Expansion coloniale de la France sous la Troisième République* (Paris, 1968); James J. Cooke, *New French Imperialism, 1880–1910: The Third Republic and Colonial Expansion* (Newton Abbot, 1971); and C.M. Andrew and A.S. Kanya-Forstner, *France Overseas: The First World War and the Climax of French Imperial Expansion* (London, 1981).

On colonial theory and policy, Henri Brunschwig, *The Myth of French Imperialism* (London, 1961), provides a magisterial interpretation and pointed the way for much later research. Raoul Girardet, *L'Idée coloniale en France* (Paris, 1972), gives an excellent synopsis, while Charles-Robert Ageron, *France coloniale ou parti colonial?* (Paris, 1978), examines the place of colonialism in French political life. In English, there is Agnes Murphy's *The Ideology of French Imperialism, 1871–1891* (New York, 1968). Raymond Betts, *Assimilation and Association in French Colonial Theory, 1890–1914* (New York, 1961), looks at the key theories behind colonial administration. On the colonial lobby, two complementary studies are Stuart Michael Persell, *The French Colonial Lobby, 1889–1938* (Stanford, CA, 1983), and Marc Lagana, *Le Parti colonial français: éléments d'histoire* (Sillery, Québec, 1990). See also Dominique Lejeune, *Les Sociétés de géographie en France et l'expansion coloniale au XIXe siècle* (Paris, 1993). On anti-colonialism, see Charles-Robert Ageron, *L'Anticolonialisme en France de 1871 à 1914* (Paris, 1973), Jean-Pierre Biondi with Gilles Morin, *Les Anticolonialistes (1881–1962)* (Paris, 1992), and Jean Lacouture and Dominique Chagnollaud, *Le Désempire* (Paris, 1993).

On attitudes to non-Europeans, see William B. Cohen, *The French Encounter with Africans: White Response to Blacks, 1530–1880* (London, 1980); William H. Schneider, *An Empire for the Masses: The French Popular Image of Africa, 1870–1900* (London, 1982); Abdelkebir

Khatibi, *Figures de l'étranger dans la littérature française* (Paris, 1987); Pierre Guiral and Emile Temime, *L'Idée de race dans la pensée politique française contemporaine* (Paris, 1977); and Léon-François Hoffmann, *Le Nègre romantique: personnage littéraire et obsession collective* (Paris, 1973).

There are various monographs on the French overseas. See, for example, David Prochaska, *Making Algeria French: Colonialism in Bône, 1870–1920* (Cambridge, 1990); Alain Lardillier, *Le Peuplement français en Algérie de 1830 à 1900* (Versailles, 1992); and Marc Baroli, *Algérie, terre d'espérances: colons et immigrants (1830–1914)* (Paris, 1992); Yvonne Knibiehler, Geneviève Emmery and Françoise Leguay, *Des Français au Maroc* (Paris, 1992); and Rita Cruise O'Brien, *White Society in Black Africa: The French of Senegal* (London, 1972). On Indochina, see Charles Meyer, *La Vie Quotidienne des Français en Indochine, 1860–1910* (Paris, 1985), and Philippe Franchini, *Saigon, 1925–1945: de la 'Belle Colonie' à l'éclosion révolutionnaire, ou la fin des blancs* (Paris, 1992). On women, see Yvonne Knibiehler and Régine Goutalier, *La Femme au temps des colonies* (Paris, 1985), and France Renucci, *Souvenirs de femmes au temps des colonies* (Paris, 1988). A still fascinating study of one of the most intriguing women in the colonies is Cecily Mackworth, *The Destiny of Isabelle Eberhardt* (London, 1951, 1977). There are countless memoirs of decidedly varying quality of men and women who lived overseas. One moving autobiographical novel is a posthumous and unfinished work of Albert Camus, *Le Premier homme* (Paris, 1994). Among other insightful recollections are Olivier Colombani, *Mémoires coloniales: la fin de l'Empire français d'Afrique vue par les administrateurs coloniaux* (Paris, 1991); Roger Curel, *Eloge de la colonie* (Paris, 1992); and Guy Georgy, *Le Petit soldat de l'Empire* (Paris, 1992).

On missionaries, a general study of Africa is André Picciola, *Missionaires en Afrique, 1840–1940* (Paris, 1987), and a biography of the most significant bishop is J. Dean O' Donnell, Jr, *Lavigerie in Tunisia: The Interplay of Imperialist and Missionary* (Athens, GA, 1979). On evangelists in Indochina, see Patrick J.N. Turck, *French Catholic Missionaries and the Politics of Imperialism in Vietnam, 1857–1914: A Documentary Survey* (Liverpool, 1987).

On the military, Douglas Porch, *The French Foreign Legion: A Complete History of the Legendary Fighting Force* (New York, 1991), provides a detailed but riveting history of the Legionnaires. On the navy, see Jean-Pierre Gomane, *Les Marins et l'outre-mer* (Paris, 1988). A readable biography of the most famous conqueror is

André Le Révérend, *Lyautey* (Paris, 1983). On administrators, the standard study is William B. Cohen, *Rulers of Empire: The French Colonial Service in Africa* (Stanford, CA, 1971); see, too, several chapters in L.H. Gann and Peter Duignan (eds), *African Proconsuls: European Governors in Africa* (New York, 1978).

On economics and empire, the major study is Jacques Marseille, *Empire colonial et capitalisme français: histoire d'un divorce* (Paris, 1984). There are relatively few business histories of colonial companies, but two particularly good ones are: Marc Meuleau, *Des Pionniers en Extrême-Orient: histoire de la Banque de l'Indochine, 1875–1975* (Paris, 1990), and Hubert Bonin, *CFAO: cent ans de compétition* (Paris, 1987). Among studies of particular colonies, see Catherine Coquery-Vidrovitch, *Le Congo au temps des grandes compagnies concessionnaires, 1898–1940* (Paris, 1972), and Martin J. Murray, *The Development of Capitalism: Colonial Cochinchina (1870–1940)* (Berkeley, CA, 1980).

Studies on the impact of France on the colonies are numerous; some, as well, examine the impact of the colonies on France. Fine examples of such research are G. Wesley Johnson (ed.), *Double Impact: France and Africa in the Age of Imperialism* (Westport, CT, 1985), and Gwendolyn Wright, *The Politics of Design in French Colonial Urbanism* (Chicago, 1991). On Indochina, there is Ngô Viñh Long, *Before the Revolution: The Vietnamese Peasants under the French* (New York, 1991). Works on the insurrections in New Caledonia and Syria are: Roselène Dousset-Leenhardt, *Colonialisme et contradictions: Nouvelle-Calédonie, 1878–1978* (Paris, 1984), and Lenka Bokova, *La Confrontation franco-syrienne à l'époque du mandat, 1925–1927* (Paris, 1990). On African troops, Myron Echenberg, *Colonial Conscripts: The Tirailleurs Sénégalais in French West Africa, 1857–1960* (London, 1991) is an excellent study, and Henri Brunschwig, *Noirs et blancs dans l'Afrique noire française* (Paris, 1983), examines other professions.

Reading on colonial culture can start with the various authors – novelists, essayists, reporters – who wrote about the empire. The relevant writings of several are available in collections, such as Albert Londres, *Oeuvres complètes* (Paris, 1992), and Guy de Maupassant, *Ecrits sur le Maghreb* (Paris, 1991). The more important novels – Alphone Daudet's *Tartarin de Tarascon*, Pierre Loti's *Le Mariage de Loti* and *Le Roman d'un spahi*, René Maran's *Batouala*, Louis-Ferdinand Céline's *Voyage au bout de la nuit*, André Malraux's *La Condition humaine*, Albert Camus' *L'Etranger* and *La Peste* – are available in various editions; the same is unfortunately not true of many others. In addition, there are biographies of many of the major writers. An authoritative analysis is Martine Astier Loutfi, *Littérature et colonialisme: l'expansion coloniale vue dans la littérature romanesque française, 1871–1914* (Paris, 1971). A perceptive general study is Edward W. Said, *Culture and Imperialism* (London, 1993).

A good starting point on the 1931 colonial fair is Catherine Hodeir and Michel Pierre, *L'Exposition coloniale* (Paris, 1991). On colonial research, there is Christophe Bonneuil, *Des Savants pour l'empire: la structuration des recherches scientifiques coloniales au temps de 'la mise en valeur des colonies françaises', 1917–1945* (Paris, 1991); Lewis Pyenson, *Civilizing Mission: Exact Sciences and French Overseas Expansion, 1830–1940* (Baltimore, 1993); and P. Lucas and J.C. Vatin, *L'Algérie des anthropologues* (Paris, 1982).

On the iconography of colonialism, see Raoul Girardet, *Le Temps des colonies* (Paris, 1979); Jacques Marseille, *L'Age d'or de la France coloniale* (Paris, 1986); and Pascal Blanchard and Armelle Chatelier (eds), *Images et colonies* (Paris, 1993). Among albums are Eric and Gabrielle Deroo and Marie-Cécile de Taillac, *Aux Colonies* (Paris, 1992), and Charles Daney, *Indochine* (Paris, 1992).

On decolonisation, recent general studies are Raymond F. Betts, *France and Decolonisation, 1900–1960* (London, 1991); Charles-Robert Ageron, *La Décolonisation française* (Paris, 1991); and Anthony Clayton, *The Wars of French Decolonization* (London, 1994). Miles Kahler, *Decolonization in Britain and France: The Domestic Consequences of International Relations* (Princeton, NJ, 1984), provides a comparative perspective. Paul Clay Sorum, *Intellectuals and Decolonization in France* (Chapel Hill, NC, 1977), looks at a specific issue. A useful collection is Charles-Robert Ageron (ed.), *Chemins de la décolonisation de l'empire colonial français* (Paris, 1986). On Indochina, see Jacques Dalloz, *La Guerre d'Indochine, 1945–1954* (Paris, 1987), and Alain Ruscio, *La Guerre française d'Indochine* (Paris, 1992). Of the large number of writings on the Algerian war, the most succinct recent account is Benjamin Stora, *Histoire de la guerre d'Algérie (1954–1962)* (Paris, 1993); in English, the most thorough is Alistair Horne, *A Savage War of Peace: Algeria, 1954–1962* (London, 1977). On sub-Saharan Africa, see Dorothy S. White, *Black Africa and de Gaulle: From the French Empire to Independence* (University Park, MD, 1979), and Prosser Gifford and William Roger Louis, *The Transfer of Power in Africa: Decolonization, 1940–1960* (New Haven, CT, 1982). A fascinating study of the New Hebrides is John Beasant, *The Santo Rebellion: An Imperial Reckoning* (London, 1984).

On France's links with its former colonies, several of the articles in Robert Aldrich and John Connell (eds), *France in World Politics* (London, 1989), provide a point of departure. Pierre George, *L'Immigration en France* (Paris, 1986), is an introduction to this issue, while Gérard Noiriel, *Le Creuset français: histoire de l'immigration, XIXe–XXe siècles* (Paris, 1988), is a study of immigration policy.

Index

Abbas, Ferhat 281
Abdallah, Ahmed 304
Abdelaziz 32, 34, 35, 204
Abd el-Khader 27, 31, 94, 204,
    215, 267
Abd el-Krim 117, 134, 136, 205,
    269
Abidjan 122, 232, 300
Abyssinia 59; see also Ethiopia
Académie Française 241, 242
Acadia 11
Adam, Paul 242–3
Adélie Land see Terre Adélie
Aden 57
administration 108–10, 308
administrators 149–54
advertising 259–60, 264
AEF (Afrique Equatoriale
    Française) see French
    Equatorial Africa
Africa 15–16, 320–3; emigration
    from 315–19; Africans 202–3;
    in literature 240–1
African Democratic Rally see
    RDA
Agence de Co-opération Culturelle et
    Technique (ACCT) 322
agriculture 165–7 passim 196,
    216, 230, 231; in the
    AEF 193–5 passim;
    Antilles 13–14; Indian
    Ocean 15–16, 61, 64, 66, 135,
    284; Indochina 181, 188–92
    passim 190; Morocco 171,
    177–9; West Africa 22–3, 38,
    49, 50, 186
aid 320
Aïn Sefra 158
Al-Atrash, Selim 209
Al-Atrash, Sultân 209, 210

Alawites 210
Algeciras Treaty 33–4
Algeria 87, 129, 152, 158, 173,
    266, 267, 323;
    administration 215; art 252,
    257; borders 294; at Colonial
    Exhibition 262–3; colonial
    policy 93–4, 109, 215;
    conquest of 24–8; economic
    policy 169–70;
    education 226;
    emigration 311–14, 315, 316;
    exports 165; Foreign
    Legion 133–4 passim;
    land 217–8; literature 237,
    238–9, 242, 245; Lyautey
    in 134–6 passim;
    independence of 296–7; law
    in 213–14; and Morocco 31,
    32; nationalism 119, 269–70;
    292–3; nuclear testing 231;
    railways 173–5 passim;
    relations with France 319–20;
    science 247, 248;
    settlement 109, 122, 123, 139,
    140–6; sport in 160;
    suffrage 119; trade 196–8
    passim; and Tunisia 30;
    war 204, 292–8; women
    in 154
Algiers 115, 152; Battle of 294;
    Camus 140–1; conquest
    of 26; culture 159, 232;
    education 155, 225, 230, 246,
    248; Free French
    government 276, 280;
    health 144, 155, 156
ALN (Armée de libération nationale)
    see National Liberation Army
Along Bay 257

Alsace 97, 100
Amsterdam Island 84
Andrianampoinimerina 61
Angkor Wat 78, 235; at Colonial
  Exhibition 262, 264
Anjouan 66
Ankazobe 135
Annaba 142; see also Bône
Annam 270; education 226;
  land 216, 219; military 148;
  missionaries 73–4, 148;
  occupation of 76, 80, 81, 87;
  rubber 190; trade 74;
  war 278–80 passim 285, 286;
  see also Indochina
Antananarivo 60, 62, 116, 225,
  232
Antarctica 84; see also Terre
  Adélie
anthropology 151, 247
anti-colonialism 111–14, 116–19,
  205; 227, 250, 267–8; and
  Colonial Exhibition 265; in
  former colonies 319–20; in
  France 283, 291, 305; in
  literature 5, 235, 243–4, 245,
  267, 297–8
Antilles 13–14, 158, 161; in
  literature 245
AOF (Afrique occidentale Française)
  see French West Africa
Apithy, Sourou-Migan 281, 299
Apollinaire, Guillaume 243, 255
Arab League 290, 293
Aragon, Louis 265
Araucania 332
Archinard, Governor 44
architecture 232–3
archives 2–3, 7
Arenberg, Prince d' 102
Argenlieu, Thierry d' 279, 287
arms trade 59
army 132–3, 137
art 243, 247, 250–6; see also
  cinema, literature, photography
assimilation 93, 110, 137, 270
Assinie 41
associated states 281, 282, 288,
  302

associated territories 281, 282,
  300
association 110, 116
astronomy 247
Atai 208, 267
Ataturk, Kemal 268
Atlas Mountains 178
Aurora University 247
Austral Islands 70
Australia 69, 95, 96, 274, 275
aviation 115–16, 236, 246

Bab el-Mandeb 57
Baker, Josephine 256
Bamako 43–5 passim, 116, 174,
  299
bananas 321
Banania 259
Bandung Conference 293
Bangkok 82, 181
Bangui 55
banking 179–83
Banque de l'Indochine 179–83,
  188, 264, 271, 287
Banque Française de l'Asie see
  Banque de l'Indochine
Bao Daï 278, 279, 285, 287, 288
Barbusse, Henri 118
Bardo Treaty 30, 290
Basilan 75
Bassas da India 84
Bastion de France 24, 25
Bataillon d'Afrique 133
Batavia 73
Batouala 243–4
Battambang 80, 181
Baudelaire, Charles 245
bauxite 166
Beauvoir, Simone de 297
Béhaine, Bishop Pigneau de 74
Béhanzin 40, 134, 204, 215, 267
Beirut 116, 208, 209, 248
Bekaa Valley 209
békés 14
Belgian Congo 50, 54, 55, 176,
  263
Belgium 193, 263, 322, 323
Bell, Prince Douala Manga 281
Ben Bâdîs, 'Abdelhamîd 270

Ben Bella, Ahmed 294
Ben Jelloun, Tahar 325
Benin see Dahomey
Berbers 106, 142, 143
Berlin Conference of 1878 29;
   of 1882 54; of 1884–85 85
Bertagna, Jérôme 143
Bertrand, Louis 242
Bertrand-Bocandé,
   Emmanuel 37
Beurs 319
Binger, Louis-Gustave 41, 42
Biskra 126
Bizerte 319
Blum, Léon 115, 118, 265
Bohn, Frédéric 183, 185
Boissière, Henri and René 85
Boiteux, Commander 44–6
Bonaparte, Jérôme 58, 94
Bonaparte, Napoléon see
   Napoleon
Bonard, Admiral 79
Bône 26, 28, 142–3, 144
Bonnier, Eugene 44–6
Bora-Bora 275
Bordeaux 170
Bouèt-Willaumez,
   Commander 40, 41, 51
Bourbon, Ile 15–16; see also
   Réunion
Bourguiba, Habib 269, 277, 289,
   290, 293
Brazza, Pierre Savorgnan de
   51–5, 104
Brazzaville 51, 116, 175, 226,
   232; conference 280, 301
breadfruit 230
Breton, André 265
British, and Aden 57; Asia 73,
   79, 82, 83; Central Africa 54,
   193, 194; China 73, 77, 83,
   181; Colonial Exhibition 263;
   colonial policy 95; East
   Africa 59; Indian Ocean
   61–6 passim; Indochina 279;
   Madagascar 276, 284; Middle
   East 83; New Hebrides 72;
   North Africa 25, 28–33 passim,
   59; Pacific 69, 70; trade 185;

West Africa 38, 42–3, 46,
   49–50
Buddhism 78, 130
Bugeaud, General 27, 31, 93
Burkina Faso see Upper Volta
Burma 82

Cabinda 54
Caillié, René 43, 103, 124–5;
   rue 324
California 178
Cambodia 77, 87, 188; at
   Colonial Exhibition 262, 264;
   education 82;
   immigrants 317; law 213;
   occupation of 78–80;
   rubber 190; settlers 148;
   trade 76; war 277–9 passim,
   288
Cambon, Paul 30
Cameroon 49; associated
   territory 281; at Colonial
   Exhibition 263;
   education 226;
   emigration 317; and
   Germany 54;
   independence 303; mandated
   territory 86, 267;
   rebellion 300–1
Camus, Albert 140, 245–7 passim
Canada 11–13, 322
canals 190–1, 231
Canton see Guangzhou
cantonnement 218, 219
Cao Bang 287
capitation 220, 223
Carbillet, Gabriel 209–10
cargo cults 275
Caribbean 13–14; see also
   Antilles
Carthage 129, 237, 290
Cartier, Raymond 283
Casablanca 34, 115, 233, 291
Casamance 36–8
Catroux, General 276
Cayenne 155
Cayor region 38
Céline, Louis–Ferdinand 245
cement 191

Cendras, Blaise 243
Central African Republic 303,
  322; see also Oubangui-Chari
Césaire, Aimé 245, 281, 298
Ceylon 329
CFA franc 321
Chad 50, 55–7, economic
  policy 192;
  independence 88, 303;
  military intervention 322;
  trade 321
Chad, Lake 46, 47, 55–6
Chagos Islands 329
Chamoiseau, Patrick 325
Chandernagore 17, 23, 289
Charles X 26, 93
Charonne, Métro 297, 324
Chasseloup-Laubat, Prosper 104,
  131
Chassériau, Théodore 252
Châteaubriand, François-René
  de 236–7
Cheik-Said 331
China, anti-colonialism 268, 282;
  decolonisation 289; trade
  73–83 passim, 179, 181, 182,
  189; war 277, 286, 287, 279,
  280
Chinese Communist Party 83
cholera 144
chotts, in Tunisia 173
Christians, in Lebanon 209
chromium 321
church, opposition to
  colonialism 118; and
  employment 222; see also
  missionaries
Chusan Island 75
cinema 258–9, 325
citizenship 212–15, 281, 289,
  311–12, 318
citrus fruit 178–9
civil service 108–9, 220, 222–3,
  309, 315; see also administration
Clemenceau, Georges 112
Clipperton Island 72, 164
cloth see textiles
coal 190
Cochinchina 73;

education 226; land 219;
  law 213; missionaries 148;
  occupation of 77, 78, 80, 81,
  87; rubber 190; settlers 148;
  trade 179; war 279, 280, 285,
  287; see also Indochina
cocoa 165, 194, 321
cod 12–13, 165, 309
code de l'ndigénat 213, 221, 281
coffee 13, 14, 165, 166, 189,
  194, 321
collectivité territoriale see
  territorial collectivity
Colomb-Béchar 32, 158, 174
Colonial Council see Superior
  Colonial Council
colonial economy 188–95
Colonial Exhibition of 1931 248,
  260–5, 324
colonial expansion, justification
  of 200–4; reasons for 97–9,
  103; by conquest 24–8, 40, 42,
  60–3, 76–8, 92, 199, 204; by
  exploration 43–6, 51–5, 78; by
  annexation 37, 39, 42, 46–8
  passim, 82; tâche d'huile
  method 106
colonial history 195; definition
  of 8
colonial government 37, 107–9,
  171, 282
Colonial League 102
colonial lobby 100–6, 111, 114,
  118, 121, 169, 185, 283
Colonial Ministry 109
colonial policy 89–90, 93–100,
  106–11, 120
Colonial Scientists, Association
  of 248
Colonial Union see French
  Colonial Union
Colonial Youth League 101
Comintern see Third
  International
Committee for French
  Africa 55, 56, 101, 102;
  French Asia 101, 102; French
  Morocco 101, 102; French
  Oceania 101, 273;

Madagascar 101
Committee of Public Safety 295
Communards 146
communists, communism 116, 118, 183, 192, 268, 272, 287, 288, 300
Community, The 302–3, 305
Comoros Islands 63–7; independence 304; referendum 302; trade 86, 87, 166, 170; women 229
Compagnie d'Afrique 142
Compagnie des Indes Orientales see East India Company
Compagnie française de l'Afrique occidentale (CFAO) *see* French West Africa Company
Compagnie Française de Suez 183
Compagnie Transatlantique 168
comptoirs, in India 17, 23, 179, 289, 317; at Colonial Exhibition 262
concessions, in China 83, 107, 289
Côn Dao *see* Poulo Condore
condominium in New Hebrides, Anglo-French 72, 107, 274, 304
Confucianism 130
Congo 35, 50, 281, 299; development 164, 192–4 *passim*; exploration 51–5; independence 303; occupation 87; railway 174–7
Congo Free State 54, 175; *see also* Belgian Congo
Congo–Ocean railway 174–7, 193
Constantine 144, 145
Constantine Plan 295
consumer goods 167–8, 183, 186, 321
contract labourers 147
copra 164, 166, 189
cork 143
corn *see* maize
Corsica 273, 291
corvée 220, 223; *see also* labour
Côte d Ivoire 41–2, 281, 299;

aid 320; coffee 165; economic policy 170; emigration 317; independence 303; military bases 322; missionaries 130; rebellion 300; settlers 311, 323; trade 183, 186
cotton 50, 83, 166, 186, 194
credit *see* loans
Creole, language 322–3
Crimean War 133, 134
Crozet Islands 84
CRUA (*Comité révolutionnaire d'unité et d'action*) *see* Revolutionary Committee for Unity and Action
Cubists 256
culture 200–4, 207, 227–8, 234–65, 322–3
currency 321; issue of 179–80, 182, 183
customs duties 29, 33, 34
customs union 169

Da Nang *see* Tourane
Dahomey 39–41, 199, 281; economic policy 170; independence 303; maize 195; missionaries 130; occupation of 87, 134; railway 174
Dakar 96, 116, 122, 148, 212, 225, 227, 232, 274
Daladier, Eugène 109
Damas, Léon-Gontran 245
Damascus 210, 211, 276
Darwin, Charles 203
Daudet, Alphone 238
de Gaulle, Charles de 274, 276–80 *passim*, 295–7 *passim*, 302–4 *passim*
decolonisation 197, 266–7, 270, 271, 280–4, 289, 298–306, 311; Algeria 296–7; Morocco 291–2; Syria and Lebanon 266, 276; Vietnam 279;
Decoux, Admiral 277, 278
Defferre, Gaston 301

Defferre law 301, 302
Delacroix, Eugène 251
Delavignette, Robert 152, 153
Delcassé, Théophile 109
demis see métis
Denmark 263
Denys, Claire 325
départements 94, 107, 215, 281, 308
départements d'outre-mer 281, 282, 302, 307–11
depression, economic 99, 118, 182, 186, 187, 191, 194, 196–7, 268, 318
députés 281, 282, 284, 285, 299
Deputies, Chamber of 109, 113, 117, 282, 284
Déroulède, Paul 100
Deschamps, Hubert 153
Deschanel, Paul 68
Désirade Island 13
Destour Party 269, 289
development 114, 137, 171–3, 230–3, 249, 283
Diego Suarez 62, 319
Dien Bien Phu 288
Diop, Birago 298
Directory, the 19
disease 144, 158, 161, 176, 195, 206, 214, 227
Djenné 44; at Colonial Exhibition 262, 264
Djibouti 57–60, 247; Colonial Exhibition 262; development of 164; independence 304; military bases 322; occupation 87; railway 164, 174; referendum 302; and Rimbaud 237; trade 170, 181, 273
Djoumbé 64–6
Dodds, General Alfred 161; rue 324
Dogon 247, 250
Dominique (Dominica) 13
DOM-TOM (*départements d'outre-mer-territoires d'outre-mer*) 307-11
Doriot, Jacques 117
Douls, Camille 126–7

Doumer, Paul 152
Doumerge, Gaston 109
Druze 84; uprising 208–12, 269
Duchesne, General 62
Dupetit-Thouard, Commander 70; rue 324
Dupuis, Jean 80
Duras, Marguerite 324
Dutch 73
Duveyrier, Henri 125–6

East India Company 15–16, 74
Eberhardt, Isabelle 156–8, 239
Eboué, Félix 274, 280
Ecole Coloniale 82, 151–2, 247, 324
Ecole William-Ponty 225
Economic and Social Investment and Development Fund *see* FIDES
economic growth 98, 113, 115, 119, 137, 160, 171–2, 189–91
economic policy 169–72, 178, 321–2
economy, French 195–8
education 111, 115, 136, 207, 224–6, 247–9 *passim*
EEZ (Exclusive Economic Zone) *see* maritime resources
Egypt 20, 59, 66, 237, 282
Einstein, Albert 118
elections 282, 284, 288, 302
El-Mokhrani 28, 215, 218
Eluard, Paul 265
Eritrea 273
Etablissements Français d'Oceanie (EFO) *see* French Oceanic Establishments
Ethiopia 59, 164, 273
ethnography, ethnographers 247, 249–50, 259
ethnology, ethnologists 151, 249
Etienne, Eugène 101–2
Etoile Nord-Africaine 119
Europa Island 84
European Community 320
Evian Accords 297, 312
exploration, Congo basin 51–4;

Indochina   78; West
  Africa   124–8
exports, imports and
  markets   98, 163, 164–9, 171,
  177–8, 186, 187, 189, 191–2,
  196, 197, 321

Faidherbe, Governor   41, 96,
  162, 223
Falkland Islands   85, 329
Fanon, Frantz   5, 227, 298
fashion   235, 325
Fashoda   47
Fathers of the Holy Spirit   128
Fauvists   256
Ferry, Jules   80, 97–100, 104
Fès   34–5, 225; Treaty of   35,
  290
FIDES (Fonds d'investissement et de
  développement économique et
  sociale)   281
Fifth Republic   215, 295, 302,
  304, 305
film   see cinema
First Empire   19–20
First World War   90, 105–6, 114,
  136, 153, 205, 223, 224, 267,
  273
fish   12–13, 48, 85, 165, 195,
  309, 311
Flatters, Paul-Xavier   174
Flaubert, Gustave   237
FLN (Front de libération nationale)
  see National Liberation Front
FLNKS (Front de Libération
  Nationale Kanak et
  Socialiste)   310
Force Noire, La   105
Foreign Legion   133–4, 286, 288,
  296
forestry   195, 216, 231
Fort-Bayard   83
Fort-Dauphin   16
Fort-de-France   245
Fort-Lamy   57
Foucauld, Charles de   130
Foureau-Lamy expedition   127–8,
  174
Fourth Republic   109, 215, 266,

280-2, 284, 295, 298, 302, 305
Fouta-Djalon   38–9
franc zone   321–2
France, Anatole   112, 118, 243
France, Ile de   15–16, 20
francisation   93, 110, 120, 267
Francophone movement   323
Free French   274, 276, 277–80
  passim, 284, 289
French, language   222–3, 225,
  228, 322
French Austral and Antarctic
  Territories   see TAAF
French Colonial Union   101,
  171, 185
French Communist Party
  (PCF)   116–7, 118, 265, 268,
  271, 281, 287, 299
French Equatorial Africa
  (AEF)   50–7, 153;
  administration   107, 108, 151;
  Colonial Exhibition   262, 264;
  dismemberment   299, 302;
  economy   192–5; economic
  policy   170, 321; education,
  225–6; health   226;
  independence   303; land   219;
  railway   176; science   248;
  status of   281
French National Front
  (FNF)   296
French Oceanic Establishments
  (EFO)   71, 131, 183, 212, 275;
  and economic policy   170; at
  Colonial Exhibition, 262; see
  also French Polynesia
French Polynesia   72, 134, 161,
  302–3, 307–11 passim
French Somali Coast   see Djibouti
French Somaliland   see Djibouti
French Territory of the Afars and
  Issas   see Djibouti
French Union   278, 280, 281–2,
  285, 288, 302, 305
French West Africa (AOF)
  35–50, 149, 153;
  administration   107, 108, 151;
  Colonial Exhibition   262, 264;
  dismemberment   299, 302;

economic policy 170, 321; education 225–6; health 227; independence 303; land 219; science 248; status of 281, 282
French West Africa Company (CFAO) 183–8
Frenchification *see francisation*
Fromentin, Eugène 237
Front National *see* National Front
fruit 165, 178–9, 186, 309
Futuna *see* Wallis and Futuna

Gabès 173
Gabon 50–1, 54, 55, 321–3 *passim*; economic policy 169–70; economy 166, 192, 193, 195; independence 303; occupation of 87; and Schweitzer 130; women in 155
Gallieni, General 63, 106, 135, 214, 245
Gambetta, Jean 129
Gambia 36, 37
Gambier Islands 70
Garnier, Francis 80, 97
gas 320, 321
Gaud-Touqué scandal 112
Gauguin, Paul 253–4
Gautier, Théophile 237
Genouilly, Rigault de 77, 131
Gentil, Commander 56
Géricault, Théodore 250–1
Germany 90, 105, 120, 267; and Central Africa 54, 193; and the Comoro Islands 66; and China 83; military expansion 273–7 *passim*; and North Africa 29, 30, 33, 35, 136; and West Africa 38, 42–3, 49–50
Ghadamès 126
Ghana 302
Gia Long 74
Gide, André 5, 118, 119, 194, 245
Glaoui, Thami el 291
Glorieuses, Iles 84
Gobineau, Arthur 203

gold 22, 41, 164, 190
Gold Coast 186, 300; *see also* Ghana
Gorée 13, 15, 36, 149, 212
governors 107, 108
Grand Bassam 41
Grande Comore 66, 304
Grande Terre *see* New Caledonia
Greater France 1–2
Griaule, Marcel 247, 250
groundnuts (peanuts) 22–3, 38, 50, 148, 166, 181, 183, 186, 195, 196
groupe colonial 101, 102–3
Groupe des indépendants d'outre-mer (IOM) *see* Overseas Independents' Group
Guadeloupe 20; citizenship 212; Colonial Exhibition 262; *département* 281, 307–10 *passim*; emigration 315; occupation of 13; trade 165, 179
Guangdong 80
Guangxi 80
Guangzhou 76, 83, 289
Guangzhouwan 83, 181, 289
Guesde, Jules 113
Guèye, Lamine 281
Guillaume, Paul 255
Guinea 38–9, 153, 186, 299, 302, 303
Guizot, François 94–5
Guyane 139; citizenship 212; Colonial Exhibition 262; *département* 281, 307–11 *passim*; gold 22, 164; military bases 134; occupation of 14; penal colony 22, 119; settlement 128, 164; trade 179; women in 155

Hainan Island 83, 277
Haiphong 73, 80, 147, 177, 181, 191, 277, 280, 286
Haiti 19; *see also* Saint-Domingue
Hangzhou 83, 289

Hanoi 116; commerce 159, 180, 181; education 225, 248; growth of 147, 159, 188, 191, 232, 233; occupation of 80, 81; settlers 147; war, unrest 271, 277, 279, 286
Hardy, Georges 152
hardwoods 166, 186, 193, 195
harkis 313–14
Haute-Volta *see* Upper Volta
head tax *see capitation*
health 111, 115, 136, 176–7, 226–7; and women 155, 230; *see also* disease
Higginson, John 72, 170
Hispaniola 13; *see also* Haiti
historiography 3–9
Hitler, Adolf 273
Hmong 140
Ho Chi Minh 5, 116–17, 270–2, 278–80, 285–8 *passim*
Holland 263
Hong Kong 73, 181, 182, 189
Houphouèt-Boigny, Félix 281, 299, 300
Hué 77; treaty of 81
Humanité, L' 265
Humblot, Léon 66

Iles Eparses 84
Illustration, L' 257, 264
Imerina 60–1
imports *see* exports
In-tassit 174
independence *see* decolonisation
India 16–17, 23, 74, 86, 179, 282, 289, 317; *see also comptoirs*
Indian Ocean 15–16, 60–7
indigénat see code de l'indigénat
Indochina 153, 161; administration 106, 107; banking 179–83; and China 279; Colonial Exhibition 262; culture 201–2, 158, 232–3; economy 188–192, 158, 165, 166, 195, 198; economic policy 169, 170, 171; education 226;

expatriates 122; Foreign Legion 134; health 227; Indochinese Federation 279, 280, 282; and Japan 273, 277–9; land 219; law 214; Lyautey 135; missionaries 129–31 *passim*; nationalism 270–2; occupation of 73–82, 88; photography 257; settlers 140, 147–8; science 247; war 223, 277–80, 285–8; *see also* Cambodia, Laos, Vietnam
Indonesia 282
industry 167, 191, 221
Institut Pasteur *see* Pasteur Institute
International African Association 54
investment 171
'invisible exports' 168–9
IOM *see* Overseas Independents' Group
Iraq 83, 276
iron 166
irrigation 171, 178–9, 189, 231
Islam and Muslims 129, 157, 158, 201, 205, 209–13 *passim*, 229, 247, 313–14, 319, 323
Istiqlal party 290, 291
Italians, in Algeria 143, 144
Italy 28–30 *passim*, 33, 66, 263, 272–3, 276, 282
ivory 57, 193, 194

Jabal Druze 209–10
Jakarta *see* Batavia
Japan 181, 192, 273, 275, 282; and Indochina 277–9
Jaurès, Jean 112, 113, 115
Javouhey, Anne–Marie 128, 156
Jesuits 247, 248
Jews 140, 142, 143, 145, 312
Joffre, Maréchal 45–6
Jouvenel, Henri de 211
Juan de Nova Island 84
Juin, General 290–1
July Monarchy 26, 94

Kabyles 28, 146, 292
Karabane 37
Karikal 17, 23, 289
Kayes 44
Kerguelen Islands 84–5, 231
Kinshasa see Léopoldville
Kitchener 47
Koh Doat 76
Korea 74, 273; war 287, 288
Kourou 309
Kunming 191
Kwangchowan see
    Guangzhouwan

La Foa 207
La Rochelle 170
labour 219–24, 281, 284;
    conditions 194
Lagrée, Doudart de 78
Lamartine, Alphonse de 237
Lambaréné 51, 130
Lambert, Henri 57–8, 170
Lambert, Joseph 61, 64–5, 170
Lamy, François 56
land 216–19, 231, 310; and
    culture 207; policy 171, 207,
    208–10 passim; grants 177, 189
Lanessan, Governor 137
Langson 81, 277
Laokay 191
Laos 87, 181; exploration 78;
    immigrants 310, 317;
    occupation of 81–2;
    settlers 148; tin 190;
    war 277–9 passim, 288
Lat Dior 38, 204
Lattre de Tassigny, Jean de 287
Lavigerie, Father Charles 128,
    129, 156
law 151, 212–14, 246, 281
Laye, Camara 298
Le Clézio, Jean-Marie 324
Le Pen, Jean-Marie 318
lead 166
League Against Colonial
    Oppression and
    Imperialism 118
League of Nations 267, 273
Lebanon 83, 86, 140, 149, 184,
    208–12, 263, 267, 310, 317, 322;
    independence 266, 276, 282
Lebon, André 102
Leclerc, General 279
Leenhardt, Maurice 249
Legey, Dr Françoise 156
Légion Etrangère see Foreign
    Legion
legislation see law
Leiris, Michel 5, 247
Lenin, V.I. 198, 267
Léopold II 54, 55
Léopoldville 50, 175
Leroy-Beaulieu, Paul 97;
    rue 324
Les Saintes Islands 13
Lesseps, Ferdinand de 54, 104
Lévi-Strauss, Claude 298
Lévy-Bruhl, Lucien 247
Liberia 183
Libreville 51
Libya 33, 272
literature 236–46, 324–5
living conditions 158–9
loans 29, 32, 62, 83, 168, 175,
    179, 180–4 passim, 284, 321
Lobaye 194
Lomé Convention 320
Londres, Albert 5, 118, 245
Lorraine 97, 100
Loti, Pierre 131, 239
Louis, Paul 99
Louis-Philippe 26, 247
Louisiana 12
Loyalty Islands 71
Luang Prabang 82
Lyautey, Hubert 32–5 passim, 63,
    106, 134–8, 158, 177, 233, 245,
    248, 260–3 passim, 324
Lyon Chamber of
    Commerce 83, 171

Maalouf, Amin 325
Macao 73, 74
Madagascar 87, 204, 319;
    administration 106, 107;
    culture 245; Colonial
    Exhibition 262, 264; economic
    policy 169–70;

education 225, 226;
emigration 317;
expatriates 122, 323;
independence 303; law 213;
Lyautey 134, 135; occupation
of 16, 60–3; nationalism 267;
science 247, 248;
settlement 16, 139;
trade 164, 165, 321;
uprising 205, 284–5; war 276
Maghreb *see* Algeria, Morocco,
Tunisia
Mahé (India) 17, 23, 289
Mahé de la Bourdonnais,
François 16
maize 189, 191, 195
Majunga 62
Makatéa 164, 166
Makoko 54, 106
Malagasy *see* Madagascar
malaria 144
Maldives 329
Mali 299; Federation 303;
independence 303; *see also*
Sudan
Malraux, André 245
Malta 141–5 *passim*
Manakara 284
Manchuria 74, 273
mandated territories 49–50, 83,
107, 208, 267, 276
manganese 321
Mangin, General 105
Manila 74
Mao Zedong 182, 286
Maran, René 243
Marchand 47
margarine 165
Marie-Galante Island 13
Marists 128
maritime resources 311
Maronites 83, 209
Marquesas Islands 70, 253
Marrakesh 127, 156, 235
Marseille 115, 170–1, 183, 260
Marseille Chamber of
Commerce 55, 170–1, 264
Marseille Society for
Geography 105

marsouins 133
Martinique 20;
administration 215;
citizenship 212; Colonial
Exhibition 262; culture 245;
département 281, 307–10
passim; emigration 315;
growth 14; Mont Pelée 246;
occupation of 13; trade 165,
179
Martonne, Edouard de 249
Marxism 117, 265, 267–8, 270,
271, 299; *see also* communism
Massu, Jacques 294, 295
Matisse, Henri 254–5
Maupassant, Guy de 237
Mauriac, François 297
Mauritania 48, 88, 126, 250;
economy 195;
independence 303; military
intervention 322;
pacification 204
Mauritius, emigration 317; *see
also* France, Ile de
Mayotte 304, 307–10 *passim*;
annexation 63–4, 95; Foreign
Legion 134, 322
Méduse 250
Meknès 251
Mekong River 73, 78, 81, 82,
191
Melanesia 71, 72, 131, 249
Melanesians 146, 147, 206–8,
218, 219, 309, 310–11; and
education 226; at Colonial
Exhibition 263
Memmi, Albert 5
menalamba 63
Mendès-France, Pierre 290
Mers-el-Kébir 275
Messageries Maritimes 168, 181,
264
Messali Hadj 270
meteorology 246–7
métis 161–2
Mexico 72, 77, 134
Michel, Louise 146
Micronesia 273; trust
territory 282

migration to colonies 138–40, 144–5, 147, 184, 309–10; from France 138–9; from India 22, 139–40, 310; *see also* settlers
migration to France, from DOM-TOMs 309; from colonies 311–19; from Europe 314–15; *see also* rapatriés
military bases in former colonies 322
military control 47, 56–7, 107, 149–50, 211; *see also* colonial expansion
military service 131–4, 223, 267, 284, 297; in Africa 105, 223, 240
mining 190, 216, 231, 308, 309, 311
mise en valeur 172, 173, 175, 181, 266
mission civilisatrice 92, 98, 104, 112, 154, 201, 222, 225, 264
missionaries 91, 101, 111, 116, 123, 128–31, 161; anti-colonialism 118; Colonial Exhibition 262; Côte d'Ivoire 41; education 224; Indochina, 73–7 *passim*, 148; Madagascar 61; New Caledonia 71, 206–7; New Hebrides 72; Tahiti 70; Togo 49; Wallis and Futuna 71; women 156, 229
Mitterrand, François 287, 300
Mohammed ben Youssef, Sultan 290, 291
Mohammed V 291–2
Moheli 64
Moncef Bey 277
Monfreid, Henri de 245
Montaignac, Marquis de 51
Montigny 76
Moors 127, 142
Mopti 44, 45
Morand, Paul 245
Morocco 86–8 *passim*, 122, 320, 323; art 251–2, 254–5, 257; Colonial Exhibition 262;

conquest of 31–5, 136, 223; culture 112, 233; decolonisation 290–2; economic policy 170; emigration 315, 316; land 216; missionaries 129; nationalism 269, 290; protectorate 107; rebellion 117, 134, 204, 205; settlement 139; trade 165, 166, 320, 321; wheat 177–8
Moulay 'Arafa 291
Moulay Hafid 34, 35, 204
Moutet, Marius 118, 249
Moyen-Congo *see* Congo
M'Poko 194
Mururoa 309
museums 247, 324
music 235, 243, 256, 325
Muslims *see* Islam
Mussolini, Benito 272
Mzabites 142, 143

Nantes 170
Napoleon 19–20
Napoleon III 75, 77, 93–4, 96, 108, 134, 144, 218
National Council of the Algerian Revolution 294
National Front 318
National Front for Kanak Socialist Liberation *see* FLNKS
National Liberation Army (ALN) 293, 297
National Liberation Front (FLN) 293–7 *passim*, 312–4 *passim*, 319
nationalism, nationalists 116, 205, 222, 227, 250, 265, 266–70, 272, 291, 305–6; Algeria 292–5 *passim*; Black Africa 298–9; Druze 209–11 *passim*; Indochina 276–8 *passim*; Madagascar 284, 285; Melanesia 208
Native Americans 140, 201, 310
'natives' 199–233, 268; reservations for 219; and photography 257–8; at

Colonial Exhibition 263
navy 131–2
négritude 205, 228, 245–6
neo-colonialism 307, 310, 320, 322
Néo-Destour Party 269, 289
Nerval, Gérard de 237
New Caledonia 72, 249, 283, 302, 304, 305, 307–11 *passim*; administration 109; Colonial Exhibition 262, 263; economic policy 170; economy 165, 166; land 218–19; law 213–15 *passim*; mining 192; missionaries 131; occupation 71; penal colony 71; railway 173; rebellion 205–8; settlement 109, 139, 140, 146–7; sport 160; war 273, 274, 275; women 155
New Hebrides 72, 170, 219, 231, 274, 275; independence 304–5
'New Imperialism' 97–100
New Ireland 332
New Zealand 69, 95
Nguyên Ai Quôc *see* Ho Chi Minh
Niamey 174
nickel 146, 147, 166, 192, 206, 273, 308, 309
Niger 46–7, 204, 303, 321
Niger River 42, 43–4, 54
Nigeria 46, 183, 186
Nkrumah, Kwame 300, 302
Norodom, King 79–80
North African Star 270
North America 10–13
Nossy-Bé 61–2
Nouméa 71, 147, 181, 205, 232, 274
nuclear testing 231, 308–9, 311

OAS (*Organisation armée secrète*) 296, 297, 312
Obock 57–9, 95, 164
Oceania *see* Polynesia, Melanesia, Pacific islands
Ogooué River 51

Olympio, Sylvanus 300
Omar, El Hadj 204
'optants' 72
Oran 26, 28, 102, 136, 144, 294
Organisation of African Unity (OAU) 304
'Orientalist' art · 251–3, 254
ORSTOM 248
Orsenna, Eric 324
Ottoman Empire 25–9 *passim*, 83, 96, 197, 198, 208, 268
Ouagadougou 174
Oubangui-Chari 50, 55, 112, 176, 192, 243, 274
Oued-Zem 291
Ouidah 39
Oujda 34, 136
Overseas Independents' Group (IOM) 299, 302
overseas territories *see territoires d'outre-mer*; *see also* associated territories, territorial collectivity

Pacific Islands 69–72, 201, 253–4, 275, 276
pacification 106, 107, 110, 174, 192, 204, 267
Palestine 83, 276
palm oil 41, 49, 50, 183, 194
Palmyra 210
Papeete 70, 181, 232
Paris Geographical Society 55, 103–4, 111, 125, 202, 324
parti colonial see colonial lobby
Pasteur Institute 247–8
Patagonia 332
Pavie, Auguste 82
PCF (*Parti Communiste Français*) *see* French Communist Party
pearls 308
Pellerin, Bishop 76
penal settlements 91, 110; Algeria, 144; Guyane 22, 119, 139, 155; Kerguelen 85; New Caledonia 71, 139, 146, 155
perfume essences 66, 166, 309
Perse, Saint-John 245, 246
Pétain, Philippe · 136, 274

Peyral, Jean 239–41
Philippeville 293
Philippines 73, 282
Phnom-Penh 148, 181
phosphate 142, 164, 166, 196, 321
photography 257–8
Phu Quoc see Koh Doat
Picasso, Pablo 255, 256
pieds-noirs 140–2, 242, 296, 312–3, 335
pirates 63, 99
Pointe-Noire 175
Poivre, Pierre 74
political rivalry 99
politique des races 106, 211
Polynesia 70–1, 131, 231, 253–4, 309; women in 155, 229; see also Tahiti
Pomaré, Queen 70, 204, 230
Pondichéry 17, 23, 180, 289; emigration 317
Popular Front 118–20 passim
Port-Etienne 48
Port Louis 16
Porto Novo 40
Portugal, Portuguese 31, 36, 37, 54, 73, 263
postcards 258
poster art 259–60
Poulo Condore 77
Pouvana'a a Oopa 302, 303
Présence africaine 298
Pritchard, George 70
Prix Goncourt 243, 324, 325
prostitution 160, 230
protectorates 107, 108, 137, 139, 215; Annam 80, 81; Cambodia 79; Cochinchina 78; Comoro Islands 66; Guinea 38, 39; Laos 82; Madagascar 62, 63; Morocco 35, 136, 290; Polynesia 70, 204; Tonkin 81; Tunisia 30–1, 290; Wallis and Futuna 71
Protet, Governor 96
Psichari, Ernest 242
public opinion 283, 287, 318

public service see civil service
Puigaudeau, Odette du 245

quadrillage 294

Rabah 56
Rabat 125, 136, 233
Rabemamanjary, Jacques 284, 285
racism 199–204, 206, 268, 318
Radicals 112, 114, 118
railways 102, 110, 136, 168, 173–7; Algeria 143; Congo 175–7, 193; Djibouti 59, 164; Indochina 80, 148, 181, 191, 277; Morocco 34; Pondichéry 180; Trans-Saharan Railway 173–175; Tunisia 30
Rainilaiarivony 61, 62
Ranavalona I 61
Ranavalona II 61
Ranavalona III 62, 63, 204, 215, 230
Randau, Robert 243
rapatriés 311–13; see also harkis
Raseta, Joseph 285
Rays, Marquis de 332
RDA (Rassemblement démocratique africaine) 299, 302
rebellion 120, 204–12, 267; in Algeria 218, 292; in Cameroon 300–1; in Côte d'Ivoire 300; in Lebanon 208–12; in Madagascar 63, 284–5; in Morocco 35, 116, 117, 134, 136, 269; in New Caledonia 146, 205–8, 310–11; in Syria 116, 208–12; in Vietnam 81, 192, 278
recession, economic see depression
Reclus, Elisée 111
Red River 73, 80, 191
Red Sea 57–8, 174
referendum 302–3; in Algeria 296, 297; in the Comoros

Islands 304; in Djibouti 304
representation, political 215,
308
research *see* science
réserves *see* native reservations
resistance, to colonial rule
204–212; *see also* rebellion
Restoration 25–6, 144
Réunion, Ile de la 61–3 *passim*,
65, 84, 87, 161, 215, 322;
citizenship 212; Colonial
Exhibition 262;
département 281, 307–10
passim; economy 165, 179;
emigration 315;
immigration 140;
railway 173; *see also* Bourbon,
Ile
Revolution, Bolshevik 265,
267–8; in China 268; of 1789,
17–9; of 1830, 144; of
1848 21–3, 93, 144
Revolutionary Committee for
Unity and Action
(CRUA) 292–3
Revolutionary League of
Vietnamese Youth 270, 271
Rhodes, Alexandre de 73
rice 135, 165, 181, 188, 189,
191, 195, 196, 284
Rif Mountains 117, 126, 136,
205
Rimbaud, Arthur 237
Rivet, Paul 247
Rivière, Henri de 81
Rivières du Sud *see* Southern
Rivers
roads 191
Rolland, Romain 118
Roman d'un spahi, Le 239–41
Roosevelt, F.D. 278
Rouan, Brigitte 325
Rouch, Jean 259
Roudaire, Captain François 173
Roux, Charles 102
rubber 38, 57, 148, 166, 181,
189–90, 191, 193, 194, 196, 231
Rufisque 149, 212
rum 165, 309

Russia 29, 82, 96, 196–8 *passim*,
267
Rwanda 322

Sahara 94, 124, 126, 127, 164,
231, 236; Trans-Saharan
Railway 173–5
Saigon 73, 116; culture 159;
economy 180, 181, 188, 191;
growth of 232, 233;
occupation of 77, 78;
settlers 147; war 279
Saint-Christophe 13
Saint-Domingue 13, 14, 18, 19;
see also Haiti
Saint-Exupéry, Antoine de 236
Sainte-Lucie 13
Sainte-Marie 61
Sainteny, Jean 279
St Joseph's University 248
St Kitts *see* Saint-Christophe
Saint-Louis 15, 21, 36, 44, 48,
125, 148, 212
St Lucia *see* Sainte-Lucie
Saint-Paul Island 84, 85
Saint-Pierre et Miquelon 12–13,
139, 307–9 *passim*; and
economic policy 170; at
Colonial Exhibition 262
Salan, Raoul 294–6 *passim*
Salkhad 210
salt mining 59
Samory Touré 42, 204, 267
sandalwood 206
Santo 305
Sarraut, Albert 109, 114, 115,
152, 172
Sartre, Jean-Paul 5, 287, 297, 298
Sautot, Henri 274
Schmaltz, Julien 250
Schweitzer, Albert 130
science 246–50
sculpture 255–6
Second Empire 108, 144
Second World War 90, 120, 182,
187, 223, 273–9
Secret Army Organisation *see*
OAS
Section française de l'Internationale

irrigation   173; and Italy
  272–3; land   216;
  missionaries   129;
  nationalism   269;
  protectorate   107;
  settlers   122, 139; war   276–7
Turks   142, 316
Tyre   209

Um Nyobé, Ruben   300–1
Union Coloniale Française   see
  French Colonial Union
Union Française   see French Union
United Nations   282, 293
United States   178, 181, 263,
  275, 278, 282, 287, 288
universities   225, 247–9 *passim*
Upper Volta   42–3, 223;
  independence   303
urbanisation   232
Utrecht, Treaty of   12

Van Vollenhoven, Joost   152–3
vanilla   165
Vanuatu   see New Hebrides
Vatican   73
Verdier, Arthur   41
Verminck, Charles-Auguste   183
Verne, Jules   236
Viaud, Julien   see Loti, Pierre
Vichy government   174, 182,
  187, 248, 274, 276, 277, 284,
  318
vieilles colonies   139, 212, 215;
  and economic policy   169–70;
  at Colonial Exhibition   262;
  départementalisation of   281
Vientiane   148
Viet Minh   278–80, 286, 287, 288
Vietnam, culture   232–3;
  economy   183, 192;
  emigration   317;
  independence   278–80, 285;
  occupation   73, 75, 77, 80, 81,
  82; missionaries   128;
  racism   201–2; relations with
  France   319, 322;

resistance   205, 270–2;
  settlers   148; war   286–8; *see
  also* Annam, Cochinchina,
  Tonkin
Vietnamese Communist
  Party   271
Vietnamese National Party   270
Vincennes   see Colonial
  Exhibition
vineyards   145
Viollette, Maurice   119
Vogüé, Melchior de   242
voting   213–15, 268, 269, 282,
  301, 308
Voulet–Chanoine expedition   47,
  111

Wallis and Futuna   71, 72, 86,
  128, 164, 275, 307–9 *passim*
war   223–4; in Indochina   182,
  192, 223; in Algeria   204; in
  Tahiti   204
water   see irrigation
welfare system   309
West Indies   173; see also Antilles
whaling   84–5
wheat   177–8
White Fathers   128
White Sisters   128, 156
wilaya   292, 293
Wilson, Woodrow   267
wine   165, 196
women   154–8, 229–30
Wuhan   83

Yanaon   17, 23, 289
Yen Bay   205, 271
Youlou, Fulbert   299
Young Algerians   270
Young Moroccans   269
Yunnan   78, 80, 177, 191, 277

Zaïre   322; *see also* Congo Free
  State
Zanzibar   64, 65
Ziguinchor   36–7
zouaves   133